Censorship of the American Theatre in the Twentieth Century

John Houchin explores the impact of censorship in twentieth-century American theatre. He argues that theatrical censorship coincided with significant challenges to religious, political, and cultural systems. Arranged in chronological order, this study provides a summary of theatre censorship in the eighteenth and nineteenth centuries and then analyzes key episodes from 1900 to 2000. These include attempts to censure Olga Nethersole for her production of *Sapho* in 1901 and the theatre riots of 1913 that greeted the Abbey Theatre's production of *Playboy of the Western World*. Houchin explores the efforts to suppress plays in the 1920s that dealt with transgressive sexual material and investigates Congress' politically motivated assaults on plays and actors during the 1930s and 1940s. He investigates the impact of racial violence, political assassinations, and the Vietnam War on the trajectory of theatre in the 1960s and concludes by examining the response to gay activist plays such as *Angels in America*.

John Houchin is Associate Professor of Theatre at Boston College, Massachusetts. He is the editor of *The Critical Response to Eugene O'Neill* (1993). His work has also been published in *The Drama Review*, *The New England Theatre Journal*, *The Journal of American Theatre and Drama*, *Theatre History Studies*, and the *Eugene O'Neill Review*.

The American theatre and its literature are attracting, after long neglect, the crucial attention of historians, theoreticians, and critics of the arts. Long a field for isolated research yet too frequently marginalized in the academy, the American theatre has always been a sensitive gauge of social pressures and public issues. Investigations into its myriad of shapes and manifestations are relevant to students of drama, theatre, literature, cultural experience, and political development.

The primary intent of this series is to set up a forum of important and original scholarship in and criticism of American theatre and drama in a cultural and social context. Inclusive by design, the series accommodates leading work in areas ranging from the study of drama as literature to theatre histories, theoretical explorations, production histories, and readings of more popular or para-theatrical forms. While maintaining a specific emphasis on theatre in the United States, the series welcomes work grounded broadly in cultural studies and narratives with interdisciplinary reach. Cambridge Studies in American Theatre and Drama thus provides a crossroads where historical, theoretical, literary, and biographical approaches meet and combine, promoting imaginative research in theatre and drama from a variety of new perspectives.

Censorship of the American Theatre in the Twentieth Century

JOHN H. HOUCHIN

CAMBRIDGE
UNIVERSITY PRESS

PUBLISHED BY THE PRESS SYNDICATE OF THE UNIVERSITY OF CAMBRIDGE
The Pitt Building, Trumpington Street, Cambridge CB2 1RP, United Kingdom

CAMBRIDGE UNIVERSITY PRESS
The Edinburgh Building, Cambridge, CB2 2RU, UK
40 West 20th Street, New York, NY 10011-4211, USA
477 Williamstown Road, Port Melbourne, VIC 3207, Australia
Ruiz de Alarcón 13, 28014 Madrid, Spain
Dock House, The Waterfront, Cape Town 8001, South Africa

http://www.cambridge.org

First published 2003

Printed in the United Kingdom at the University Press, Cambridge

Typeface Adobe Caslon 10.5/13 pt.   *System* LATEX 2$_\varepsilon$ [TB]

A catalogue record for this book is available from the British Library

ISBN 0 521 81819 2 hardback

To my wife
Pamela Spring Newton
For her love and support

Contents

Acknowledgments

I began researching this topic in 1994. Initially, I wrote articles on isolated examples of theatrical censorship that occurred in the early part of the twentieth century. I naively concluded that really there were not enough examples of this kind of activity to support a book-length study. Of course, there was the opposition that plays by Ibsen and Shaw encountered in the first decade of the century, but these were the results of slow-dying Victorian prudery. I knew about attempts to stop *Hair* and *Oh! Calcutta!* in the South, but I assumed that these campaigns represented conservative religious biases that had retarded the intellectual and cultural development of that region for over a century. Surely the protection afforded by the First Amendment would not have permitted very many egregious attempts to suppress stage plays. I quickly changed my mind. As I continued to research this topic, I was astonished at the staggering number of instances where senators, representatives, popes, legislators, teachers, district attorneys, judges, bishops, school boards, and private citizens had attempted to alter or suppress theatrical productions. Moreover, efforts to censor shows made headlines in major newspapers for weeks at a time, particularly if the offenders were arrested and tried. Thus, the sheer number of investigative articles, editorials, and letters to the editor that appeared in metropolitan dailies was immense. And then there were pro and con essays that appeared in news magazines, theatre journals, law reviews, and organizational newsletters. With the advent of the information age, National Public Radio and Cable News Network, not to mention numerous websites on the Internet, broadcast assessments, interviewed principals, and presented editorial opinion. By the time I began to write this book in 1997, I was no longer worried about a scarcity of data. I was, however, concerned about my ability to condense this mountain of information into a volume whose length would not cause publishers to laugh hysterically at my pretentiousness.

I am indebted to Cambridge University Press for making this project a reality. Don Wilmeth, editor of Cambridge's Studies in American Theatre and Drama, and Victoria Cooper, my editor at Cambridge, have been particularly patient and encouraging. I am also indebted to the administration of the College of Arts and Sciences at Boston College – former dean Father Robert J. Barth, S.J., Dean Joseph F. Quinn, and Dean of Graduate Studies Michael Smyer – for providing me with material and intellectual support that enabled me to complete this protracted investigation.

I am also grateful to the dozens of research librarians at the University of Texas at Dallas, Southern Illinois University, the Billy Rose Collection at Lincoln Center, and the Harvard Theatre Collection. I am particularly thankful to the staff of the Thomas P. O'Neill Library at Boston College who helped me locate the material that gave this study the breadth and depth that it possesses.

Numerous colleagues have also taken time to read my drafts and discuss my ideas. I would especially like to acknowledge Stuart Hecht, John Mahoney, Scott Cummings, Luke Jorgensen, Crystal Tiala, Howard Enoch, Paul Doherty, Brian Hughes, Sarah Blackstone, and Alex Argyros. There is another group of people whose help proved invaluable, my Boston College research assistants: Diane Bronowicz, Kristina Smarz, Kelly Fitzgerald, Krista Clarkson, Kate Bailey, Alison Haislip, Katheryn Davis, and Lindsey Macauley. They ordered, read, summarized, and catalogued scores of books and articles. Their efforts have been greatly appreciated.

Finally, I want to thank my wife, Pam. She read and edited hundreds of pages and we discussed the topic for hundreds of hours. As a psychoanalyst she was particularly interested in the psychological aspects of censors – their need for control as well as their compulsion to preserve the status quo. Her insight, not to mention her love and support, were inestimable.

Introduction

This is a book about censorship. Specifically, it is a history of the censorship of theatre in the United States in the twentieth century. It will explore how major attacks on theatre reflect correlative crises in the larger culture. In other words, it is my argument that attempts to censor performance erupt when the dominant culture construes its laws, rituals, and traditions to be in the process of significant change. Rarely does the collective mind of a community encountering such transformations embrace them as a natural, evolutionary process. Rather, it attempts to halt or reverse these shifts by reverting to the rituals or philosophy of a purer, Golden Age.

Such behavior is indicative of a conservative society, one whose energy is used to maintain its political, moral, and social infrastructure. This type of society resists economic innovation and the rapid reordering that accompany such transformations. Its teachers in its schools do not encourage originality or radically new ideas. Instead, they emphasize rote learning of established principles and theorems. Its ministers preach that the relationship between gods and humans is fixed, does not evolve, and is not open to interpretation. Salvation is obtained by strict adherence to established principles. Speculation and experimentation are apostasy and inevitably lead to the spiritual demise of individuals and the communities that support them.

The conservative community cannot tolerate untrammeled innovation and does not believe that the future holds the answer to its problems. As Karen Armstrong has surmised, the conservative spirit depends upon mythology for its direction. Instead of looking for something fresh or innovative, it seeks direction from the past. It directs its attention to sacred beginnings, to a primordial event. The past tells the community what is constant, what has always been. It asserts that current and future stages of society are pale shadows of a putative Golden Age and its leaders look for their inspiration in the deeds of historical presidents, kings, generals,

and saints. By studying the Golden Age, professors will become philoso-
phers, priests will become prophets, and citizens will become patriots. More
importantly, by embracing ancient ritual practices and mythical narratives,
individuals will acquire a sense of meaning that resonates deeply within
their unconscious mind and their leaders will retrieve a clear, precise tem-
plate that maps out how social, political, sexual, and economic relationships
should be conducted. In short, embracing the past will clarify the future.[1]

Understandably, the conservative community fears artists, particularly
theatrical artists. Throughout history these individuals have generated intense public adulation, but the political, religious, and social leaders of the
conservative community typically characterize them as immoral, pernicious,
or subversive. They fear that these artists will teach the faithful to imagine
new systems, rewrite laws, and overturn the old order.

Theatrical artists, especially actors, embody the archetypes of play and
display, and possess a primal energy that only can be described as vivid,
alive, and passionate. They speculate, hypothesize, and pretend. Their raw
personae seem to embrace the world as it is and they are sensually aware of
the nature that surrounds them. Many choose to ignore socially or politically
created boundaries and their lives are often unconventional or "messy." The
characters that they portray on stage debunk ancient rituals and ignore
accepted traditions. Their offstage lives appear to be anarchic and are
studded with illicit activities and stormy confrontations with authorities.
And, while religious and political leaders demand morality, accountability,
and restraint, actors frequently symbolize sensuality, license, and abandon.
They may respect the past, but they are ultimately concerned with the
present and the future.

In short, censors have traditionally viewed theatre as a volatile, unstable
entity that might, as Richard Schechner has said, "come tumbling back into
reality." They worry that actors and audiences are porous and that the fiction
of the stage might be acted out as a reality in non-theatrical space and time.
Or, as Edward Albee recently said, "Unfortunately, people tend generally
to want passive experiences. That's the thing about a movie – you go to it
and it is totally safe because it's not happening. A play is dangerous, and
that's one problem that people have with plays: They are active; they are in
the present tense; they are happening – they have not happened – and stuff
can go wrong."[2] These concerns were particularly true in the United States
in the twentieth century, a turbulent one hundred years in which theatrical
artists aggressively challenged virtually every social convention that had
been established during the Victorian and Edwardian eras. During the first

decade of the century, dramatists disputed the notion that biology was destiny and created female characters, who abjured passive, maternal roles. By the end of the century, bold and open discussions of lesbianism had become part of the established dramatic canon. In the 1930s playwrights, directors, and producers collectively questioned the capitalist economic paradigm and became part of a revolution that significantly altered the relationship of the federal government to its citizens. Radical theatre artists reemerged in the 1960s and introduced guerrilla tactics, nudity, and rock music into theatre. Not only did they challenge the political and military power structures that ruled the nation, but also they deconstructed the conventions of theatre itself. By the 1990s, much theatre in the United States bore little resemblance to that which was being produced one hundred earlier.

Theatre, however, only reflected the often violent transitions that were taking place in the larger culture. By the last decade of the nineteenth century, urban centers began to grow exponentially, their populations swelled by immigrants from Eastern Europe, and the culture of the city virtually replaced the agrarian ethos in the imagination of the nation. Rampant capitalism, with its emphasis on productivity at any cost, replaced a simple subsistence economy. Traditional Protestant teachings, which posited a doctrine of absolute right and wrong, gave way to moral relativism. As the twentieth century progressed, the telephone, radio, television, and the Internet brought previously isolated communities into intimate contact with one another. What we saw and learned often generated fear, anger, and disgust. The internal combustion engine, interstate highways, airplanes, and space shuttles allowed us to travel through the solar system as easily as we could drive across town. But the imperative of speed robbed us our quietude. Military forces and nuclear weapons have made the United States the most powerful nation on earth, but sadly have not been able to protect it from forces that hate and fear it.

It has been an explosive century with each decade providing some with hope and others with the threat of annihilation. In order to achieve the former and avoid the latter, the conservative community in the United States (which is actually a multifaceted manifestation) sought solace and protection by embracing the past. Religious conservatives demanded that the faithful should return to the teachings of the Bible, to the fundamentals of Christianity that had been preached for hundreds of years. They demanded theological orthodoxy and rejected any speculation or experimentation. Social conservatives decried feminism and called upon women to resume their traditional roles of mothers and wives. Cultural conservatives deplored the polyglot culture that emerged during the late twentieth century and longed for the day when English-speaking Caucasians would again dominate the nation. Legal conservatives demanded that the judiciary interpret the Constitution in accordance with the intentions of the "Founding Fathers." Only by understanding the intentions of these eighteenth-century leaders, they claimed, could the citizens of the twentieth and twenty-first centuries lead lawful, meaningful lives.

In the final analysis, censors in the twentieth century feared that theatre had the capacity to eradicate the boundaries between classes and genders, instigating political and sexual anarchy. They believed that actors, directors, and playwrights had the capacity to replace old mythologies with systems that would undermine traditional edifices of power. These opponents of theatre knew, sometimes better than its allies, that theatre was alive, often erotic, and always sensual, and that it had the power to transform audiences and bring about change. It was these characteristics that ultimately disturbed censors, and it was these characteristics that they sought to suppress.

Structure and focus

This study focuses on theatrical censorship in the United States from 1900 through 2000. An introductory chapter summarizes anti-theatrical biases of the eighteenth and nineteenth centuries in an effort to create a historical context for the ensuing investigation. Chapters two and three cover the period from 1900 to 1930. They reveal that censorship during the first thirty years of the century was aimed largely at productions that discussed sexual topics that threatened the dominant moral paradigms of the nineteenth century. Chapter four focuses primarily on attempts by the federal, state, and local governments to silence theatre deemed politically subversive. Chapters five and six investigate how sexually transgressive theatre became a metaphor for political radicalism and moral anarchy.

Although I have sought to present what is a comprehensive study of American theatrical censorship, I do not attempt to address the suppression of other areas of communication. Columnists, authors, publishers, screen writers, photographers, television producers, and rock singers have often been the targets of various local, state, and federal investigators who were displeased with what these individuals had to say. Each medium, however, utilizes a more or less unique communicative ontology that, while it may overlap into other media, employs an idiosyncratic system of signs and symbols. Therefore, an attempt to study the entire range of censorial activities in the United States would necessitate a multitude of volumes authored by dozens of experts. In the same vein, high-school principals and various municipal groups exercise much theatre censorship informally. With few exceptions I have elected not to include these events. While they make for interesting reading, they tend to mirror other major trends that are already being assessed.

While many of the efforts of censors will seem absurd to students of theatre, I have endeavored to remain even-handed, limiting my personal comments to situations that warrant interpretative observations. I also discuss at some length a number of court decisions, delve into religious history, and examine political events. By so doing, I am not attempting to pass myself off as a legal or religious scholar. I have simply attempted to describe several historical developments that have annexed theatre into their orbit.

While this work may raise more questions than it answers, I trust that it will reveal some of the shifting tides of censorship during the twentieth century in the United States as it attempts to connect these events to the cultural, religious, and political currents that shaped them.

I

Overture: theatrical censorship from the Puritans to Anthony Comstock

The Massachusetts Bay colony

Any discussion of theatrical censorship in the United States must begin with the religious sects that settled the colonies of British North America. They transported the anti-theatrical feelings of radical English Protestants to the New World and inscribed their attitudes into colonial law. More importantly, they forged a bond between secular and religious authorities that permitted (and encouraged) judicial and executive units to suppress any individual or group that challenged the moral topography as described by mainstream Christian teaching. While the Constitution may have prevented the establishment of a national religion, very few citizens questioned the right of governmental units to defend the moral status quo.

The stage, for English Puritans, represented a chaotic and anarchic site, exempt from the laws of the state and of God where sexual, social, and religious transgressions could be practiced with impunity. It was the church of Satan and undermined the authority of true Christianity. The Puritans who sailed for North America brought these prejudices with them, and the English government that approved of and protected theatre was an ocean away. Although there were specific instances of anti-theatrical activity in most of the English colonies in North America, the vast majority of theatrical censorship emanated from the Puritan plantations of New England and the Quaker commonwealth of Pennsylvania. The flood of immigrants into North America began in 1630 and, by 1640, over 18,000 English citizens had settled along the Atlantic seaboard. While many of the early settlers were entrepreneurs seeking their fortune in the New World, there were several thousand who sought to establish a "New Jerusalem." These religious dissidents believed that England would soon encounter God's wrath. In their opinion, neither the Anglican Church nor the monarchy was willing to purge the English Church of its popish traditions and purify the land of its immorality. And, when the first shareholders of the Massachusetts Bay Company landed in New England in 1630, they promptly limited franchise to church members. In so doing, the Puritan leaders of this enterprise insured that governance of the colony would not fall into the hands of the irreligious.[1]

Within the first fifty years of the colony's existence, this alliance between magistrates and ministers made itself conspicuously evident. Virtually every practice or celebration, secular or religious, which was not specifically accounted for in the Bible, was rigorously proscribed. In 1634, the General Court passed sumptuary laws forbidding the purchase of woolen, silk, or linen garments with silver, gold silk, or thread lace on them.[2] The celebration of Christmas, nicknamed "Fools tide," was outlawed. Scripture had not specified when Christ was born, and the colony's leadership asserted that the Roman Church's designation of December 25 was merely an excuse to celebrate the "Old Saturnalia of the Heathen."[3] Dancing posed a slightly different problem. Although Increase Mather characterized it as the "Devil Procession," it could not be completely outlawed because it had been practiced in the Old Testament.[4] However, the General Court did preclude dancing on the Sabbath as well as "gynecandrical" or mixed-sex dancing.

In 1684, Charles II rescinded the original charter of the Massachusetts Bay Company and converted Massachusetts from a private to a royal colony. Official Puritan control ended and a cultural thaw ensued. The colony's population continued to swell, but these new English immigrants were mostly Anglicans, and they brought with them a liberal spirit. Dancing schools flourished. Boston boasted of four in 1720 and eight by 1730.[5] Churches purchased organs as services became more resplendent.[6] Secular music also flourished. Outdoor concerts began in 1729 and increased dramatically during the 1730s. Faneuil Hall was built in 1742 and in 1754 Concert Hall opened. By mid-century, concerts had become an established part of Boston's cultural life.

Theatre, however, in no way benefited from this cultural awakening. In 1714, word spread that some students might petition the city council to use Boston Town Hall to present a play. When Samuel Sewall heard this rumor he wrote to Isaac Addington on March 2 to express his indignation:

There is a rumor, as if some design'd to have a Play acted in the council-Chamber, next Monday; which much surprises me: And as much as in me lies, I do forbid it. The Romans were very fond of their Plays: but I never heard they were so far set upon them, as to turn their Senate-House into a Play-House. Our Town-House was built at great cost and charge, for the sake of very serious and important Business . . . Let it not be abused with Dances, or other scenical divertissements . . . Let not Christian Boston go beyond Heathen Rome in the practice of shameful vanities.[7]

Clearly, tax revenue could only be used to support "very serious and important business," and, unlike Athens (or "Heathen Rome" for that matter), Boston was unwilling to elevate theatre to that status. It was a bias that would prove difficult to eradicate.

In the meantime, the southern colonies demonstrated that they were capable and desirous of integrating pleasure and leisure into their world. Because of the agricultural economics of the region, farms spanned thousands of acres. Owners lived in their great houses with their families. Although they entertained guests, they were, for the most part, isolated. Thus the annual convening of the colonial assemblies was eagerly anticipated for the socializing it provided for planters and their families, and was routinely celebrated with races, parties, concerts, and eventually with plays.

Perhaps the only case of attempted theatrical censorship in the southern colonies occurred in Accomac County, Virginia, in December 1665. Three young men enacted what turned out to be the first English-language play in North America, *Ye Bare & Ye Cubb*. One, Edward Martin, demanded that they be punished. The presiding Justice of the Peace thought otherwise and ordered Martin to pay the court costs.[8] Eventually Charlestown, Williamsburg, Annapolis, and Fredericksburg would all boast a public eager for plays, but the most important developments in colonial theatre occurred further north – in Philadelphia.

The Company of Comedians from London

Until about 1720, Philadelphia bore the stamp of its founding colonists. Visitors found neither great wealth nor abject poverty, but reported that the Quaker citizenry was dull and austere. As Carl Bridenbaugh has noted: "There was little gaiety and less elegance; a dreary commercialism, clothed in the austere garb of Quaker principles, permeated the very air."[9] Quaker opposition to theatre, clearly the result of that denomination's Puritan heritage, was a significant feature of the legal history of the colony. William

Penn railed: "How many plays did Jesus Christ and his apostles recreate themselves at? What poets, romances, comedies, and the like did the apostles and saints make or use to pass away their time withal?"[10] Consequently, he explicitly prohibited theatre in Pennsylvania when he drafted the first *Frame of Government of Pennsylvania* in 1682, long before any colonists or actors had even arrived:

> Thirty-seventh. That as careless and corrupt administration of justice draws the wrath of God upon magistrates, so the wildness and looseness of the people provoke the indignation of God against a country: therefore . . . all prizes, stage plays, cards, dice, may-games, masques, revels, bull baitings, cock-fightings, bear-baitings and the like, which excite the people to rudeness, cruelty, looseness and irreligion, shall be respectively discouraged, and severely punished.[11]

When Charles II granted Penn a charter, however, he cleverly reserved for the Crown the privilege of revoking any legislation enacted in that colony. William and Mary, exercising this royal prerogative, rescinded Penn's anti-recreation provision in 1693. The colonial Assembly, dominated as it was by Quakers, continued its efforts to ban theatre, and passed "An Act against Riots, Rioters, and Riotous Sports, Plays and Games" in 1700. Once again the Crown, this time Queen Anne, revoked the law in 1705. Still undaunted, the Quaker Assembly passed two more acts against "Riotous Sports, Plays and Games," one in 1706 and the other in 1711, both of which were vetoed.[12]

During the next fifty years, however, a conflation of economic and political events transformed dreary Philadelphia into what Henry Steele Commager described as "an American Weimar."[13] The Quaker policy of religious tolerance, Philadelphia's advantageous location at the mouth of the Delaware River, and abundant farmland, which stretched for hundreds of miles beyond, attracted thousands of immigrants. Although Pennsylvania's prosperity benefited most sectors of society, it transformed many merchants and their families into a mercantile aristocracy. Men such as Samuel Carpenter, Samuel Richardson, Isaac Norris, Edward Shippen, William Frampton, and Richard Hill moved to Philadelphia from other colonies to increase their wealth and ended up as heads of mercantile dynasties.

Philadelphia also developed a cultural environment unrivaled by any English city except London. Among its more prominent institutions were its Library Company (1742); the American Philosophical Society (1744); and the College of Philadelphia, which began life as the College, Academy, and Charitable School of Philadelphia (1755), to which was added a medical school in 1765. By 1776, Philadelphia could also boast of seven newspapers, which accounted for about one-seventh of all the journalistic output of the continent.[14]

Philadelphia's preeminence extended into the arts. During the decade of the 1750s more than a dozen artists of prominence lived and worked in that city. Benjamin West began his illustrious career there and went on to become president of the Royal Academy in London. Among his contemporaries were James Claypoole, John Meng, Henry Bembridge, Pierre du Simitière, and Charles Willson Peale. Penn's city even surpassed Boston in musical activity. By the outbreak of the Revolution, all denominations, save the Quakers, had added sumptuous musical offerings to their services. Private concerts had begun as early as 1739 and, by 1769, the Italian virtuoso, Giovanni Gualdo, had initiated a public subscription series. By 1776, the city boasted over thirty music teachers and several serious composers of whom Francis Hopkinson was probably the best known.[15]

This liberal, intellectual, and cultural climate combined with economic prosperity prompted Walter Murray and Thomas Kean to organize the first company of professional actors in British North America. The company produced plays at a warehouse owned by future mayor, William Plumstead. The warehouse, like the Elizabethan public theatres, lay outside the city limits, and was thus immune to official municipal sanctions. Although Addison's *Cato*, presented in August 1749, was the only play that was certainly produced, there were probably others because the company remained in Philadelphia at least until January 1750. Although the city council could not close the theatre, it condemned the company's performances and charged the local constabulary to watch them carefully. Sensing that the religious climate was still inhospitable to theatre, Murray, Kean, and their company left Philadelphia for New York in February.[16]

While Philadelphia was spawning, albeit grudgingly, the first professional theatre company in British North America, Massachusetts took steps to insure that the same blight would not infect its precincts. In March 1750, the General Court of Massachusetts passed an "Act to Prevent Stage-Plays and other Theatricals." It provided punishment for anyone who for any reason allowed performers to use "any house, room or place," for "acting or carrying on any stage-plays, interludes or other theatrical entertainments whosoever." It also forbade any person to act in or witness said activities.[17]

The impetus for the passage of such a law is not precisely known, but interest in theatre was certainly on the rise. Lillo's *The London Merchant* was printed in the *Boston Weekly Journal* in 1732. A poem in the April 23, 1750 issue of the *Boston Evening Post* alluded to the fact that private performances periodically took place in the city. William Clapp argued that "two young Englishmen, assisted by some volunteer comrades from the town" had presented Otway's *The Orphan, or Unhappy Marriage* at the Coffee House in State Street early in 1750.[18] And, of course, the Murray–Kean Company had been active in Philadelphia in 1749 and had begun to produce plays in New York in March 1750. Irrespective of the specific provocation, the "Act to Prevent Stage-Plays" remained in force for the next forty years.

However, the entire colonial theatre environment was on the brink of change. In 1751, William Hallam, an actor–manager at the New Wells Theatre in London, was forced to close his theatre. By that time, thousands of English citizens had immigrated to the New World and British actors were already performing in Jamaica. Hallam thus went about assembling a company to travel to the North American colonies. In May 1752, the Company of Comedians from London managed by Lewis Hallam, William's brother, set sail. The company landed in Yorktown and traveled overland to Williamsburg where Hallam immediately applied for permission to build a theatre. After some initial complications, the London Company opened its first production, *The Merchant of Venice*, on September 15, 1752.[19] From this moment until 1774, the censorship of theatre in British North America would be almost exclusively aimed at this company.

The Williamsburg season lasted eleven months and was, by all accounts, extremely successful. However, the population of Virginia was not numerous enough to provide sufficient income for the company, and it departed for New York. Once again the company overcame initial opposition and commenced a prosperous run on September 17, 1753.[20] Sometime before the end of the New York season, Hallam received an invitation to perform in Philadelphia, which was extended by "several gentlemen of that city." They suggested that he apply directly to Governor James Hamilton "for permission to open a theatre in that city, and pledged themselves for the success notwithstanding any opposition from the followers of Penn."[21]

Although the Assembly's efforts earlier in the century to ban theatre had been unsuccessful, the colonial governor, who was appointed by the Penn family, still possessed the authority to prohibit the company from appearing. Arguments both for and against this visit were sent to various newspapers in an attempt to influence Hamilton's decision. One series, which appeared in Benjamin Franklin's *Pennsylvania Gazette*, was particularly revelatory because it placed these competing agendas in stark relief. An opponent of theatre who identified himself only as "A.B." maintained that theatre in

England was so foul that it was "impossible to enter it, and not come out the Worse for having been in." He called it the "great Corrupter of the Town" and a "Shame to our Nation and Religion." Finally, he claimed that actors, whom he called the "very Dregs of Human Nature," would make it their business "to debauch your Minds by their lewd Compositions, and wanton Gesticulations."[22]

His remarks were rebutted the following week by "Y.Z.," who sardonically characterized his opponent as one of the "gloomy spirits" who painted the Creator "as a sour morose Being, disgusted with Cheerfulness and Gaiety in his Children." Such people, he continued, "are often fighting against nature and reason, embracing things that are painful, because they are disagreeable." In his closing, he departed from his attack on "gloomy spirits" to introduce a crucial defense of the London Company. He equated theatregoing with the all-important Enlightenment concept of personal freedom, which could not be abridged because of religious disapproval:

> We are happily situated in a *free country*, under a *good prince*, and a *mild government*; and it is not at present unlawful for any man, or set of men, to be entertained in any manner not injurious to their neighbors . . . let not those who have fettered themselves by their own too rigid rules, and themselves cannot enjoy entertainments of a more agreeable kind, how much soever they desire them, envy those that have preserved their liberty, nor endeavor to deprive them of it.[23]

Clearly, the upcoming visit of the London Company had prompted the clash of two opposing ideals. The first privileged the Church and the state. To "A.B." and his colleagues, individual choice based upon the desire to experience personal pleasure was unthinkable. The prevailing order – "our Nation and Religion" – could not endure the resulting chaos. He argued that such institutions needed and demanded uncritical submission from citizens and congregations in order to survive. Unapproved behavior was the "great Corrupter" and could not be countenanced.

On the other hand, "Y.Z."'s laissez-faire attitude toward theatre was indicative of Enlightenment ideals. Within this construct, the rights of the individual were privileged above the needs of the state and the demands of religion. A secular state was to protect the rights of its citizens to pursue life, liberty, property, and happiness, provided, of course, these pursuits did not interfere with the rights of others to exercise those same privileges. The jurisdiction of the Church was to be limited to parochial matters. Morals were to be governed by the laws of nature, which were determined by scientists, not churchmen. Thus, it would be immoral to prohibit or in any way obstruct a citizen from engaging in pleasurable entertainments, including the theatre.

Although Governor Hamilton sided with "Y.Z." and the other liberals of Philadelphia, he was not entirely comfortable. He warned the company that it should offer "nothing indecent or immoral," and limited its engagement to a mere twenty-four performances. He also required it to post a cash bond and perform "one night for the benefit of the city." Hallam, too, was aware of the inhospitable climate, and he, like Murray and Kean, used William Plumstead's warehouse, which insured that the city council would not interfere. The company opened its first Philadelphia season on April 15, 1754. The program consisted of *The Fair Penitent* and *Miss in Her Teens*, which was presented "before a numerous and polite Audience, who responded with universal applause."[24]

On June 19, 1754, the first Philadelphia season came to a close with a performance of Colley Cibber's *The Careless Husband* for the Charity School. The company's effort netted £100 for the school, a sum that indicated the theatre was filled to capacity.[25] In October 1754, it opened its first Charleston season, and in January 1755 Hallam took the company to Jamaica. There the intrepid manager contracted yellow fever and died. His widow married David Douglass who had operated a relatively prosperous theatre in the West Indies, and in 1758 they returned to the North American colonies.

In mid October, the Douglass Company disembarked in New York. The new manager, having spent several years in the leisurely, hospitable climes of Jamaica, was not accustomed to the bureaucracy of North America. Upon his arrival, he began to build a new theatre on Kruger's Wharf, but his application to perform was denied. While it was possible that Douglass offended some religious sensibilities, no such objections appeared in the New York papers. More than likely, Douglass, a foreigner and an itinerant, had failed to acknowledge the policing function of the local magistrates. He worsened his situation by publishing a letter in the *Mercury* in which he claimed he would not open a theatre but rather "An Histrionic Academy," in which he would deliver "Dissertations...Moral, Instructive and Entertaining." When authorities responded even more harshly to this ruse, he resorted to a strategy that has been the refuge of so many artists – self-inflicted, public degradation. He claimed that he had not intended to circumvent the law nor had he intended to affront the "Gentlemen, on whom I am dependent for the only means that can save us from sure ruin." He concluded by asking their favor and begging their forgiveness.[26] Apparently the gesture of public obeisance soothed the magistrates and the Douglass Company opened in New York on New Year's Day, 1759. There were no further incidents and, by all accounts, it was a successful season.

Douglass wanted to play in Philadelphia that year and accordingly petitioned Governor William Denny for permission – well in advance of his arrival. He intended to build a theatre on Society Hill, which also lay outside the city limits. When word leaked out that such a project was in the making, Quakers, Presbyterians, Lutherans, and Baptists petitioned the governor to halt construction. The "Synod of Ministers" claimed that plays were "fatal sources of obscenity; inveterate enemies to virtue and devotion." They demanded that the Assembly "preserve the honour of the deity, the interests of religion and virtue, and the public safety" by putting a "stop to such pernicious plays in this province, in the present and future times."[27]

When Denny failed to act on the petition, the Assembly passed an "Act of the More Effectual Suppressing and Preventing of Lotteries and Plays" on June 20, 1759. The act called the erection of the theatre a "scandal of religion," and accused the London Company of seducing the "weak, poor and necessitous" to neglect their "labor and industry" by attending the theatre.[28] The governor neatly sidestepped the issue. He approved the act, but changed its effective date to January 1, 1760, thereby allowing the company to perform for six months. Not unexpectedly, the Crown vetoed the measure in September.[29]

Encouraged by his successes in Quaker Pennsylvania, Douglass decided to venture into Puritan New England, not Massachusetts, but Newport, Rhode Island. Here, the "shores of Narragansett Bay were blown by breezes of tolerance . . . which were to the actor folk invigorating."[30] Douglass and his company arrived in the late spring of 1761, but had neglected to secure references from the governor of Virginia. A company member then rushed south to secure the necessary document. In the interval, Douglass advertised that on June 10 in the Kings Arms Tavern he would present a series of *Moral Dialogues in five parts depicting the Evil Effects of Jealousy and other Bad Passions, and proving that Happiness can only Spring from the Pursuit of Virtue*. Taken together these "moral dialogues" constituted *Othello*. By using the familiar rhetoric of the Enlightenment and by avoiding the words "acting" and "plays," he hoped to deflect any hostility to his venture until an official permit was issued.[31]

The *Dialogues* were well received, but public response was not uniformly positive. At a town meeting in August, angry citizens voted to ban the players. Irrespective of this negative decision, Douglass began work on a theatre on Easton's Point. Exactly what prompted Douglass to oppose the Newport citizenry in such a blatant manner is a mystery. B. W. Brown speculates that Douglass trusted that Newport's wealthy citizens could control and ultimately change public opinion over time. This hypothesis may indeed be accurate. Influential Philadelphians had managed to overcome vigorous opposition and the same situation may have obtained in Newport. Nonetheless, a great deal of the credit had to go to Douglass. His company performed during September and October, the months that the General Assembly was in session. During that time, he made sure that all the Rhode Island lawmakers received passes and before leaving he produced two benefits for the poor. Douglass' first New England season had been profitable and surprisingly peaceful.[32]

From Rhode Island, Douglass took his company to New York, where he began construction on a new theatre at the corner of Nassau and Chapel (now Beekman) streets. As a result of England's decision to withdraw its troops to the Caribbean to fight the French, New York was sinking into a deep recession. It is at this point that the economic argument against theatre began to be advanced. Merchants claimed that it siphoned off too much money from the city, tempted men and women to spend frivolously, and deprived the poor of needed assistance. Thus, troublesome economic conditions began to take on the dimensions of a moral emergency, and theatre was now blamed for financial as well as spiritual destitution. Consequently, Douglass could only obtain permission to perform in the city for two months or until December 1761.

He managed to extend his company's stay in New York, but on December 21, only three days after the original deadline had passed, a withering attack appeared in *Weyman's Gazette*. It accused dramatic performances of tempting "servants and apprentices to embezzle their masters property; inflaming the passions of youth by scenes of obscenity and lust; [and] instilling a strong relish for a voluptuous and indolent life." Finally, the writer accused the London Company of earning in excess of £6,000 which he compared to stealing.[33]

Usually, Douglass held his temper when confronted with such absurdities. On this occasion, he vehemently rebutted his opponent. He detailed his expenses and calculated that the company would only share 620 pounds; and, in a rare attack, he claimed that his actors had earned this small sum more honorably than "those who have raked together thousands by an inflexible attachment to their own dear interests, by oppressing the fatherless and widows, and unfeelingly grinding the face of the poor."[34]

By the time Douglass finally departed New York in April 1762, much of the heated acrimony had vanished. He returned to Newport in early June and ventured on to Providence after a few performances. Unfortunately, Providence was not Newport and he completely misjudged the tenor of the population. On July 19, the town voted to petition the General Assembly to outlaw theatre in Rhode Island. Douglass defied the mandate, as he had in Newport, and continued to produce plays. The anti-theatrical residents of Providence made good on their promise. On August 24, a petition signed by over 400 male citizens was presented to the General Assembly:

> petitioners in this county, humbly conceiving that so expensive amusements and idle diversion cannot have any good tendency among us, especially at this time, when this colony as well as others is laboring under the grievous calamity of an uncommon draught and a very great scarcity of hay and provisions. Wherefore your petitioners pray that you will ... make some effectual law to prevent any stage-plays, comedians, or theatrical performances being acted in this Colony in the future.[35]

The exact connection between the dramatic enactments of the London Company and the "uncommon draught" and "scarcity of hay" was never clarified, but the petition was approved without debate. There would be no more professional theatre in New England until after the Revolution.[36]

Douglass took his company south for the next four years – to Virginia, South Carolina, and finally Jamaica. During this hiatus, anti-British feeling erupted as a result of the Stamp Act. In spring 1766, an amateur company was performing *The Twin Rivals* in New York at the Chapel Street Theatre. The radical "Sons of Liberty" decided that theatre, like tea, was a British export and should be boycotted or destroyed. They had already burned playbills along with some tax stamps, and had prevented a performance on April 9. The company tried to perform again on May 5, but the "Sons" invaded the house about the middle of the first act. They demolished the interior and unceremoniously dispersed the actors and audience. During the fray one boy was killed.[37]

The American Company in the virtuous republic

The violent responses to the Stamp Act convinced Douglass that the interests and safety of his company would be better served if he allied himself more conspicuously with his adopted homeland. He thus renamed his theatre the American Company and changed his repertory. He decreased the number of royalist, authoritarian tragedies that depicted the evils of rebellion and civil disorder. He replaced them with main pieces and farces that upheld family order, thereby suggesting that Douglass was attempting to appeal to his audience's increased interests in prosperity and stability rather than the authority of monarchs. Prominent in his new repertory were plays by Richard Cumberland, David Garrick, Oliver Goldsmith, and Hugh Kelly, as well as the ballad operas of Isaac Bickerstaff and the semi-operatic adaptations of Shakespeare's *The Tempest* and *Cymbeline*. Yet his opponents in Philadelphia refused to be mollified by Douglass' conciliatory gestures, particularly when it became known that Douglass planned to build a theatre in Southwark when he returned there in the fall of 1766.[38]

Well-rehearsed religious diatribes once again appeared. They alleged that theatre was irreducibly degenerate and asserted: "If you live in the use of this diversion, you have no grounds to hope, that you have the spirit and heart of a Christian."[39] Not surprisingly, the theatre building itself was also the target of significant antagonism. It was labeled the "devil's abode, where he holds his filthy court of evil Spirits."[40] Another adversary indicted it as the "sink of corruption and debauchery."[41]

However, the most heated opposition to the Douglass Company came from radical American Whigs who feared that theatre would spoil the virtue of Americans. American Whigs, who had for some time been influenced by radical English Whigs and Augustan satirists, concluded that England was irredeemably corrupt, dangerously diseased, and eaten away by vice, greed, and luxury.[42] Thus, many observers concluded, Americans were more capable than the British of establishing the much-longed-for "virtuous republic." In order to create this idealized state, America needed a citizenry willing to sacrifice private desires for the public good. As Benjamin Rush declared, a citizen had to become "public property [and] his time and talents – his youth – his manhood – his old age – nay more, life, all belong to his country."[43]

America, however, was already showing signs of internal decay. Instead of practicing temperance, industry, and frugality, Americans had been seduced by luxury, individualism, and social rivalries. The position of the arts in this discourse was equivocal, at best. John Adams, despite his sensuous attraction to the world of art, remained suspicious. He argued, "The more elegance, the less virtue, in all times and countries," and railed that painting, sculpture, music, gardens, and furniture were "bagatelles introduced by time and luxury in change for the great qualities and hardy, manly virtues of the human heart." Thus, conservative religious opposition to theatre merged with a generalized cultural paranoia to create what Gordon Wood called "secular Puritanism."[44]

Within this paradigm, the pleasure and delight offered by theatre were thoroughly incompatible with rectitude and "manly virtues":

> At a time, when pleasure seems to be the grand idol of our cares, and dissipation the object of our wishes, it is really a matter of serious concern, to behold the great encouragement that is given to follies and diversions, of every kind, in this city...I believe I shall not stand in single in the opinion, when I assert, that PLAYS have an evil tendency to corrupt and debauch the mind...When we examine the rise and fall of states, and trace the causes by which whole nations have sunk at once from the height of glory into more than Gothic barbarity, we shall find them to be principally owing to the luxury and effeminacy of the times.[45]

The concept of "republican virtue" also incorporated significant concern for security. The colonial middle class, a sizable population, which included prosperous small merchants, tradesmen, and craftsmen, routinely voiced these concerns. For this group, any decline of "republican virtue" signified fiscal as well as political and religious degeneration. Wastefulness and frivolity, once only personal flaws, were now regarded as palpable threats to the community.

A contributor to the *Gazette*, who called himself "The Censor," castigated "Masters of Families [who] are complaining of the great scarcity of money, and of the degeneration of trade, and are watching their expenses" for "giving encouragement to a set of strolling comedians."[46] "A Friend to All Mankind" condemned the wealthy because they "leave the poor and distressed without alms, and turn a deaf ear to their affecting supplication. – Good God! To what a depth of insensibility are these unhappy people [theatregoers] fallen."[47]

It was, however, well-to-do middle-class sons who were at the gravest risk. Because they had not been tempered in the fires of worldly competition, they were too naive to withstand the temptations proffered by the theatre. A lengthy poem published in the *Gazette* in April 1767 warned that dire economic consequences awaited young men who frequented the theatre. It read in part:

> Lo! Sons of trade from the paths of profit stray,
> Charmed with the Pleasures of the attracting PLAY.
> What will those sons by passion's slaves commence?
> Unhinged from business, headlong in Expense?
> On rising Youth Profusion's Floods will press,
> Plunge them in Vice, and whelm them in Distress;
> Licentious revels! Blending night and day,
> Till truth and trade, and industry decay;
> Till lavish waste shall feel its galling loads,
> And bold advent'rers rob the public road.[48]

Irrespective of the frenzy and pitch of the discourse, the American Company opened its third Philadelphia season in November 1766. It was arguably the single most successful season in the brief history of colonial theatre. The company gave approximately 100 performances of forty-two plays, between November 14, 1766 and July 6, 1767.[49] Judging from the number of complaints about young people in attendance, apprentices and servants were as well represented as the gentry.

The American Company returned to New York in December 1767 when Douglass opened the John Street Theatre. He remained there until August 1768. In spite of new financial hardships brought on by the Townshend Acts and some isolated antagonistic criticisms, the season was peaceful. It finally seemed that theatre had become, if not universally approved, at least tolerated. For the next six years, Douglass and the American Company performed without any significant interference.[50] The Revolution, however, was at hand and, on October 20, 1774, the Continental Congress, in session in Philadelphia, resolved to close all theatres "in order to encourage frugality...and discountenance and discourage, every species of extravagance and dissipation, especially all horse racing, and all kinds of gaming, cock fighting, exhibition of shows and plays, and other expensive diversions and entertainments."[51] Following this Congressional fiat, the American Company withdrew to the more hospitable confines of Jamaica where it remained until 1784.

During the war, theatre was a favorite pastime of British officers who produced a significant number of plays in Faneuil Hall in Boston, in the John Street Theatre in New York, and in the Southwark Theatre in Philadelphia. The Americans, in spite of the Congress' prohibition against theatre, also presented plays. Perhaps the most famous production occurred on May 11, 1778, in Valley Forge to celebrate the French and American alliance signed in February of that year. Washington, an inveterate theatregoer, ordered a grand military fête to celebrate the signing of the treaty, and a performance of Addison's *Cato* was the centerpiece of the festivities.[52]

Congress' opposition to plays was blatantly ignored on other occasions as well. In Philadelphia, during September and October 1778, American officers produced plays to benefit "families who have suffered in the war for American liberty."[53] This continued defiance by American officers clearly outraged Congress, which was meeting at the time in Philadelphia. On October 12, it passed a second resolution that left no doubt that a moral as well as a political revolution was being waged, and that theatre threatened both. The statement opened by reiterating that "true religion and good morals are the only solid foundation of public liberty and happiness," and went on to outlaw "theatrical entertainments, horse-racing, gambling, and other such diversions" because they were "productive of idleness, dissipation and a general depravity of principles and manners."[54] When rumors of performances persisted, Congress passed an even harsher sanction. It threatened persons holding official positions in the new government who "act, promote, encourage or attend such plays" with immediate dismissal.[55] Nonetheless, many of the former colonies blatantly disregarded Congressional prohibitions and theatrical entertainments – approved, produced, and attended by Americans – continued in New York, Annapolis, Baltimore, and Portsmouth, New Hampshire.

Professional theatre in the new nation

With the end of the war came freedom – and confusion. The population was physically and emotionally exhausted. The economy was on the brink of collapse and social chaos reigned. The former colonies (now states) were not yet a nation. Although the patriots had fought to liberate themselves from the "yoke of British Tyranny," it was far from clear how this newfound freedom would manifest itself. In the minds of many, luxury and pleasure were equated with corruption and social decay, and had to be combated if the Republic was to fulfill its destiny. For these critics, theatre epitomized this decadence. By promoting a spirit of play rather than productivity, by encouraging imaginative processes, rather than practical skills, it embodied all of the dissolute impulses that had debilitated other powerful nations, including England.

Ironically, the supporters of dramatic entertainment also acknowledged the tendency of theatre to debase its audiences. They, however, assured the public that this powerful force would be carefully regulated and used only to advance public and private morality. Theatre was to be an engine of virtue, with noble heroes and heroines functioning as unimpeachable standards by which all citizens could measure the worth of their own actions.

The opponents of theatre were not convinced and pitched battles – particularly in Pennsylvania and Massachusetts – soon erupted. In 1779, Pennsylvania had followed the lead of the Continental Congress and enacted its own anti-theatrical legislation. In an effort to purge the citizenry of any lingering attachment to English culture, it prohibited "acting, showing or exhibiting any tragedy, comedy, tragi-comedy, farce, interlude or other play." In July 1782, John Henry, who, before the war was the leading actor of the American Company, petitioned the Assembly to repeal the 1779 anti-theatrical law. His appeal was rejected. A year later, the petition of another actor, Dennis Ryan, was also denied. Early in January 1784, Lewis Hallam, Jr., who had taken over the management of the American Company from Douglass, also requested that the Assembly relax its injunction, but to no avail. Undaunted, Hallam performed *A Lecture upon Heads* from April 1 to June 9 at the Southwark. A blatant subterfuge, *Lecture* was an entertainment consisting of satirical and serious recitations, songs, dances, and speeches that had been occasionally performed by Douglass when authorities would not permit him to produce plays.[56]

A fully reconstituted American Company, under the direction of Hallam and Henry, returned in December and remained until July 1785. Advertisements were purposefully obfuscated in order to evade authorities. Thus, the company would perform "pantomimical finales" and "dialogue and dumb show," in addition to "lectures." In September 1786, the Assembly, smarting from Hallam's circumvention of the law, strengthened the 1779 legislation. It extended the list of offenses to include pantomimes, and set the fine for producing any type of performance at £200 per occurrence.[57]

Irrespective of these new prohibitions, Hallam and Henry, and their company returned for two weeks in January 1787 and for a longer stay in June of that year. Although under the interdiction of the Assembly, they nonetheless presented full-length productions, which they described as "Spectaculum Vitae": *Jane Shore* became *The Penitent Wife; or Fatal Indiscretion*; *The School for Scandal* was changed to *A Comic Lecture in five parts on the Pernicious Vice of Scandal*; and *Hamlet* was transfigured into *Filial Piety*.[58]

In its battle with the Assembly, the company, which had since been renamed the Old American Company, was given crucial support by General Washington. During June 1787, the Constitutional Convention was

in session in Philadelphia, and Washington and his wife attended performances on three occasions, each of which was widely publicized. The
importance of these events can hardly be overestimated. As a man who was
admired by nearly every citizen in the new nation, his approval immeasurably enhanced the position of theatre and placed significant pressure on the
Assembly to rescind this legislation.[59]

In March 1788, Hallam and Henry once again petitioned the Assembly
to nullify the anti-theatre law. On this occasion the examining committee
reported favorably to the full Assembly, calling the stage "a great mart of
genius," and a "natural and necessary concomitant of our independence."[60]
The resolution was tabled. By far the most important development within
this contentious period was the appearance of the Dramatic Association.
Organized and supported by some of Philadelphia's most influential citizens, its avowed purpose was the repeal of the 1786 anti-theatre law. Its
arguments, though varied, rested on a theme that had come to dominate
many debates about freedom – the right of citizens to exercise personal
preference when choosing how to spend leisure time. In a petition signed
by over 2,000 residents, the Dramatic Association stated that those who
wished to prohibit drama sought to deprive their fellow citizens of rational
enjoyment, and thus "abridge the natural right of every freeman, to dispose
of his time and money, according to his own taste and disposition, when
not obnoxious to the real interests of society." Most importantly, it warned
that, if this type of social control were permitted, it would be extended into
other disputed areas of life:

> If, indeed, a mere difference of opinion shall be thought a sufficient foun-
> dation to curtail our rights, and diminish our enjoyments, the boasted
> liberality of the present age, will be eclipsed by the furious bigotry of the
> middle centuries; and the same authority which proscribes our amuse-
> ments, may, with equal justice, dictate the shape and texture of our dress,
> or the modes and ceremonies of our worship. This, however, is an evil
> which, we are confident, cannot receive the countenance of a legislature,
> elected to ensure the equal rights of the citizens of a free commonwealth.
> The claim of superior wisdom, virtue, and patriotism, arrogantly enforced
> will there be disregarded.[61]

By linking the establishment of the theatre to freedom of choice, the Dramatic Association appealed to an irreducible precept of liberty for which
the Revolution had been waged and upon which the new Republic had
been founded. The Assembly finally consented and, on March 2, 1789, a

bill to repeal the 1786 law against theatre passed by a 35 to 27 vote.[62] However, the Assembly, still convinced that a theatre left to its own devices bred chaos, was determined to protect the "morals, peace and order of society." Thus, the new legislation empowered the president of the Supreme Executive Council, the Chief Justice of the Supreme Court, and the president of the Court of Common Pleas for the County of Philadelphia to license any drama that was to be presented.[63] Although circumscribed, professional theatre could once again be presented openly in Philadelphia. No longer in need of subterfuges, the Old American Company proudly announced that its next play, *The Roman Father*, would be presented at the Southwark Theatre "By Authority." Soon, a similar battle would commence in Boston.

The General Court of Massachusetts had passed "An Act to Prevent Stage-Plays and other Theatrical Entertainments" in March 1750. Bostonians put together their first organized effort to repeal the act in 1767. Joseph Tisdale, a Boston merchant, spoke before the House of Representatives supporting a measure to rescind the 1750 law.[64] While Tisdale garnered some support from the more socially minded delegates from Boston and Salem, he could not overcome the combined prejudices of the Congregational clergy and representatives from rural Massachusetts. The measure failed.

The first post-war attempt to legalize theatre came in June 1790 when Hallam and Henry petitioned the General Court to open a theatre. The petition was summarily ignored, but the discursive treatment of theatre took an ironic turn. Prior to the Revolution, American patriots associated theatre with the decadent, dictatorial English monarchy. After the Revolution, those who favored legalizing the stage characterized themselves as freedom-loving Americans, and likened their opponents to the despotic regime that had just been defeated:

> THEATRE: The question which is to be agitated this day, is not, whether a theatre shall be erected in this town, or not. It is, whether the citizens of the metropolis will any longer silently submit to an infringement on their natural and imprescribable rights. Whether the slavish restrictions of a law, made when the state was under the dominion of a foreign monarch, and that a period when the rights of man, and of citizens, scarcely known, were but little understood, shall any longer block the record of time.[65]

On October 26, 1791, the residents of Boston, in a town meeting, appointed a committee to advise its legislative representatives regarding repeal of the Act of 1750. On November 9, the day that the report was to be announced, an article appeared in the *Columbian Centinel* that set the tone for the ensuing debate. In rhetoric reminiscent of the radical broadsides of 1774, it exhorted Bostonians to fight for theatre as one of their unalienable rights: "*Citizens of Boston!* Be firm as you ever have been − It would be arrogance to recommend to you coolness and manly dignity. It is not for a *Theatre* you will contend − It will be for the RIGHTS of MEN! In their cause you have ever acquired honour, and ever will."[66]

In article after article, the merits and demerits of theatre were hotly debated. Proponents consistently goaded legislators with the fact that theatre was now legal in other states: "Is the Legislature of Massachusetts less enlightened than that of Pennsylvania, or will it be less liberal?"[67] Regional rivalries were exploited. When the *Centinel* reported that Connecticut and New Hampshire permitted theatre, it asked, "whether the citizens of Boston are not as virtuous and discerning, and possess as much taste and regard for propriety, as their neighbors?"[68] The clergy was also targeted: "Is it because we have committed the care of our souls to them that they mean to take care of our bodies also? Are we not able to take care of ourselves and our purses? Or do they suppose if we spend our money at the theatre, we shall have none left to give them?"[69]

The repeal of the anti-theatre law of 1750 was introduced into the Assembly in January 1792. John Gardiner, an avid proponent of this cause, presented an impassioned plea. His appeal was later printed and distributed throughout Boston. He described his effort as an attempt "to dispel the dark fogs of an absurd, blind superstition," and predicted that the "dark gloomy bigot must soon go off the stage of life." Not unaware of the keen concern for financial gain among Massachusetts's businessmen, he closed by enumerating the several economic benefits that would accrue if a theatre were built.[70] In spite of his prodigious efforts − the published form of his address exceeded 100 pages − his motion was denied by a vote of 99 to 44.[71]

Irrespective of the Assembly vote, Bostonians were determined to have theatre. In late August, Alexandre Placide and Joseph Harper opened the New Exhibition Room in Board Alley. Their initial offerings consisted of tightrope-walking, tumbling, acrobatics, a few musical pieces, and recitations.[72] Although the entertainments lacked sophistication, the *Centinel* reported that the boxes were filled with genteel women and that "the place will continue to be frequented by the amiable fair and encouraged by the judicious and enlightened of both sexes."[73]

The original company only numbered five members, but soon began to grow as word spread that there was a theatre in Boston. From August 28 to October 24 the company's membership grew to twenty-one. By October it had launched a regular repertory season, and, in the four months between September and December, Placide and Harper presented twenty-five full-length plays, thirty-five afterpieces, four full-length French operas, and a full-length comic opera.[74]

Some Bostonians, however, still objected to the fact that an illegal theatre was operating in Boston. The most ardent opponent of the New Exhibition Room was none other than Governor John Hancock. He considered the presentation of plays a direct challenge to the authority of the state and ordered Boston officials to close the theatre. On December 5, 1792, during a performance of *The School for Scandal,* Boston's sheriff arrested Harper. The audience on that evening, composed primarily of young men, was incensed at being deprived of their entertainment. They stormed the stage and tore down the arms of the state and a portrait of the governor that hung in front of the stage box.[75] Harper was released the next morning on a technicality. He took part of the company and went to Providence, Rhode Island. Placide traveled with the remaining members to Salem. On December 21, an irate citizens committee, which included John Quincy Adams and Paul Revere, initiated a move to revoke the 1750 anti-theatre law. In February, the legislative process began once again. A committee wrote out a new bill and on March 27, after gaining approval in the House of Representatives, it was sent to the Senate where it was passed the same day. On March 28, Governor Hancock reported back that he did not intend to sign the bill, but would make no objections to it. Although not officially repealed until 1806, the 1750 law prohibiting theatre in Massachusetts had been, for all intents and purposes, nullified.[76]

The Board Alley Theatre remained in operation until June of that year when it was demolished. In the April 23 issue of the *Centinel*, it was announced that a subscription drive for a new, elegant home for dramatic performances was to be launched. The Boston Theatre, later known as the Federal Theatre, was designed by none other than Charles Bullfinch and opened on February 3, 1794. With this event "legal theatre" commenced in Boston. Its subsequent journey, however, was anything but smooth.

Idealists who maintained that the drama would play a significant role in their plan to create a rational and progressive society had led the battle for theatre in eighteenth-century North America. Throughout this conflict, however, it was always assumed that the new American culture would propagate a continuation of classical European traditions. Such was not the case. The idealism of the Enlightenment gave way to the democracy of popular culture in the second decade of the nineteenth century. Advocates of theatre would go on to lament that drama, like other arts, had been vulgarized and that a universal barbarism had engulfed the nation. Theatre artists who embraced classical traditions found themselves in an increasingly hostile environment, isolated from the mainstream of American culture, which was being shaped by a materialistically minded public.

Despite the nagging sense that theatre was potentially subversive, Americans, during the first two decades of the nineteenth century, had begun to lay aside their religious concerns and accept theatre as a significant means of cultural expression. However, the acceptance of theatre did not mean that all controversy ceased. On the contrary, violent antagonisms erupted with alarming frequency. And, while the content of plays was not a particularly distressing issue, concern about audience behavior increased significantly. Given the traditions that informed the behavior of working-class audiences in early nineteenth-century auditoriums, theatre reformers were faced with a daunting challenge.[77] During the colonial period and for the first two decades of the nineteenth century, theatres were dominated by the tastes of the urban gentry who built them. During the 1830s and 1840s, however, theatres became embroiled in what Sean Wilentz called the "great transformation." During this historical moment American upper, middle, and working classes began their confrontational formative process, and theatre quickly became a hotly contested site as an ever-increasing number of skilled and unskilled workers vigorously challenged the aristocrats that controlled it.[78]

The early years of the Bowery Theatre clearly demonstrated this process. The Bowery opened in June 1826 and Philip Hone, the aristocratic, ex-mayor of New York, laid the cornerstone. In his dedicatory speech he outlined his expectations for the theatre:

> When preserving its natural purity under the influence of correct taste, the drama has never caused the blush of shame to tinge the cheek of modesty... It is therefore incumbent upon those whose standing in society enables them to control opinions, and to direct the judgment of others, to encourage by their countenance and support, a well regulated theatre, in order that this popular amusement, innocent and laudable, when properly conducted, may not denigrate into licentiousness by seeking its patronage from corrupt taste and vitiated indulgences.[79]

For four years the Bowery "never tinged the cheek of modesty," and was on the verge of bankruptcy. In 1830, Thomas Hamblin became manager and abruptly unveiled a new strategy that would have a significant impact on the composition of the Bowery's audiences and on the way other New York theatres conducted business. He turned almost exclusively to melodramatic and equestrian spectacles, and reinvested his profits in publicity, scenery, and costumes in order to attract working-class audiences who lived in that area. Walt Whitman's elegiac description of the Bowery's audience aptly described the popularity of Hamblin's plan:

> well dressed, young and middle-aged men, the best average of American-born mechanics – the emotional nature of the whole mass arous'd by the power and magnetism of as mighty mimes as ever trod the stage – the whole auditorium and what seeth'd in it and flushed from its faces and eyes to me as much a part of the show as any – bursting forth in one of those long-kept-up tempests of hand clapping peculiar to the Bowery – no dainty-kid-glove business, but electric forces and muscle from perhaps 2000 full-sinew'd men.[80]

The vast majority of these "full-sinew'd men" were the Bowery B'hoys, who had become the topics of travelogues, dime novels, police gazettes, and plays. They first became noticeable in the 1840s when a large percentage of the New York working class was composed of young single males. They had migrated to the city to find work, lived in boarding houses, and gathered together in saloons and theatres. They valued self-help, independence, fairness, generosity, and, most of all, egalitarianism. They vigorously opposed any form of pretense or class distinctions. Theirs was a distinctly masculine culture that defined itself by rowdy behavior. Typically, the B'hoys ran with the fire companies, which by the 1830s had become clubs for young workingmen, and often preferred brawling with other fire companies to extinguishing fires. By the late 1840s the B'hoys had become the subject of so much popular discourse that they had been transformed into a cultural icon. They became the representation of what was good and bad and even what it meant to be an American.[81]

For the B'hoys, the theatre was merely an extension of the street or the marketplace. The pit was their exclusive preserve where they ate, drank, shouted, and fought. When not engaging in these activities, they might lift a stranger over their heads and pass him back and forth until they were exhausted. And all of these activities transpired during the course of the performance. The B'hoys reveled in the traditions of audience sovereignty and frequently demanded specific tunes, called for encores, and demanded that management and actors appear before the curtain to justify certain decisions.

Although the B'hoys may have ruled the pit of several American theatres, working-class males ruled little else. During the 1820s, expanded markets, improved transportation systems, and the advent of modern manufacturing precipitated the demise of the craft system, transforming labor into a market commodity. In addition, massive immigration continued to drive down already depressed wages. By the late 1830s, the antagonisms between workers and aristocrats had reached critical mass. As Peter George Buckley has so painstakingly described, the debate over the relative propriety or impropriety of audience behavior in New York theatres during this period indicated the presence of a highly charged political and social semiotic system that signified deep social divisions:

> Because of the public nature of the early nineteenth-century stage – with its mingling of classes and its active rights of audience sovereignty – theatre culture became a sensitive index to class formation, especially as manifested in the battle for control over the public sphere of politics, the press and the streets. Here, the theatre was not just a mirror but a central ground for the struggle.[82]

By the early 1840s, New York's upper classes, in an attempt to distance themselves from workers and immigrants, moved northward out of the Bowery. In addition, they constructed for themselves the Astor Place Opera House, a home for Italian opera and a cultural oasis for fashionable New Yorkers. The Opera House thus signified, in a material sense, aristocratic exclusiveness and superiority.

This cleavage was further exacerbated by a furious theatrical rivalry that had developed. Edwin Forrest, the first native-born "star" of the American stage, whose powerfully robust style greatly appealed to working-class audiences, particularly the B'hoy, was at his apogee. William Charles Macready, the famous English actor who was noted for his carefully fashioned Shakespearean portrayals, was the favorite of New York's elite, and his chief rival. The volatile working-class audiences of lower New York took a dim view of this support. They interpreted this approval as an attempt of the upper classes to dominate theatrical tastes just as they had asserted their control of the economy. On May 7, 1849, both actors were in New York and both were slated to perform Macbeth, with Macready's performance to occur in the Opera House. Forrest's supporters infiltrated the auditorium, greeted the actor with hisses and boos, hurled fruit, eggs, nuts, and chairs, and eventually halted Macready's performance.

Macready was determined to leave the city but was persuaded by forty-seven prominent citizens to continue his engagement. On May 10, Macready's supporters were prepared for any eventuality. Police arrested ticket holders who appeared to be troublemakers and 200 militiamen guarded the theatre. The sight of these soldiers guarding Macready and his supporters enraged the crowd of 5,000 that had gathered and they unleashed a barrage of cobblestones. The panicky soldiers, after once having fired over the heads of the attackers, aimed a volley at the densely packed attackers. At least twenty-two people were killed.

There are very few historical events that clearly signal a radical cultural shift. The Astor Place Riot is one such occurrence. It spelled the end of the era of audience sovereignty and resulted in a plethora of laws designed to restrict the audience. The reformation of audiences was not, however, an isolated social phenomenon. It was part of a desire to rehabilitate all of American society and included the moral purity movement, sabbatarianism, temperance, and Sunday-school campaigns. Some supporters of social reform were sincerely interested in the spiritual and material well-being of the working-class poor who were flooding into large east-coast cities. Others insisted that the new industrial economy required a sober, disciplined, and dependable work force in order to generate profits. Still others feared that the "masses" intoxicated with dreams of democracy would seize control of all institutions. Irrespective of the stated goals of the reformers, one issue clearly emerged. The "dangerous classes," the hordes of poor, would have to be transformed into honest, sober workers, who were sexually continent, frugal, and dedicated to family, workplace, and church. Otherwise they would have to be banished to the margins of society and denied access to the community of citizens.[83]

As early as the 1850s, state legislatures began to define a ticket as a temporary license that could be revoked at any time for any reason.[84] After the Civil War, these bodies appropriated for themselves the right to license theatre buildings and enacted regulations governing "way, manner, and place wherein it could be presented." They could grant or withhold discretionary licenses at will, and those who violated the terms of their license were liable to criminal prosecution. Moreover, state governments frequently delegated this authority to towns and cities thereby insuring the closest possible scrutiny.[85]

Thus, censorship of the American theatre began with fiats designed to control audiences not actors, and by 1890 American theatre auditoriums had been completely transformed. Audiences were licensed to sit quietly and witness the performance. Any response other than polite applause might be regarded as dangerous and result in eviction. Rather than participants in a theatrical event, theatregoers were transmuted into docile consumers and managers had become policemen.[86]

Legislation certainly speeded the gentrification of theatre. But the process of transforming theatres from sites of male, working-class solidarity into havens of middle-class respectability had commenced before the Civil War. Perhaps the most crucial figure during this period was P. T. Barnum, whose "Lecture Room" played a critical role in this evolution. In 1841 when Barnum purchased Scudder's Museum, which he renamed the American Museum, it was a potpourri of natural and man-made curiosities – skeletons, mineral specimens, stuffed birds, plant life, and a few pieces of randomly collected art work. Barnum, however, was already an experienced entrepreneur and showman, who had demonstrated an uncanny ability to read social trends. He clearly understood that his fortune lay within burgeoning bourgeois society and deftly exploited their class anxieties. This group, as Bruce McConachie points out, had been influenced by a number of forces that quickened "the consciousness of urban Americans" about the widening gap between the "unwashed" and the "respectable." Riots, slums, and massive immigration defined the former, while the latter described its members in terms of segregated housing, distinctive fashions, and newly acquired white-collar jobs. Early advertisements depicted his audiences as well-dressed, white families and promised to exclude anything that would corrupt their refined sensibilities. And, if middle-class audiences complained that their gentility might be compromised by his "freaks," he need only remind them that Tom Thumb had had an audience with Queen Victoria to assuage their anxieties.[87]

It was, however, his ability to attract middle-class women that proved to be the key to his success. As early as 1845 he had already begun to advertise for the "right" type of woman by promising to exclude the "wrong" type from his exhibition area. He boldly proclaimed, "No admittance for FEMALES OF KNOWN BAD CHARACTER, or other improper persons, so that Ladies and Families will be perfectly safe, and no more exposed to evil companions than in their own Parlors."[88]

He expanded upon this strategy when he opened his newly renovated "Lecture Room" in 1850. Although this space was one of the finest production facilities of the period, he never advertised it as a theatre. The middle class held theatres in very low esteem and would never deign to enter one, but they flocked to Barnum's "Lecture Room," a "home for moral drama." He reiterated this point at the opening night ceremonies on June 17, 1850 when an actress proclaimed:

> Here vice shall be portrayed, with such a mien
> That all shall hate it when it once is seen–
> And virtue, with its rich rewards and fun
> Nightly before this altar you shall see.[89]

He refused to sell alcohol and would not tolerate rowdy or boisterous behavior, thereby removing the markers of male dominance from his theatre. Moreover, by refusing to admit prostitutes, he severed his theatre's longstanding association with commercialized sex.

The premiere production, *The Drunkard; or, The Fallen Saved* by W. H. Smith, became the first play to run in New York for 100 uninterrupted performances. He followed with biblical dramas such as *Joseph and His Brethren* and other melodrama staples such as *The Soldier's Daughter*, *A Mother's Prayer*, *The Pioneer Patriot*, and *Charlotte Temple*. Eventually, he mounted H. J. Conway's happy ending adaptation of *Uncle Tom's Cabin* in 1853.[90]

Theatre in the American Museum had become, in Robert Allen's words, "sanctified and feminized."[91] Although critics attacked Barnum for claiming that his productions were actually dramatized sermons, he constantly reassured his patrons that his Lecture Room was morally superior to a common theatre:

> The most fastidious may take their families there, without the least apprehension of their being offended by word or deed; in short, so careful is the supervision exercised over the amusements that hundreds of persons who are prevented visiting theatres on account of the vulgarisms and immorality which are sometimes permitted therein, may visit Mr. Barnum's establishment without fear of offense.[92]

Although Barnum was the most successful of the entertainment entrepreneurs to mine middle-class morality, he was not alone. As early as 1837, Noah Ludlow had banished prostitutes from the third tier in his theatre in St. Louis and in all other cities that his company toured, including Mobile and New Orleans. J. H. Hackett banned prostitutes when he reopened the Howard Athenaeum in 1846.[93] Even the Bowery Theatre took advantage of the popularity of the sermonizing tone of melodramas and mounted its own production of *The Drunkard* in July 1850.[94] Perhaps the one production that might arguably claim to have made American theatre respectable for the middle class was George L. Aiken's adaptation of *Uncle Tom's Cabin*, which originally opened in September 1852 in Troy, New York, and then, on July 18, 1853, at Purdy's National Theatre. William Lloyd Garrison's *The Liberator*, a periodical hardly given to praise of theatre, extolled the production because the audience left the auditorium "as gravely and seriously as people retire from a religious meeting."[95] A later review noted that there were Quakers, Methodists, Baptists, Presbyterians, and Congregationalists in attendance.[96] There was no doubt that there was a willing and able audience ready to frequent theatre, if only they could be guaranteed that their values would be preserved and enhanced.

By 1860, theatre in America was well on its way to severing its connections with aggressive working-class males, alcohol, and prostitutes. Like the bourgeois culture that it buttressed, the gentrified theatre of the second half of the nineteenth century defined itself by obviating all that was dirty, noisy, vulgar, or sexually provocative.[97] However, the campaign to purify theatre was by no means complete, and in 1868 the advocates of respectability suffered a setback. That year George Wood contracted Lydia Thompson and her burlesque troupe, soon to be known as the "British Blondes," to appear at the newly renovated Banvard's Museum and Theatre. While legal sanctions of burlesque would not proliferate until the twentieth century, the responses to Thompson and her company are crucial. They marked the first instance that the issue of female representation dominated the anti-theatrical discourse in the United States. It was an issue that would be debated for over 100 years.

When Thompson first appeared in New York, she was thirty-two and married to her manager, Alexander Henderson. She had toured Europe in 1859 and had starred in a number of successful extravaganzas in London for the next five years. She sailed for the United States with four other actors who had achieved considerable fame as burlesque performers: Ada Harland, Lisa Weber, Pauline Markham, and Harry Beckett, the only male member of the company. Her publicist, Archie Gordon, emphasized the company's overwhelming sexual charisma, which he claimed might paralyze the entire nation.[98]

Their premiere production, *Ixion*, opened on September 28, 1868, and all 2,265 seats in Wood's house were sold. The play itself, by F. C. Burnand, was a general lampoon of classical culture composed in rhymed pentameter and making generous use of puns. However, Burnand's play was probably no more than a skeletal structure to which were appended topical allusions, popular songs, dances, and even more outrageous puns. The women played all of the male roles, and recent divorce cases among the elite as well political scandals were favored as subjects. Contemporary tunes were given new, more topical lyrics, and dances, particularly parodies of minstrel show jigs, were especially popular. Thompson's costume probably consisted of a stylized Greek tunic, tight at the waist and extending to a few inches above the knees with a scooped but not revealing neckline. She also wore tights and ankle-high boots. Although photo documentation of the other performers does not indicate their costumes for *Ixion*, they were probably no more revealing than those worn by the ballet dancers of the period.[99]

The initial critical response to Thompson's company was favorable: "their success was unbounded. The wildest symptoms of delight burst forth as each individual of the new company appeared, and Miss Thompson, Miss Markham and Miss Weber were nearly lost in several floral avalanches, which occurred during the progress of the entertainment."[100] Thompson played Ixion and was praised for her ability "to swear, swagger, and otherwise be masculine."[101]

Ixion played at Wood's until December 28 when another Thompson burlesque replaced it. During these months Wood's did the best business of any theatre in New York, grossing nearly $47,000 in October, $46,000 in November, and $40,000 during the third month of the run. Two days before *Ixion* closed, it was announced that Thompson's company would open *The Forty Thieves; or, Striking Oil in Family Jars* on February 1 at Niblo's Garden, possibly the finest theatre in the United States. Recently, Niblo's had gained a reputation for staging lavish spectacles and had just ended a fifteen-month run of the fantasy extravaganza *The Black Crook*. Now its large stage and technical resources were placed at Thompson's disposal.[102]

Before *Ixion* closed at Wood's, however, the response to Thompson's company had begun to shift. In November, the *New York Times* lamented the deplorable condition of theatre. The writer complained that in the past he defended theatre as a school of morals and manners. After admitting that there was still some theatre that did not "outrage the human sense of decency, or the public intelligence," he launched into a furious attack on "glaring and flaunting spectacular shows":

Look at the sensual exhibitions of the feminine form! Listen to the sala-cious music! See the appeals to the sensational and the pandering to the base and vulgar elements of human nature! Hear the gross innuendo, and notice the foul suggestion! Who will deny that these things are immensely damaging to the public taste and terribly ruinous to the public morals? It will not do. It cannot continue. It must not be tolerated ... the indecency calls for the severe condemnation of all who have a true appreciation of dramatic art, and who believe that the theatre, instead of being the enemy of public morality, should be its exponent and support.[103]

Although the author did not mention burlesque explicitly, there is little doubt that the "sensual exhibitions of the feminine form" and "salacious music" referred to these performances. Burlesque was obviously the "wrong theatre." Like the Roman mimes and medieval "Feast of Fools," burlesque depicted an inverted, topsy-turvy world. In this particular re-visioning of normative society women who were obviously women, but who had learned how to "swear, swagger, and otherwise be masculine" played men. They distorted classical tradition to fit their own designs, mutilated language by means of outrageous puns, and generally challenged the hegemony of middle-class propriety.

During 1869, burlesque became the entertainment rage of New York. After Thompson departed from Wood's Theatre, a new company headed by Mr. and Mrs. W. J. Florence produced *Field of the Cloth of Gold*. On February 18, Elise Holt, another English burlesque performer, opened the New Waverly Theatre with *Lucretia Borgia, M.D.* Burlesque was so popular that it itself became the subject of burlesque. In March Tony Pastor staged *Romeo and Juliet; or, The Beautiful Blonde Who Dyed (Her Hair) for Love.* Meanwhile, each new production employed lavish staging, costumes, dances, and music.[104]

The ever-increasing popularity of burlesque combined with Thompson's opening in Niblo's Garden unleashed a wildly hostile discourse. Richard Grant White, writing in 1869, called it "monstrously incongruous and un-natural ... the result is absurdity, monstrosity. Its system is a defiance of a system. It is out of *all* keeping.'[105] Virtually every newspaper that had praised Thompson's company now characterized the British Blondes as carriers of a vile, indecent, impudent, sexually perverted disease.

Olive Logan, an actress and feminist, carried on a sustained and passion-ate attack against burlesque. As an actress she detested "leg business" and "yellow haired nudities" because they demeaned and compromised honest, young women who sought careers in theatre. Instead of artistry, she argued that the only attributes needed by the women of burlesque were a comely body and shamelessness:

1. Is your hair dyed yellow?
2. Are your legs, arms, and bosom symmetrically formed, and are you willing to expose them?
3. Can you sing brassy songs and dance the can-can, and wink at men, and give utterance to disgusting half-words, which mean whole actions?[106]

For Logan, burlesque performers were not artists who had acquired complex skills through arduous practice. Quite the contrary! These women were "a disgrace to the dramatic profession" responsible for driving "actresses who love virtue better than money...into the streets."[107]

These women, however, signified much more than the exaltation of talentless performers; they were a threat to all American women. Burlesque performers purposefully displayed their bodies – primarily their legs – to enhance their popularity. As Robert Allen has explained, their legs became a "synecdotal sign of the lower body and of female sexuality in general hence the symbolic transformation of mid-thigh pantaloons and opaque tights into complete nudity."[108] Although Logan also objected to the ballet dancers in *The Black Crook* because their costumes were too revealing, she admitted that the ballerinas at least represented "imps and daemons," who silently danced and silently exited. The women of burlesque did not even pay lip service to the convention of characterization:

> The nude woman of today represents nothing but herself. She runs upon the stage giggling; trots down to the footlights, winks at the audience, rattles off from her tongue some stupid attempts at wit...and is always peculiarly and emphatically herself, – the woman, that is, whose name is on the bills in large letters, and who considers herself an object of admiration to the spectators.[109]

The "admiration" of which Logan spoke was clearly not honorific. Burlesque performers compounded the damage caused by their immodesty by colluding in their own objectification. Not only did they titillate audiences with their appearance and demeanor, they were brazenly themselves. They even established eye and verbal contact with spectators to enhance their appeal. These performers, at least as Logan read them, merely stimulated audiences by calling attention to their exposed bodies. Logan, like many other nineteenth-century American feminists, were of the opinion that male sexual passion was irrational and dangerous. The burlesque performers brazenly energized this passion and thereby worked to the detriment of all women. Burlesque, as an entertainment form, was based on sexual difference, irrationality, and the display of female sexuality, and was emblematic of all that American reformers opposed.[110]

Obviously, the "nude women" were equated with prostitutes, and the discursive treatment of both revealed intense anxiety over the place of women and the role of sex in mid nineteenth-century America. Like prostitutes, these women traded on their ability to stimulate male audiences by their verbal brashness and displaying their bodies – the bolder the presentation, the greater the rewards. However, prostitutes and, ultimately, burlesque performers were regarded as agents of chaos who threatened to overturn this newly ordered middle-class society. Both signified the antithesis of the idealized "Victorian woman," a middle-class construct who was responsible for maintaining the sanctity of home and family and upholding the moral standards of society. Unfortunately, the visibility of prostitutes who freely walked the same streets as "respectable women" in every major American city served to confute this paradigm. Their presence served as a reminder that sex did not belong exclusively to the private context of marriage. Rather, it was a commodity which, like any other, could be negotiated and purchased. Prostitutes also highlighted the inequities brought on by a patriarchal hierarchy. Although white men enjoyed sexual, political, and economic freedom, the jobs available to women, the places they could go, and the influence they exercised were severely constricted. Finally, prostitutes, in a time of unexplained cholera epidemics and a growing incidence of syphilis, became symbolic of disease. If the theatre were to become a respectable institution, worthy of middle-class patronage, prostitutes (read the "nude women" of burlesque) would have to be banished from the stage, just as they had been removed from the third tier. Thus, the challenge posed by the appearance of transgressive women on the burlesque stage resonated throughout the larger culture, as the female body became contested political terrain. Whatever group controlled the representation of women would also dictate the limits of erotic expression and boundaries of sexual relationships. As the nineteenth century drew to a close, the debate over female representation began to dominate the trajectory of the censorship discourse in the United States.

Enter Anthony Comstock, who, just four years after the appearance of Lydia Thompson and her "British Blondes," became the first federally appointed censor in the history of the United States. More than any other individual in the nineteenth century, Comstock expanded government control over sexual representation and contraception. By so doing, he and his colleagues hoped to force society to conform to a single, fundamental, homogeneous, overarching moral paradigm. While Comstock himself was more concerned with restricting books, magazines, and reproductions of nude women than theatre, his ability to involve governmental entities, particularly the federal government, in policing the representation of the female body had profound repercussions.

Born in 1844 in New Canaan, Connecticut, into a strict Congregationalist family, Comstock was an unremarkable child and served without distinction in the Civil War. Although his diaries revealed a young man obsessed with sensual temptation, he apparently never yielded. He married in January 1871 and until 1872 was employed as a dry-goods clerk in New York City. Thus far, nothing indicated that he would ever distinguish himself, but on March 3rd of that year he began a quest that would occupy him for the rest of his life. Having become aware of the presence of obscene literature, and "in the spirit of an avenger of wrongs done to young men, the clean-lived young Connecticut Christian started on the trail of those worse than murderers."[111] Accompanied by a reporter from the *New York Tribune*, he gathered enough evidence to have a book dealer and six associates arrested for selling obscene material. Comstock was utterly convinced that obscenity – in pictures, magazines, newspapers, and books – was the most virulent foe that Christian Americans would ever battle. It caused crime, debased the institution of marriage, and threatened to corrupt children, particularly young males, the future of the nation and the race.[112]

Later in the spring of 1872 he received his first backing – from Morris K. Jessup and Robert R. McBurney, respectively, the secretary and president of the YMCA. Shortly thereafter, the YMCA established its Committee for the Suppression of Vice, the first of many such community organizations in New York. But these crusaders would not stop at the local level. Late in 1872, Comstock traveled to Washington to lobby Congress to pass "An Act for the Suppression of Trade in, and Circulation of Obscene Literature and Articles of Immoral Use," unofficially dubbed the "Comstock Law." The act had one overriding objective – to prohibit the use of the mails to disseminate any obscene material. When the law was passed, Anthony Comstock was appointed a special agent of the Post Office Department and granted the authority to enforce this law.

To Comstock it did not matter if a book was actually obscene, contained a few suggestive passages, or merely sported a racy title. A provocative title or suggestive images rendered the entire work obscene. In 1913, two years before his death, he claimed that his total number of arrests would fill a passenger train of sixty coaches, containing sixty people each. He also bragged that he had seized 139,000 obscene books, 194,000 lewd photographs and pictures, and 60,000 articles made of rubber and used by both sexes for immoral purposes.[113]

Comstock's career as America's most famous prude might seem laughable today had he not seen to it that information about contraception and abortion was also defined as an obscenity. Neither he nor his YMCA associates saw any difference between smutty photographs, sex aids, and efforts to limit the size of families. Women who wanted to control their bodies and the size of their family were obscene and, as such, punishable by law. To this end he hounded Ann Lohman, a.k.a. Madame Restell, New York City's most famous abortionist, until she committed suicide. He was also responsible for the indictment of Margaret Sanger who, to avoid trial, fled to England in September 1915.[114]

However, Comstock's overriding concern was the promiscuous distribution of inexpensive editions of tawdry dime novels and cheap reproductions of provocative European art. And it should come as no surprise that Comstock's paranoia flourished during a period when literacy, transportation, and communication technologies were advancing at an exponential rate. Railroad tracks and telegraph lines criss-crossed the nation. Public schools produced, if not a sophisticated population, at least a literate one. Advances in printing made low-cost books, magazines, newspapers, and photographic reproductions available for a few pennies. In Walter Kendrick's opinion, this democratic distribution of information conjured up "nightmarish images of a world without structure…where all barriers had been breached and all differences leveled."[115] Comstock and his supporters reacted to this rapid onset of modernity by seeking to resuscitate the moral certitude that dominated much nineteenth-century thought and behavior. By returning to the moral strictures of the past, he hoped to dictate the direction that future generations would follow.

While Comstock occasionally railed against gambling and intemperance, he, like his Edwardian generation, defined immorality in purely sexual terms and exerted tremendous effort in an attempt to prescribe the depiction of the female body. As was evident in the furor that erupted over burlesque, displays of women, who offered erotic possibilities, had to be suppressed if traditional moral injunctions were to be preserved. Nineteenth-century theatre rarely challenged these attitudes, but the same cannot be said of the twentieth century. Beginning in 1900, a steady stream of producers and playwrights who had been influenced by European naturalists began to challenge this bourgeois moral paradigm, and the battle between the guardians of the past and the heralds of the future would shortly commence.

2

Bad girls, tough guys, and the changing of the guard

Olga Nethersole, *Sapho*, and the Moral Reform movement

By the 1900s, the evolving American culture began to clash with the fixed certitudes preached by establishment politicians and moralists. At the eye of the storm was the "New Woman." These women, mainly white and middle class, graduated from high school and attended colleges and professional schools in record numbers. Many entered new fields such as anthropology and sociology, and were among the first to propose that gender distinctions were socially constructed. They demanded the right to vote, birth-control information, and abortion services.

Social conditions in large cities also induced significant concern. Single men and women, who had flooded into metropolitan areas for jobs, began to dominate the social landscape. After work and on weekends they crowded into the scores of dance halls and amusement parks that had sprung up across the nation. They flocked to vaudeville theatres and to the newly operational movie houses that provided cheap entertainment. Here, they engaged in improvised courtship rituals without the supervision of parents, teachers, and ministers. At the same time, the commercial sex industry flourished as the glut of male workers and immigrants created a fertile market for brothel owners and independent female entrepreneurs.

Middle-class moralists interpreted these cultural shifts as an attack on society's ethical armature and mounted a series of counteroffensives aimed at keeping Victorian morality firmly in place. They targeted gambling, alcohol, prostitution, immigration, and homosexuality and enlisted the aid of willing public officials who attempted to suppress transgressive behavior. Thus, by the beginning of the twentieth century, maintenance of middle-class morality had become a significant component of the national political agenda.

The appearance of naturalistic plays on the American stage added more fuel to this already intense fire. European naturalism never completely took root in the United States, but it nonetheless exerted significant influence. A number of foreign plays and a few authored by Americans attempted to depict an unvarnished view of society, one that was governed by passions and greed. As a result, a genre of aggressive plays that depicted men and women in a less than ideal light began to appear. And, as theatre began to challenge middle-class notions of propriety, it, too, became a target of these reformers.

The furor that such campaigns could generate was clearly demonstrated shortly after the turn of the century when *Sapho* opened on February 5, 1900, at Wallack's Theatre. Adapted by Clyde Fitch from the novel by Alphonse Daudet, it told the story of an ill-fated love affair between a notorious *femme fatale*, Fanny Le Grande, and a young student, Jean Gaussin. Olga Nethersole, a British actress/manager, produced *Sapho* and starred as Fanny. She had distinguished herself by portraying problematic female characters whose checkered pasts often caused turmoil and grief. Among her most famous roles were Paula Tanqueray in *The Second Mrs. Tanqueray*, Camille, and Carmen in a dramatic version of the opera that she commissioned.

What transpired during the next three months as a result of this production was the first theatre scandal of the twentieth century, one that rivaled the frenzy caused by Lydia Thompson's "British Blondes." Vice crusaders waged a furious assault on *Sapho*, and Olga Nethersole, an unmarried, successful, female entrepreneur, was held responsible for this moral contagion. The collective press of New York railed that *Sapho* was coarse, unsavory, and indecent. The *New York World* in particular launched a withering attack.[1] Characterizing the production as the "*Sapho* plague," the *World* published anti-*Sapho* petitions that were updated daily, persuaded dozens of clerics to preach against the production in spite of not having seen it, and convinced scores of women to appeal to Nethersole to close her play because it was a "menace to society."[2] Due largely to the *World*'s continuing attacks, Nethersole and her male lead, Hamilton Revelle, as well as the theatre manager and her personal manager, were arrested for corrupting public decency. They were indicted and tried as "persons of wicked and depraved mind and disposition... intending to debauch and corrupt the morals as well of youth [*sic*] as of divers other persons and to raise and create in their minds inordinate and lustful desires."[3]

Sapho, as well as dozens of the other controversial plays produced over the next two decades, challenged entrenched and interlocking paradigms that had defined women for nearly a century. More specifically, *Sapho* challenged the belief that prostitutes were victims of male aggression, shattered the myth that sexually transgressive women endured unspeakable punishments, and depicted sexual conduct that was thoroughly incompatible with prevailing middle-class demands for emotional restraint. Finally, *Sapho*'s corrosive messages were the products of an unmarried, female artist who, in the opinion of her accusers, possessed no regard for public decency or morality.

By contemporary standards, it is difficult to understand why *Sapho* caused such uproar. It appears sentimental and predictable, with an ending that confirms the female's maternal role and reaffirms her complete dependence on males. Fanny Le Grande is an infamous courtesan with many conquests to her credit, among them a poet, whose love poems to her are known throughout the country, and the sculptor Caudal, who created a statuette of *Sapho* for which Fanny modeled. In addition, we learn that Fanny has an illegitimate son whose father, Flamant, has been carted off to prison for forging bank notes to finance their affair.

At a raucous Parisian party, she meets and falls in love with Jean Gaussin, a student several years her junior. The first act ends with Jean sweeping Fanny into his arms and whisking her up a long flight of stairs, to spend a torrid night together. It was this scene more than any other to which *Sapho*'s opponents most strenuously objected. Fanny's love for Jean transforms her. Although she knows that he will not marry her, she convinces him to allow her to live with him, and becomes a thoroughly conventional domestic partner. Jean, however, cannot forget that Fanny has a notorious past and eventually learns that she has a child whose father is in prison. When Fanny sends for her son against his wishes, Jean can no longer control his jealousy and anger. He rails that he has been betrayed and, in spite of tearful protestations from Fanny, leaves her and her child.

She attempts suicide but is saved by her son and her neighbors. Meanwhile, Flamant is pardoned, returns to Fanny, swears his undying love and, since a wealthy friend has coincidentally died leaving him his entire estate, pleads for her and their child to leave with him. Fanny feels unworthy of his devotion because she does not love him. For the sake of her son, however, she accepts his proposal in spite of Jean's unexpected reappearance and protestations of love.

Olga Nethersole believed that the story of Fanny Le Grande conveyed a significant moral lesson to audiences. She reasoned that a story of a selfish, decadent woman who transformed herself into an exemplary wife and mother would inspire other morally deficient women to undertake the same process. Her adversaries, on the other hand, treated *Sapho* as part of a widespread, pernicious assault on the social and moral ballast of the nation.

As is the case with most aggressive censorship efforts, the crusade against *Sapho* was the result of a convulsive backlash that sought to protect established social norms. Throughout the nineteenth century, reform groups in the United States worked to combat social ills such as slavery, alcohol, gender inequality, prison abuse, and child neglect. These conditions were thought to be humanly created deviations from the natural order, that, if not corrected, would retard cultural advancement, threaten health, obstruct the spread of knowledge, and generally lower the morals of society. The Social Purity Reform Movement, perhaps the most popular and politically influential of these efforts, believed that it was the special mission of women to reform and protect the morals of society.[4] This movement was born during the Second Great Awakening, a religious revival that emerged in the northeastern United States in the 1830s and attracted tens of thousands of Protestant women. Although the movement was not bound by traditional Christian dogma, its members nonetheless retained a religious zeal that characterized many later reform efforts:

> As pragmatists, with a religion of morality and humanity, they constructed the religious foundations of modern society. The concept of social purification released religious energies for social tasks. It appealed to churched and unchurched, to traditional religionists and secular progressives. It functioned, therefore, as a force for integrating apparently disparate reforms...Briefly, purity reform, in a time of stress and flux, promoted social cohesion and formulated a new social consciousness.[5]

Nowhere was its fervor more evident than in efforts to protect the sanctity and preeminence of the family. And, for social-purity reformers, the most dangerous threat to wives, mothers, and families was prostitution. In the first decades of the nineteenth century, prostitutes were believed to be morally bankrupt females, predators who ravaged society. They were responsible for disease and crime, destroyed homes, promoted the sexual double standard, and debauched innocent women.

By the outbreak of the Civil War, however, female reformers had modified this assessment. According to John D'Emilio and Estelle Freedman, the model of the depraved woman was replaced with that of the female victim:

Unlike male reformers, who usually portrayed the prostitute as a source
of depravity and a threat to men's health, these women claimed a sympathy with the prostitute...Rather than condemning the "fallen women,"
female reformers promised to uplift her and restore her to true womanhood. In the name of gender solidarity, they launched an attack on male
sexual privilege.[6]

In 1834, women in New York who shared these views organized the
Female Moral Reform Society. Its aggressive leaders traveled the countryside organizing auxiliaries and attempting to transform prostitutes
into morally respectable women, whether or not they actually sought
transformation.[7]

While many reformers noted that poverty had driven women into prostitution, they refused to acknowledge that the economy of commercial sex
was far more appealing than the economy of morality. They preached that
female factory workers and domestics were driven into prostitution because
greedy employers forced women to work long hours in wretched conditions
for paltry wages. Women could escape such conditions only by turning to
prostitution. Thus, the prostitute was depicted as a victim rather than an
economic pragmatist making the best of a bad situation. Ironically, such
a view even advanced the cult of true womanhood. As long as prostitutes
could be characterized as having been forced through chicanery or violence
into abhorrent situations, the paradigm of the pure woman, secure in her
home with her husband and family, remained the standard by which all
women were measured.

Irrespective of these inconsistencies, the campaign to reform prostitutes
presented an opportunity to challenge male political and economic hegemony. By 1839, the Female Reform Society included hundreds of chapters.
Yet it was through their publications – *Friend of Virtue* in Boston and *The
Advocate of Moral Reform* in New York – that moral reformers successfully promoted a nineteenth-century version of sexual politics. As Barbara
Hobson illustrates, the articles, editorials, and stories linked prostitution to
"male sexual dominance in economic, political and social life, and viewed
the sexual double standard as an extension of imbalance of power between
the sexes."[8]

Equally as important, the *Friend of Virtue* and *The Advocate of Moral
Reform* advanced a discourse that was not only popular, but carried with
it an air of historical as well as religious authority. Seducers were either
depicted as callow lovers or powerful, upper-class males who eventually
abandoned their prey. Victims were generally orphans or the daughters of

widows who had left their safe rural homes in search of employment in the city. A grim fate awaited these helpless women. A fallen man could be re-habilitated and reintegrated into society.[9] Fallen women, although pitiable, were tainted for life and eventually succumbed to madness or suicide – or both.[10]

After the introduction of the penny presses in the 1830s and 1840s, these cultural stereotypes dominated popular fiction. American readers were del-uged with such tales of feminine virtue and masculine treachery as *The Eastern Belle, or, the Betrayed One*; *A Tale of Boston and Bangor*; *The Mysteries of Boston, or, A Woman's Temptation*. Meanwhile, playwrights continued to make the heroine's struggle to maintain her virtue the central issue of the drama. David Grimstead notes: "Virtue and the heroine stood almost indis-tinguishable at the center of the melodrama, the one the personification of the other."[11] Like the stories found in the *Friend of Virtue* and *The Advocate of Moral Reform*, play after play warned women to beware of men. If per-chance this warning was not heeded, madness and death inevitably resulted. These paradigms became so firmly entrenched in the American conscious-ness that a transgressive woman who did not suffer this fate violated not only theatrical conventions, but the "natural" order as well. Playwright Bronson Howard, writing in 1886, indicated how thoroughly this notion had been embraced:

> In England and America, the death of a pure woman on the stage is not "satisfactory," except when the play rises to the dignity of tragedy. The death, in an ordinary play, of a woman who is not pure ... is perfectly satisfactory, for the reason that it is inevitable. Human nature always bows gracefully to the inevitable. The only grief in our own lives to which we can never reconcile ourselves are those which might have been averted. The wife who has once taken the step from purity to impurity can never reinstate herself in the world of art on this side of the grave; and so an audience looks with complacent tears on the death of an erring woman.[12]

It was thus impossible to combine virtue and vice in the same heroine. The "pure woman" and her degenerate sister had to remain separate and distinguishable, forever standing in binary opposition. But the character of Fanny exhibited behavior that blurred the carefully delineated boundaries that separated virtuous women from fallen women, and women from men. In the first scene the audience learns that Fanny behaves more like a sexu-ally privileged male, capriciously seducing then discarding lovers. In keeping with her character, she stealthily pursues Jean, a naive student newly arrived from the country. She awakens in him a dormant lust and easily transforms him into an aggressive, predatory male whose passion she welcomes. Obviously, Fanny is not a victimized female forced to surrender her virtue. Although Fanny is later transformed into a dutiful, self-sacrificing partner, her initial behavior demands retribution. Fanny, however, not only survives, she prospers. Like the male protagonists of the period, she is reintegrated into society through the auspices of a forgiving and wealthy Flamant. Meanwhile, Jean, like so many doomed heroines, is abandoned by his lover and disowned by his family. *Sapho*'s message was revisionist – and subversive. Fanny was a fallen woman, but she was also repentant, redeemable, and capable of maternal devotion. More insidiously, it implied that other women might behave in the same manner without fear of punishment.

Critics who opposed *Sapho* immediately complained that it would permanently debase audiences, particularly the young. William Winter wrote that this production polluted youthful minds with a "needless and harmful knowledge of the seamy side of life, with the tainted suggestion of a leering debauchery and the noxious vapors of impudent vice."[13] The *World* published shrill warnings from hundreds of public officials, teachers, and ministers. The city superintendent of schools told parents: "To see it may ruin the life and happiness of a boy or a girl forever. The seductive portrayal of vice on the stage is the most dangerous, and unfortunately the most successful, method by which the spirit of evil tempts to their ruin those whose characters are as yet unformed."[14] In an article entitled "*Sapho*-Crazed Women Throng to See Nethersole Play," concern was voiced that young women had already been corrupted:

> The great preponderance of the spectators were women [*sic*]...What was the tone of the house? To express it in one word one would say the people were very "knowing." Every phrase with a salacious meaning thinly veiled – or deeply veiled, or not veiled at all for that matter – earned its reward in knowing snickers and giggles.[15]

As a result, priests, rabbis, and ministers urged "pure young women" to avoid the play by reiterating the commonly held belief that the progress of society depended upon female moral superiority. As one cleric maintained:

> The character of *Sapho* is an unnatural one. It disgraces womanhood – it is a character that is absolutely pernicious and a libel on God...The presentation upon the stage of such a character as *Sapho* can have but one effect – the lowering of the standard of womanhood. This means a severe blow to society.[16]

However, to locate the *Sapho* discourse exclusively within the evangeli-cally driven Social Purity Reform Movement would be misleading. It was also a product of class formation. By the 1870s, sexual practices in middle-class marriages had become a matter of private control. Erotic pleasure, romantic intimacy, and emotional bonding emerged as legitimate motiva-tions to engage in sexual activity. But sex was to be indulged in "legitimately and temperately," and was valued for the "spiritual completeness that it of-fered." Predictably, middle-class wives vigorously objected to "unrestrained animal passion" because such behavior defiled their "best feelings" for their partners.[17]

However, the growth of commercialized sex, particularly in working-class districts, severely compromised middle-class emphasis on legitimacy and restraint. The ample number of dance halls, concert saloons, and all-male bars offered their single and married clientele numerous opportunities to see erotic displays, purchase titillating books or pictures, and have access to prostitutes. The rapid development of technology, particularly after the Civil War, provided even more opportunities. Advances in printing permit-ted cheap reproduction of erotic literature, and an efficient postal system allowed for quick and inexpensive dissemination.

These developments did more than threaten the idealized status of sexual relations in middle-class marriages. Privacy and self-control had come to symbolize class superiority, but it was feared that commercialized erotica was too alluring and too widespread to be resisted by society in general. If this situation went unchecked, America would be transformed into a chaotic society governed by passion and caprice rather than order and reason. Thus, a painfully ironic condition arose within the middle class. While claiming control of their own private sexual practices, they simultaneously demanded laws to proscribe similar behavior among workers and the poor. Their eagerness to adopt this position betrayed their fear that sexuality would pass irreversibly out of the private control of the family and into the public domain of the marketplace.[18]

Sapho depicted precisely the type of woman that middle-class moralists feared. Fanny's romantic exploits were virtually a matter of public record. Her lovers had all been illustrious men and her liaisons with them the topic of endless café gossip. The poetry that extolled her beauty was the common property of all those who could read, while numerous copies of the *Sapho* statuette circulated freely throughout France. Even Jean's father owned a reproduction of Fanny's body. Not only had she been a personal sexual object for the numerous men who had actually caressed her, but also a mass-produced sexual object, embraced by thousands whom she had never met.

Perhaps more dangerous than Fanny's public indiscretion was her uncontrollable passion. Unbridled ardor dominated her life with Jean, and at one point she even crawled and wailed at his feet, pleading hysterically for him to remain with her. Moreover, she transformed Jean into a man so thoroughly controlled by his emotions that he abandoned her because he was so jealous of her previous lovers. Fanny and her relationship obviously demonstrated little of the control so crucial to the middle-class claim of emotional superiority. Not surprisingly, she was roundly vilified:

> Fanny Le Grande is a selfish animal from the time she persuades her unwilling but weak victim to say "yes" to her pleadings to the end ... *Sapho* is the quintessence of animalism and selfishness. In these two qualities we find the motive, from beginning to end, of her relations with Jean ... Does she stop for one moment to consider to what depths she is dragging him, the only man she has ever met to whom she could apply the words truth and honor? Not she. She fairly forces herself upon him, although at times he turns in disgust, until by clinging lips and arms he yields.[19]

Jean and Fanny's relationship, fueled as it was by emotion and lust, rather than rational considerations, was incapable of fulfilling any familial or community imperatives. Uncontrolled and unrestrained, it threatened to contaminate the lives of anyone who came into contact with it.

Apparently, the portentous threats posed by *Sapho* only whetted the appetite of New York audiences and interest was intense from the very beginning of the project. Opening night was sold out five days in advance. Droves of ticket scalpers and booksellers hawking copies of Daudet's novel gathered to capitalize on the production's notoriety. The *New York Times* dismissed audiences as a "great crowd of loungers" attracted by the "salaciousness of the play."[20] Nonetheless, audiences continued to grow. By early March, crowds were so numerous that they filled the lobby and spilled into the street, necessitating extra policemen to clear the way for cable cars.[21]

A kind of "*Sapho* mania" began to set in. A few days after the opening, anti-vice crusaders in Boston, Buffalo, Baltimore, Chicago, Cincinnati, St. Louis, Providence, and Brooklyn informed the *World* that *Sapho* would be suppressed in their cities. The "*Sapho* plague" claimed victims nonetheless. One J. J. Rosenthal bought the American rights from Nethersole and Fitch, and was in the process of sending out four touring companies only twelve days after opening night.[22] Meanwhile, two other *Sapho* adaptations were announced, including one that promised to emphasize "every indecent feature of the novel" and give "special prominence to the heroine's immoral relations with Jean."[23] A production cropped up in Elizabeth, New Jersey, which the mayor threatened to close if wholesale deletions were not made.[24] At least four different burlesques of *Sapho*, including *Sapolio*, by Weber and Fields, and another produced by students of Columbia College, appeared in New York.[25] Those who opposed the production had only to point to this bedlam to justify their contentions that the theatre, as well as the moral order, was in peril.

This carnival-like atmosphere and the resulting diatribes, accusations, arrests, and trials were undoubtedly sparked by the production itself. That Olga Nethersole, producer and star of *Sapho*, was an unmarried professional woman provides the entire episode with a cultural resonance that transcended its importance as an isolated theatrical scandal. By 1900, the specter of the "New Woman" thoroughly permeated American culture. By the turn of the century, the majority of high-school graduates were women and 80 percent of colleges, universities, and professional schools admitted women. Many were suffragists, but all asserted that women would no longer walk in their mothers' footsteps. Many women remained single to pursue professional careers. Those who married dramatically altered their maternal role. The "New Woman" gave birth to fewer children – only 3.5 per family in 1900 compared to 7 in 1804. As a result, married women enjoyed more leisure time that they gave to volunteer associations such as conservation, suffrage, and civil rights groups. Much of the mass media was thoroughly enamored by the "New Woman" and depicted the modern mother as active outside the home, physically fit, independent, and intelligent. Clearly, women had begun to lay claim to prerogatives previously enjoyed exclusively by men.[26]

However, this revolution created a significant backlash from conservative apologists. An incident sparked by James Cardinal Gibbons, Archbishop of New York, was typical of the period. In his sermon of February 4, 1900, just one day before *Sapho* opened, he indicted the "New Woman" for the "wrecks of families in our country."

> I regard woman's rights women and society leaders in the higher walks of life as the worst enemies of the female sex. They rob woman of all that is amiable and gentle, tender and attractive...and give her nothing in return but masculine boldness and brazen effrontery. They are habitually preaching about woman's rights and prerogatives, and have not a word to say about her duties and responsibilities. They withdraw her from

those sacred obligations which properly belong to her sex and fill her with ambition to usurp positions for which neither God nor nature ever intended her ... Her heart is abroad. It is exulting in imagination, in some social triumph or reveling in some scene of gayety and dissipation ... I speak the sober truth when I affirm that for the wrecks of families in our country woman has a larger share of the responsibility.[27]

During the next week, in addition to its denunciations of *Sapho*, the *World* printed heated rebuttals to the Cardinal's claims. On February 11, it devoted two full pages to the controversy, reprinting the entire text of Gibbons' sermon, as well as thirteen responses representing the entire political spectrum. Given the volatile conditions surrounding the emergence of educated, assertive, and independent women, it is understandable that Olga Nethersole quickly became the focus of this controversy.

As an actress, Nethersole was of the Romantic school and emphasized physical abandon and the vivid display of passionate extremes. Described as having a "weakness for warm plays," she played volatile tempestuous women such as Camille, Carmen, Paula Tanqueray, and now Fanny Le Grande. Although reports of her acting are not extensive, Edward Dithmar regarded her as a "rough spasmodic actress, fit only for melodrama."[28] William Winter said her performance in *Sapho* was "violent, hysterical and raucous," while characterizing the acting generally as "shockingly indelicate and offensive."[29] In an extremely revealing commentary, an unnamed writer for the *World* conflated her passionate acting style with the behavior of sexually transgressive women in general: "Her voice, her eyes, her lips, her movements – all exaggerate the coarseness and vulgar suggestion of the class of woman she represents."[30] Obviously, the semiotics of Nethersole's portrayal of Fanny struck a very tender nerve among her detractors. On or off the stage, displays of passion and desire signified moral bankruptcy and impending sexual anarchy. Or, as Cardinal Gibbons might have stated, "masculine boldness and brazen effrontery."

In spite of dozens of articles and petitions, Nethersole steadfastly defended her integrity by taking advantage of contemporary beliefs that women were morally superior to men. She blamed narrow-minded males for fabricating the current scandal, while maintaining that the great numbers of women who had seen *Sapho* proved it was a moral play:

That there were more women than men present at the matinee today only proves, in my mind, that my play is a moral one. I thank these women one and all. Women see all that is good in life; men only that which is bad. All of the abuse I have had since I started to produce *Sapho* has come

from men, and was started by those supposed to be the best of men–
ministers . . . What can be more noble in life than a woman who is trying
to be good? There is a moral in *Sapho*. Nothing is immoral that points to
a moral.[31]

The *World* filed a formal complaint with the police and Nethersole was
arrested on February 20. She labeled the charges "villainous, perjurious and
un-American" and refused to be driven from the stage.[32] To the great dismay
of her detractors, she continued to act the role of Fanny after she was released
on bond. Finally, the police closed the production on March 5. Nethersole
would not be silenced and opened *The Second Mrs. Tanqueray* on March 7.
She appeared as Paula Tanqueray, a role nearly as controversial as Fanny. In
April she even sued the Revd Dr. Chalmers Easton, a Washington minister,
because he characterized her as personally lewd in a sermon. Although he
responded that he was referring to the character of Fanny, she refused to
drop the suit until he tendered his explanation from the same pulpit.[33]

The copious publicity coupled with the thinly veiled character assaults
transformed the ensuing trial into a meta-theatrical event that was nearly
as popular as *Sapho*. The courtroom was packed with reporters and fans,
creating the impression that a different, more surrealistic version of *Sapho*
was being enacted in the time and space of the real world. Costumes were
described in exhaustive detail, long portions of dialogue were reported, and
movements were debated to determine whether or not they were seductive.
Moreover, Nethersole's courtroom attire and deportment were meticulously
delineated in the daily papers. It seemed as if the press wanted to determine
if Olga Nethersole could portray Olga Nethersole with more delicacy than
Fanny Le Grande. Surely, such a spectacle proved to censors that theatre, left
to its own devices, might easily spill over into the "real world" and completely
transform it.

Nethersole was acquitted on April 5 and resumed playing Fanny two days
later. That evening her first entrance was greeted with "violent applause"
causing her to "bow her acknowledgment fully twenty times before the
play could proceed."[34] These spontaneous bursts of appreciation continued
unabated for the duration of the run. She revived the play in January 1901 in
Brooklyn, for which she published a souvenir book containing over a dozen
photographs of her as Fanny Le Grande.[35]

In the years to come, at least six other versions of *Sapho* were copyrighted,
and dozens of touring companies added it to their repertoire. In order to
obtain licenses in other cities, however, scandalous scenes, particularly the
end of Act I, had to be deleted. Such omissions were invariably greeted with

boos and hisses from members of the audiences who expected to see some "fireworks."[36]

Anthony Comstock versus George Bernard Shaw

Although the efforts to proscribe *Sapho* and punish Olga Nethersole failed, conservative moralists continued to attack productions that depicted transgressive women. In 1905, another battle, virtually identical to the *Sapho* campaign, erupted. On this occasion, vice crusaders were enraged when the economic advantages of organized prostitution were extolled, and the adversaries were none other than Anthony Comstock and Bernard Shaw.

Comstock rarely concerned himself with performance. Outside of railing that the 1893 Chicago World's Fair be razed because of the presence of the notorious "hoochie-coochie" dancers, he barely even acknowledged the existence of theatre. In 1905, however, he became the catalyst in the second major censorship battle of the twentieth century. During September of that year, the actor/producer Arnold Daly successfully presented Shaw's *Man and Superman*. Later that month Professor A. E. Bostwick, head of the circulating department of the New York Public Library, withdrew the published edition of the play from general circulation and placed it in the closed stacks. He justified his action by claiming children needed to be protected from Shaw's corrupting philosophy.

When this news reached Shaw, he automatically assumed that Comstock was responsible and penned a sarcastic response:

> Comstockery is the world's standing joke at the expense of the United States. Europe likes to hear such things. It confirms the deep-seated conviction of the Old World that America is a provincial place, a second rate town civilization after all.[37]

Comstock countered with characteristic spleen:

> I had nothing to do with removing that Irish smut-dealer's books from the Public Library shelves, but I will take a hand in the matter now. I see this man Shaw says . . . that he knows that his works can probably do harm to weak and dishonest people. Well, that lays him, his works, his publishers, the people who present his plays and all who or which has anything to do with the production or dissemination of them liable to the law which was made primarily to protect the weak. He convicts himself . . . This Shaw is outside our rules.[38]

The battle had begun. The *New York Times* editorialized, "let us not be forced to diet of treacle always. Let us have a drama of red corpuscles, the men who write our plays face the problems of existence fearlessly and express them freely and openly."[39] *Theatre Magazine* claimed that Shaw was the most brilliant playwright alive and that he was capable of genuine service to mankind, but that he was too often interested "in setting the world on fire merely to see it burn." The *New York Mail* claimed that Shaw was jealous of America's innocence, as opposed to the jadedness of the Old World.[40] Even the *Chicago Tribune* entered the fray. In an article, which sounded as if it could have been written by Comstock, the paper asserted: "Literary smut, even though it is the product of genius, is unfit for general reading."[41]

In mid-October, amidst the heated controversy over *Man and Superman*, Arnold Daly announced that he would present *Mrs Warren's Profession.* Suddenly, the stakes were raised. In this play, Shaw argued that, as long as a male-dominated economy kept women poor, prostitution was a reasonable career option. Now, the debate over Shaw was annexed into the ongoing controversy over commercialized sex.

Mrs Warren's Profession differs from *Sapho* in that Fanny Le Grande is a courtesan who grants sexual favors in return for gifts and acclaim. She is, in essence, an independent entrepreneur whose liaisons are motivated by a combination of adventure and love. Shaw's heroine, Mrs. Warren, is exactly the opposite. She is a bottom-line capitalist who has escaped the oppression of factory work by selling sexual favors. Now she operates a string of European brothels.

Moreover, Shaw had the temerity to portray a society intellectually and financially dominated by women. Mrs. Warren is not a debased, avaricious brothel-keeper. She is an astute businesswoman who understands the connection between sex, power, and wealth.[42] Vivie, her illegitimate daughter, is attractive and intelligent, and has just graduated with high honors from college. The men, however, are virtually impotent. The Revd Samuel Gardner, an Anglican clergyman had, as a young man, been one of Mrs. Warren's lovers. He and his son Frank live near the summer cottage Vivie has rented and that Mrs. Warren visits during the course of the play. Frank, a fatuous boy who ardently courts Vivie because he needs a rich wife, is unaware that he may be her half-brother. Sir George Crofts, Mrs. Warren's companion and business partner, is a brusque, humorless Philistine. Praed, also a friend of Mrs. Warren's, is a well-meaning but ineffectual artist who has nothing to offer except advice.

The tone of the play is witty and thoroughly disrespectful of bourgeois values. Although Mrs. Warren admits to Vivie that she had taken advantage of opportunities that certain men presented to her, she brags that she is now a wealthy businesswoman. Vivie, however, rejects her mother's philosophy and wealth, and sets out on her own. The final scene, in which they part, presumably forever, contains pain and resentment, but no easy sentiment. Each is fiercely committed to her own journey. Mrs. Warren continues as Europe's most successful madame and Vivie will chart her own course. Clearly, these two women had broken the cultural molds that had previously confined their gender.

Comstock, when he heard of the plot – it is doubtful if he ever read the play – wrote Daly to warn him against producing one of "Bernard Shaw's filthy products." Daly, who also played Frank, countered that the play would be regarded as a "strong sermon and a great moral lesson" and invited Comstock to attend a dress rehearsal.[43] Comstock responded with a second letter that stated intent was of no concern to the law. If the production harmed public morals, the producer would be treated as if he willingly meant to do so.[44]

On October 27, *Mrs Warren's Profession* previewed in New Haven. The reporter for the *New Haven Register* was outraged: "The play itself is fit for publication only as a document for the sociologist and reformer. Acted it is incredibly worse. The full force of the utterances and gestures only add to its vulgarity." Although New Haven's Mayor Studley had neither seen nor read the play, the reports of his friends and colleagues convinced him that it was not fit for public presentation. "The play is well written," he maintained, "and well acted, but rotten. It is nothing that this city ought to license."[45]

Exasperated, Daly returned to New York and commended his play into the hands of the critics. "If the press of New York condemn the play," he stated, "we shall take it off at once. If they uphold us, we will fight. I shall take the press opinion as the verdict of the people."[46] Police Commissioner William McAdoo was not mollified. He seized a copy of the script, expunged any lines which he considered too risqué and threatened to close the production if they were spoken.[47]

Crowds responded to the controversy and began to gather outside of the Garrick Theatre shortly after 6:00 P.M. opening night. Several extra uniformed policemen were brought in from surrounding precincts to keep traffic moving, but to no avail. Dense throngs on 35th Street between Sixth and Seventh Avenues blocked carriages carrying ticket-holding patrons from reaching the curb. Mary Shaw (no relation to the author), who played Mrs. Warren, and her fellow cast members required the assistance of billy-club waving policemen to reach the stage door. Scalpers hawked $3 orchestra seats for as much as $35. Second balcony seats, ordinarily 50 cents were sold for $5. Between 2,000 and 3,000 people had to be turned away.[48]

Critics and editorial writers thought *Mrs Warren's Profession* was too blunt and shocking. While they agreed that it might be of some worth as a social document, it would likely corrupt innocent audience members by stimulating their curiosity about sexual issues. The *Times* fumed:

> Mr. Shaw takes a subject decayed and reeking and analyzes it for the edification of those whose unhealthy tastes find satisfaction in morbific suggestion...whatever its merits or demerits as a play for the closet or as exposition of the author's views upon a sociological question, [it] has absolutely no place in the theatre before a mixed assembly.[49]

The *Herald* critic labeled the play "the limit of indecency" which no amount of editing could purge of its filth:

> The whole story of the play, the atmosphere surrounding it, the incidents, the personalities of the characters are wholly immoral and degenerate. The only way successfully to expurgate *Mrs Warren's Profession* is to cut the whole play out. You cannot have a clean pigsty...Does not this literary muck leave a bad taste in the mouth? Does it not insult the moral intelligence of New York theatregoers and outrage the decency of the New York stage? There was not one redeeming feature about it last night, not one ray of sunshine of cleanliness to lighten up the moral darkness of situation and dialogue, not the semblance of a moral lesson pointed.[50]

Thus, any play which discussed prevailing sexual inequities, criticized male-dominated society, or challenged middle-class morality was scorned for being "decayed and reeking," "a pigsty," and "literary muck."

McAdoo attended opening night armed with the version of the text that he himself had expurgated to make sure that the forbidden lines were not spoken. Although the cast had altered the lines accordingly, the police commissioner still decided the play was obscene. Charging that it was "an offense to the morals of the public," he ordered it closed and issued warrants for the arrest of the theatre owner, its manager, the cast, and Daly. In the meantime, Daly reneged on his promise to let the critics decide the fate of his production. Swayed by the demand for tickets, he opened the box office on the morning of the 31st hoping that some compromise with McAdoo might be negotiated. Such was not to be the case. At 4:00 P.M. he was ordered to close the box office and refund the $10,000 he had received for tickets.[51]

When Comstock was informed that *Mrs Warren's Profession* had been closed, he smugly responded:

> I had full confidence that Mr. McAdoo would do his duty. And now I will do all in my power to help him see to it that Arnold Daly and those associated with him in the production get the limit of the law ... An example should certainly be made of the guilty persons.[52]

Shaw's response was uncharacteristically somber. He professed pride in his play and argued that it had made him more friends than any other play he had written. He then commented on the central philosophy of the play and what he considered to be the prime motivation for censorship throughout history – the maintenance of power by the powerful:

> It will be seen more and more clearly that the police, doubtless with the best intentions, are protecting not public morality but the interests of the most dangerous class, namely the employers who pay women less than subsistence wages and overwork them mercilessly to grind profits for themselves out of the pith of the nation. Naturally, they raise the clamor of immorality and disgusting dialogue.[53]

In July, after several delays, the Court of Special Sessions acquitted Daly and his co-defendants of presenting an indecent and immoral play. Justice Olmstead, in his majority opinion, held that the play did indeed address issues that offended public morals and portrayed indecent characters. There was, however, nothing offensive about the language of the play nor were there any indecent actions performed on stage. He further stated that virtue may not have been given its just reward, but that vice was painted in such an odious light that it could not have possibly stimulated impure thoughts in the mind of the audience. And, since the law did not forbid disgusting an audience, he had to acquit the operatives.[54]

The censors had their way in spite of the acquittal. Daly announced that he would keep *Mrs Warren's Profession* off the boards because the notoriety connected to the play would call the motives of the producers into question. Moreover, he voiced concern that all of the attendant publicity would at-tract audiences interested in the play's sensational reputation rather than its dramatic and social message. In the spring of 1907, *Mrs Warren's Profession* reopened in New York, with Mary Shaw once again playing the lead. The publicity surrounding the closing and subsequent trial had given the production an unsavory reputation and it played barely two weeks. However, the production toured the Midwest and west and enjoyed remarkable success, thanks in no small part to Mary Shaw's commitment to the play and its message. Like Olga Nethersole with *Sapho*, she believed that *Mrs Warren's Profession* was a "woman's play – one in which the theme "appeals more powerfully to women than to men." Accordingly, she took her case to women's clubs in every major city she visited. She explained how the play's message affected all women and asked their cooperation. She claimed that none of the hundreds of women to whom she spoke ever objected to the play. "On the other hand," Shaw commented, "it was most unusual to find a man who was not shocked by it. I could explain this in only one way – the story was too truthfully told, too awful in its true presentation of a great fact in society."[55]

Irish Americans and *The Playboy*

Not all controversial plays of this period centered on female sexual transgressiveness. The Abbey Theatre of Dublin began a tour of the United States in 1913. Included in their repertoire was John Millington Synge's *The Playboy of the Western World*, a play that incited the Irish population of nearly every city in which it played. Set in the Aran Islands, where Synge spent several years living among its peasant population, its hero is Christopher, a young man given to spinning outrageous lies. His only redeeming quality is his verbal skill, which transforms these fabrications into tales of rare poetic beauty. He appears at a pub and boasts that he has murdered his father and that the police are on his trail. When his father arrives instead of the police, he does indeed try to kill him, but is restrained by some of the patrons.

In Dublin working-class Irish vigorously protested the character Synge had created. They complained that Christopher, because he was brutal, duplicitous, and cowardly, was not a true Irishman. Rather, he was a deviant creature concocted by Synge to heap ridicule on Irish men. Similar demonstrations of outrage were expected when the play opened in Boston on October 16, 1911. Although it prompted heated debate, it generated nothing close to a riot. The morning after opening night, the *Boston Globe* published interviews with several prominent male Irish Americans and the opinion seemed to be evenly split. Some labeled Synge a great imagistic poet and urged Irish audiences to enjoy the humor and the poetry of *Playboy* with an open mind. Others assumed a rigidly nationalistic attitude. One contributor claimed:

> *The Playboy of the Western World* has not a single situation – no, nor even a single line that is truly Irish. The play is a lie from beginning to end. That a people so deeply religious as the Irish, so teeming with filial and parental love...should ever be portrayed on the stage as Synge portrays them in this play almost makes one ashamed of the warm reception it received... If I did not enter here and now a vigorous protest against this shocking travesty, this disgusting burlesque, this lying, and not simply playful caricature upon the Irish race...I should fear than my Irish ancestors would rise up and call me a reprobate.[56]

Nonetheless, the reviewer for the *Boston Herald* described *Playboy*, as an "extraordinary work: a work of rare literary merit that is unusually effective on the stage."[57] The *Boston Evening Transcript* called it "adroitly dramatic, adroitly theatrical from beginning to end."[58] Even the secretary of the mayor, who served as unofficial city censor, ruled that "obscenity must be sought elsewhere."[59]

Playboy met with a markedly different response when it moved west. Audiences rioted in New Haven. Before the play opened in New York, the United Irish-American Societies of that city condemned it as "immoral and not true to Irish character" and the *Gaelic American* called the production a "monstrosity" and a "challenge to the Irish people of New York."[60] As soon as the first lines were uttered on opening night, November 27, 1911, a barrage of vegetables and eggs was hurled from the balcony and gallery of the Maxine Elliott Theatre. The actors scurried for cover in the wings, but the stage manager insisted that they continue the play. When the actors resumed, a more intense assault commenced, only this time stink bombs were lobbed into the audience and onto the stage. Ushers grabbed the assailants and unceremoniously threw them down the stairs of the theatre. The police were slow to respond in spite of repeated appeals from theatre staff. By the time the act ended, the vegetable throwers had been expelled. But, when it was announced that the act would be repeated, booing and hissing resumed and accompanied the play to its conclusion.[61]

Lady Gregory, author of much of the company's repertory and one of the Abbey's founders, and her guest, former president Theodore Roosevelt, attended the November 28 performance. Also in the audience was former police commissioner now Chief Magistrate McAdoo who, at the request of Mayor Gaynor, was there to determine if the production was immoral or

indecent. Hisses, groans, coughs, and sneezes greeted the actors, but uniformed policemen who were also in attendance ejected those who protested
too vigorously.[62] McAdoo found the production unobjectionable and subsequent performances were attended by quiet, attentive audiences. Perhaps
the significant number of uniformed and plain-clothed police convinced
any would-be protesters that their cause was not favored.[63]

Playboy's supporters claimed that the complaints of the "Irish patriots"
only served to confirm Synge's thesis – that many Irish were violent, ignorant
and censorious:

> Nobody doubts that the purpose of the Abbey Theatre and its play-
> ers is wholly artistic . . . But a few quarrelsome Irish patriots, who claim
> American citizenship, though obviously they do not value it, declare that
> posture of events, the characterization, and some of the text of *The Playboy*
> misrepresent Ireland, which they hold to be a land devoid of crime and
> violence, free from evil passions, full of brotherly love and virtue. The
> patriots invade the theatre, pelt the actors with missiles, and try to howl
> down the performance . . . These particular adherents, however, have gone
> about the business in a way that will strike the world as particularly
> Irish, and by their violence, their interference with the pleasure and busi-
> ness of others, have helped to justify the portrayal of ruffianism in the
> play.[64]

The New York pattern repeated itself when the company traveled to
Philadelphia. Dozens of police were in evidence at the Adelphi Theatre
the night of January 14, 1912. Ten minutes into the production, Joseph
McLaughlin, national vice president of the Ancient Order of Hibernians,
rose and shouted, "I protest." He was not able to continue his speech because
a number of uniformed police descended upon him and removed him from
the theatre. At that point, disruptions in other parts of the house commenced. Police removed the protesters, but each action prompted more
demonstrations. Eventually, order was restored, and the performance continued. The next night the confrontation became more violent as opponents of *Playboy* booed and hurled eggs onto the stage. The protesters
were evicted, but the crises rapidly escalated. An outraged citizen filed a
complaint that *Playboy* was "disgustingly immoral, blasphemous [and] obscene." Accordingly, the cast was arrested, but was later released on $500 bail
each.[65]

When informed of the actors' arrests, Bernard Shaw once again reiterated
his dislike of the United States:

The occurrence is too ordinary to be worth any comment. All decent people are arrested in America. For that reason I refused all invitations to go there. Besides, who am I that I should question Philadelphia's right to make itself ridiculous? It is a dangerous country for genuine Irishmen and Irishwomen. American Gaels are the real playboys of the Western World.

Playboy encountered similar problems in Chicago, but the tour's notoriety gradually abated. By the time it returned to New York in February 1913, the *Times* described the auditorium as "quiet as a millpond."[66]

The response to American naturalism

Playboy's detractors denounced it as immoral, but Synge's play did not threaten virtue. The resistance it engendered was due to the portrayal of the hero as cowardly and violent. In this respect, *Playboy* has to be considered a product of European naturalism, a literary genre advocating that life be depicted truthfully, without any idealization or regard for moral sensibilities. Characters in naturalistic dramas were governed exclusively by instincts, environment, and heredity. Transcendent spiritual values, if they existed at all, were treated as anachronisms, while compassion and goodness were mocked as fantasies. Needless to say, a world ruled by this grim materialistic philosophy incensed traditional moralists. Even Pope Pius X protested that naturalism was the "ever-increasing evil of the present day, and which breathing only the love of pleasure and sensuality, weakens and enervates the minds of men ... [and] effaces the sense of the most sacred obligations."[67]

Naturalism as it existed in France, Germany, or Russia never made a profound mark in the United States. Its brutal assessment of human nature was too forbidding to America's reform-minded, optimistic middle class, who believed that the combination of reason, moral suasion, and legislative action would bring about a perfected society. There was, however, one exception. Americans became obsessed with the graphic portrayals of moral degeneracy. The fact and fiction of prostitution, illegitimate children, sexually transmitted diseases, and adultery captivated the American public.

Turn-of-the-century drama had addressed some of these topics, but their treatment was oblique and circumspect. Public discussion of sexual topics was still taboo. By the beginning of the 1910s, however, new dramatic trends, influenced by naturalistic demands for truth, had begun to make an impact. Plays such as *Sapho, Mrs Warren's Profession, Man and Superman, The*

Shewing Up of Blanco Posnet, *Ghosts*, as well as less-well-remembered works such as Stanislaus Stange's *Divorce* (1909), Eugène Walter's *The Easiest Way* (1909), Clyde Fitch's *The City* (1909), Bayard Veiller's *Within the Law* (1912), and Edward Sheldon's *Romance* (1913) disquieted a genteel theatre public. To many, this new direction meant that theatre would be transformed from a platform for moral uplift into an agent of degeneracy and social disorder. Thus, civic and religious groups, dominated primarily by middle-class female reformers, set about insulating their communities from the pernicious effects of this type of drama.

On April 25, 1910, a committed group of citizens gathered at the Art Institute of Chicago and, by the time the meeting was adjourned, the Drama League of America had come into being. Given the harsh rhetoric generated by Comstock and other vice crusaders, the aims of the Drama League were positively benign. Its organizers aimed to create an organization with a chapter in every major city in the nation. The chapters would stimulate an interest in the "best drama," and "awaken the public to the importance of the theatre as a social force and to its great educational value if maintained on a high level of art and morals." Like the temperance, suffrage, and purity reform movements, the Drama League was committed to the betterment of society. In the words of one speaker, revitalizing the drama was "one with the cause of every worker for social betterment...it is the awakening of social consciousness, the sense of civic responsibility, the knowledge that in our pleasures no less than in our work, our acts do inevitably make or mar the lives of our fellow men."[68] The Drama League did not attack shows it considered demeaning or immoral. To do so would have only provided bad shows good publicity. Instead, it promoted productions that it considered worthy, and refused to comment on others. Although the reputation of the Drama League suffered from the perception that its members were meddlesome "do-gooders," its membership swelled from 10,000 in 1910 to over 100,000 in 1914. Thus, an endorsement from the Drama League meant a financial windfall for any New York touring production.[69]

However, it was in New York, the theatrical center of North America, that the most intense reform campaigns were mounted. And it was the Roman Catholic archdiocese that most ardently crusaded against immoral plays. In 1911, the American Federation of Catholic Societies named a dozen plays that were polluting the minds and souls of theatregoers:

When such plays are praised and heralded as attractions we feel that producers and managers are menacing the public morality and the welfare of the nation. For these plays being based on abominable sexual perversity and setting up a standard of morality which is open licentiousness will gradually accustom the spectators first in thought, then in deed to discard all Christian modesty and will thus prove grave to the nation.[70]

However, it was the presence of women and girls in audiences, "the modest and shame-faced," that keenly disturbed Catholic moralists. Not only were these women relinquishing their moral superiority and endangering their souls, they were also making it worthwhile for greedy managers to exhibit "immodest and shameless productions."[71]

As a result of this situation, John Cardinal Farley, Archbishop of New York, established the Catholic Theatre Movement in December 1912 to oppose these "immodest and shameless productions." Enthusiastically headed by Miss Eliza O'Brien Lummis, an influential advisor of the Cardinal, its goal was "to censor plays to which the general public is invited."[72] While Lummis ardently objected to cabaret, burlesque, lewd dancing, and scanty costumes, "problem plays" were her primary concern. In these presentations, issues were "discussed openly as though it were a philosophical thesis, and the sex problem is solved by deciding against virtue." Public discourse and representation of sexuality was thus inexorably linked to the loss of virtue. Dubbed the "conspiracy of silence," this suppression of public discussion of sexual concerns betrayed a belief that immorality was the fault of external conditions. If individuals could be permanently sequestered from a contaminated environment, they would remain pure. If, on the other hand, men, women, and children were exposed to sights and sounds that hinted at moral relativism, they would be incapable of resisting such powerful temptations. Accordingly, the Catholic Theatre Movement (CTM) wanted state authorities to establish censorship boards for "permanent and Christian regulation of the stage." By so doing, the CTM hoped to insure that modesty of dress, virtuous behavior, pre-marital sexual continence, conjugal fidelity, permanence of marriage, and the sanctity of the family would be the only issues discussed on stage.[73]

Sex plays of the 1910s

Clearly, American theatre in the 1910s was evolving in a direction that alarmed middle-class moralists. That alarm turned to panic when a spate of "sex plays" appeared on Broadway and portrayed the sullied, lurid world of criminal sexuality to the great delight of New York audiences. The first of these was Eugene Brieux's *Damaged Goods*. Arguably the most provocative play of the period, *Damaged Goods* was the most forthright discourse on syphilis to reach American audiences.[74] Advocates claimed that the fortress of silence surrounding this disease would at last be breached. *Damaged Goods* would explain that upstanding middle- and upper-class men, women, and children were all at risk. Moreover, it would dispel the myth that syphilis was God's punishment for profligacy. Opponents of the play, while not opposed to this goal, completely dismissed theatre's ability to promote social transformation:

> [The theatre's] mission is aesthetic, not ethical, and it fulfills its mission best when it provides intelligent diversion for all sorts and conditions of men. When the stage tries to teach, particularly when it tries to treat seriously of subjects generally considered too delicate for common conversation, it may accomplish some good, but it invariably causes harm, too, by its general appeal to the merely curious and morbid minds.[75]

The play itself is a protracted lecture that attempts to dispel commonly held beliefs about syphilis. The first act takes place in a physician's office. A character known only as "Doctor" tells George Dupont that he has contracted syphilis, but that he can be cured with the proper drugs. However, the Doctor forbids him to marry. Dupont argues that he is a moral man and has never been with a prostitute. His physician curtly dismisses his protestations as irrelevant and explains that prostitutes are not exclusively to blame. The disease, he explains, does not respect social or economic status. Dupont, however, ignores the Doctor. He marries and promptly infects his wife and their unborn child. Brieux virtually abandons the plot in the third act in favor of an extended explanation by the Doctor to Dupont's father-in-law about the steps to be taken to protect the general public from syphilis. These include sex education for youth, pre-marital health tests for men and women, and elimination of the myth that the "dreaded disease" is God's punishment of immorality.

The situation and dialogue in *Damaged Goods* were considered too inflammatory and shocking for the general public. Thus, only private performances sponsored by the Sociological Fund of the Medical Review of Reviews were announced. Composed of legislators, physicians, social workers, educators, and students in these fields, these audiences were adjudged serious and sober enough to withstand the harsh message of the play.[76] Critical response was generally favorable. Eventually *Damaged Goods* was opened to the general public. While the houses were good, the play ran for only sixty-six performances.

The white slavery controversy

Damaged Goods, while possibly the most serious play of the decade to address sexual issues, was only one of hundreds of tracts that dealt with heretofore unmentionable sexual topics. For the most part, this discourse was subsumed under the topic of "white slavery." As originally used, the term described the brutal kidnapping and transformation of innocent Caucasian women into prostitutes.[77] In general, the media gleefully supported the notion that a monolithic vice empire controlled a network of brothels in the United States and Europe. Between 1908 and 1914, respected newspapers as well as tabloids such as the *Police Gazette* churned out hundreds of sensationalist articles alleging a widespread traffic in young white women. Reginald Wright Kauffman's immensely popular novel, *The House of Bondage,* went through fourteen editions in only two years. Between 1909 and 1914, twenty-two white slave exposés were published and disseminated throughout the country. Many came with lurid, multicolored covers and proffered titles such as "The Great War on White Slavery," "Fighting for the Protection of Our Girls: Truthful and Tasteful Accounts of the Hideous Trade of Buying and Selling Young Girls for Immoral Purposes," and "Graphic Accounts of How White Slaves are Ensnared and a Full Exposition of the Methods and Schemes Used to Lure and Trap Girls."[78]

Replete with "case histories," these narratives featured dark-skinned alien "procurers," in search of poor, innocent girls newly arrived in the city. They would lead the unsuspecting women into the clutches of heartless brothel-keepers, who were protected by corrupt police and politicians. On occasion, relatives or sweethearts would arrive to save the heroines from contamination. If, however, they arrived after the heroine was defiled, prison and/or death and/or madness was their certain fate.

While there were indeed cases of abduction and imprisonment in "houses of bondage," the white slavery panic was quickly transmuted into an all-encompassing metaphor signifying widespread anxiety over profound shifts in American society.[79] Among these were the staggering number of immigrants arriving from southern and Eastern Europe (the "dark skinned procurers"), rapid growth of commercialized sex, the shift from an agrarian into an industrial economy, and the spread of syphilis. Feminists, too, incorporated this metaphor into their civil rights discourse. For these women, white slavery denoted male domination of every aspect of society. Consequently, they supported the publication and performance of these narratives not as art, but as an affirmation of the suffragist effort to liberate women from male dominance. By graphically depicting the results of male lechery, they hoped to illustrate the need for moral as well as social, political, and economic reform.

The white slavery panic was further fueled by the appearance of hundreds of thousands of young, unmarried working women indulging in the world of nighttime amusements that proliferated shortly after the turn of the century. In New York, women congregated with each other – and with men – in social clubs, in one of the over 500 dance clubs that dotted Manhattan, at amusement parks such as Coney Island's Steeplechase Park, Luna Park, or Dreamland, at vaudeville theatres, and at the newly operational movie theatres, which provided cheap entertainment.[80]

Panic-stricken purity crusaders watched helplessly as thousands of single, young women eagerly engaged in mixed-sex leisure activities. Tract after tract warned these women to abjure their desire for pleasure and remain within the safe precincts of their homes or settlement houses. If they yielded to their instincts, moral degeneracy was their certain fate. Thus, white slavery came to signify much more than the abduction of young women for immoral purposes. It encompassed an extensive litany of horrors that emerged as profound shifts in American culture became apparent.[81]

Theatre producers and playwrights enthusiastically participated in the white slavery panic. Whether motivated by a genuine concern for the safety of women or tempted by the potential profits such productions might yield, dozens of plays dramatizing female sexual abuse were churned out. Critics almost uniformly rebuked such productions as crass, vulgar enterprises that had thoroughly contaminated the theatre. Moreover, they attacked producers and playwrights for their failure to support traditional moral standards. *The Nation* claimed the current vogue of plays was a dual assault on morality and aesthetics: "Not all of us admit that the claims of art, for its own sake, absolve its practitioners from the established restraints of decency and the recognized laws of beauty."[82] The Catholic Church was unrelenting in its denunciation of these productions. It indicted them as a "riot of moral filth, gruesomeness and infidelity" and called for police investigations. It fumed: "In view of this public shamelessness, one naturally asks are there any lower depths of indecency into which the drama is going to descend?"[83]

Given the highly charged atmosphere surrounding white slavery and the opposition of critics and moralists, public officials began to monitor any presentations that addressed the vice discourse. The four plays that received the most attention all premiered within fifteen months of one another:

The Lure by George Scarborough opened at the Maxine Elliott Theatre on August 15, 1913; on September 2, Bayard Veiller's *The Fight* premiered at the Hudson Theatre; an adaptation of Reginald Wright Kauffman's *The House of Bondage* opened at the Cecil Spooner Theatre at 163rd Street on December 9; and Rachel Marshall and Oliver Bailey's *The Traffic* opened at the New York Theatre on November 16, 1914. It was, however, *The Lure* and *The Fight* that generated the most controversy. *The Lure* is a melodrama that features a working-class girl, Sylvia, whose mother is dying because she cannot afford proper nourishment or medicine. Sylvia discovers the card of an older woman who always had "extra work for girls in the evening." When she calls upon this benevolent matron, she is deftly imprisoned in the woman's house. Unfortunately, Sylvia's captor has transported some of her charges across state lines to conduct business, thus making her guilty of a federal offense under the Mann Act (1910), which forbade, under heavy penalties, the transportation of women from one state to another for immoral purposes. As luck would have it, Sylvia's beloved is a federal agent who raids the house and succeeds in rescuing her from her lurid fate.

The Fight describes the mayoral campaign of a young feminist in a Colorado town that is beset with vice and corruption. She runs on a reformist platform and encounters opposition from both local and national politicians who profit from these illegal activities. The most controversial scene takes place in a house of ill repute where the candidate has trailed her opponents. She accuses them of corrupting young women and the community for their own profit, and proceeds to victory.[84]

The most encouraging critics admitted that these plays possessed some grim power. Others claimed that, no matter how serious the intent, such displays tempted young people to indulge in whatever corrupt activity that was represented. Still others claimed that the producers only cared about turning a profit:

> The motive in all this display of indecency on the stage is necessarily the touchstone of its moral intent, and that motive is, without any concealment at all, mercenary. Theatrical managers did not tumble over each other in the rush to see who could first produce the most "risky" play, because they had suddenly found artistic salvation. It was merely the jingle of the guinea that made them prick up their ears.[85]

On September 6, Chief Magistrate McAdoo issued summonses to Lee Shubert (*The Lure*) and William Harris (*The Fight*). Shubert, upon hearing that such a process had begun, responded indignantly: "This is a shame and an injustice... The play is a great moral lesson."[86] The foremost suffragists in New York, all of whom had been invited to attend a performance before the arrest warrants were issued, seconded Shubert. Mrs. Mary Garrett Hay, president of the Women's Suffrage Party, commented: "To my mind it is a moral play. Girls, go see it and see it with wide open eyes."[87] McAdoo, when asked his opinion of the feminists' assertion, responded, "We do not need... to uncover a sewer to convince people as to its filthiness, nor to warn those of ordinary cleanly habits against getting into it." He concluded by asserting that the citizens who saw *The Lure* were only expressing their private opinions. He, on the other hand, was a public official obligated to protect the citizenry from indecent and immoral activities. Thus, McAdoo, because he was a public official, believed he was endowed with keener powers of moral discernment than average citizens. While he never claimed that he was a censor, he justified his actions by claiming that some productions were as infectious as sewers and, in the name of public health, he was obligated to suppress them.[88]

The *Times* also indicted feminists for naively supporting a moral contagion:

> The present disposition of women to countenance plays treating subjects which until lately were considered unfit for public discussion follows naturally on the discussion of the subjects on the lecture platform and in books and magazines. From the first, sensible onlookers have seen that this movement must have evil results... It is, therefore, most discouraging that women of good character, who generally hold to a serious view of duty, should, under a delusion that good can come out of evil thus exposed, lend their countenance to the exploitation of such filthy stuff.[89]

It probably came as no surprise to readers that producers had been accused of greed. To suggest that suffragists were as guilty as producers was another matter entirely. One cannot help but recall Cardinal Gibbons' indictment of suffragists because their "masculine boldness and brazen effrontery" was responsible for the "wrecks of families in our country" (see above pp. 49–50). Clearly, feminists were not to be trusted with moral or aesthetic leadership of American culture.

Lee Shubert and William Harris quickly moved to have their cases transferred from McAdoo's jurisdiction to the Court of Special Sessions, which required a grand jury indictment before a trial could be held. The two producers then offered this twenty-three-member panel the opportunity to attend a private performance of each play and decide whether or not they were indecent. In the meantime, the productions were withdrawn. The producer of *The Fight*, reading the handwriting on the wall, eliminated the controversial second act, which shows the candidate in the bordello confronting conspirators. In Veiller's rewrite, the candidate merely describes the altercation. When the grand jury viewed the revised version of the play, they found nothing objectionable and elected to drop all charges. Shubert showed the unexpurgated version of *The Lure* to the grand jury on September 12, but did not want to risk a negative verdict. Four days later, he informed District Attorney Bostwick of his intention to rewrite the offensive scenes, which, like those in *The Fight*, took place in a house of ill repute.

Neither producer graciously accepted defeat, and both were more than willing to enlist the aid of feminists to advance their claims. Harris invited twenty-four prominent suffragists to attend *The Fight* on October 7. On October 14 the delegation stated that the play was "frank in its treatment of white slavery," and agreed that neither the characters nor the dialogue were indecent.[90] Not to be outdone, Shubert hosted a rally of 800 feminists. Sponsored by the Women's Political Union, this gathering merged support for the frank discussion of the dangers of white slavery with support for suffrage. One after another, speakers asserted that "votes for women" would eliminate prostitution. The Revd. Dr. Anna Shaw, president of the National American Women's Suffrage Association, attacked the "smug hypocrisy," which ignored the economic conditions that drove women into prostitution. Olga Nethersole reminded the women that the attack on *Sapho* bore a striking resemblance to the current campaign against the white slave plays.[91] A few days later, Mrs. Emmeline Pankhurst, the famous English suffragist, was a guest at the Maxine Elliott Theatre. After the final curtain, she congratulated the production saying: "The stage has at last awakened to its mission as a factor in public education and is presenting the sordid truths of life in a courageous fashion."[92]

A few weeks later, the actress Cecil Spooner and her manager Joseph Cone added more fuel to the white slavery fire when they opened *The House of Bondage*. Adapted from Reginald Wright Kauffman's notorious best-selling novel, the play tells the story of a girl who leaves her home in rural Pennsylvania to find work in New York. She becomes attached to a man who entices her into a house of ill repute; the play chronicles her descent into the horrors of prostitution.

The production opened on December 8 at the Cecil Spooner Theatre, a facility managed by the actress that she renamed for herself. Spooner had saturated Harlem and the Bronx, where the theatre was located, with extremely provocative posters advertising her white slave drama. Complaints were filed with the police before the play premiered claiming that it would likely be indecent. A deputy police commissioner attended the opening, judged that the play was offensive and had warrants issued. The next night, as the curtain was about to rise, police walked backstage and arrested Spooner and her manager. She was not permitted to change into street clothes, and both were escorted to the waiting patrol wagon. Spooner's husband and business partner told the audience what had transpired, calling it a "form of persecution which many artists are obliged to suffer." The audience shouted and booed in protest, and streamed out of the theatre only to discover Spooner being hustled into the patrol wagon. The crowd followed the wagon to the precinct house where they cheered as Spooner and Cone emerged. The duo was subsequently released into the custody of their attorney until the next afternoon when they would have to appear before Chief Magistrate McAdoo.[93]

Rather than close her play or go to jail, Spooner elected to purge *The House of Bondage* of those scenes to which the police had objected. On December 10, an altered version was presented. After the third act, Spooner stepped in front of the curtain and detailed her encounter with the police to an audience that numbered 2,500. She complained that she had been treated outrageously, and urged her patrons to write to the mayor on her behalf. A man rose to support her saying that she had been harassed because the play had revealed the connection between police officials and vice kingpins. The audience applauded and the show continued. Police officials were also present to witness the revised play. They complained that more revisions were needed and that new warrants would be issued.

The threat of more arrests apparently had the desired effect. When *The House of Bondage* moved to the Longacre, a Broadway theatre, on January 14, 1914, the offensive scenes had been eliminated. Mainstream critics unanimously scored the production. Alan Dale, however, went even further. In his signed column, he called the new version "just a cheap, garish, ill-written, senseless and impossible 'mellerdrammer,' worse than anything shown in the 'ten, twent, thirt' theatres." More importantly, he indicted female audiences for supporting these plays:

> Anybody who paid more than a quarter to see yesterday's matinee ... must feel like kicking herself around the block. For it was a female audience. Don't imagine that men endured the piffle I saw yesterday. They didn't.

Nearly the entire audience was composed of women, ready with their handkerchiefs and sometimes even ready with their laughter. There is no accounting for taste.[94]

The expurgated version of *The House of Bondage* ran for only eight performances and closed on January 27.

Early in the fall of 1913, *The Traffic* opened on the west coast and slowly wound its way eastward. In November, it reached Chicago arriving there shortly after *Damaged Goods* had closed. It tells the gruesome tale of a young woman who seeks work to pay for her sister's medical treatments. She falls in love with a man who pays for the girl's care, but, in turn, convinces her to become a prostitute to repay him. Her recovered sister, who is only fourteen, is also led into the brothel, which prompts the police to raid the house. During the mayhem, the heroine kills her lover. She has, however, become too cynical and too dependent on drugs and alcohol to respond to protestations of love from the physician who treated her sister. In the last act she is tried for murder and convicted.

Judging from the response of one critic, white slavery as a component of feminist semiotics was as controversial in Chicago as it was in New York:

> With the appearance of *The Traffic* ... the "white-slave drama" reared its scarlet sociological front in our midst ... this eruption of propaganda for sexly reform had a slightly fatiguing effect upon me, and the many assurances from high authorities that such revelations make for the purification of the male heart and the emancipation of the female soul fail to relieve my tedium. I, for one, am sick of the talk of white slavery, and not all the eloquence of Mrs. Pankhurst can interest me in the subject.[95]

By the time *The Traffic* reached New York in November 1914, white slave plays had been denounced as "detestable sociological conferences" that had broken "the barriers of restraint and good manners."[96] *The Lure, The Fight*, and *The House of Bondage* had already closed and *The Traffic* expired after only eight performances.[97]

It is difficult to assess the relevance of the white slave plays. Were they tawdry manipulations of national panic? Brooks McNamara, one the most informed of the Shubert scholars, completely dismisses Lee Shubert's sanctimonious defense of *The Lure* as a Barnum-like ruse meant only to stimulate ticket sales.[98] Were they unconscious attempts to restrict female sexual freedom? Joan McDermott and Sarah Blackstone certainly believe that was the case.[99] Or were they perhaps the faint beginnings of American dramatic naturalism? Although they adhered to a melodramatic formula and capitalized on media generated hysteria, these plays nonetheless introduced middle-class Broadway audiences to the seamy underbelly of commercial sex. It is conceivable that they might have been a seedbed for more serious investigations of human sexuality. However, fierce opposition to these plays completely preempted such possibilities. Theatre's mission, as the anonymous *Times* editorialist asserted, was "aesthetic, not ethical."[100] Frank discourse concerning the human condition was not yet an option for the drama.

However, the white slave plays signified that a profound shift in the direction of American theatre had occurred. During the period from 1875 to 1920, the nation's cultural, social, and political aspirations had been determined by a small group of ministers, teachers, politicians, lawyers, and business leaders. But, from 1920 to 1929, a new generation seized control of the culture. No longer would the elite be able to dictate what was and was not tasteful, suitable, uplifting, or appropriate. Women were out and about, electing to attend entertainments that their parents decried. A new economy, defined by mass production and consumption, captured the imagination of the populace. In turn, "the crowd," "the mob," "the horde," as they were disparagingly called, exercised significant influence on culture. They challenged fixed and rigid rules regarding such disparate areas as religion, sport, dress, and leisure. These cultural insurgents also launched an intense attack on traditional moral standards. F. Scott Fitzgerald and Hollywood stars now set the moral norms for this generation. Yet this shift did not go unchallenged. It met stiff resistance from political and religious leaders who fiercely battled to preserve the values of the past, the values that the youth of the twenties sought to destroy. Not surprisingly, theatre occupied a central role in this discourse.

3

Flappers and fanatics

The twenties roar

By 1920, New York had become the unquestioned theatrical center of the United States, completing a process that had begun after the Civil War. In 1920, 150 plays were produced on Broadway and steadily rose until the 1927/28 season when 280 were produced. As might be imagined, the New York theatre provided something for virtually everyone. A new generation of producers, playwrights, and designers had witnessed the disaster of war, revolution, and the loss of ideals, and attempted to transform theatre into a forum where this new and uncomfortable discourse might take place. George Cram Cooke and Susan Glaspell along with their colleagues at the Provincetown Playhouse introduced New York audiences to Eugene O'Neill and proved that American playwrights were indeed artists. The Theatre Guild and its directors, Theresa Helburn, Lawrence Langer, Lee Simonson, Philip Moeller, and Maurice Wertheim, established an art theatre that was thoroughly professional – and successful. And Robert Sherwood, Sidney Howard, Rachel Crothers, Maxwell Anderson, John Howard Lawson, and Eugene O'Neill introduced New York audiences to a frank and often brutal portrayal of the human condition.

By no means, however, did these young Turks unseat the entrenched Broadway establishment who thought of theatre as a commercial enterprise, not social work. Lee and J. J. Shubert owned over 100 theatres nationwide, including a dozen in Manhattan, and kept them filled with revues and musical comedies. George M. Cohan frequently had three or four productions running simultaneously. Florenz Ziegfeld and Earl Carroll kept audiences sated with lavish revues that featured nude females in exotic settings and Al Woods produced what seemed to be a never-ending stream of bedroom farces.

Clearly, New York theatre reflected the multiplicity of cultural, social, and political agendas that emerged during the twenties, without a doubt the most tumultuous decade the nation had ever experienced. These years were characterized by social invention, popular ideology, generational conflict, and, above all, mass consumerism. Due to mass production, brought about by technological advances and the increasing efficiency of labor, total industrial production increased by over 60 percent, far outstripping the growth in population. Profits, dividends, salaries, and industrial wages grew appreciably. Consumer credit was dramatically extended. As a result, advertising and salesmanship came to be regarded as patriotic enterprises. For the first time in American history, spending, rather than saving, came to be identified with prosperity.[1]

Perhaps the most stunning example of this enhanced consumerism was the purchase of automobiles, the "supreme machine of the Twenties [sic]." The automobile provided middle- and working-class Americans with a freedom and mobility once reserved for the aristocracy and were purchased at an astounding rate. In 1895, there were four motorcars registered in the United States. By 1927, there were in excess of 16 million.[2]

The twenties was also the decade of heroes. The exploits of Red Grange, Babe Ruth, Bill Tilden, Jack Dempsey, Henry Ford, and, of course, Charles Lindbergh, were followed with almost religious devotion. The public's desire to entertain itself seemed unquenchable as crossword puzzles and mah-jong became obsessions, and college football, as well as professional baseball, boxing, golf, and tennis attracted huge audiences. As a result, spending on amusement and recreation rose by 300 percent from 1919 to 1929. The most popular of all mass entertainment was the movie. Although the educated and upper classes shunned films, workers and immigrants who knew little English flooded into the newly erected movie palaces which provided overstuffed seats and liveried attendants all for only 50 cents. Each week about 100 million Americans went to the movies, a number about equal to the population. The flapper, the bootlegger, the vamp, the befuddled cop, and the corrupt politician, all reflections of modern life, constantly reappeared to tease and entertain the film audiences of the twenties.[3] As one observer stated, the new generation had distinguished itself from its forebears by proving that "unremitting toil is not necessarily a law of human destiny."[4]

The twenties also bred a generation of pessimistic, cynical intellectuals who reviled the carnival atmosphere that evolved after World War I. They believed the war had been fought not to secure freedom but to preserve

corrupt political structures. Ezra Pound railed that Europe and America
had sacrificed its young to preserve a decaying nineteenth-century culture
or, as he termed it, "a bitch gone bad in the teeth."[5] George Santayana
hypothesized that, prior to 1917, America believed itself to be the land
of goodwill, free from poisons. During the next two years, its optimism
disappeared as it encountered one of the "heredity plagues of mankind."[6]
F. Scott Fitzgerald declared that a new generation had grown up to find
"all Gods dead, all wars fought, all faiths shaken."[7] Gertrude Stein simply
called these Americans the "lost generation."[8]

Yet there was a larger, conservative sector of the population who resented the cynicism of urban intellectuals, chastised the middle class for its
shocking indulgence, and loathed the immigrant swarm. They turned to
the past for their values, and sought to rekindle patriotism, fundamental
religion, frugality, sexual continence, and abstention from alcohol. Sinclair
Lewis called these conservatives "villagers" and H. L. Mencken dispar-
aged them as "boobs." As a group these Americans lived in cities that
numbered less than 10,000. While intellectuals rejected the war because
the peace had not gone far enough, the villagers feared that it had gone
too far by threatening national sovereignty, as in the proposed League of
Nations.[9]

While the villagers might have appeared foolish and backwards to
sophisticated urbanites, they were hardly the simpletons that Mencken
depicted. Villagers won almost every major political engagement of the
decade, including the election of three Republican presidents. Their
insistence that America belonged to white, Protestant, northern Europeans
led to a resurgence of the Ku Klux Klan.[10] Their isolationist policies kept
the United States out of the League of Nations, ignited the "Red Scare"
of 1919, and resulted in legislation that accounted for the arrest and
deportation of thousands of immigrants who dared to criticize the
government.[11]

It was Prohibition, however, that most clearly delineated the villagers
from their urban opponents. This "noble experiment" was largely the creation of provincial, Protestant, white America. The voting in the House
of Representatives bears out this observation. Of the 197 representatives
who voted for passage of the Volstead Act, 129 hailed from towns of less
that 10,000, and 64 were from villages of less than 2,500. Out of the 190
who opposed the amendment, 109 came from cities of over 25,000. As
more than one historian has observed, Prohibition was a measure passed by
"village America against urban America." Throughout the decade, whether

a political candidate was "wet" or "dry" in large measure determined whether he supported the conservative agenda of the village or could be counted among the "mongrels" that inhabited the cities.[12]

Aside from specific political issues, conservatives in the 1920s worried that the individual autonomy that the young had appropriated for themselves undermined the fixed moral absolutes upon which the national ethos rested. They refused to entertain the possibility that standards of behavior were socially constructed; and, for them, the appearance of flappers, jazz babies, the Charleston, rumble seats, raccoon coats, hip-flasks, Fitzgerald novels, and Hollywood sex symbols was tantamount to anarchy. As one agitated critic believed, youthful disregard for traditional authority echoed Satan's challenge to God:

> Laws, which mark the decent restraint of print, speech and dress, have in recent decades been increasingly disregarded. The very foundations of the great and primitive institutions of mankind – like the family, the Church and the State – have been shaken. Nature itself is defied. Thus the fundamental difference of sex is disregarded by social and political movements that ignore the permanent differentiation of social function ordained by God himself.[13]

It was, however, the sexual mores of this modern generation that most profoundly disturbed their elders. Sexual activity was no longer limited to the confines of marriage or the deviant behavior of prostitutes, procurers, and their clientele. Sexual satisfaction came to be regarded as a value in itself and a critical component of personal happiness. Moreover, the burgeoning consumer economy described human relationships in terms of uncontrollable sexual impulses. Popular songs and magazines taught that love occurred in a flash and was the product of chemistry, not social considerations. Films promised to introduce audiences to previously unseen sexual exploits. Contemporary dances were exuberant and provocative, and the enclosed automobile provided privacy and marked the end of courtship conducted under the watchful eyes of parents. Moreover, women had shortened their skirts, bobbed their hair, discarded their corsets, liberally used make-up, and had taken up smoking, drinking – and golf.[14]

Nudity and sexuality on the stage

Although sexual themes and transgressive women had appeared on stage during the 1910s, many producers and audiences in the twenties seemed utterly obsessed with nudity, sexual situations, and blunt language. The battles that evolved proved that not all of the villagers lived in small towns. The revues of the period appropriated the successful formula perfected by Florenz Ziegfeld in his *Follies*. They presented beautiful women in lavish settings and skimpy costumes. The Shuberts' first effort, *The Passing Show*, opened in 1912 and they produced various reprises of their hit reviews throughout the teens and twenties. At first, *The Passing Show* featured burlesques of current Broadway hits, and was intended to provide simple entertainment for the "tired businessman." Successive editions included more and more women in briefer and briefer costumes. By the early twenties, the Shuberts incorporated nude women in a variety of scenes that included hanging like tassels from chandeliers and posing as apples, grapes, and cherries in a fruit basket.[15] The Shuberts' main competitor was Earl Carroll, whose *Vanities* featured virtual nudity as his female performers were frequently displayed in G-strings and a few well-placed feathers or beads. Complaints were lodged with the police department who dutifully attended performances to make sure that Carroll's brief costumes did not disappear entirely. Carroll was never charged with any city or state crime. He did, however, attract the attention of the federal government. At a post-performance party, a young woman entered a bathtub purportedly filled with champagne, and Carroll was tried for violation of the Volstead Act (1919), which prohibited the manufacture, sale, or transportation of alcoholic beverages in the United States.

Although these displays of nudity agitated some cultural critics, they rarely incurred official sanctions. Displays of the nude women, while they might have been daring, did not necessarily challenge the existing moral paradigm. These revues represented women as harmless objects of sexual desire, affirmed male heterosexual hegemony, and reiterated that America was a land where fantasies became reality. Although Carroll and later the Shuberts staged numbers in which the women moved, for the most part they remained motionless and silent, erotic objects rather than people.

Plays that featured fully developed characters who defined themselves by their sexual behavior met with an entirely different response. It was these representations that ran afoul of Section 1140-a of the New York State penal code. It read, in part, that any person who participated in any capacity in a "play, exhibition, show or entertainment which would tend to the corruption of the morals of youth or others...shall be guilty of a misdemeanor." In essence, this piece of legislation allowed prosecutors to file charges against a play if it merely exhibited the *tendency to corrupt a child*. Whether or not a child had actually seen the play or, for that matter, had actually been corrupted, was immaterial. If a play might or could pollute a youthful mind, it might be legally proscribed. In October 1921, Al Woods, one of Broadway's most successful producers, encountered the full force of Section 1140-a. During that month he opened his comedy, *The Demi-Virgin*, and it was greeted with a chorus of calls for official censorship. Woods began his career in 1905 as a producer of blood-and-thunder melodramas. After the popularity of this genre of plays waned, he switched to sex farces, which reached their height of popularity in the early 1920s. Playwright Avery Hopwood was his chief collaborator. Although he died in an accidental drowning in 1928, he contributed thirty-three plays to the New York stage and in 1920 had four Broadway shows running simultaneously. The typical Woods–Hopwood farce took place in upscale surroundings and was peopled with witty and eccentric characters. The dialogue was sophisticated and riddled with light profanity and double-entendre. Although the central theme was sex, the frantic efforts of the central characters to engage in illicit activities never quite came to pass.[16]

In *The Demi-Virgin*, two Hollywood idols have just married. On their wedding night, the beautiful film star, Gloria Graham, deserts her husband, Wally Dean, when she receives a call from an old flame. Not knowing whether or not the union was ever consummated, movie columnists label her a "demi-virgin." The cast included types who were easily recognizable to a modern audience. There is a Charlie Chaplin type, a "Perils of Pauline" serial heroine, and a Mary Pickford ingénue. The most disturbing character, however, is "Fatty Belden," an obvious impersonation of Fatty Arbuckle, who is portrayed as a womanizing, booze-guzzling profligate.

The two most troublesome scenes are a game of strip-poker played by five starlets and an encounter in which Wally threatens to make Gloria pay her "marriage debt." In typical Woods–Hopwood style, the dialogue promised more titillation than the performance delivered. The starlets stripped only as far as their underwear and Wally never really intended to "have his way" with Gloria. In fact, when she returns to him in the last act, he reveals that their divorce was never finalized.

Although critics claimed the show was indecent, *The Demi-Virgin* might never have attracted the attention it did had it not been for events in Hollywood. Just fifteen days before *The Demi-Virgin* opened, the Fatty Arbuckle scandal hit the papers. Arbuckle had been accused of manslaughter in connection with the death of a young film actress, Virginia Rappe. The papers claimed that Arbuckle had pushed a Coke bottle into Ms. Rappe's body during a brutal sexual assault. Actually, she had gone to see Arbuckle because she was pregnant and unmarried, and needed to borrow money. He endured three trials and was finally acquitted when it was determined that the prosecution's case was based on perjury. Nonetheless, Arbuckle's career was ruined and the studios decided it was time to clean up their act, both on and off the set. In 1922, the newly formed Motion Picture Producers and Distributors Association (MPPDA) hired Will Hayes, the architect of Warren G. Harding's landslide 1920 election victory and former head of the Republican National Committee. The MPPDA wanted Hayes to rehabilitate the crippled film establishment and paid the nonsmoking, teetotaling, church-going Hayes $100,000 per year to police the morals of Hollywood. The Hayes Office immediately drew up a list of over 200 people who were banned from films because they drank too much, used drugs, or were promiscuous. He enacted the "seven foot" rule that prohibited any kiss from lasting more than seven feet of film. He demanded that actors' contracts contain "morals" clauses that provided punishment for performers who engaged in "lewd behavior."[17]

It is impossible to link the Arbuckle episode and the subsequent decision of film producers to police themselves directly to the subsequent calls for theatre censorship in New York. However, the climate that these events created clearly made a volatile situation unstable. When *The Demi-Virgin* opened in Pittsburgh on September 26, the Director of Public Safety ordered Woods to cut some lines and episodes. When the producer refused, his show was closed. Hopwood was incensed, but Woods was delighted that his production had received a "million dollars worth of advertising."[18] The show opened in New York on October 18. Reviews generally dismissed the show as a sly attempt to cash in on the notoriety generated by various Hollywood scandals. Alexander Woollcott called Hopwood's characters a "bit gaudy and prankful" but generally a "moral lot."[19] The *Variety* critic congratulated Hopwood for having balanced on "two wheels around the dangerous curves of dialogue" and suggested that the "matinee crowd" would have a "lot of laughs."[20] The reviewer from the *Commercial* was obviously not amused with the play's sexual innuendo. He claimed that Woods and Hopwood had given the censorship movement "a powerful impetus." He condemned the play as "unadulterated smut, bordering on the pathological," and claimed that it contained "neither wit, wisdom, nor plot," and was "designed to carry all the vulgarity that could be spread over an evening."[21] Apparently Chief Magistrate

McAdoo and several other citizens agreed with the outraged critic, and Woods and Hopwood were summoned to his office on November 3 to answer complaints that *The Demi-Virgin* constituted an "immoral exhibit." Woods refused to make any changes in the script, thereby forcing a trial.[22] The preliminary hearing got under way on November 7. McAdoo listened to the testimonies of those who opposed the production. Chief among the plaintiffs was John S. Sumner, who succeeded Anthony Comstock as Secretary of the Society for the Suppression of Vice. The Chief Magistrate, however, refused to hear testimony from those in the field of theatre. He claimed that it was his duty "to judge this play as it would appeal to the intelligence of ordinary men and women."[23] On November 14, McAdoo found Woods guilty of presenting an obscene play, set bail at a thousand dollars, and bound him over for trial in the Court of Special Sessions.

In the meantime, *Variety* reported that all of the publicity had brought a "golden stream to the *Demi-Virgin* box office."[24] McAdoo insisted that Woods close the play, but the latter refused. All the while, Woods advertised *The Demi-Virgin* as the most famous play in America.[25] The trial was to begin on November 28, but in an attempt to close Woods' show before that date, Commissioner of Licenses, John Gilchrist, entered the fray when he revoked the occupancy license of the Eltinge Theatre. He maintained that his authority to take such action did not depend on any court decision. Instead, he claimed that a 1913 ordinance granting commissioners of licenses the authority to revoke movie-theatre licenses for fire and safety violations also extended to the legitimate stage.[26] Woods appealed to the New York State Supreme Court for an injunction and won.[27] *The Demi-Virgin* continued to play as usual. In the meantime, the grand jury met to draw up an indictment on December 23. It heard testimony from McAdoo, Sumner, and several policemen who had attended the show. In a surprise move, it gave Woods an early Christmas gift by dismissing the case on the same day.[28]

Wood's problems were not yet over. The Supreme Court vacated its injunction, thereby clearing the way for Gilchrist to close *The Demi-Virgin*.[29] Woods took his case to the federal Appellate Court. This panel disagreed with Gilchrist's interpretation of the New York City ordinance as it applied to live theatre. It completely ignored Gilchrist's allegation that *The Demi-Virgin* was immoral. Instead, it focused on the dangers of having one person establish moral standards for all theatre in New York. It declared:

It is a most dangerous power to vest in a single individual...It seems an extraordinary interpretation of this law to hold that power to censor all other plays than motion picture plays is given to a single individual whose appointment by the Mayor is not subject to confirmation by any municipal body, with no standard to guide his action and with no provision either for a hearing before the commission or for a hearing to review his determination.[30]

Although the license commissioner would remain a central figure in future censorship questions, this decision marked a significant victory for producers. Prior to this ruling, the commissioner need only hint that a theatre license was in jeopardy and owners would insist that plays be altered or withdrawn. Now this power had been drastically curtailed. Woods' production closed quietly at the end of the season on June 3, 1922. It had been performed nearly 300 times to over 200,000 people.[31]

Play censors and play juries

The battle over censorship had barely begun. Governor Nathan Miller opposed censorship. Nonetheless, several pieces of legislation had been considered in Albany during *The Demi-Virgin* escapade, and it surely seemed that some type of official control would be established.[32] Opponents of censorship insisted that a censor would be too frightened to permit a discourse relating to the body or sexual relations, and insisted that they would merely "scour the drama of every stray reference to the fact that men and women have a sexual character and can have sensual desires."[33] Alexander Woollcott warned that a state censor would "be unable to distinguish between a beautiful but uncomfortable play... and mere vulgarity."[34] A commentator for *The Nation* argued in terms that still resonated in the 1990s:

A stage...that promises to keep clean and refined...must avoid the new, close its doors to genius, deny the creative spirit, and league itself on principle with rigidity and spiritual sloth...To silence the arts at all is to be in danger of silencing them altogether; to attempt to curb the creative processes is to misconceive of their very nature and to substitute a machine for an organism, death for life.[35]

The anti-censorship voices encountered foes who were equally passionate. Among the most vocal was Dr. John Roach Straton, pastor of the Calvary Baptist Church, who garnered extensive publicity for his virulent denunciations of the stage from his pulpit. He blamed theatre for the escalating divorce rate, for debauching young audiences, and for luring parishioners from Sunday school. He claimed that conditions on the American stage had destroyed "those female graces and charms that God has designed for pure and holy ends." Moreover, he peppered his opposition with a goodly amount of anti-Semitism:

> the theatre today has fallen almost entirely into the hands of a small group of Jews. It is very unfortunate for any one race to have control of the whole of the theatrical business…The American people ought to have an American Theatre…It is amazing that the American people have permitted such control and they ought to cast off that bondage.[36]

Chief Magistrate McAdoo provided even more ammunition. In a lengthy article published in the *Saturday Evening Post* in January 1922, shortly after Woods had been acquitted by the grand jury, he explained the dangers posed to the public by theatre. McAdoo claimed producers had openly attacked orthodox morality by claiming that traditional standards of decency were no longer operative. Without specifically naming Woods, he indicted "some producers" for "the undressing of women on the stage." He promised that, were it not for the law, "some of these people would not hesitate to produce a play giving an exhibition of entire nudity, and carry the scenes and language to any limit." He complained that producers were corrupting reputable actors and objected that "decent clean-living people" were being subjected to such filth.[37]

McAdoo, however, stopped short of demanding an official state censor. Instead, he sanctioned a plan that had been proposed by several organizations representing playwrights, producers, and actors. As he explained it, an independent committee would advise the police commissioner as to whether or not a play fell within the law. If this committee decided that the play was immoral, it would have to close. If the decision were inconclusive, the play would be allowed to continue its run.

The basic tenants for the "Play Jury," as this committee came to be known, were formulated on January 24, 1922. A jury pool composed of several hundred citizens from various professions would be assembled. In order to maintain objectivity, no one associated with theatre or reform organizations would be impaneled. If complaints were received, a jury of twelve, who were unknown to one another, would be asked to attend the production in question and to decide, individually and in private, whether or not the show was indecent. In this way, the profitable effects of publicity and court actions would be avoided. The Authors' League of America, the American

Dramatists, Actors' Equity, and the Producing Managers' Association agreed to close "convicted" productions regardless of other contractual obligations and to waive claims for damages. The city, in turn, agreed to relinquish prosecutorial authority.[38]

The case against Jews and African Americans

When the first test case emerged in the middle of the 1922/23 season, it became evident that the city did not intend to abide by the rules it had accepted. On December 20, 1922, Sholom Asch's *The God of Vengeance* opened at the Provincetown Playhouse. Produced by Alice Krauser, it starred the legendary Austrian actor Rudolf Schildkraut. It had received its European premiere in 1907 at Max Reinhardt's Deutsches Theater where Schildkraut also played the leading role. Throughout the next decade, it was translated into several languages and performed in Russia, Austria, Poland, the Netherlands, Norway, Sweden, and Italy. In New York, it became a staple of the Yiddish repertory shortly after its German premiere.[39]

A variation of the brothel plays that had been so controversial in the 1910s, *The God of Vengeance*, according to Harley Erdman, represented "Asch's contribution to European naturalism at its seamiest."[40] The play tells the story of Yankel, a Polish Jew who, along with his wife Sore, operates a brothel in their basement. He is obsessed with guilt, but refuses to give up his business because it is too profitable. If, however, he can preserve the purity of Rifkele, his daughter, and deliver her as a virgin to a respectable husband, he may be able to redeem himself. In order to bless this plan, he purchases a Torah that he believes will protect Rifkele from any contamination. However, Yankel fails to realize that his daughter is in love with one of his own prostitutes, Manke. In two intimate scenes, Manke and Rifkele kiss, caress each other, and pledge that they are bride and bridegroom.

The God of Vengeance contained more than enough provocation for censors. Aside from the theme of homoerotic love, it dealt with prostitution, took place in a brothel, and clearly implied, as had *Mrs Warren's Profession*, that the respectable "upstairs" was supported by the sordid "downstairs." Most importantly, for Jews at least, it placed perhaps the most sacred object in Jewish tradition, the Torah, in a situation that was potentially blasphemous.

Although critics from the major dailies did not make a habit of reviewing downtown productions, Schildkraut's American premiere provided a powerful incentive. Response to the play was generally uneasy. While

Schildkraut was praised, many reviewers could not bring themselves to discuss the content of the play. Burns Mantle completely skirted the blatant depiction of lesbianism as did Heywood Broun. The latter warned his readers that the scenes between Manke and Rifkele "made us a little sick" and cautioned, "The American stage has not yet achieved absolute frankness in dealing with the more traditional vices. We can afford to wait until that fight has been won before venturing into decadence."[41] The *Sun*'s critic reiterated the theme of sickness when he warned audiences that they should "have a strong, shock-proof stomach" if they wanted to attend *The God of Vengeance*.[42] The *Evening Post*'s critic was one of the few papers to mention the amorous encounter between the two young women. He flatly states that Rifkele "falls a victim to a Lesbian," but does not explain how or why this extraordinary event occurs.[43] The noted attorney and sometimes producer Harry Weinberger assumed control of the production and moved it to the larger Greenwich Village Theatre and then to the Apollo Theatre on Forty-Second Street, where it opened on February 19, 1923. The latter move, however, proved to be the undoing of the production. Had the production remained in the bohemian confines of the Greenwich Village, it might have completed its run without interruption. The move from downtown to uptown, from the margins to the mainstream, galvanized resistance to the play. Arthur Hornblow, one of the very few critics who reviewed the Apollo production, protested that Jews and Village bohemians had polluted the "august sanctity of a 42nd Street home" and chastised the police for "allowing a thing of this sort" to be continued before heterosexual audiences.[44]

Unbeknownst to Hornblow, however, the authorities had already begun to investigate *The God of Vengeance*. The inquiry, however, was not prompted by the Society for the Suppression of Vice. Rather, the revered Rabbi Joseph Silverman, rabbi emeritus of the prestigious Temple Emanue-El, who believed that this play was anti-Semitic, filed the initial complaint. Considering the fact that the author, producer, and all but one member of the cast were Jews, it may be difficult to interpret this indictment. However, *The God of Vengeance* was intended to be a naturalistic treatment of Eastern European Jews. When these Jews migrated in great numbers to the United States of America in the first two decades of the century, they generated a great deal of mistrust. In New York, they lived in ghettos on the Lower East Side, spoke Yiddish, preached radical politics, supported modern art, and rejected assimilation. Consequently, their sense of how to perform their ethnicity differed considerably from more conservative Jews whose ancestors had migrated from northern and central Europe during the mid-nineteenth century. These Jews had made assimilation into white, Protestant society a major goal. They identified with middle- and upper-middle-class propriety, had reformed their worship, actively supported philanthropic causes and participated in the arts. Displays that connected Jews with prostitution, brutality, or perversion might tarnish the image they had striven to create.[45]

Moreover, plays such as *The God of Vengeance* could only fuel the anti-Semitism fire that was threatening to burn out of control. The Ku Klux Klan had made significant political advances by offering to protect Americans from the Jews. Moreover, Attorney General Palmer hailed the Immigration Act of 1919 as a means of ridding the nation of these "aliens of misshapen caste of mind and indecencies of character," who were attempting to establish a reign of terror in the United States.[46] Clearly *The God of Vengeance* was a product of this foreign culture that both offended and frightened the assimilated Jews.

Acting on Rabbi Silverman's complaint and without any input from the Play Jury, the grand jury began secret deliberations. However, the charge that *The God of Vengeance* was racially offensive could not legally enter into its deliberations. That body could only act if the penal code's prohibition against "impure theatrical productions" had been violated. But the fact that the play's central characters were a brothel-keeper and several prostitutes, that one of the scenes depicted the rooms in which the women plied their trade, and that the play featured a lesbian seduction provided more than enough justification for the grand jury to act. The fact that "upstanding" Jews supported this action against "corrupt" Jews only strengthened the case.

On March 6, 1923, the police appeared backstage and announced that theatre owner Michael Selwyn, producer Weinberger, and the twelve-member cast had been indicted by the grand jury. At Weinberger's request the play continued uninterrupted. No arrests were made, and the fourteen who had been indicted appeared the next morning in the Court of General Sessions. All pleaded not guilty and returned to the theatre to give their matinee performance.

The production had closed before the trial commenced in May 1923. Weinberger, who defended himself and his colleagues, never really had a chance. The trial judge would not allow testimony from expert witnesses such as Eugene O'Neill and Elmer Rice or from several prominent Jewish leaders. He ruled that these individuals had seen the play after the indictments were issued and that changes in the production had been made. Weinberger countered by attempting to convince the jury that the accused play was no more indecent than the Bible or Shakespeare. Assistant District Attorney James G. Wallace, a pivotal figure in later censorship trials, responded that "ideas of public decency in Shakespeare's time were different from those of today" and should anyone attempt some of his plays in their original form "they would surely be prosecuted." The judge, in his charge to the jury, argued that Shakespeare's decision to write "salacious plays" was not a defense. He instructed the jurors not to consider the "literature of the world," only the play on trial. "The people of New York," he said, "are anxious to have pure drama. They want decent plays. We are opposed to immoral and indecent productions... Even though a moral lesson is sought to be taught, it cannot be taught by words or lines or actions that might amount to immorality or obscenity."[47]

Not surprisingly, the jury took only 90 minutes to reach its verdict. Schildkraut and Weinberger were both found guilty and fined 200 dollars. The remaining defendants were given suspended sentences. Many observers used the trial to prove that existing laws prohibiting immoral theatrical productions made creation of an official censor unnecessary. The *Times* even took the opportunity to warn artists that they were not beyond the law. "There is a penal code," a writer noted, "to which painters and writers and playwrights and actors and theatrical managers must pay due regard."[48]

Weinberger was outraged. He claimed that any group, whether it be Jewish, Catholic, or Ku Klux Klan, that had been offended now had the right to suppress a play by claiming it was immoral.[49] Other members of New York's theatre community were equally shocked. A critic for *The Nation* demanded to know why the latest Shubert revue, which featured a female chorus who wore nothing above their waists other than a "slender bit of chiffon," went unchallenged, while *The God of Vengeance*, "one of the most effective of moral plays," had been judged obscene.[50] Even Heywood Broun, whose review of the production was decidedly unflattering, opposed the verdict:

> We want to know specifically and precisely just what harm has been done to the community by the production of *The God of Vengeance*. The nature of the play was fully discussed after the first night. People who went thereafter wanted to be shocked. Very probably they were. What of it?[51]

Although the conviction was eventually overturned by the Court of Appeals, the cast of *The God of Vengeance* was the first company of actors to be convicted of presenting an indecent performance.

Still, shrill complaints about the immorality of modern theatre continued to proliferate. Arthur Hornblow protested that the graveyard seduction scene in Elmer Rice's *The Adding Machine* was an "episode so foul as to be absolutely inexcusable." If the authors and producers did not stem "the rising flood of stage filth . . . the authorities will be forced sooner or later to interfere in the interest of public order."[52] *Theatre Magazine* observed: "a flood of filth and indecency has lately descended on the American theatre," and speculated, "official control seems the only remedy."[53] In all, seven separate agencies concerned themselves with the proliferation of so-called dirty plays. These included a police committee, the Social Service Commission of the Episcopal Church, the New York Federation of Churches, the Play Jury, the Methodist Episcopal Board of Temperance, Prohibition and Morals, Dr. S. Edward Young's Society for the Prevention of Crime, and the Society for the Suppression of Vice.

John Sumner, secretary of the last, was far more brutal in his attacks on theatre than any of his colleagues. He frequently used the metaphor of a "sewer" to impress upon readers that uncontrolled theatre was a menace to the health of the community and maintained that offending producers should be "clubbed into a sense of decency."[54] Although he claimed to support pure theatre, he contended that several external forces had corrupted it. First, there were the newspapers, which, instead of denouncing immoral productions, increased their circulation by publishing photographs "of half naked stage beauties in rotogravure sections." Secondly, he blamed "feminine independence" for creating a receptive audience. To remedy this situation he urged that women be reeducated to use their free time not for amusement, but to work at tasks "they disdainfully call drudgery." Finally, like John Roach Straton, he indicted New York's Jewish producers and urged Americans to rescue its theatre from "foreigners":

> It is up to the people who take pride in the stage and what it was before a money-mad, un-American and brutish element took over its control . . . [They are] the "belly element," the gross and mercenary crew who are dragging the good name of the American stage in the mud and mire of foreign perversity.[55]

As the decade progressed, more ethnic and racial controversies erupted. In February 1924, Eugene O'Neill's *All God's Chillun' Got Wings* became the target of a fierce, racially motivated campaign. The play, which was produced by the Provincetown Playhouse, tells the tragic story of a black man, Jim Harris, and his white wife, Ella Downey. At the insistence of George Jean Nathan, the play had been published in the February issue of H. L. Mencken's *American Mercury*. Even many who approved of the play as literature were scandalized to learn that a white actress, Mary Blair, was cast opposite the young Paul Robeson and that during the course of the production she would kiss his hand. Soon after the production was announced, the *Brooklyn Eagle* printed a story, founded on rumor, that the actress Helen MacKellar had indignantly rejected the role because of that scene. Although the Provincetown denied the rumor by explaining that Blair had been offered the role of Ella first, opposition grew. When playwright Augustus Thomas was asked his opinion of the project, he responded that he never would have written such a play, and that a white man in blackface should play Jim's role. "The present arrangement," he said, referring to the interracial casting, "has a tendency to break down social barriers which are better left untouched."[56]

William Randolph Hearst's *New York American* attacked the upcoming production on a daily basis. A member of the Play Jury, although he had not read the script, reiterated that he was opposed to any kind of immorality and advised that the production be prevented. John Sumner, in the name of community safety, claimed that such a play might cause race riots and urged the police to close it before it opened. Protests from black and white clergymen were received at City Hall and the mother of one of the Caucasian children who played in a brief prologue withdrew her daughter from the play. A barrage of hate mail claimed that O'Neill was a "disgrace to his race and religion" and accused him of being a "Jewish pervert masquerading under a Christian name in order to do subversive propaganda for the Pope." There was even a bomb threat stating that the theatre would be full of dead people if the play opened.[57]

O'Neill, somewhat disingenuously, explained that *All God's Chillun' Got Wings* was not about race but "humanity." He insisted Jim and Ella were not symbols of their race, but individuals facing relational crises that any couple would face. He admitted that their problems were the result of their "racial heritage." He insisted, however, that he was interested in the struggle of human beings to forge a relationship in spite of insurmountable obstacles:

> I admit that there is prejudice against the intermarriage of whites and blacks, but what has that to do with my play? I don't advocate mixed marriage in it. I am never the advocate of anything in any play – except humanity toward Humanity.[58]

Although the mayor had no legal authority to close the production, he discovered a loophole that might derail it. Only the mayor's office could license the appearance of child actors. Since the play contained a scene showing Jim and Ella as children, the Provincetown Playhouse applied for the appropriate permission. A few hours before opening, the theatre received a reply from the mayor's office. The application had been rejected. No reason was given.[59] When the curtain rose, director James Light appeared and explained that the prologue could not be played because of the mayor's action, whereupon he read the scene. Police ringed the theatre on opening night to ensure that no children appeared in the production and that no bombs were thrown. The producers, distrustful of the police, hired their own security force, a former boxer and his crony.[60]

For all of the threats, the run of *All God's Chillun' Got Wings* was uneventful. O'Neill even seemed disappointed. He wrote to a friend, "When the play opened, nothing at all happened, not even a senile egg. It was a dreadful disappointment for all concerned, particularly the critics, who seemed to feel cheated there hadn't been at least one murder that first night."[61]

While most supporters of censorship shied away from overt racist indictments, they were seldom willing (or able) to consider artists who were probing the dark recesses of human behavior as anything other than perverts, who wanted to overturn the moral order. They refused to acknowledge that theatre was a symbolic crucible in which social and political formations were examined. These advocates of censorship denied that stage plays that featured violent or sexually transgressive behavior were observations and explorations of humanity. Instead, they, like all censors before them, imagined that anarchistic forces that employed theatre as their principal weapon were attacking their culture and traditions. In their opinion it was the duty of art and artists to support the normative culture. Any attempt to change, challenge, or confuse these constructs was considered blasphemous and treasonous.

War stories on stage

Thus far in the decade, controversial plays had been accused of immorality, blasphemy, anti-Semitism, debunking marriage, and encouraging miscegenation. In September 1924, in one of the most bizarre episodes of theatre censorship ever recorded, a production was accused of slandering the United States military. On the 3rd of that month, *What Price Glory* by Maxwell Anderson and Laurence Stallings opened at the Plymouth Theatre and was arguably the most compelling example of American naturalism to appear during the decade.[62] The play is set in France during World War I. The thin plot involves two marines, Captain Flagg and Sergeant Quirt, who battle for the affections of Charmaine, an innkeeper's daughter. The anemic story was, however, only an excuse for the actual theme of play. The remaining marines in Anderson and Stallings' piece were not the selfless patriots who populated previous American war dramas. They were crude, disorderly men trapped in an absurd situation that at any moment could claim their lives. They were "grunts," small cogs in a giant war machine that would willingly sacrifice them to achieve an abstract political objective. Stallings, a reporter for the *Globe* and a former marine who had lost his leg in the war, wrote the majority of the dialogue. He peppered it with expletives that had never been used in a Broadway theatre. These soldiers were cynical men who completely rejected the patriotic rhetoric of politicians. They cursed and grumbled incessantly and their only real concern was the length of their next liberty.

New York critics were astonished. George Jean Nathan called its humor "Rabelaisian," and claimed that its "drunk and bawdy" laughter revealed "a sweeping understanding, a sweeping sympathy, and an enveloping ironic pity."[63] Stark Young also alluded to its Rabelaisian qualities and called it a "war play without puerilities and retorts at God and society, and not febrile and pitying, but virile, fertile, poetic."[64]

Although *What Price Glory* was regarded as a stunning artistic success, there were those who took umbrage at its non-heroic treatment of the military. Admiral Charles Plunkett, ranking naval officer in New York State, although he had not seen the play, complained to Mayor Hylan that *What Price Glory* had maligned marines. The mayor immediately ordered the Commissioner of Licenses to investigate the complaint. By September 25, Commissioner of Licenses William F. Quigley had assembled a panel consisting of Admiral Plunkett, General Robert Bullard, ranking army officer in New York, the Police Commissioner, the Corporate Council, and a representative from the Department of Justice to investigate these charges. Yet the maintenance of Marine Corps honor was not the city's only objective. The police announced that they would use a newly enacted amendment to the penal code to suppress productions that they deemed offensive. Originally intended to deal with jostling in order to arrest pick pockets, this amendment, as interpreted by the District Attorneys of the five boroughs, permitted police to press misdemeanor charges against anyone displaying offensive conduct or using unpleasant language in public.[65]

Fearing the worst, Arthur Hopkins, producer of *What Price Glory*, altered the most offensive lines of the production, but officials still took issue. The navy complained to the Department of Justice, "The Marine Corps and the army of the United States are belittled to the public, the play showing that they are drunkards most of the time, and that there is a lack of discipline and respect which tends to bring discredit and reproach upon the army and Marine Corps." Moreover, the complaint asserted that *What Price Glory* had violated Section 125 of the National Defense Act that prohibited anyone except an enlisted man or officer from wearing the uniform of the army, navy, or marines.[66]

Supporters of the play were incredulous. Numerous letters and editorials accused the military investigators of prudishness, childish peevishness, and outright ignorance. One observer who was particularly outraged claimed that Stallings and Anderson's play simply revealed the "official hypocrisy" of the military, which "treats Defense Day as if it were an autumn festival to celebrate peace and plenty, and advertises poison gases as if they were to be kept in the family medicine chest along side soothing syrups."[67] Eventually, the United States District Attorney forwarded the complaint to the Judge Advocate General's desk where it was mercifully allowed to die. *What Price Glory* continued to run, finally closing after 299 performances, the second longest run of the 1924/25 season.[68]

Clearly, Anderson and Stallings' rendering of the marines had touched a nerve. Once again, a naturalistic drama had challenged officially sanctioned images of good and evil. *What Price Glory* shocked audiences by portraying soldiers not as idealistic warriors seen on recruiting posters, but as crass, rebellious men caught in an absurd and deadly situation.

While *What Price Glory* was enjoying a successful run, producer William Brady attempted to capitalize on its notoriety by opening *Simon Called Peter*. Brady's effort lacked the raw power of the former play and was instead a tale of wartime seduction – with one interesting twist. The target of the seduction was an army chaplain. Peter Graham is a chaplain in France during the war. He worries that his charges do not heed his advice because he is too aloof, and decides to socialize with them in order to know them better. Through them he meets a nurse, Julie Gamelyn, with whom he falls in love and with whom he spends a week in a London hotel. The most controversial moment of the play comes when a cabaret singer attempts to seduce Graham in a torrid scene in which she strips to the waist. The play ends with Graham leaving the ministry in order to marry Julie.

Although the play was credited with having some effective moments, it was not enthusiastically received. The New York clergy, however, were extremely agitated that one of their own had been presented in an unflattering light. Sensing an opportunity to reap a significant publicity harvest,

Brady presented a special matinee for the clergy of Manhattan that was accompanied by a panel discussion. John Roach Straton did not attend. Instead, he sent a letter of condemnation that Brady took great pleasure in reading from the stage. It said, in part, that commercial theatre producers put on "the most salacious, absurd and even indecent productions," that the "moral life of actors and actresses were deplorably low," and that the contemporary theatre was one of the "deadliest menaces to the health of civilized society."[69]

The Play Jury again

Simon Called Peter generated clerical opposition, but the story of a minister falling in love during wartime reaffirmed rather than challenged the existence of romantic love. Other plays completely dismissed such bourgeois notions. Beginning in November 1924, a series of dramas that portrayed a society dominated by passion and greed premiered in New York. On November 11, O'Neill's *Desire Under the Elms* opened at the Greenwich Village Theatre. New York critics were, by and large, neutral or worse. The *Morning Telegraph* refused to accept the aesthetics of its naturalistic design. "The play will be hailed as realistic," wrote Fred Niblo. "No one will call it an entertainment, but at the slightest suggestion of its foulness, many will rise to exclaim: 'But that's life – that's real.' Sure. So is a sewer."[70] Stark Young, while not enthusiastic, praised O'Neill for his "lack of sentiment," "mature conception," and "imaginative austerity."[71] It was Joseph Wood Krutch, however, who appreciated *Desire Under the Elms* for its brutal power. "The meaning of his work," he wrote, "lies not in any controlling intellectual idea and certainly not in a 'message,' but merely in the fact that each play is an experience of extraordinary intensity."[72] But this brutal catalogue of incest and infanticide was not the only problem play to open during this period.

Sidney Howard's *They Knew What They Wanted*, in which a bride sleeps with a field hand rather than her husband on her wedding night, premiered thirteen days later. In December, *The Harem* and *Ladies of the Evening* opened. In the former, a woman disguises herself as a sultan's concubine in order to seduce her own husband, and the latter features several racy scenes with streetwalkers. In February 1925, William Brady, in association with Al Woods, opened what was probably the tawdriest show of the season. *A Good Bad Woman* tells the story of a former burlesque performer and street prostitute, Eileen Donovan, who returns to her hometown. She hides her past and takes a job as a companion to a wealthy woman. She seduces the woman's son but later finds out that he is in love with a young lady who is married to a callous physician. She pities the boy and arranges to have the girl's father discover herself and the doctor in a compromising scene. The father is outraged and kills the husband, allowing the lovers to be united. Eileen, however, returns to the street.

The play received universally unfavorable reviews, but garnered extensive publicity. As attendance soared, the *New York World* launched a furious campaign that endorsed censorship. New York's ministerial fraternity, led by Reverend Straton, also voiced its disapproval. It accused District Attorney Joab Banton of having been cowed by powerful producers and demanded that he enforce the law "regardless of how high up or influential particular law-breakers may happen to be."[73]

Yielding to the pressure, District Attorney Banton initiated yet another drive to purify the stage. At first he took matters into his own hands. He claimed that there were thirteen offensive shows in New York that would either have to alter their scripts or face formal charges. Brady and Woods' *A Good Bad Woman* topped his list. The two producers consented to rewrite their show, but the District Attorney responded that is was "irreclaimably vicious" and would have to be withdrawn. Brady and Woods decided not to oppose Banton and announced that *A Good Bad Woman* would close on February 21. Banton then turned his attention to *The Harem* and *Ladies of the Evening*, both produced by David Belasco. Rather than face a court battle, the latter gladly consented to delete any offensive material.[74]

Alarmed that Banton might proclaim himself a censor, representatives from Actors' Equity, the Authors' League, the Drama League, and various reform groups petitioned the District Attorney to reactivate the long dormant Play Jury to make decisions about issues of stage morality. Banton welcomed this suggestion. He admitted that indictments and trials were time consuming, the inevitable publicity generated sizable audiences, and punishment, if any, was generally minimal. Finally, on March 13, after weeks of delay, three Play Juries were dispatched, one each to *The Firebrand*, *They Knew What They Wanted*, and *Desire Under the Elms*. To the great disappointment of those who wanted these plays removed from the stage, each was acquitted. A particularly long and passionate kiss in *The Firebrand* was ordered shortened and the latter two were completely exonerated. Public response was mixed. District Attorney Banton refused to comment, but Governor Al Smith seemed pleased that he would not have to deal with the matter of New York theatre in Albany. He commented at a Friars Club dinner that he opposed all forms of censorship and told reporters that the public would eventually ignore entertainment that did not "appeal to the higher senses." Brady said the verdicts were "comical" and claimed that "a jury which would called *Desire Under the Elms* guiltless... would have pinned a medal on *A Good Bad Woman*." John Sumner was disappointed, but agreed not to file complaints against any play that was acquitted. Kenneth Macgowan, producer of *Desire Under the Elms*, called the verdict "perfectly proper and natural... now the play and its author have been vindicated."[75] New York's religious leaders, on the other hand, were indignant. Cardinal Hayes fumed that the "panderers to filth" deprived parents and children of their liberty to attend theatre because "they are afraid of what they are going to see."[76] Speakers at a New York conference of Catholic men proclaimed that the plays were "not fit to be seen by savages" and argued that the Play Jury was a tacit admission that local authorities could no longer prevent "indecent and blasphemous productions."[77] At a meeting of the New York Federation of Churches, reformers demanded the abolition of the Play Jury because it was little more than a "bargain with lawbreakers" and urged city officials to prosecute producers in accordance with the penal code.[78]

The verdicts of the Play Jury, impartial citizens who had rendered unbiased judgments, had failed to mollify reformers. Clearly, it was not equity that was desired, but punishment. The stage, if it depicted characters and situations that offended or challenged established social constructs, had to be suppressed.

Bad girls, angry men, and the Padlock Law

For the next few months, stage controversies subsided. The only murmuring came when *They Knew What They Wanted* was awarded the Pulitzer Prize. *Theatre Magazine*, for one, wondered how an award meant to honor a work that raised "the standards of good morals, good taste and good manners" could possibly have been given to a play in which a young bride consummates her marriage not with her husband but with a "young roustabout."[79] During February, the caldron started to bubble again as racially motivated censorship once again appeared. On the 9th, Belasco opened *Lulu Belle*, a "protracted odyssey of a mulatto courtesan, reeking with Billingsgate."[80] The title character is a cabaret dancer who seduces a barber and convinces him to leave his wife and children. She then becomes enamored of a prizefighter who helps her rob another man. She finally ends up in the bedroom of a French *vicomte* where she is strangled by the barber she deserted. For the production, Belasco supplied realistic depictions of tenement houses, cabarets, crap games, wedding parties, and fire-escape confrontations. At one point a Ford even cruised across the stage. Most striking, however, was the use of a huge African American cast to provide the sordid detail of the "downtown colored district of New York."[81] The *Bookman*'s reviewer noted that Belasco's cast "must have depopulated several cotton growing states, not to speak of emptying Harlem's black belt nightly."[82] Arthur Hornblow commented the casts of other objectionable plays were composed of "white players" and indecencies had been kept "in the family so to speak." But Belasco had mixed the races, thereby attempting to emulate Harlem cabarets "where black-and-tan performers draw the midnight pleasure seekers."[83] Clearly, *Lulu Belle* was a troublesome play. Blacks and whites had been graphically portrayed as inhabiting a violent, sexually charged world. Belasco, whether for profit or art, had created an environment that eliminated carefully demarcated racial boundaries. Although the costumes were revealing, the plot outrageous and the dancing provocative, the District Attorney inexplicably chose not to act and *Lulu Belle* completed a run of 461 performances.[84]

During the next ten months, however, the New York theatre scene was punctuated by a series of raids, closures, and trials unparalleled in the decade. This period revealed yet another permutation in the censorship battles being fought in New York. As Marybeth Hamilton has pointed out, the "dirty play controversy" was as much about the struggle for control of Broadway as it was about the division between "prudes and progressives." It was fought out among three groups – moral reformers, progressives, and Mae West's "wise cracking" fans – all of which sought to control who wrote, produced, and viewed Broadway plays.[85]

The turmoil involved four plays – *Sex*, *The Captive*, *The Virgin Man*, and *The Drag*. The first was written by one of the most notorious figures of the period, Mae West, who summed up her aesthetic philosophy rather succinctly. "People want dirt in plays," she said, "so I give 'em dirt. See?"[86] Her first play, *Sex*, was written in 1924 and 1925. She claimed that it was inspired when she observed a particularly pathetic prostitute negotiating with some sailors on a New York pier. James Timony, her lover/accountant/attorney, Matilda, her mother, and a Pittsburgh theatre owner, C. W. Morgenstern, formed the Moral Production Company to produce the show. Although she had appeared in vaudeville and revues since she was sixteen, the role of Margie Lamont, a Montreal prostitute, marked her debut in a stage play. West originally intended to title her play *The Albatross*, but director Edward Elsner told her that she had a unique sexual quality that he could only describe as "low sex." His depiction appealed to her and she changed the name to *Sex*, which, in her opinion, more accurately described the theme of the play.[87]

Sex opened at Daly's Theatre on April 26, 1926. The plot was scabrous, even for the twenties. Margie becomes involved with a gigolo who seduces Clara Stanton, one of New York's social elite, whom he then begins to blackmail. Margie rescues Clara from the plight but, instead of receiving gratitude, she is accused of being part of the conspiracy. She revenges herself by seducing Jimmy, Clara's son, and threatens to marry him. When she meets a long-time sailor boyfriend, she abandons her plan and follows his ship to Trinidad.

West's portrayal of Margie drew much of its disturbing power from her plainspoken definition of prostitution as an economic and specifically working-class activity. The dialogue never tried to hide that she took money for sex and it was this fact that accounted for much of the play's off-color humor. West made it clear that prostitution was a meeting of bodies and an exchange of cash. Margie Lamont was not a romanticized courtesan. She was paid labor and lived at the bottom of the economic ladder.[88]

The critical response to *Sex* was universally negative. The *Times* considered it a "crude and inept play, cheaply produced and poorly acted."[89] *Billboard* wrote that *Sex* was the "cheapest most vulgar low show to have dared to open in New York this year."[90] The *New Yorker* dismissed it as "a poor balderdash of street sweepings and cabaret sentimentality, unexpurgated in tone, singing, sobbing and writhing as hard as it can to work on the biological facts of life."[91] *Variety* 's reviewer was even more indignant. He labeled it "a nasty red-light district show . . . the dramatic garbage of the year" and called West an "exhibitionist."[92] In spite of (there were many who said because of) the avalanche of bad publicity, *Sex* remained opened and played to capacity houses.

The following September, what was arguably the most controversial Broadway production of the decade, *The Captive*, opened at the Empire Theatre. *La Prisonnière*, as it was known in Europe, was written by Edouard Bourdet, translated by Arthur Hornblow, Jr., and directed and produced by Gilbert Miller for the Charles Frohman Company. It had opened in Paris in March 1926 and was immediately hailed by French critics as one of the greatest dramatic masterpieces of all times. Reinhardt, who had originally produced *The God of Vengeance*, staged *La Prisonnière* in Berlin and Vienna. During that season it also opened in Belgium, the Netherlands, and Switzerland.

Like the controversial *The God of Vengeance*, it dealt with a lesbian relationship. Unlike its predecessor, however, the principles in this drama belonged to the European gentry, not to the coarse, grasping Polish Jewry. Moreover, Bourdet penned a nearly antiseptic drama that was devoid of the histrionics and sexual displays of Asch's work. The heroine, Irene De Montcel, rarely speaks of her passion for her lover, Madame d'Aiguines. She only shows the depressive effects of being unable to see d'Aiguines. What the audience learns of the two women comes from the men in the play. The infamous Madame never appears.

The story of *The Captive* concerns Irene (played by Helen Menken), an agitated young woman whose father insists that she join the family on his new assignment with the Foreign Service in Rome. Determined to remain in Paris, she feigns interest in Jacques (played by Basil Rathbone), a suitor favored by her father, and gambles that her father will not force her to leave if he believes a marriage is in the offing. She convinces Jacques to help her carry out this charade but, as the first act curtain falls, the audience sees her caress a corsage of violets that she has been wearing and lift the phone to make a call.

The second act reveals the crux of the action. Irene is now married to Jacques but refuses to have a sexual relationship with him. Instead she spends her evenings at the home of Monsieur d'Aiguines who happens to be Jacques' former schoolmate. Jacques believes his wife is having an affair with his old friend, but in a tense meeting, d'Aiguines confesses that it is not he whom Irene visits, but his wife. In an impassioned speech he warns Jacques that such women, whom he calls "shadows," can destroy everything that a man has worked to create:

> D'AIGUINES:... They must be shunned, let alone... We don't know anything about it. We can't begin to know what it is. It's mysterious – terrible! Under the cover of friendship a woman can enter any household, whenever and however she pleases – at any hour of the day – she can poison and pillage everything.[93]

The third act reveals that Irene has ceased visiting the d'Aiguines' home and has attempted to become a dutiful wife and homemaker. She cannot, however, return her husband's passion. When Irene leaves to consult an interior decorator, Jacques' former mistress pays a visit in order to retrieve some incriminating love letters. Although she protests at the beginning of the scene that she does not want to rekindle their relationship, he convinces her of his love and, before she leaves, they agree to meet. Irene returns in an agitated condition and asks Jacques to take her away from Paris. She has accidentally met Madame d'Aiguines. The latter has divorced her husband, but is seriously ill and will not leave for Switzerland unless she can effect reconciliation with Irene. Jacques is unconcerned and explains that he can no longer help her and leaves to dress for his meeting with his lover. At that moment a box of violets arrives. Irene hastily grabs her hat and coat and exits, Jacques returns in time to hear the door slam. He informs his servant that, like his wife, he, too, will be leaving for the evening.

The Captive typically provoked schizoid responses from critics. Few reviewers even mentioned the word "lesbian" for fear their columns would be censured for being as salacious as the play. And, while the play was generally praised as an outstanding work, its subject matter was condemned. Gilbert Gabriel praised Bourdet, Miller, Menken, and Rathbone, but obliquely lamented that the "sweet young things" whom he overheard discussing the play were in danger of being irredeemably corrupted.[94] Arthur Hornblow, whose son translated *La Prisonnière*, praised it as an "unusually fine play... absorbing in its human interests, tremendous in its climaxes, fascinating in its almost pitiless dissection of a woman's soul in torment." In the same sentence, however, he claimed it was a "morbid, repellent, unsavory story" and ended his review by complaining that the times were so decadent that "from now on, our wives, sons, and daughters, are free to discuss at the breakfast table the gangrenous horrors of sex perversion."[95] George Jean Nathan revealed himself as more of a homophobic than his other colleagues. After admitting that Bourdet had written a great play, Nathan attacked it for the very reasons he admired it. He claimed that shows such as *Sex* were harmless because they were trashy and provided only moronic diversion. *The Captive*, he argued, was far more subversive precisely because it was so well written and performed so masterfully. Specifically, he complained that Bourdet had created dramatic work that covertly, but perhaps unintentionally, encouraged women to become lesbians:

> To put it plainly, it [*The Captive*] is the persuasive advancement of the assurance that a degenerate physical love between women is superior to the normal physical love of the opposite sexes... Art or no art, the fact remains that Bourdet's play amounts in simple [*sic*] to nothing more or less than a document in favor of sexual degeneracy, concealed though it be in a smoke-screen of detraction and in the pink mists of protestation.[96]

The Captive was, nonetheless, an overnight sensation and grossed an amazing $14,000 for its first five performances.[97] Although sex plays did not dominate Broadway, they were extremely visible and profitable and, during the next month, pressure began to mount on city officials to curb these dramas once and for all. On December 28, in response to this pressure, Mayor Jimmy Walker summoned Broadway producers to City Hall to warn them that there would be serious consequences if they continued to produce "sex plays." William Randolph Hearst, a long-time adversary of Walker and his mentor Governor Al Smith, in an attempt to embarrass them both, claimed that the mayor would not act forcefully:

> Mayor Walker has taken the first step in assembling the managers and play producers of New York to advise them to be decent. But it is a useless and insufficient step if the Mayor is going to stop there; because some of these managers will NOT be decent, and the others will not take the trouble to COMPEL them to be decent [sic]. Mayor Walker has put his hand to the plow, and he should not turn back...The public expects him to proceed with it and to succeed with it. He will disappoint the public, and to a degree lose their respect, if he fails or falters. He may have to resort to drastic action; but whatever is necessary to be done must be done, for the credit of the city and the welfare of its people require that this great and menacing evil...be ended promptly.[98]

Events then progressed at a whirlwind pace. On January 20, *The Virgin Man* opened. An anemic farce that featured a Yale undergraduate pursued by three women, it received generally poor notices. Nonetheless, another sex play had opened. The next day, John Sumner echoed Banton's call for censorship. Hearst, who had been organizing pro-censorship committees across the state, enthusiastically supported Banton's and Straton's position, but his motives were far from altruistic. His target was Governor Al Smith. He and Hearst had been bitter political enemies since 1922 when the former foiled the latter's plan to capture the Democratic nomination for Governor and then refused to support his efforts to run for senator. Smith further alienated Hearst when he convinced Tammany to shift its support in the 1925 New York mayoral campaign from incumbent John Hylan, whom Hearst backed, to State Senator Jimmy Walker, who was eventually elected.[99] Now Hearst saw an opportunity to deal Smith a public relations setback as Governor as he readied his campaign for the 1928 Democratic presidential nomination. On January 26, State Senator Abraham Greenberg drafted a comprehensive theatre censorship bill. It would allow the State Motion Picture Commission to police "all dramas, musical plays, playlets and theatrical productions of every kind."[100] Greenberg's bill was all but assured of passage. By demanding that the bill become law, Hearst hoped to place Smith, an ardent foe of censorship, in a lose/lose situation. He would either have to veto a popular piece of legislation or sign a bill that he philosophically opposed. In either instance, the Governor would be compromised.

Matters seemed to go from bad to worse very quickly. Only one day after Greenberg announced his intentions, Mae West let it be known that she intended to open *The Drag* in February. Hoping to cash in on the popularity of the homosexual theme of *The Captive*, West concocted a raucous tale of homosexuality and transvestitism. Rolly Kingsbury, the son of a wealthy judge, is married to the daughter of a Park Avenue doctor. The marriage, however, is only a ruse to hide his homosexuality and the majority of the play focuses on scenes that depict the gay subculture of New York. West called the play an educational drama because of two brief opening scenes that argue that homosexuals were victims of a curable disease, not criminals. The play, however, is short on education and long on titillation. *The Drag* was a flamboyant spectacle that utilized every homosexual cliché that West could concoct. She and her director, Edward Elsner, assembled a supporting cast of sixty men recruited from Greenwich Village clubs. According to the January 12 issue of *Variety*, Elsner permitted this chorus to "cavort and carry on as they like." The results, he claimed, were "natural and spontaneous."[101]

These "natural and spontaneous" rehearsals yielded two lengthy scenes. The first, lasting for most of the second act, shows four of Rolly's friends visiting his apartment to discuss the party they will attend the next night. The dialogue is raunchy and riddled with sex insults and descriptions of dresses the men will wear, and is punctuated with screams, squeals, and shrieks. West also included a number of songs as the performers gathered round the piano. One, intended as a gibe at *The Captive*, was entitled the "The Woman Who Stole My Gal."[102] The climax of the play was a "drag ball" that featured the principals and thirty chorus members, dressed in evening gowns and tuxedos, dancing to an onstage jazz band, performing drag sketches, singing, and exchanging crude sexual quips.[103]

When word spread of what West had in mind, producers and theatre owners panicked. Under the guise of instituting a self-policing process, they met at the Hotel Astor on January 28. However, it was Mae West who was their target. If *The Drag* opened in New York, the Greenberg measure would certainly be enacted. In a rare moment of solidarity, they pledged that West's play would not find an available theatre. In order to prevent future crises, they elected Winthrop Ames to chair a committee of producers and owners to pass judgment on productions that were planning to open in New York.

One day before Greenberg formally introduced his bill, *The Drag* opened for previews in Bridgeport, Connecticut, where it was advertised as a "homosexual comedy drama more sensational than *Rain* or *Sex*."[104] *Variety*, which had been tracking the progress of the production, sent a reviewer to the opening. The resulting observations were anything but kind. *The Drag* was accused of being a "cheap and shabby appeal to sensationalism done without intelligence or taste." The reviewer was not opposed to the depiction of homosexuals, when "handled with discretion and tact." However, he objected bitterly to West's treatment of the topic:

> this play is utterly insincere and everything urged in its favor is phony, the object being an inexpressibly brutal and vulgar attempt to capitalize a dirty matter for profit and without a shred of decency in purpose or meaning ... The whole venture is without justification and merits the unqualified condemnation of the public.[105]

When *The Drag* appeared headed for Broadway, Governor Smith, already the target of Hearst's editorials, pressured Mayor Walker and District Attorney Banton to use existing city and state laws to suppress troublesome plays. Although Smith did not specify exactly how to proceed, he apparently favored a hand-picked squad of men from the police force and the District Attorney's office to close the offending productions.[106] The New York dailies began to report that raids on various shows were a foregone conclusion. Only the specific productions remained a secret. Walker, never one to take a direct hit, chose this precise moment to leave New York for a vacation in Cuba and left Assistant Mayor McKee and Banton in charge of the operation.

In a sudden burst of activity, on February 9 police squads descended on three productions, *The Captive*, *The Virgin Man*, and *Sex*. The raid at Daly's Theatre, where *Sex* was playing, became its own drama as the police and actors performed for reporters and passers-by:

> Outside the theatre an enormous array of cameras pointed at the stage door. This was taken as further evidence that the majesty of the law was about to be vindicated and about 1000 onlookers were there when the calcium drumfire began. There were faint cheers and murmurs as 12 policemen and twenty-three victims made their way through the crowd to ten taxicabs that had been hastily summoned. Etiquette prevailed to the end. The policemen handed the women of the company into the cabs with ceremonious gallantry and the scene shifted to Night Court.[107]

The mood, however, soon changed to one of uncompromising seriousness. Banton vowed to prosecute the productions personally and seek jail sentences in every instance. The raids, combined with the resolve of the Ames Committee, quickly buried *The Drag*. On February 12, Morgenstern announced that he could not find a theatre, had disbanded the company and would make no further effort to produce the show in New York. The District Attorney, however, could not keep the raided shows closed. Within forty-eight hours, all three productions had obtained restraining orders to prohibit any further police action. Predictably enough, the intense publicity provided a significant increase in attendance. *The Captive*, which had been playing to capacity houses, began selling all of its standing room tickets. *Sex* experienced a 20 percent increase in business and *The Virgin Man*, which had announced that it would be closing, was able to continue its run.[108]

The next few weeks were filled with furious activity. The producers, cast and playwright of *The Virgin Man* were arraigned.[109] William Dugan, author and co-producer of the play, demanded that his partner close the play. When his colleague refused, he attacked him backstage as the audience waited for the play to begin. The police finally intervened, hustling Dugan off to the nearest station house. He later remarked: "The authorities are mad. They are real mad. They're going to get somebody, and it isn't going to be me."[110]

Clearly, Dugan believed the police meant to punish the accused principals as a warning to others who wanted to produce shows that contained blatant sexual themes. His assessment was accurate. On March 29, Dugan and his two producers were found guilty of having given immoral performances, fined $250, and sentenced to the workhouse for ten days.[111]

The case of *The Captive* was even more entangled. Fearing that the censorship bill would gain more momentum the longer Bourdet's play ran, officials took swift action. Stories began to circulate that Miller might close his production voluntarily in order to avoid prosecution. At first he denied the rumors, but on February 16 Miller withdrew *The Captive*. Horace Liveright, producer and publisher, immediately announced that he would take over the production.[112] However, the court blocked Liveright's plan. Miller had agreed, as part of his settlement, not to sell the production's scenery. Moreover, the cast had been granted immunity from prosecution on the stipulation that they not appear in any subsequent productions. Finally, Liveright was informed that he was still under investigation for publishing *Replenishing Jessica*, a novel that the grand jury had declared obscene, but for which he was never prosecuted.[113] Defense attorney Arthur Hayes who had been part of the defense team for the famous "Scopes Monkey Trial," equated

New York authorities with those in the South. He said, "We laugh at those people in Tennessee, but we do the same thing in New York. In Tennessee, it was held you should keep people ignorant to save their souls. Here the police attempt to say you should keep them ignorant to save their morals."[114] Hayes appealed to the New York State Supreme Court to issue an injunction to forbid the city from interfering with *The Captive*. Justice Jeremiah Mahoney refused the petition and ruled that *The Captive* was immoral. His opinion echoed the troubled observations of New York's critics. The play had "excellent literary quality" and he professed that it might not harm "a mature and intelligent audience," but he held that it might have "dangerous effects on some persons in an indiscriminate, cosmopolitan audience."[115]

Action against *Sex* also proceeded. West, Timony, John Cort, part owner of Daly's Theatre, and twenty members of the cast had been arraigned. On March 19, however, Morgenstern announced that he was voluntarily closing *Sex*. West, he said, was "tired out after her year's work in the play." He added that she had been exceedingly "unnerved by the developments of the past month [and] in need of rest."[116] If their strategy had been to have charges against West and her cohorts dismissed, it failed. A trial date was set for March 28.

The Wales Padlock Law

In the meantime, efforts to pass a censorship bill in Albany hit a snag. Satisfied that city authorities were capable of controlling the theatre, Greenberg withdrew support from his own bill. However, Assemblyman Edward Jenks, chairman of the Judiciary Committee, assumed sponsorship of the measure and scheduled hearings for March 9. Sidney Howard, Frank Gillmore, Theresa Helburn of the Theatre Guild, Owen Davis from the near moribund Ames Committee, and Revd Charles Gilbert, representing Episcopal Bishop William Manning, all spoke against the measure. If the Jenks Bill became law, they asserted the state would have to erect a censorship bureaucracy so immense that it would collapse of its own weight. Furthermore, they argued that New York could not remain the center of American theatre if such restrictions were put in place.

Supporters of the Jenks Bill were equally as impressive. John Sumner, Revd John Roach Straton, and Monsignor Michael Lavalle, representing Francis Cardinal Hayes, spoke in favor of the legislation. They argued that the Play Jury had been ineffective and that the public should not fear censorship because, after all, every law was a form of censorship.[117]

The Jenks Bill received a favorable recommendation from the committee, but never reached the floor of the Assembly. There were, however, other plans afoot. Neither Governor Smith nor Mayor Walker wanted to establish a censorship bureau, but both, particularly the former, wanted to be regarded as a champion of morality. District Attorney Banton had the answer. Banton, a Democrat, immediately submitted a compromise to the Republican leadership of the Assembly as soon as it became apparent that a rigorous censorship bill had some support. He proposed that the Licensing Commissioner be given the power to revoke a theatre's license for up to a year if an offending production were convicted of obscenity under prevailing city statutes. Thus, a theatre owner who leased his building to a production that contained "any obscene, indecent, immoral or impure drama, play, exhibition or tableaux," would suffer significant financial loss if the show were found guilty of corrupting public morals. Even if an offending production closed before it was brought to trial, as was the case with *The God of Vengeance*, owners still ran the risk of losing their theatres for a year if that show was convicted.[118] The Wales Padlock Law, named for State Senator Roger Wales, passed with bi-partisan support on March 23.[119]

In a lengthy letter to the *Times*, Assistant District Attorney Wallace, who had prosecuted *The God of Vengeance*, promised that serious producers had no reason to fear that gross injustices would be visited upon them, but his explanation was not exactly reassuring. He stated that his office would only prosecute immoral plays. However, he reminded his readers any indecent and obscene part of any play rendered the entire production culpable. Thus, a few risqué lines or a revealing costume would be grounds for prosecution. As Wallace explained: "If a play contains obscene matter which tends to corrupt, then the play as a whole tends to corrupt." Wallace particularly liked the second feature of the bill that made it a misdemeanor to present any play dealing with "sex perversion or sex degeneracy." Now dramas dealing with homosexuality could be prosecuted because homosexuality, after all, was legally defined as a perversion. His closing statement was chilling. He maintained, "There is, therefore, in the present law nothing to cause alarm to *right thinking* people [emphasis mine]."[120]

Banton was ecstatic. He declared: "Nudity and naughtiness have legally come to an end forever in New York's public entertainments, whether in

theatres or in night clubs."[121] More thoughtful observers worried that indecency could never be legally defined:

> no legal definition has ever been framed which makes possible any objec-
> tive test. The opinion of one set of twelve jurors may very well be different
> from that of another set, and so, even though indecency upon the stage
> may be a recognized crime, no crime has been committed until a court
> has decided that a given performance is indeed indecent.[122]

The District Attorney's office was inclined to ignore the subtleties of
moral relativism. It merely sought convictions and *Sex* was Banton's primary
target. After all, the Assembly had approved the Wales Padlock Law on
March 26, but Governor Smith had not yet signed the measure when the
Sex trial began on March 29. Thus, Banton desperately needed a conviction
to prove to the Governor and the Assembly that he was capable of activating
the punitive features of the law.

Throughout the trial animosities between the defense attorneys and Assistant District Attorney Wallace, threatened to explode in the courtroom.
Defendants were cautioned by the judge to refrain from making snide remarks about the prosecutor. Wallace eventually became so agitated that
he challenged his adversaries to meet him outside, whereupon bailiffs had
to separate the attorneys. The defendants were also tense. Timony took a
rosary out of his pocket and began to pray while the jury deliberated. Barrie
O'Neal, the leading man, broke into tears and had to be consoled by West.

The verdict was virtually a foregone conclusion. West and her fellow
defendants were convicted of producing and/or appearing in an indecent
production. Prosecutor Wallace claimed that the conviction proved that
"dirty plays can be successfully prosecuted before juries and that the stage
can be kept clean without censorship," and he urged the governor to sign
the padlock legislation.[123] On April 20th, West, Morgenstern, and Timony
were sentenced to ten days in jail and fined $500 each. The remaining
nineteen defendants were given suspended sentences.[124]

The *Sex* convictions apparently convinced Governor Smith that New
York City authorities were capable of convicting transgressive theatrical
productions in courts of law. He gladly signed the Wales Bill on April 7.
By so doing he proclaimed local authorities could effectively police theatres
and that a state censor was unnecessary.[125]

West, Timony, and Morgenstern began serving their sentences on
April 21, the latter two at the Tombs and the former at the Women's
House of Detention. They were given "housecleaning duties," mopping

and sweeping. Because Timony demonstrated "initiative and ambition," he was promoted to the boss of his squad. West performed similar duties and her only complaint dealt with the comfort of her prison garb.[126] Upon her release, she maintained that she had gathered enough material for a dozen plays. She also said that she had "gained a new slant on life," and that she was going to devote some of her time to philanthropy. True to her word, she handed the warden a check for $1,000, a fee she had received for writing an article on her experiences in jail. He immediately announced that the money would be used to start a "Mae West Memorial Prison Library."[127] Although District Attorney Banton had won this match, the two adversaries would soon meet again.

For nearly a year, the obscenity debate vanished from the theatre scene. Then came *Maya* by Simon Gantillon and the insidious power of the Wales Law became immediately apparent. *Maya* was produced by Actor–Managers, a group of serious-minded artists previously associated with the Neighborhood Playhouse, and opened at the Comedy Theatre on February 21, 1928. Gantillon had penned a sentimental piece in which the clients of a Marseilles prostitute symbolically transform her into women whom they have loved, hated, lost, or deserted. *Maya* had been presented in twenty European cities in twelve languages, and many New York critics were as enthusiastic as their European colleagues. Alexander Woollcott was in awe. He claimed, "The pageant of Maya's Days and Nights [*sic*] has been wrought with simplicity, imagination, reticence and compassion – above all compassion. It is saturated with ancient sentiment . . . At best the Gantillon play is something done once more. But done, I think, most beautifully."[128] Brooks Atkinson wrote somewhat enigmatically, "Artistically it is a triumph of understanding over characters and environment."[129] Other critics took issue with the play's excessive sentimentality. Gilbert Gabriel labeled it a "string of flatly sympathetic vignettes of the oldest profession on earth, a lot of lusterless scraps of art laid on the doorstep of a seaport brothel, [and] many tears shed bitterly, maudlinly and mostly in vain."[130] John Anderson was similarly unimpressed. He called it "a repetitious and threadbare play, hunting through a haystack of episodes for a scant glimmer of interest."[131]

Although *Maya* might not have been universally lauded as great theatre, very few critics suggested that it was indecent. Police department critics thought otherwise. On February 23, James Sinnott, secretary to the Police Commissioner, saw a performance of *Maya* and reported to his superior that it was indecent.[132] Assistant District Attorney Wallace then attended and decided the play could be successfully prosecuted. The District Attorney's office contacted Lee and J. J. Shubert, who owned the Comedy Theatre, to inform them that charges were about to be filed. The Shuberts immediately informed Helen Arthur, manager of the *Maya* production, that they would be evicted. Arthur was stunned. Aside from vague reports in some of the dailies, she had no idea that an investigation had even begun, yet alone been concluded. Nor did she know that the District Attorney had approached the Shuberts. When she contacted her attorney to determine if there were any recourse, she was informed that her booking contract included a clause that stated any public objection over her production would result in her eviction.[133] Although religious, educational, and business leaders formally protested the District Attorney's action, and critics John Mason Brown and Barrett Clark circulated a petition among their colleagues, *Maya* closed on March 3.

The District Attorney and the Police Commissioner had now established themselves as unofficial censors. They only had to intimate that a show was obscene to persuade frightened theatre owners to evict troublesome tenants. The state had not instituted an official censor, but it had clearly established a censorship mechanism.

The press was outraged. "This is censorship in its worst form, irresponsible and obnoxious," wrote the *World*. "It does not even give the producers of the play their day in court. Instead it so terrorizes the owner of the theatre with its threat of a year's padlock that he does not dare take the risk of letting the case be taken to court."[134] Heywood Broun wrote, "The Wales law is, of course, thoroughly vicious and unfair."[135] Barrett Clark accused the prosecutor's office of attacking small producing companies because they did not have the resources to defend themselves in court, and dared the District Attorney to challenge the Theatre Guild.[136]

Clark was soon to get his wish – sort of. In late April, Lee Shubert and his general counsel, William Klein, filed a complaint with District Attorney Banton that two Theatre Guild productions – Eugene O'Neill's *Strange Interlude* and Ben Jonson's *Volpone* – contained "immoral and obscene situations." As Klein complained, the District Attorney was "making fish of one and fowl of the other."[137] Banton agreed to investigate but speculated that the action was motivated by professional jealousy.[138]

Assistant District Attorney Wallace represented Banton at both performances. He reported that neither play "would tend to the corruption of the morals of youth and others." Nonetheless, Wallace's report noted that there "are some lines in each play which are coarse and which offend good taste" and he demanded that these lines "be renovated and perfumed." The Guild agreed.[139] Now the full effect of the Wales Padlock Law was evident, but the District Attorney's Office was not the only adversary. Anyone for any reason could file a complaint with the police, and owners might elect to close shows long before any crime had been proven.

Mae West again

Shortly after the District Attorney had disposed of *Maya* and concluded that the case against *Strange Interlude* and *Volpone* was a non-issue, his old nemesis Mae West confronted him once again. During the spring of 1928, West appeared as Lil in *Diamond Lil*, which she also authored. The play, a mixture of comedy and melodrama, contained an array of prostitutes, madams, pimps, drug dealers, thieves, and up-town swells. The production was an amazing success, drawing accolades from critics who, only a few months before, had excoriated her for her acting and her writing. The role of Lil transformed West into a Broadway star. Although pleased to garner the attention and money that came with stardom, she was not about to surrender her reputation as Broadway's bad girl. During the run of *Diamond Lil*, she had been busy writing a play that would once again rekindle the image of her as a purveyor of smut, and lead to an even more sensational trial. *The Pleasure Man*, as this play was eventually called, was culled from her vaudeville experiences and purportedly revealed the backstage life of one of these theatres. In many respects, *The Pleasure Man* is a reworking of *The Drag*, but there is one crucial change. The protagonist, Randy Terrill, is a heterosexual matinee idol who seduces willing fans and naive showgirls. When one of these women becomes pregnant, he refuses to honor his promise to marry her. She has a back-alley abortion and dies. Her brother, the house electrician, castrates Terrill and he dies. It was not, however, the heterosexual violence that disturbed critics. Rather, it was the presence of another troupe of transvestites. *The Pleasure Man* unfolds through a series of back-stage scenes that reveal, along with Terrill's abusiveness, the cavorting of five transvestites as they trade gossip and insults while dressing for their performance. Particularly offensive is a drag party in Act III where Terrill's murder takes place.

The Pleasure Man opened at the Bronx Opera House on September 17, 1928. Most of the metropolitan dailies regarded the premiere as a tryout and did not send critics. Jack Conway of *Variety* was one the few who made the trip uptown. His review was entitled:

OH, MY DEAR, HERE'S MAE WEST'S NEW SHOW –
GET A LOAD OF IT AND WEEP.

He called it the "queerest show you've ever seen. All the queens are in it."
After belittling everyone associated with the production, he ended with
some begrudging praise for West.

> The thing ran for two-and-a-half hours. It needs plenty of cutting and
> re-writing, but will it get the pennies. You and I should have a piece . . .
> That West girl knows her box office and this one can't miss, and if you
> think it can, hope you get henna in your tooth brush. But don't miss it,
> because you must see it to appreciate the strides we girls are making.
> You can't possibly imagine it. And go early, some of the lines won't
> last.[140]

It continued its run in Queens and opened in Manhattan on October
1 at the Biltmore Theatre. The critics were unimpressed. Gilbert Gabriel
indignantly railed: "No play in our times has had less excuse for such a
sickening excess of filth. No play, I warrant, has set out to sell muck to
the jeerful."[141] The *Times* claimed it was "a coarse, vulgar and objectionable
specimen of the author's theatrical writings. As a play it is as bad – a hodge
podge, scrambled in theme and poorly written."[142]

Although the district attorneys in the Bronx and Queens permitted *The
Pleasure Man* to be presented after certain line changes had been made,
Manhattan authorities were not nearly as accommodating and Mayor
Walker gave orders for the show to be raided. After the curtain fell on
opening night, uniformed and plain-clothes officers arrested the entire cast,
crew, and orchestra – fifty-six persons in all. West, who was still performing
in *Diamond Lil,* arrived at the 47th Street precinct house after finishing
her show and was also arrested. After arranging a $500 bond for each of
her company, she was released. The next day Nathan Burkan, her attorney
and a specialist in theatrical cases, filed for an injunction restraining police from interfering with the production and a performance was given on
October 2.[143]

The next day, at the request of Mayor Walker and District Attorney
Banton, the Appellate Division of the New York State Supreme Court
vacated the temporary injunction. The cast, unaware of the Supreme Court's
decision, began the performance, but police charged down the aisles and
unceremoniously halted the show. Once again the company was transported
to the 47th Street Precinct House where they were arraigned. Without the

protection of a restraining order, Burkan admitted that it was futile to reopen the show and announced that it was closing.[144]

Mayor Walker took credit for the raid. While claiming he was a liberal and a supporter of theatre, he drew the line when blatant homosexuality was displayed:

The action taken by the police in the *Pleasure Man* simply demonstrates that this Administration is determined to put an end to this type of salacious performance in violation of the law ... We shall not have disgusting or revolting degenerate plays for public exhibition in this city. The efforts of the police and what they will do have my hearty support ... anything so offensive to the decency and morality of the citizens of this community cannot continue in this town while I am Mayor.[145]

More than likely, Walker's actions were not the result of a sudden concern for the maintenance of New York's moral fiber. Nineteen twenty-eight was an election year. Al Smith was running for president and Franklin Roosevelt for governor. According to the *Evening Post*, the mayor had told the Police Commissioner that "any dastardly drama even slightly odorous was not to be tolerated on Broadway this season. New York must be good in Presidential years."[146]

West completely ignored the possibility that the attacks aimed at her were politically motivated. Instead she defended herself against charges that she had mounted another version of *The Drag*. She asserted that the leading character in *The Drag* was a "homosexualist." *The Pleasure Man*, on the other hand, was about a "normal man and women." As for the transvestites, she claimed that they were a common feature of the American entertainment scene:

I have some lady impersonators in the play. In fact, I have five of them. But what of it? If they are going to close up the play and prevent the people from making a living because they take the part of female impersonators, then they should stop female impersonators appearing on the Keith circuit ... How many thousand female impersonators you think there are in this country? Are they going to put them all out of business?[147]

That West actually intended to present an objective portrayal of transvestites is unlikely, but she completely missed (or avoided) the seminal issue that vice crusaders intuitively comprehended. Audiences that saw transvestites perform on the Keith Circuit witnessed a seamless mold created by men who had carefully folded their masculinity into a female form. Moreover, the final product was largely a fiction designed to appeal to male sexual fantasies. West's scenes revealed a previously hidden juncture, an intersection where male and female traits mingled improvisationally. More disturbingly, she disclosed that the desirable "female" who appeared on the vaudeville stage was not only fashioned by men, but was, in reality, clearly a man who sought out the attentions of other men.

West's trial did not begin until March 1930. By then, Roosevelt had been elected Governor of New York, but Smith had lost the presidential election to Herbert Hoover. Jimmy Walker was under investigation for graft, and the nation was sinking into the Depression. Irrespective of these momentous events, Assistant District Attorney Wallace stepped forward to prosecute Mae West for obscenity. On this occasion, Wallace was no match for Burkan. He attacked Wallace's assertion that transvestitism was degenerate, citing that female impersonation had been a theatrical tradition for centuries. He completely compromised the prosecution's chief witness, Captain James Coy, who had led the raid. When Coy cited lines that he considered indecent, he got the Captain to admit that he could neither see nor hear well enough to take notes, and that his testimony had been based on a fellow officer's transcriptions. Burkan then asked Coy to imitate the female impersonators. He eagerly obliged and pranced around the courtroom, hands on hips, to the uncontrolled glee of the spectators. Wallace retaliated by insisting that the dialogue and gestures used in the play were filled with lurid meanings and called an "expert" to interpret these lines to the jury. Burkan strenuously objected, claiming that Wallace was trying to "poison the atmosphere of the court." He argued: "If the words of the play have double meanings that are commonly known, no expert is needed. If these words are in Chinese, it might be in order for the state to call in an interpreter." Judge Amedeo Bertini overruled his objection and the expert witness was allowed to explicate the text, but the defense attorney retaliated. He gained the court's permission to stage an acrobatic act that the prosecution claimed was indecent. Predictably, the act contained no indecencies. Wallace angrily protested that it was not the same performance that his witnesses had seen. The trial ended with each attorney accusing the other of lying to the public.[148]

The jury, after deliberating for ten hours, informed Judge Bertini that it could not reach a verdict and all charges were dismissed. The judge was obviously frustrated. He complained that a court of law, by its very nature, was not equipped to judge the "words, intonations, gestures and actions" of a theatrical production. Instead he encouraged state lawmakers to establish a "system of censorship."[149] The jury concurred and called upon the legislature to establish a censorship mechanism that would decide the suitability a play before it opened:

> The jury in this case, by its inability to agree on any verdict [,] failed to perform the duty expected of it by the public and left this most important subject in a most uncertain and unsatisfactory status. The undersigned members of the jury deem it their duty to urge upon you the desirability of your recommending some effectual measure of censorship of all plays presented in New York. The failure to agree tends to demonstrate that censorship of plays by criminal litigation is not the most effective and most reliable means of assuring the playgoing public of New York that no play will be presented that tends to corrupt the morals of the young.[150]

When the defendants in the *Sex* and *Virgin Man* cases were convicted within the traditional criminal justice process, editorialists praised the court system. Now that West had won acquittal within that same system, the judge and dissenting members of the jury claimed that the criminal justice system was incapable of protecting the public. In its place, they wanted a new, extra-legal arrangement where adjudicators were committed to protecting an abstract moral code rather than interpreting the law. In short, theatre was too amorphous and too mercurial to be controlled by traditional legal measures. A censor, operating outside of the legal system, was needed if the moral order was to be protected from performers.

The strange journey of *Strange Interlude*

Although New York was the center of theatre and theatrical controversies during the twenties, other cities also became embroiled in controversy. Perhaps the most contentious of these episodes occurred in Boston in 1929. The Massachusetts State Legislature, in order to streamline the censorship process, had empowered Boston's mayors with the right to revoke theatre licenses *for any reason whatsoever* in 1904. When Mayor Malcolm Nichols threatened to exercise his authority if the Hollis Theatre allowed O'Neill's *Strange Interlude* to open, he ignited one of the most rancorous disputes of the decade. Produced by the Theatre Guild, O'Neill's controversial "woman's play" had escaped the wrath of District Attorney Banton. Although some critics doubted its greatness, it won the Pulitzer Prize for 1928 and ran for 414 performances. By the time it was scheduled to open in Boston, September 30, 1929, it had been seen by an estimated 1,500,000 people in Los Angeles, Seattle, Detroit, Tacoma, Columbus, Kansas City, and

Washington, DC. Internationally, it had been performed in state theatres in Stockholm, Budapest, and Vienna. The Lord Chamberlain had approved it for production in London and it was slated to open in Berlin in 1930. When the production reached Boston in September 1929, Mayor Nichols decided that *Strange Interlude* was a "disgusting spectacle of immorality" and refused to license the production.[151]

John Casey, the mayor's "theatrical advisor," aided him in his decision. Appointed by Mayor Patrick Collins in 1904 because the latter did not want to attend theatre on a regular basis, Casey, a former drummer in burlesque pit bands, was a censor in all respects save title. Casey's standards were simple. He steadfastly maintained: "Nothing should be placed upon the stage of any theatre anywhere to which you could not take your mother, sweetheart, wife or sister." To this end, he instituted his eight-point "Code of Morals" by which he judged theatrical productions. His "Code" forbade: lascivious dialogue, gestures, or songs intended to suggest sexual relations; performance in the aisles or auditorium; bare female legs; one-piece union suits worn by women; depictions of drug addicts; all forms of "muscle dancing"; profanity; and the portrayal of a moral pervert or sex degenerate, meaning a homosexual.[152]

The Theatre Guild, however, claimed that neither Casey nor Nichols informed them that there were any problems with *Strange Interlude*. Nor did they imagine that a Pulitzer Prize-winning play by America's most noted playwright would be objectionable. Thus, when Mayor Nichols and Casey announced the ban, the Guild's leadership was taken completely by surprise. Theresa Helburn, the Guild's executive director, and Lawrence Langer, a member of the board of directors, immediately issued a joint statement expressing their dismay. They called the mayor's action "undemocratic" and that it "arbitrarily disregards the opinion of thousands of respectable Boston citizens." Helburn and Langer explained that advertising for *Strange Interlude* had begun in May and that no complaints had been voiced during the intervening period. They pointed out that 7,000 advance tickets totaling approximately $40,000 had been sold and that the text had been on sale in Boston book stores for nearly two years without generating any complaints.[153]

Perhaps hoping to embarrass the mayor into relenting, the press claimed that the issue of censorship had once again made Boston the laughing-stock of the nation. As the *Boston Herald* noted, "[The mayor] will make the City a subject of national and international contempt and ridicule"[154] A sarcastic editorial in the *Boston Globe* congratulated censors for having created the "most famous urban advertising slogan known to modern times 'Banned in Boston.'" The writer went on to encourage authorities to continue to suppress any work that was remotely suggestive, particularly great works of art. Only by such action would Boston's "banner" be circulated throughout the world.[155] The *Boston Transcript* quipped, "Boston is rapidly becoming a city where it's criminal to deny that there is a Santa Claus or that the stork delivers babies."[156]

Guild officers Theresa Helburn and Lawrence Langer, and critic Walter Pritchard Eaton took to the radio to try to persuade the mayor to change his mind. Eaton, a member of the panel that had nominated O'Neill for the Pulitzer, organized a Citizens' Committee of approximately 300 who inundated the mayor with appeals to recant. The Guild's board of directors even retained counsel to prepare an appeal to the federal Court of Appeals challenging the mayor's constitutional right to suppress a play before it had been performed.[157]

Although the press continued to assail the mayor, he received significant support from Boston's clergy who unleashed a furious indictment of the play that read like a checklist of most feared sins of the period. They claimed that it endorsed atheism, debased marriage, condoned abortion and encouraged infidelity. One minister agreed that Americans badly needed instruction regarding sexual relationships but argued that such a responsibility should "not be commercialized and turned over to some hirelings who for an admission fee into some theatre are willing to undertake the task."[158] Still another warned that "radical exponents of a so-called new morality" supported *Strange Interlude*. While he admitted that it was a masterful piece of literature, he cautioned that the results of O'Neill's "psychological surgery on decaying souls should not necessarily be displayed on the stage" and that its "underlying immorality unconsciously lingers as a justification for overthrowing the sanctities."[159]

Not all clerics backed the mayor. One declared that the prohibition of *Strange Interlude* was a "spent illusion on the part of Mayor Nichols and Censor Casey."[160] Another cautioned: "It is dangerous to keep the people in ignorance of the great questions of sex. Of course, there are perils in all education, but they are not to be compared to the perils of ignorance."[161]

Although the Guild had threatened to sue the mayor in federal court, the inevitable delays meant that the production would have to be canceled. Instead, the Guild decided to open *Strange Interlude* in Quincy, a depressed suburban city about fifteen miles south of Boston. Unlike Boston's chief executive, the state legislature or that city's charter had not granted Quincy's mayor, Thomas McGrath, any special censorship authority. Instead, those powers lay with the Licensing Commission, which, after seeing a play, might revoke the license of the theatre if the production was deemed obscene. Mayor McGrath, however, was exceedingly shrewd. Wishing to shield himself and the Commission from pressure, he appointed a twenty-five member "play jury" that would pass on the appropriateness of *Strange Interlude*.[162] Quincy merchants were elated. Business along Hancock Street, where the Quincy Theatre was located, was depressed and the estimated $3,000 per week that audiences would spend seemed to outweigh the elevated moral considerations voiced in Boston.[163]

Only one possible snag remained – the ministers of Quincy. As soon as it was announced that *Strange Interlude* would premiere in their city a number of clerics raised an enormous hue and cry. Was Quincy to receive the "refuse of Boston" one outraged pastor asked. "If it's too vile for Boston, then it's too vile for Quincy."[164] Another wrote that he hoped the mayor would regain his senses and recognize that *Strange Interlude* "does violence to the marriage ideals of the Catholic Church of which the Mayor is a loyal member and tries to make an abhorrent and unnatural moral code seem reasonable and attractive."[165]

The Guild leaders obviously anticipated the Quincy ministers would involve themselves in the debate and acted quickly to neutralize whatever negative feelings they might possess. On the 24th, Eaton and Robert Sisk, a member of the Guild's board, sent a letter to each cleric in Quincy. They explained that the majority of opposition from Boston's clergy was the result of excerpts from the play that had been taken out of context. Eaton and Sisk characterized O'Neill as a "serious-minded and sober writer, whose purpose is to try to illumine some of the problems of the modern world as he sees them. Supplying cheap excitement is no part of his purpose." They stressed that the issue at hand went beyond the right of the artist to express himself. They cautioned: "It really involves the whole question of free speech and hence can at one moment involve the press and pulpit as well as the stage." Finally, they urged the ministers to refrain from expressing their opinion until after opening night.[166]

On the 26th the Quincy Ministers' Association held a closed-door meeting at which the mayor spoke. Although the majority of opinions were negative, none of the clerics had seen or read the play. For this reason, they declined to issue an opinion until the production opened. "In view of the fact that our municipal authorities have granted permission for the presentation of *Strange Interlude* in our city on Monday evening next," their statement read, "the Quincy Ministers' Association feels it to be inadvisable to take any action until after that presentation."[167]

On September 30, 1929, fifteen days after Mayor Nichols barred *Strange Interlude* from Boston, it opened in Quincy. The audience that night was, according to one critic, "ninety-nine and some tenths percent pure Bostonian."[168] When Mayor McGrath entered the auditorium he was greeted with an enthusiastic ovation and he, like his fellow audience members, remained for the entire five and one-half hour performance. The audience appeared attentive throughout but not overly enthusiastic, but when the curtain descended it greeted the cast with fourteen curtain calls.[169]

However, Mayor McGrath seemed to garner more attention than the actors. After the final ovation, the mayor was besieged with well-wishers who thanked him for providing a home to *Strange Interlude*. When reporters finally succeeded in spiriting the mayor away from his admirers, they began to press him for his opinion. His response left little doubt that *Strange Interlude* could play as long as the Guild wanted to keep it running.[170]

Strange Interlude ran for a month, one week longer than anticipated. Viewed from one perspective, both Mayor Nichols and the Guild could claim ideological victories. The mayor could boast that he had prevented *Strange Interlude*, with its display of decadent and degenerate modern lifestyles, from playing in Boston. The Guild could counter that it had protected serious aesthetic expression from assault by providing the citizens of New England with access to one of the world's finest plays. Yet, as a writer for the *Evening Transcript* noted, the citizens of Boston remained victims because the city's arbitrary and unreasonable censorship policies were still intact. Serious modern drama that probed the dark psychological recesses of human beings would be suppressed, while the "flashy and trashy" would be tolerated.[171]

As this observer correctly surmised, the notion of obscenity as applied to *Strange Interlude* did not mean the depiction or description of sexually taboo events. O'Neill and the Guild remained decorous and cautiously circumspect in language and staging. The play's obscenity lay in what Mayor Nichols called its "theme." *Strange Interlude* offended its detractors by subjecting fixed moral precepts to intense scrutiny. In the end, O'Neill pronounced these standards to be hypocritical, debased and corrupt. This was the obscenity that Mayor Nichols, Casey, and their ministerial allies perceived. And theatre in Boston would not escape such morally motivated judgments until 1970.

During the twenties the small claque of moralists, educators and politicians momentarily lost control of theatre. The tastes of the broad masses determined what was produced and plays that debunked traditional moral standards grew in popularity. It is true that many of these – *Sex*, *The Virgin Man*, *The Demi-Virgin*, *Lulu Belle*, etc. – clearly exploited the public's curiosity about sex. Many others, however, used theatre to probe the darker aspects of human nature. *Desire Under the Elms*, *Strange Interlude*, and *They Knew What They Wanted* challenged traditional notions of love, family, and motherhood, *The God of Vengeance* and *The Captive* introduced audiences to lesbian love. *What Price Glory* depicted a grimly, non-heroic vision of war.

With the arrival of the 1930s, an entirely different theatre ethos appeared. The Depression, radio, and the "talkies" conspired to deal professional theatre a near deathblow. Audiences dwindled, theatres closed, and scores of playwrights, directors, and actors left for Hollywood. Moralists still sought to suppress plays that offended middle-class sensibilities, but the federal government soon entered the censorship wars. Congressmen grew fearful that a newly instituted, politically charged theatre might drive bitterly frustrated workers into a revolutionary frenzy. For the first time in the history of the nation theatre assumed a politically aggressive posture and the ensuing battle lasted for the next thirty years.

4

Have you now or have you ever...

Professional theatre in the Depression

Upon accepting the Republican nomination for president in 1928, Herbert Hoover announced that the United States was "nearer to the final triumph over poverty than ever before in the history of any land." Apparently the American electorate agreed, for Hoover solidly defeated the Democratic candidate, New York Governor Al Smith. As the 1920s drew to an end, it seemed that big business had solved America's social problems. The booming consumer economy allowed corporate leaders to proclaim the triumph of industrial capitalism. On the surface, their claims were justified. Living standards had risen at home, and America's diplomatic and military conquests had secured numerous international investment opportunities as well as the acquisition of cheap raw materials. The "labor problem" also seemed to have been resolved. Militant labor activists had been driven underground by the post-World War I "Red scare" and the welfare policies of many large businesses softened the animosity that characterized earlier interactions between labor and management.

But all was not as it seemed. Beneath the veneer of prosperity, American society was riven by economic and social conflicts. Hoover knew that the economy was in trouble, but did nothing for fear of dampening the enthusiasm necessary to maintain the speculative boom of the era. By 1928, the rapid industrial expansion that had fueled the optimism of the previous years was waning. Construction slowed, consumers reduced their spending, and manufacturers' inventories began to swell. In 1929, industrial corporations reduced production and began to lay off workers. By that summer, the nation was in the midst of a recession. In September, investors began selling their stocks. The trend escalated rapidly and on October 24, 1929 a rush of sell orders at the New York Stock Exchange sent prices tumbling. As fear and panic spread, directors of the exchange and concerned bankers tried to stabilize the situation, but by the next week it was clear that the market had crashed.

Few people were directly affected by the precipitous downturn of stock prices because the vast majority of Americans did not own stock. Nonetheless, a severe economic slump ensued as corporations drastically curtailed production and fired millions of workers. Between October and December the number of unemployed soared from fewer than 500,000 to more than 4 million. By the spring of 1933, 15 million were unemployed and countless more were working only a few hours per week. Real wages declined by 16 percent and between 1929 and 1933 the gross national product fell 29 percent. Construction was down 78 percent, manufacturing 54 percent, and investment an unbelievable 98 percent.[1] Breadlines and soup kitchens sprang up in large cities. So many men sold apples on street corners that the Census Bureau counted apple selling as a job. President Hoover defended this action by claiming, "Many persons left their jobs for the more profitable one of selling apples."[2]

Although the Depression had a disastrous effect on professional theatre, the popularity of live performance had already been damaged by the advent of radio and "talking films." The first modern receiving sets were placed on the market in 1925, and by 1926 readings of plays and sermons, concerts, and live coverage of sporting events were reaching in excess of 15 million listeners in the United States and Canada. During the Depression when money was scarce, the radio literally brought a world of entertainment into Americans' homes.[3]

"Talking films" posed an even more formidable challenge to theatre. Outside of New York in 1920, nearly 1,500 theatres were available for touring productions. In 1930, there only about 500. Many were converted to movie houses and the rest were simply demolished because they could not compete with the new medium.[4] In New York, the combined effects of radio, the "talkies," and the Depression significantly altered the demographics of professional theatre. During the 1930/31 season, there were 190 productions, a drop of fifty compared to the previous year. In 1938/39, only 80 new shows were produced. The Shuberts with all of their holdings in and out of New York went into receivership. The Stage Relief Fund was organized by Rachel Crothers to help needy theatre workers pay their food, gas, electric, and medical bills. Actress Selena Royle founded the Actors' Dinner Club where performers could purchase a meal for 1 dollar. Those who could not afford to pay ate for free. During an especially severe winter at the depth of the Depression, 150,000 meals were served, 120,000 of them at no cost.[5]

The reformist agenda

As the Depression worsened, a deep, wide, and permanent chasm opened between those who demanded revolutionary changes within the economic and cultural infrastructure of the nation and those who believed that a return to discipline and traditional virtues would speed recovery. For the most part, those who advocated the latter course of action dominated the cultural and political landscape; and, while most nationally organized censorship targeted the film industry, professional theatre, even in its wounded condition, continued to provoke the ire of moralists. In spite of the Wales Padlock Law, theatres in New York still pushed the limits of propriety. Shortly after Mae West was acquitted of charges of indecency in connection with *Pleasure Man* in April 1930, police stepped up their surveillance of questionable dramas. Captain James J. Coy, who had led the raid on West's play, was on hand to observe Norman Bel Geddes' production of Gilbert Seldes' adaptation of *Lysistrata*. Brooks Atkinson had called it "horseplay broader than a Second Avenue burlesque, full of rough and tumble bawdry." Surprisingly, Coy reported he had found nothing objectionable in the production.[6] Such was not the verdict when Earl Carroll opened his latest edition of *Vanities*. Claiming that he was only meeting "America's demand for sophisticated entertainment," Carroll presented several women clad in nothing but a few strategically placed fans and veils. One "costume" particularly disturbed the police. It consisted of a single small fan carried by Faith Bacon. After keeping the show under surveillance for several nights, the police raided the July 9th matinee and arrested eight females and one male for performing in an indecent show. After some initial objections, Carroll gave Ms. Bacon a larger fan, added more fabric to the remaining costumes, eliminated some of the bawdier jokes, and reopened his revue within a week.[7]

Catholic clerics were particularly outraged that both productions remained open. Cardinal Hayes launched a venomous attack. He called New York theatre "an outrage of public decency" that was the "dishonor of America's finest, noblest and most hospitable city."[8] Equity responded immediately and accused the archdiocese of lobbying for a censor, a charge that the Cardinal's representatives denied.[9] The New York theatre establishment was not convinced and continued to challenge the prelate to make good on his claim that the theatre was totally corrupt.[10] The police seemed buoyed by the Cardinal's attack. Barely a month after the Hayes assault, *Frankie and Johnnie* by John Kirkland previewed in Jamaica, New York. Set in a waterfront bar in St. Louis, the play depicted the grim lives of dock-workers, waitresses, and prostitutes. After the third performance, police raided the play and arrested fifteen persons connected with the show be-cause the language was too coarse. The offensive lines were altered and the play opened for a brief Broadway run.[11] The same fate awaited *Bad Girl,* an adaptation of a novel by Nina Delmar. In this moderately successful drama the pregnant heroine contemplates an abortion because she fears that her new husband does not want a baby. She changes her mind only to discover that he is happy at the prospect. The District Attorney objected to some of the lines and a scene in a maternity ward. The producers executed the necessary changes and the production was allowed to continue, whereupon the prosecutor quipped "*Bad Girl* is a good girl now."[12]

In spite of the fact that a combination of religious diatribes and police raids seemed to keep the stage free from offensive costumes and dialogue, agitation for stricter controls once again emerged. In January 1931, Seabury Mastick, state senator from Westchester, informed the public that he was about to introduce a censorship bill in Albany. Leaders of the the-atrical power bases once again convened to derail this latest legislative effort to control New York theatre. Lawrence Langer, fresh from his *Strange Interlude* battle in Boston, represented the Theatre Guild. Frank Gillmore spoke for Actors' Equity. Edward Childs Carpenter, Mark Connolly, and Elmer Rice advanced the cause of the Dramatists' Guild and Dr. Henry Moskowitz was the advocate for the League of New York Theatres. Collec-tively, they vowed to fight state censorship, but were undecided as how to proceed. Playwrights were opposed to any censorship whatsoever and in-sisted that public taste would modify wrongdoings committed by producers or playwrights. Others present hoped to resurrect the old Play Jury system in the hopes that a self-censorship mechanism would stave off state im-posed proscriptions. The latter plan was adopted and presented to Senator Mastick. Apparently satisfied with these efforts, he withdrew his proposal in order to give this committee time to put together another self-policing plan.[13]

New York, however, was not the only city to attempt to suppress stage productions. In Boston City, Censor John Casey required that all chorus girls wear stockings. Chicago police charged the stage of Cohan's Grand Opera House in the middle of *Sketchbook,* another Earl Carroll review, and arrested the twenty-nine members of the cast. It was rumored that a skit that satirized Chicago's crime reputation provoked the raid.[14] The rumor seems to have been true. In April, Mayor Cermak threatened to close any play that injured Chicago's good name.[15] In Pittsburgh, the public safety director threatened to suppress the touring production of *Lysistrata* if the "dirt and vulgarity" were not removed. "It's the rottenest show I ever saw," the director said. "It is vulgar to the core." As a result, the famous helmet scene and several suggestive properties were deleted.[16] In Los Angeles, the entire *Lysistrata* cast of sixty-five was arrested. The local producer obtained a restraining order preventing police from making further arrests, but the show was raided a second time. Although the commanding officer was cited for contempt, this harassment disrupted ticket sales and *Lysistrata* was forced to close.[17] Although the producer and cast were acquitted of all charges one month after *Lysistrata*'s demise, city officials once again demonstrated that they could use private judgment to suppress plays that challenged the prevailing moral and social order.

In New York, theatre faced a reformist tidal wave. In early 1932, Judge Samuel Seabury began investigations aimed at convicting Jimmy Walker, New York's playboy mayor, for "malfeasance, misfeasance, and nonfeasance." This situation placed Franklin Roosevelt, Governor of New York and the leading candidate for the Democratic presidential nomination, in an impossible situation. If he removed Walker from office, he might lose the support of Tammany bosses, all of whom supported the mayor. If he allowed Walker to retain his post, Republicans would claim that he was as corrupt as Walker. The mayor, however, saved Roosevelt the agony of making this decision. He resigned on August 14, 1932 and sailed for Europe ten days later.[18] Roosevelt won his party's candidacy for president, but Tammany had been thoroughly discredited and political reform became the mantra of New York candidates for political office.

In November 1933, Fiorella La Guardia, the candidate of the "Fusion Party," composed of disaffected Democrats and Republicans, was elected mayor and a new era of reform took root. Cleansing New York's performance scene was one of the new mayor's primary objectives. He appointed Paul Moss Commissioner of Licenses and, in spite of the 1922 State Supreme Court decision that limited the powers of this office, La Guardia endowed him with the authority to revoke the licenses of theatres that housed offensive productions. In January 1935, Moss met with Frank Gillmore, Henry Moskowitz, and Roger Baldwin, executive director of the American Civil Liberties Union. Although the specifics of the discussion were not fully disclosed, there was no doubt that the commissioner announced that he would determine what was and was not going to appear in New York theatres.[19]

In accordance with this new reformist agenda, the police raided Minsky's Republic Theatre, arrested three dancers, and revoked the theatre's license in April 1935.[20] Minsky's attorneys successfully challenged Commissioner Moss' authority to revoke theatre licenses without a conviction, but producers had been placed on notice. Clearly, nude or semi-nude women were equated with the decadence and permissiveness of the twenties and Walker's administration. They would no longer be tolerated. It was equally clear that, in spite of the courts, Moss would play a pivotal role in this purge.[21]

Banned in Boston

Although most charges of indecency were linked to the display of women, in Boston any play that questioned the authority of traditional religion or the cruelty of the dominant heterosexual culture was banned as indecent and perverted. In 1935, two such productions came under attack. The Abbey Theatre's production of Sean O'Casey's *Within the Gates*, an abstract drama dealing with the inability of traditional religion to address contemporary issues, was to premiere at the Shubert Theatre in January. Many Boston clerics objected to its alleged slanderous treatment of Christianity and complained to Mayor Frederick W. Mansfield. The mayor attempted to reach some sort of compromise. He suggested that certain offensive lines be deleted from the text. The producers consented and the mayor agreed to allow the play to open. The ministers, however, were unmoved and demanded that Mansfield ban the play. Unable to withstand the pressure, the mayor withdrew his permission. While the Methodist and Episcopal spokespersons claimed that it was "a vulgar play, serving no decent purpose [and] might affect unhappily the young people who see it," Roman Catholic clergy fomented the most heated opposition.[22] They took particular umbrage at O'Casey's claim that religion was "good-natured and well-intentioned [but] unable to find a word or invent an action that will help give meaning to life."[23] The insulted clerics claimed that "all right-minded citizens . . . would protest the sympathetic portrayal of the [play's] immoralities." And countered that religion was an "effective force in meeting the problems of life."[24] In the opinion of Boston's clerical establishment, *Within the Gates* challenged the hegemony of orthodox religion and had to be completely suppressed. And they called upon civic officials to enforce their religious agenda.

The uproar over the mayor's latest use of his unilateral censorship authority raised even more flap than the *Strange Interlude* episode. Mansfield, in
order to conciliate his very vocal opponents, promised never to close another
production before it opened. The mayor, like many other politicians, soon
forgot his promise. Later in 1935, another theatrical production threatened to
compromise the morals of Bostonians. On this occasion the offending play
was Lillian Hellman's *The Children's Hour*. Produced by Herman Shumlin
in conjunction with the Theatre Guild and Theatre Society, the production
opened in New York on November 20, 1934. It is the story of two women,
Karen Wright and Martha Dobie, who operate a New England boarding
school. A vengeful student tells her grandmother, an influential patron of
the school, that the women are carrying on an "unnatural relationship."
The grandmother then informs her friends, who promptly withdraw their
children from the school, causing its swift demise. The women sue for libel,
but lose. After their defeat, Martha confesses that she has been in love with
Karen. She leaves the room and commits suicide.

In spite of its obvious melodramatic ending, *The Children's Hour*, for
the most part, generated enthusiastic responses. Burns Mantle claimed it
"struck Broadway like a thunderbolt" and named it one of the ten best
plays of the 1934–35 season.[25] *Time* praised Hellman for adroitly weaving
the "arcane criminality of childhood, to the no less delicate subject of female
homosexuality."[26] Stark Young called the final act "adolescent banality," but
gave the overall production high marks.[27] Brooks Atkinson, who also chastised Ms. Hellman for not ending the play prior to the gunshot, nonetheless
praised her for writing a "venomously tragic play," that was supported by
the "deadly accuracy of its acting."[28]

The Children's Hour was scheduled to open in Boston on January 6, 1935 at
the Shubert, the same theatre that was to have housed the ill-fated *Within
the Gates*. City censor Herbert L. McNary, whose official title was Commissioner of Licenses, had seen the play in New York. He subsequently
informed Mayor Mansfield that it dealt with lesbianism and in his opinion
"was not a proper presentation for a Boston theatre." In spite of his promise
to permit controversial shows to open before passing judgment, the mayor
announced on December 14 that the play was "unfit for public presentation"
and that he was "unalterably opposed" to its presence in Boston. The mayor
was so adamant that he would not even accept Shumlin's offer to bring
the entire production – sets, costumes, and actors – to Boston at his own
expense for a private performance for the Board of Censors.[29] The mayor
was unmoved.

Once again, Bostonians were stunned. Yet, after having had no discernible effect on decisions regarding *Strange Interlude* and *Within the Gates*, public complaints diminished in number and volume. An editorial writer for the *Boston Post* lodged the most ardent protest when he wrote: "*The Children's Hour*, despite what his Honor has heard to the contrary, is not a dirty play. It is a sincere, brilliant and powerful tragedy, written delicately and played impressively."[30]

A. G. Munro, manager of the Shubert Theatre, would have been within his legal rights to open the show and have the full Board of Censors, consisting of the mayor, the chief justice of the municipal courts and the police chief, rule on its suitability. But, if the censorship panel returned an unfavorable verdict, his theatre would lose its license. Munro was unwilling to take that risk and reluctantly informed the producers that *The Children's Hour* could not open at his theatre.

Shumlin, unlike other New York producers who had been kept out of Boston, did not take the matter lightly. He filed suit in federal court against Mayor Mansfield and Commissioner McNary for $250,000 in damages.[31] He also petitioned the federal District Court to enjoin the City of Boston from interfering with the production. The ensuing trial clearly revealed the capricious, arbitrary nature of Boston's censorship policies. McNary testified that he had seen the play in New York. He also admitted that outside of a single "God damn," only one moment in the play disturbed him – the whispering scene. In order to convince her grandmother that the school was an abusive environment, Mary maintains that Miss Dobie and Miss Wright engaged in "unnatural relations." When asked to explain what she meant, the child whispers the information into her grandmother's ear. The gesture profoundly disturbed McNary. When asked what about the whispering offended him, he responded: "The need for whispering." For the commissioner, this brief dumb show signified that unspeakable acts had been described during the silent interlude. McNary was not apparently concerned that the accused women were blameless and that the most perverse character in the play was a vengeful ten-year-old girl who fabricated malicious lies. That moment had transformed an effective drama into a discourse about perversion and he dutifully reported to the mayor that the production would be inappropriate for Boston.[32] Mayor Mansfield subsequently took the stand. He explained that McNary's misgivings led him to believe the play violated a Massachusetts law that prohibited the "portrayal of a moral pervert or sex degenerate on stage."[33] For that reason he warned the producers that *The Children's Hour* was not acceptable for Boston. He reminded the court that he had not legally "banned" the production. He had simply informed producers that the censorship commission would review the play. Munro had cancelled the production, not the mayor. Federal Judge George Sweeny agreed with the defendants and refused to grant an injunction.

However, Judge Sweeny was careful to point out that his ruling did not imply the play was indecent. That decision would have to be rendered by the censorship commission.[34] Obviously, officials in Boston used their power to shield conventional morality and religion from any questions that might be generated by theatre. It was a power that would prove to be virtually unassailable.

A long and winding road

The mayors La Guardia and Mansfield were not the only municipal chief executives who altered the course of Depression theatre. In September 1935, *Tobacco Road* opened in Chicago. Adapted by Jack Kirkland, author of the notorious *Frankie and Johnnie*, from Erskine Caldwell's novel of the same name, it had been running in New York since December 1933. *Tobacco Road* told the story of Jeeter Lester and his family, hardscrabble Georgia farmers who in the best of times barely eke out a hand-to-mouth existence. Now that they are caught in the grips of the Depression, they teeter on the brink of starvation. While Caldwell and Kirkland occasionally blame capitalism for the Lesters' fate, they actually create a grim naturalistic comedy whose characters are the products of an absurd biological and naturalistic determinism.

Although Jeeter frequently speaks of and appeals to a transcendent God, he has never allowed his religious beliefs to dictate an ethical course for his life. He is a liar, a thief, and a philanderer. He has sold his twelve-year-old daughter, Pearl, to his neighbor, Lov Bensley, to be his wife. When Lov enters the scene to demand that Jeeter make Pearl behave like a wife, he steals the bag of turnips that Lov is carrying. When Pearl runs back home to be with her mother, he offers Lov his older daughter, Ellie May, who has been afflicted with a harelip, at no charge. Lov refuses to take Ellie May and offers to buy Pearl again for $2 a week, and Jeeter willingly accepts. He refuses to feed his pellagra-stricken mother hoping to kill her. After she wanders into the woods, presumably to die, Jeeter muses that he will probably go look for her someday. Dude, his son, accidentally kills his mother when he backs over her with a car. Neither he nor his father is unduly upset. Jeeter simply tells his son to bury her in a deep hole. When Pearl finally escapes from Jeeter and Lov, he sends Ellie May to live with him saying, "Be nice to him and maybe he'll let you stay. He'll be wanting a woman pretty bad now."[35]

With the exception of Henry Hull, who portrayed Jeeter, virtually every aspect of the New York production received negative reviews. Kirkland, who owned the production, and his partners, did not give up. They lowered ticket prices and advertised aggressively. Eventually the public took notice and transformed *Tobacco Road* into New York's most popular theatre attraction. The producers mounted a west coast tour that had been on the road twenty weeks before it wound its way into Chicago. Then on October 21, 1935, after the production had already been playing for six weeks, Mayor Edward Kelly attended a performance. Upon seeing the show at the Selwyn Theatre the mayor fumed, "Chicago had always been a liberal city . . . but liberalism does not condone filth . . . It is an insult to decent people."[36] Kelly initially attempted to have the producers volunatarily withdraw the play. When they refused, he simply revoked the license of the Selwyn, making it impossible for that or any other play to be mounted in that theatre.

Mayor Kelly had not been petitioned by a ministerial coalition, by teachers, or by social organizations who feared that the reputation of the city might be injured if such a show were allowed to continue. He had been personally offended. Something (or a number of somethings) had profoundly upset his moral and aesthetic compass. Perhaps the mayor resented the fact that the author and adapter had created a darkly comic universe driven by abject poverty, parental cruelty, and insatiable sexual appetites. Perhaps he felt that Kirkland and Caldwell had not subjected Jeeter to the moral and ethical condemnation his behavior merited. Perhaps he feared that the chaos and immorality of *Tobacco Road* needed to be suppressed before they corrupted the entire nation.

Of course, it is impossible to determine why precisely Mayor Kelly arbitrarily asserted his executive purview, but exercise it he did and a battle royal commenced. The producers hurried to federal court to seek a restraining order and found a comrade in the person of Judge William H. Holly. The city attorney argued that the court had no authority to challenge the mayor's right to revoke theatre licenses. Judge Holly tersely responded:

Do you mean to say that Mayor Kelly can step into any theatre, and arbitrarily decide for himself the play should be closed without the court having any jurisdiction? Could the mayor order *Alice in Wonderland* closed merely because he thought it should be closed?[37]

The next day Judge Holly found for the plaintiffs, but the city was not done. It appealed to the United States Circuit Court of Appeals to set aside Holly's order. The court agreed with the city and issued a writ of supersedeas. Then, on November 21, the Court of Appeals, without ruling on whether or not the play was obscene, simply upheld Mayor Kelly's right to revoke the license of the Selwyn Theatre. *Tobacco Road* remained closed in Chicago.[38]

Marching to the left

The attempts of municipal and state officials in Boston, New York, and elsewhere to prevent theatre from engaging in meaningful cultural interrogation were by no means new. Since 1900, reformers had undertaken such crusades. Their zeal met with periodic success, particularly outside of New York. The Depression, however, provided these reform efforts with new momentum. The nation's crippled economy was blamed on the excesses of the twenties. Free spending and hedonism had caused this collapse and only a return to traditional values would correct the situation. Theatre, like other components of the culture, would have to be reformed and purified. Yet moral reformers (and those politicians who sought their votes) were not the only forces that believed theatre needed to be controlled. During the thirties, government officials at all levels feared that a revolution, led by American workers, was a distinct possibility. Consequently, theatre that sympathized with workers or advocated collective labor action was indicted as an engine of that revolution and was brutally attacked.

American professional theatre had rarely concerned itself with realistic depictions of working-class issues. It was the middle and upper classes that bought theatre tickets and they, for the most part, wanted to be amused. It is true that O'Neill, Howard, Anderson, Hellman, and a handful of others attracted audiences with serious compelling drama. But most producers, with the exception of the Theatre Guild, generally shied away from controversial issues in favor of easily digestible dramatic fare. After all, they, like other businesspersons, measured their success by profit not public edification. During the Depression, producers became even more conservative.

Investment capital, while still available, had greatly decreased, and movies could provide audiences with more spectacular entertainment for a fraction of the price of a theatre ticket. Thus, commercial producers were extremely reluctant to support "relevant theatre."

Yet the Depression had created a volatile climate. Hundreds of thousands of working-class Americans with and without jobs began to blame the capitalist economic system for the current conditions, and it was these antagonisms that militant theatre artists began to address. These productions depicted bosses as entrenched, wealthy, and politically influential individuals who owned and operated immense industries as private fiefdoms. Workers, on the other hand, were portrayed as victims standing on the precipice of economic disaster. While these dramas may have oversimplified the economic algebra of the period, they nonetheless announced that the economically disenfranchised were on the verge of revolution.

The radical theatre of the 1930s was the product of actors, poets, novelists, and academics who wanted to use the drama as an instrument of societal change. In many respects it self-consciously modeled itself after the aggressive agit-prop groups of Russia and Germany that employed theatre to advance revolutionary political agendas. While most of its practitioners were not card-carrying members of the Communist Party, they were nonetheless emotionally and intellectually committed to Marxist philosophy. And it was this connection that would haunt performers in the United States for the next three decades.

Throughout the Depression, the Communist Party articulated a platform that called for management of the economy by the central government and the unionization of all workers. It blamed the disastrous state of the economy on capitalism and called for a top to bottom overhaul of the American political system. It staged a series of rallies dubbed "International Unemployment Days" and "Hunger Marches," which it used to demand direct government aid to workers and a cessation of lay-offs. In city after city, the turnout at these rallies far exceeded expectations as tens of thousands marched in the streets of New York, Boston, Chicago, Detroit, and Milwaukee. In New York, Chicago, Chattanooga, and Atlanta, Communists convinced African Americans and whites to work together on Unemployment Councils. In the rural south, they organized black sharecroppers, an effort that resulted in gun battles with landowners and police.[39]

Unwittingly, President Roosevelt advanced the Communist agenda by supporting its chief concern – unions. During the first 100 days of his first administration, Roosevelt approved dozens of new relief programs.

One of the most important, the National Industrial Recovery Act (NIRA), stated that employees had the right to organize and bargain collectively through representatives of their own choosing, free from the interference, restraint, or coercion of employers. The NIRA thus enabled organizers to portray joining a union as a patriotic contribution to the national recovery effort, rather than a revolutionary act. As a result, three times as many workers went out on strike in 1933 as in 1932. For many employers, acknowledging the right of workers to organize spelled irretrievable disaster and they resorted to force to prevent such an eventuality. Strikes of taxi drivers in New York, shipyard workers in New Jersey, aluminum workers in Pennsylvania, and copper miners in Montana resulted in violent confrontations. Transportation workers were engaged in a four-month state of siege with police and National Guard troops before they were allowed to unionize in Minneapolis. San Francisco longshoremen, who attempted to form a union, closed down the entire waterfront. When the police attempted to break the strike, riots ensued. In Toledo, workers at the Electric Auto-Lite Company and the Toledo Edison Company battled Ohio National guardsmen carrying rifles, bayonets, gas bombs, and machine guns to gain the right to unionize.[40]

The labor movement was also enhanced by the passage of the Wagner Act in 1935. Arguably the most pro-labor bill ever enacted by the United States, it granted workers the right to select their own union by majority vote and to strike, boycott, and picket. Supporters of the measure argued that a strong labor movement would uphold wages thereby preserving purchasing power of workers. Most importantly, they insisted that the legislation permitted workers' grievances to be addressed within the capitalist system. Its opponents claimed that it was promoting a Communist revolution in the United States. Although Roosevelt did not completely sympathize with every aspect of the Wagner Act, he nonetheless signed it into law on July 5, 1935. By so doing he linked his administration to the goals of organized labor and was repaid with significant support during his subsequent reelection campaigns. At the same time, he galvanized a powerful coalition of businessmen and Congressional conservatives that would oppose him at every turn. It was against this backdrop of political antagonisms that the upcoming battles over workers' theatre would be fought.

The growing militancy of workers had a direct impact on the direction of American theatre as hundreds of proletarian production groups emerged to transform theatre into an agent for social change. Beginning in 1930, dozens of troupes such as the Workers' Laboratory Theatre and the Proletbühne performed militant labor chants at union meetings and rallies. The leftist New Theatre League came into being solely to organize the hundreds of groups that had appeared nationwide. It held conferences, sponsored publications, and operated script bureaus. Its membership included the Rebel Players of Los Angeles, the Blue Blouses of Chicago, and the Solidarity Players of Boston as well as New York groups such as the Theatre of Action, Theatre Collective, Negro People's Theatre, and Theatre Advance and Artef, a Yiddish ensemble.[41]

Although the majority of these companies were amateur, several entered the professional arena. The Workers' Laboratory Theatre, hoping to appeal to a wider audience than the labor movement, changed its name to the Theatre of Action. Its most successful production, *The Young Go First*, a play about young men who worked in the government's Civilian Conservation Corps (CCC), was produced with a full Equity cast and union stagehands. The Theatre Union produced seven widely acclaimed dramas. Among them were George Sklar and Albert Maltz's anti-war drama, *Peace on Earth*, which opened in November 1933. Supported by scores of workers' organizations and radical political groups, it played for 143 performances. *Stevedore*, its next production, was one of the most provocative plays of the period. It told the story of a black dockworker who brings longshoremen of all races together to fight corrupt bosses.[42]

The Group Theatre was, by far, the most renowned of the politically committed professional ensembles. It produced three of the most socially relevant plays of the decade – *Awake and Sing*, *Waiting for Lefty*, and *Till the Day I Die*. All were written by Clifford Odets and produced in 1935. The Group Theatre proved that leftist political ideology held significant popular appeal. Aside from spawning dozens of amateur and professional companies, the political activism of the thirties inspired a number of playwrights to craft didactic plays around proletarian subject matter. Chief among them were Arthur Arent, Albert Bein, Marc Blitzstein, Michael Gold, Paul Green, Lillian Hellman, DuBose Heyward, Langston Hughes, Sidney Kingsley, John Howard Lawson, Albert Maltz, Clifford Odets, Paul Peters, Elmer Rice, Irwin Shaw, Claire and Paul Sifton, George Sklar, John Steinbeck, and John Wexley.[43]

Clearly, worker militancy had generated a type of theatre heretofore unknown in the United States. Not only did it promote labor unions, racial tolerance, and radical economics, it challenged the paradigm of commercial theatre that had, with few exceptions, dictated dramatic production since the late eighteenth century. Archibald MacLeish, writing *in New Theatre*, the most influential leftist theatre journal of the period, exuberantly proclaimed that commercial theatre, with all of its "appurtenances, paraphernalia, tricks and grimaces," was dead. With its demise, worker/artists could gain control of the "means of production" and create "a theatre for art."[44]

However, politically aggressive theatre was not universally welcomed and often triggered violent response from those conservative forces that it assailed.[45] Police in Los Angeles, San Francisco, Newark, Boston, Philadelphia, and New Haven routinely revoked performance permits and/or raided productions by workers' theatres. In Hollywood, members of a pro-German gang kidnapped and severely beat the director of the Hollywood Group Theatre because they objected to a scene that defamed Hitler in Odets' *Till the Day I Die*. In Washington, DC, New Theatre Group secured the sponsorship of four Congressmen for its production of *Lefty* and had rented a church-owned hall for the occasion. On the day the production was to have opened, the Hearst-owned *Washington Post and Times Herald* screamed that Communists were invading the capitol. Hearst operatives attempted to convince the United States Attorney to investigate the performance. They asked the sponsoring Congressmen why they lent their names to Communist propaganda and attempted to get the church that owned the theatre to cancel its contract. Church and government officials refused to be bullied and the performances took place.

The federal government and the federal theatre project

Although workers' theatre appealed to left-leaning playwrights and thousands of economically disenfranchised Americans, the New Theatre League and its member theatres never forged a cohesive, well-financed, professional theatre network capable of articulating their activist agenda on a national scale. That situation changed radically on April 8, 1935, when Roosevelt signed the bill that authorized him to spend $4.8 billion to eliminate unemployment. But, rather than dole out money to the destitute, the legislation was designed to employ 3.5 million able-bodied workers in a vast array of projects financed by the federal government. With the stroke of a pen the federal government became the largest employer in the United States.

The largest share of the appropriation, $1.39 billion, was earmarked for the Works Progress Administration (WPA), established by executive order the following May. Roosevelt appointed Harry Hopkins, a former social worker who had directed the Federal Emergency Relief Administration, to head the WPA. Congress, aside from approving its appropriation, exercised no control over this vast bureaucracy, which was responsible for employing hundreds of thousands of workers. To Republicans and conservative Democrats the WPA undermined the free-enterprise system and signified that the country, under Roosevelt's leadership, was traveling a path toward socialism.

Hopkins, basking in the president's reflected glory, spent very little energy attempting to mollify Roosevelt's critics. Instead, he moved quickly and aggressively to put federal reemployment programs in place. Although Roosevelt's opponents generally disapproved of Hopkins' initiatives, one program – Federal No. 1 – profoundly disturbed them. With the blessing of the president, Hopkins established Federal No. 1, or Federal One as it became known, to reemploy artists, musicians, writers, and theatre professionals. But Hopkins intended for Federal One to spearhead a cultural revolution, which would create a "cultural democracy." He wanted the Federal Writers', Music, Art, and Theatre Projects to transform the vast panoply of American traditions into paintings, dramas, symphonies, and stories that were capable of speaking to diverse audiences spread across the nation. Hopkins, for his part, claimed that Federal One would ultimately benefit the free enterprise system by creating a vast market that would continue to consume art, music, theatre, and literature after federal sponsorship had ended.[46] WPA critics were far more skeptical. They believed that Federal One was little more than a clever ruse to spread the president's socialist agenda.

By far the most disturbing component of Federal One was the Federal Theatre Project (FTP), which quickly established a significant performance network. Hopkins formally unveiled the FTP in the summer of 1935. He described as "free, adult, uncensored" theatre that would not blindly follow the New York commercial model. Hopkins, however, stunned the theatrical community when he chose Hallie Flanagan, who had been his classmate at Grinnell College in Iowa, to lead the FTP. Since her graduation, this forty-five-year-old academic had taught high school and college drama. She was part of George Pierce Baker's Workshop '47 at Yale. In 1926, she was the first woman to be awarded a Guggenheim Fellowship, which she used to study theatre in Europe and the USSR. On her return, she wrote and directed *Can You Hear Their Voice?* for the Experimental Theatre at Vassar. Based on Whitaker Chambers' description of the Arkansas drought, it borrowed heavily from techniques developed by German and Soviet agit-prop ensembles. In *Voices*, she dramatized the disparity between the living conditions of rich and poor and, in the process, created one of the most widely acclaimed experimental theatre pieces of that period. Most importantly, to Hopkins at least, she shared his vision that a federal theatre would speak to all Americans. Upon her appointment he told her:

> This [the FTP] is not a commercial theatre... It's got to be run by a person who sees right from the start that the profits won't be money profits. It's got to be run by a person who isn't interested just in the commercial type of show. I know something about the plays you've been doing for ten years, plays about American life. This is an American job, not just a New York job. I want someone who knows and cares about other parts of the country. It's a job just down your alley.[47]

Flanagan, like Hopkins, was committed to employing out of work theatre artists, and with Hopkin's blessing imprinted the FTP with an idealistic stamp that conservative Congressmen vehemently opposed. She wanted the FTP to be a vital populist theatre that was accessible to everyone. She envisioned an egalitarian theatre that would create a "new era of nationalism" based not on the purity of any racial or cultural stock but on the "classless, inclusive character of the national experience." She wanted the FTP to forge a newer, more critical, more political culture where decisions and directions that affected all citizens could be openly discussed.[48]

At first, Broadway producers proved to be the FTP's most ardent opponents. They wanted the federal government to underwrite their productions and allow the New York Broadway theatre establishment to resuscitate the American theatre. They were not interested in Flanagan's social agenda or her vision of a national network of subsidized theatres. To them she was an amateur from a girls' school and had no idea of how to produce within the hard-core environs of professional theatre.

The theatrical unions ultimately proved to be more of a challenge than the New York producing establishment. Equity feared that the government's lower wage scale might induce commercial producers to clamor for reduced salaries.[49] The International Alliance of Theatrical Stage Employees (IATSE), the stagehands union, proved to be particularly vexing. It had forbidden its members to file for relief. As a result, stagehands had to be hired as non-relief workers and listed, per union demands, as supervisors – the highest pay scale. In addition, IATSE members would not work on the same crew with non-union stagehands, whom they considered amateurs. For this reason, the New York unit was constantly in financial turmoil, a situation that opened them to charges of malfeasance during the budget hearings of 1939.[50] More troublesome still was the Socialist-inspired Workers' Alliance.

Organized in 1935, it enrolled most of the non-union WPA workers by convincing them that individuals who were not represented by a union would be utterly powerless against the massive WPA bureaucracy. Convinced by the Alliance's doomsday rhetoric, scores of clerks, janitors, timekeepers, stenographers, and washroom attendants quickly enrolled. As a result, beleaguered FTP officials were constantly barraged by hundreds of union demands and complaints.[51]

For a number of reasons, the FTP was not in a position to oppose the authority of the unions. The Roosevelt administration had signaled its support for labor by endorsing the National Industrial Recovery Act (1933), Wagner Act (1935), and the Emergency Relief Appropriations Act (1935), which created the WPA. During the intervening months between the organization of the FTP and the 1936 presidential elections, organized labor, particularly the radical Congress of Industrial Organizations (CIO), which was strongly committed to the Communist Party, supported the president with time and a considerable amount of money. As a result, FDR garnered 60 percent of the popular vote and carried every state but Vermont and Maine. The Democrats gained twelve more seats in the House and seven in the Senate, giving the president's party a Congressional majority of nearly 80 percent.[52] Although the WPA could not by law operate a closed shop, Hopkins clearly reiterated the administration's commitment to unions. He told Hallie Flanagan exactly how the FTP should regard unions. "We're for labor, first, last, and all the time," he said. "The WPA is labor – don't forget that. We're going to cooperate with all these unions."[53] It is no wonder that the FTP's future Congressional adversaries felt justified in accusing the agency of being an advocate of the radical labor movement.

While negotiations with the New York professional theatre establishment were frustrating, the challenges posed by the WPA bureaucracy seemed insurmountable. Roosevelt had committed to reemploy 3.5 million Americans and Congress had approved an appropriation of nearly 5 billion dollars to carry out this task. Consequently, WPA administrators had little sympathy for Flanagan's cultural agenda and had no patience for the lengthy interview and audition process that project coordinators demanded in order to protect the artistic integrity of their productions. By November 1935, the FTP had hired only a fraction of the 13 thousand workers it was supposed to employ. Tensions ran so high that WPA administrators threatened to close the project. From the very inception of the FTP, it was clear that the reemployment goals of the WPA could never be fully integrated into Flanagan's hopes for a national professional theatre.[54]

Although active FTP projects developed in Atlanta, Seattle, Hartford, Cincinnati, Detroit, and Boston, other communities in the United States did not have enough unemployed theatre professionals to merit the establishment of a fully developed FTP center. This situation was made more difficult by the WPA's insistence that workers could only be hired in the city where they had registered for relief. Thus, when the available jobs in Chicago were filled, qualified actors could not move to Dallas to obtain a position, even though the Dallas project might have desperately needed applicants. As a result, the vast majority of resources went to Los Angeles, Chicago, and especially New York – cities that possessed a large number of unemployed theatre professionals.

In spite of the bureaucratic maze erected by the WPA and the demands of the unions, the FTP had hired thousands of workers in over a dozen cities by the end of 1935. A year later it had produced over 200 shows in nearly 40 theatres in 22 cities.[55] However, the seeds of discord had been sown long before anyone could enjoy these successes. Shortly after her appointment, Flanagan met with Elmer Rice whom she had selected to direct the critically important New York project. One of their most pressing challenges was employment of thousands of eligible actors. One obvious solution was a "Living Newspaper," which would dramatize current events. Both Rice and Flanagan were familiar with this theatrical technique used by Socialists and Communists to spread information, education, and propaganda throughout central Europe. Basically, the American version of the Living Newspaper, like its European cousin, employed brief, staccato scenes structured like sketches in vaudeville or burlesque. Like newsreels, they had an invisible announcer or narrator titled the "Voice of the Living Newspaper." Scenery was sparse and consisted mostly of interlocking platforms, while slides were used to provide specific data. Scenes were accompanied by music and built to a comic or dramatic punchline that ended in a blackout. In this way productions could be rapidly altered to include a constant flow of information. Rice invited American Newspaper Guild Vice President Morris Watson to help supervise the 243 actors, journalists, and other theatrical personnel.[56]

The Living Newspaper attempted to educate and empower the audience by explaining a social problem and exhorting them to solve it. Yet, from its inception, this activist project generated opposition. The Living Newspaper's first production, *Ethiopia*, depicted the Italian invasion of that country. Two days before opening night, Jacob Baker, director of Federal One and Hopkins' assistant administrator, canceled the production, claiming that it would damage relations with Mussolini. Rice was livid. In protest he invited the press to a dress rehearsal and then promptly resigned. His statement to the press indicated that the chemistry created when art was combined with politics was unstable and extremely volatile. He accused Baker of creating a "smoke-screen to conceal the real issue – freedom of speech." He claimed that Baker had not made his decision until Rice told him of two upcoming FTP productions. The first was *Class of '29*, an exposé about the failure of government relief programs to end unemployment. The second was *South*, a Living Newspaper that depicted lynching, racial discrimination, and the plight of sharecroppers in the southern states. In Rice's words, the Living Newspaper would be "hitting the Democratic Party where it lived" and might cost the administration the support of southern Congressmen.[57] It would not be the last time this radical production unit would raise the ire of bureaucrats and politicians.

Although the Living Newspaper had to delay its premiere, other projects in New York moved forward and, by March 1936, thirty-six plays were in rehearsal. More than a dozen rehearsal halls had been rented and six theatres were in operation. The "Negro Unit," under the supervision of John Houseman, had already produced Orson Welles' "voodoo" *Macbeth* at the Lafayette Theatre in Harlem. Virgil Geddes headed the Experimental Theatre and was in the midst of rehearsing *Chalk Dust*, a bitter commentary on the educational system. A German group was producing Kleist's eighteenth-century comedy, *The Broken Jug*. The Poetic Theatre was staging W. H. Auden's *Dance of Death* and the Popular Price Theatre was readying its now famous production of T. S. Eliot's *Murder in the Cathedral*, as well as the controversial *Class of '29*.

While some of these productions stimulated mild controversy, the Living Newspaper once again created an enormous storm when its first fully realized production, *Triple-A-Plowed Under*, was criticized because it espoused Communism. It opened on March 14, 1936, and ran until May 2. In twenty-six scenes, it showed the plight of farmers between 1920 and 1936. However, it focused its political attack on those who opposed the Triple-A or Agricultural Adjustment Act, including the Supreme Court, which declared it unconstitutional. The Triple-A was a key feature of the first Roosevelt administration. It aimed to raise farm prices by paying farmers not to plant crops and, in the cases where crops had been planted, plow them under. The play featured 100 actors who played roles of farmers, urban workers, Supreme Court justices, and senators, as well as Thomas Jefferson, Al Smith, Secretary of Agriculture Henry Wallace, and Communist Party Secretary Earl Browder. The play closes with a scene in which characters from the previous scenes debate the situation. Just as it becomes clear that nothing will be accomplished by working through traditional political channels, the "Voice of the Living Newspaper" announces the latest news from the radical Farmer-Labor Party. The farmers and laborers then reach out to one another in a show of solidarity as the curtain falls.

Unlike *Ethiopia*, *Triple-A-Plowed Under* did not incite government censorship, but it nonetheless generated a great deal of bitter dissension. When the show went into rehearsal the Federal Theatre War Veterans' League set itself up as a watchdog group to combat Communist infiltration of the FTP. It took great umbrage at the presence of Browder's character, and claimed "government buildings, time and money are used to promote communistic propaganda." Letters of protest were sent to Hopkins and on opening night 300 members marched to the Biltmore Theatre to protest the play their employer had produced. During the performance, a veteran rose and shouted, "Let's all sing the 'Star Spangled Banner.'" Another loudly heckled Browder's speech. As Flanagan recalled: "The actors [were] full of misgivings, the audience full of tension and the lobby full of police."[58] Even Congressmen became involved. Robert Low Bacon (R-N.Y.) complained that the play was "pure and unadulterated politics," and called the FTP the "flower of American Brain Trust Communism."[59]

Triple-A polarized New York critics. Most conservative writers dismissed the production as New Deal propaganda. John Mason Brown concluded his review by wondering if *Triple-A* should not have been called a "'Living Editorial' for the Administration, rather than a 'Living Newspaper.'" and worried that such spectacles would incite people to rebel against the profit motive.[60] The Hearst-owned *New York Evening Journal*, a notorious anti-New Deal paper, called the production "a precious piece of Raw Deal propaganda ... the most outrageous misuse of taxpayers' money that the Roosevelt Administration has yet been guilty of." It also complained that *Triple-A* smelled of Communism and advocated class warfare.[61]

Leftist critics generally applauded *Triple-A* for daring to speak the truth and praised it for being an instructive and objective presentation of the facts. Some even went so far as to complain that the play was too objective and that theatre sponsored by a democratic government could never present vital political opinions for fear of offending some party or constituency:

> instead of containing too much propaganda, it contained too little. In other words, it was more like a newspaper than a play. It was far too impartial for drama ... The production of plays is not a democratic function.[62]

The fact that the Living Newspaper had unveiled a production that was open to so many interpretations indicated that it was a well-conceived piece of serious theatre. It had stimulated the type of discussion that Flanagan desired and proved that theatre that grappled with common, every-day problems could attract enthusiastic audiences. However, Flanagan's "people's theatre" generated serious concerns. It angered administration crit-ics who claimed that the New Deal, like Stalin's regime, had transformed theatre into a vast propaganda machine. The fact that Flanagan had vis-ited Russia and had lavishly praised its theatre only fueled this paranoiac speculation. Surely, Roosevelt, Hopkins, Flanagan, the WPA, and the FTP were engaged in a dark conspiracy that would use theatre to undermine the sacrosanct principles of free enterprise and private property.

Triple-A was followed by *1935*, an attempt to create the dramatic equiva-lent of an actual newspaper. Accordingly, it was composed of news stories, editorials, cartoons, and features that recounted the major events of that year. Although it contained some strident social commentary, the urgency of its message was buried amidst a heap of unrelated comic, satiric, and gen-eral interest skits. It ran for only eighteen nights, from May 12 to May 30. It was followed by arguably the most controversial of all Living Newspapers, *Injunction Granted*. Written by Arthur Arent and the Living Newspaper staff, it was directed by Joe Losey. In twenty-eight scenes lasting 90 min-utes, *Injunction Granted* begins in seventeenth-century England and ends in 1936 in the United States. It basically states that labor unions are the only hope of American workers. To prove its point it depicts attempted strikes, aborted labor legislation, court-ordered injunctions to break strikes, police attacks on strikers, and distortion of pro-union legislation by the courts. It is the last scene, however, that most clearly indicates that *Injunction Granted* is not concerned with journalistic objectivity. Scene twenty-eight ends with an inflammatory speech by an actor portraying John L. Lewis, president of the radical CIO, speaking to steel workers who are attempting to organize in the face of aggressive opposition. According to *Injunction Granted*, only labor unions can provide safety and prosperity for American workers.

Flanagan had seen some rehearsals, but was livid when she attended opening night. She claimed that Watson and Losey had made substantive changes that altered the objective nature of the production. She claimed it was "bad journalism and hysterical theatre" and told the two men that she would not permit the Federal Theatre to become a political pawn of the Democratic Party, the Republican Party, or the Communist Party.[63]

Many liberal and pro-labor critics praised the play, calling its treatment of the issues "biting and powerful." Although some found its treatment of the unions biased, it was praised as having a "vitality, an excitement and an interest seldom found in the more commercial Broadway offerings."[64] Mainstream critics, however, considered the play too radical. Brooks Atkinson said that it would brand the FTP as a political insurgent. He claimed: "It [is] intemperate in its point of view and hysterical in expression."[65] *Commonweal* described it as propaganda and, as such, it had "no place in a taxpayers' theater, and as art it has no place in a theatre at all."[66]

All the while, Congressional displeasure mounted as rumors about Communists in the FTP began to spread. By the summer of 1936, Congressman James J. Davis (R-Penn.) wondered aloud why the administration had permitted a woman, who was infatuated with the Soviet Union, to use taxpayers' money to attack the United States.[67] The controversy swirling around the FTP was further magnified in the fall of 1936 when it opened Sinclair Lewis' *It Can't Happen Here* simultaneously in twenty-two theatres in eighteen cities on October 27. Adapted from his 1935 novel of the same name, Lewis tells the story of a fascist takeover of the United States by President "Buzz" Windrip who is aided by a brutal paramilitary unit, the Corpos. His opponent is a small-town newspaper editor who leads the underground.[68]

While the topic of the play caused a significant amount of uneasiness, the date of the opening – less than two weeks before the 1936 presidential elections – prompted a heated discourse. The amount of interest in this project, as well as its multiple layers of interpretation by political commentators, theatre critics, and feature writers, was astonishing. Some observers claimed that it was New Deal propaganda intended to celebrate Roosevelt on the eve of the election; others thought it was aimed at his defeat. Some thought it proved that Communists controlled the FTP; others maintained that it was unconsciously fascist.[69]

It Can't Happen Here was undoubtedly the theatrical event of the year. By opening night, over 78,000 lines of copy had been devoted to the production. It was performed in Yiddish and Spanish, and adapted for FTP's Negro company in Seattle. Over 300,000 people saw the production in New York alone where it was performed over 300 times by four companies. Many of the local companies mounted touring productions that played in smaller cities. All in all, *It Can't Happen Here* played nationwide for more than 260 weeks, or the equivalent of 5 years.[70] Flanagan was justifiably proud when she wrote in *Arena* that hundreds of thousands had seen a play describe how dictatorships become established when there was a "sudden silencing of free voices:"

In producing that play the first government-sponsored theatre of the United States was doing what it could to keep alive "the free, inquiring, critical spirit" which is the center and core of a democracy.[71]

However, the FTP's very successful production of *It Can't Happen Here* was fraught with alarming implications for conservative ideologues. Whether or not the FTP intended to espouse any particular political doctrine or position was of little consequence. In addition to being one of the New Deal's most controversial programs, it had now become one of its most visible. It had generated unprecedented interest in a hypothetical political scenario. Might it not, if it chose, generate the same excitement for an actual event – or person? Although the Living Newspaper's stance tended to insult and agitate conservatives, its impact was more or less limited to New York. Now the FTP had created a nationwide network that could be used to duplicate and magnify any message it chose. For Flanagan, this capacity meant that the FTP could sow the seeds of a "free, inquiring, critical spirit" nationwide. For the opponents of the New Deal, it meant that the government was financing the transmission of radical messages that would inevitably bring about the downfall of the capitalist system.

Shortly after *It Can't Happen Here* closed at the Adelphi, the Living Newspaper unleashed another assault on the capitalist system. On February 23, 1937, it premiered its fourth "edition," *Power*, which targeted private utility companies and defended the Tennessee Valley Authority. *Power* was the most sophisticated Living Newspaper to date, combining statistics, projections, imaginative staging, and music. Its message was clear. Electric power belonged to the people, who were urged to use the political system to wrest it from the control of private utility companies. *Power* ran until July 10 in New York, playing to over 76,000 people. *Power* was one of Flanagan's favorite productions. She boasted that it proved that "our playwrights and playgoers cared about economic and social plays" and encouraged audiences "to understand the natural, social, and economic forces around them and to achieve through these forces a better life for more people."[72] Harry Hopkins was even more enthusiastic. After opening night he told the cast:

> I want this play and plays like it done from one end of the country to the other ... Now let's get one thing clear: you will take a lot of criticism on this play. People will say it's propaganda. Well, I say what of it? The big power companies have spent millions on propaganda for the utilities. It's about time that the consumer had a mouthpiece.[73]

Hopkins' prediction was accurate. *Commonweal*, *Stage*, *Time*, and *Herald-Tribune* called it propagandistic, but other critics were more liberal in their estimations. *Newsweek* hailed it as "theatre with a purpose." The *Times* called it "the most indignant and militant proletarian drama of the season," and *The Nation* praised it as "a unique piece of art... *Power* makes an impact on the mind comparable to the best polemic."[74]

Power may have been less inflammatory than the Living Newspaper's previous works, but other events had already conspired to weaken the FTP. The WPA itself was in grave danger. Buoyed by his overwhelming victory in 1936, the president introduced legislation to add four more justices to the Supreme Court to insure that New Deal legislation would not be declared unconstitutional. His plan exploded in his face and he lost credibility as well as significant Congressional support. On the defensive, the president sought to mollify conservatives by agreeing to cut spending as a means of balancing the budget. Upon hearing the president's conciliatory message, conservative Congressmen immediately targeted the WPA appropriation.

When rumors spread that Project One might be cut, FTP audiences and casts staged all-night sit-ins in theatres as a protest and 44th Street was filled with protesters. On May 27, 7,000 employees of the arts projects staged a one-day strike causing massive confusion.[75] But these strikes could not compare to those taking place in the Midwest. The CIO, assuming that the Roosevelt administration was powerful enough to support its union-organizing efforts, led massive strikes against General Motors and the steel industry including US Steel, Bethlehem, and Republic. However, the administration, hobbled by the "court packing" fiasco, sat on the sidelines as anti-labor forces mounted brutal counter-attacks against strikers. In the minds of many Americans, a revolution was afoot. The Roosevelt administration, with its pro-union policies, had greatly contributed to the current unrest, and the FTP, with its anti-capitalist living newspapers urging worker solidarity, was soon to be trapped in a web spun by Roosevelt's political foes.

In the midst of the most violent labor unrest ever experienced in the United States, the FTP production of *The Cradle Will Rock* started rehearsals. The story of a union-organizing drive taking place in the mythical Steel Town, USA, it echoed the real-life struggle of steel workers that was taking place in the Midwest. Written by Marc Blitzstein, directed by Orson Welles and produced by John Houseman, it was slated to premiere on June 16, 1937, at the Maxine Elliott Theatre. However, on June 12, Flanagan received a memorandum from the WPA. It stated that impending cuts and reorganization made it impossible to open any new exhibition, concert, or play before July 1, the beginning of the new fiscal year.[76] It was obvious that WPA officials feared that *Cradle*'s aggressive pro-labor message combined with the one day walk-out staged by FTP employees would further prejudice lawmakers, causing them to reduce the WPA funding even more dramatically. Welles, along with Archibald MacLeish, flew to Washington on the 13th to meet with WPA officials and, in a particularly sharp exchange, Welles informed Hopkins' assistant that if *Cradle* failed to open as scheduled, he and Houseman would produce it privately. The threat had little impact and Welles flew back to New York. The next day both men started telephoning everyone they knew telling them that if they wanted to see *Cradle*, they had better come to that evening's dress rehearsal.[77]

On June 15, WPA police took charge of the Maxine Elliott Theatre with orders not to allow government property to be used or removed. Welles, Houseman, and Blitzstein turned the ladies' dressing room into a makeshift office and the search for a vacant theatre began. As if matters needed to be made worse, the musicians' union and Actors' Equity announced that if Welles and Houseman independently produced *Cradle*, their members would have to sign new contracts and be paid union scale, a financial impossibility. At this point, it was decided to forgo an orchestra. Blitzstein would play the score on a piano played on a bare stage. Welles and Houseman assured the actors that they could sing their roles from their seats in the auditorium. After all, Equity had only forbidden them to appear "on stage." On the evening of the 16th, ticket holders gathered outside the theatre and began to grow restless. Some of the cast went out to entertain them and reassure them the show would take place – somewhere. According to Houseman, it was 7:20 when the "miracle" occurred. An unidentified theatre real-estate broker who had spent the entire day on the phone informed them that the Venice Theatre was available. They informed the cast, many of whom were still unsure about disobeying their union, and emerged from the Maxine Elliott. They told the crowd that the show would take place, twenty-one blocks up Seventh Avenue and the now famous parade of cast, crew, and audience to the Venice Theatre commenced.[78]

By the time the entourage arrived, it numbered more than 2,500 and, in defiance of the fire code, filled the aisles when all the seats were taken. Curtain was postponed until 9:00. At 9:01 Welles and Houseman walked onto the stage and introduced Marc Blitzstein to the audience. The composer then took his seat at an ill-tuned upright piano. One by one the actors began to sing their roles and move through the auditorium. A primitive hand-held spotlight illuminated Blitzstein and a few musicians defied their union and accompanied the composer. Houseman's description of the audience's response is worth noting:

> There were no "bugles, drums and fifes" that night – only Marc's pounding of an untuned piano before a wrinkled backdrop... As the curtain fell and the actors started to go back to their seats, there was a second's silence – then all hell broke loose. It was a glamorous evening and the cheering and applause lasted so long that the stagehands demanded an hour's overtime – which we gladly paid.[79]

Houseman gleefully announced that *Cradle* would continue to run. The show would have eleven more performances. Then the cast would return to the Maxine Elliott where, under WPA regulations that limited absences to twelve days, the FTP would have to take them back.[80]

Welles and Houseman "officially" opened *The Cradle Will Rock* under the banner of the Mercury Theatre in December 1937. Although the emotional frenzy of June 16 could not be repeated, critics still praised its energy and commitment. The *Sun* said it was an "angry, frequently effective musical satire, done barely on a bare stage to the music of a piano which, like the production itself, is stripped to its essential anatomy."[81] Brooks Atkinson described it as "the best thing militant labor has put into the theatre yet... What *Waiting for Lefty* was to the dramatic stage, *The Cradle Will Rock* is to the stage of the labor battle song."[82] Stark Young, never a fan of workers' theatre because of its lack of subtlety, was full of praise:

> In the freedom, bright courage and innovation that Mr. Blitzstein and his director, Mr. Orson Welles, have imparted to this venture, in which all sorts of power and beauty appear, partly achieved now, partly as prospects for the future – we may feel high hopes... it is... a living theatre thing; they are rarely found.[83]

Cradle took on a life of its own – and therein lay the danger. Although the FTP had officially washed its hands of *Cradle*, it had nonetheless provided the initial funding for the project and was unable to suppress it. Once again, theatre that advocated economic solutions to social problems that challenged the capitalist ideology had generated immense interest. Moreover, Welles, and Houseman had proven that such dramas could be commercially successful. Clearly, the FTP, while attempting to provide a forum for previously unheard American voices, had transformed itself from an anemic producer of obscure plays into a powerful advocate for social transformation.

Flanagan's vision of a popular activist drama reached its apogee with the final Living Newspaper production, *One-Third of a Nation*, which opened at the Adelphi Theatre in New York on January 17 and ran until October 22, 1938. It was seen by nearly 220,000 people and was adapted by FTP companies in Cincinnati, Seattle, New Orleans, Detroit, Portland, Philadelphia, Hartford, and San Francisco. Basically, *Nation* examines the lack of affordable housing in New York from 1605 until 1937 and supports public housing. Unlike other Living Newspapers, however, it does not attack capitalism. In it, the Little Man, a generic citizen, is given a history lesson regarding land grants, real estate development, land speculation, and tenement housing legislation. Eventually, he advocates government assistance as the common person's only means of obtaining decent, safe housing and urges collective action on the part of the spectators if they want to solve the problem. In spite of the fact that it did not attack political parties or individuals, *Nation* still managed to irk several members of the Senate who objected to being represented on stage. Specifically, Senators Bailey of North Carolina and Andrews of Florida castigated the FTP for quoting their opposition to federal housing. Senator Andrews was particularly irate and demanded the name, address, and salary of every actor, writer, and producer of the play.[84]

Congressional retaliation

While the FTP was pursuing its goals for a populist theatre, Congress was focused on internal political subversion. During the early thirties there existed a palpable fear that foreign subversives were bent on destroying American democratic institutions. From a distance of over sixty years, it is tempting to dismiss these concerns as another instance of American xenophobia. Yet Communists and Fascists openly preached their messages. Radicals were in control of many trade unions and pro-Hitler sympathizers staged rallies and operated youth camps. Many Congressmen began to panic.

One of the most vocal advocates of Congressional action was Samuel Dickstein (D-N.Y.), an aggressive and often abrasive representative. His district ran along the East River from Chatam Square to East Houston and was home to tens of thousands of Eastern European Jewish immigrants. During the early thirties, Dickstein was concerned that anti-Semitism was on the rise in New York and the nation. After participating on several committees that investigated subversion, he introduced a bill in April 1937 to give Congress the authority to investigate any organization that distributed "slanderous or libelous un-American propaganda."[85] Yet the Dickstein bill, which was aimed at "Nazi rats, spies and agents," was soundly defeated. Liberals felt that such investigations would target Communists, and Congressional conservatives would not support the "Jew, Dickstein."[86]

Ironically, the Dickstein initiative was resuscitated by Martin Dies, an ambitious Congressman from east Texas. Dies' father had represented the same district from 1909 to 1919. Dies, Sr. mistrusted immigrants, despised Bolsheviks, and broke with Wilson over the League of Nations. Dies initially proclaimed himself a New Dealer and cruised into office on the coattails of Franklin Roosevelt in 1932, but he quickly shed his liberal skin. The younger Dies was fond of quoting his father, displayed a suspicion of big cities, big capital, and big government, and perennially proposed to deport foreign nationals. Dies desperately wanted to head a Congressional committee. He had noted that colleagues such as La Follette, McCormack, and Fish had attracted significant national attention and assumed that he could garner similar accolades. Supported by majority leader Sam Rayburn and Vice President John Nance Garner, both Texans, and House speaker William Bankhead, Dies introduced a virtual carbon copy of Dickstein's bill calling for Congressional investigation of subversives. Yet the new anti-Roosevelt coalition of Republicans and southern Democrats that began to form in 1937 trusted the conservative Dies far more than the liberal Dickstein. Ironically, the Dies/Dickstein bill was greatly aided by its co-sponsor from New York, who lobbied his liberal colleagues. The measure establishing the House Committee on Un-American Activities (HUAC) was passed by a vote of 191 to 41 in May 1938.[87]

The composition of the first committee must have been a severe blow to Dickstein. Dies was named chairman and the bill's co-sponsor was omitted from the roster. The remaining Democrats included John Dempsey (D-N. Mex.) and Arthur D. Haley, (D-Mass.), both lukewarm New Dealers, and Joe Starnes of (D-Ala.) and Harold Mosier (D-Ohio), both conservatives. The two Republicans, Noah Mason of Illinois and J. Parnell Thomas of New Jersey, were ardent opponents of Roosevelt.[88]

While the authorizing legislation charged HUAC with investigating a broad spectrum of political subversion in the United States, its members subtly altered that mandate. Within months of its inception, it became clear that the committee cared less about unearthing subversion than with using its investigative powers to wound the Roosevelt administration by linking it with radicals. The committee, while too small to take on the entire New Deal, targeted the WPA, especially Federal One and attempted to convict the president of advancing the socialist agenda through national arts programs. If he were able to achieve this goal, he would not only catapult himself into the national spotlight, he would also advance the presidential aspirations of his chief mentor, Vice President Garner. If Roosevelt decided not to run for a third term in 1940, Garner would be the likely Democratic candidate. By linking the administration to radicals, Dies just might be able to embarrass the president enough to prevent him from running. Such a coup could have increased his political stock exponentially.[89]

Of course, Dies asserted that the Committee would investigate Fascist as well as Communist subversion. He even announced that he would begin an investigation into pro-German propagandist, George Sylvester Viereck, who was ready to embark upon a journey to visit Hitler. Viereck claimed that he was only going to Germany to pay his respects to the former Kaiser and Dies dropped the investigation. On the other hand, J. Parnell Thomas, who could discern a Communist plot in the fall of a sparrow, left no doubt whom he would target. Even before hearings began, he demanded "a thorough cleaning of the Federal Theatre Project." The FTP, he claimed, "has become part and parcel of the Communist Party, spreading its radical theories through its stage productions."[90]

The Committee began hearings on August 12, 1938. On the 16th, Walter S. Steele, chairman of the American Coalition Committee on National Security, which he claimed represented 114 patriotic organizations, set the tone for the majority of the pre-war hearings. He gave nearly 200 pages of spoken testimony and another 200 pages of written reports, all of which were entered into the record. In them, he purported to identify every Communist and leftist organization in the United States as well as their leaders. His list included all of the controversial groups such as the American Civil Liberties Union (ACLU), the CIO and its member unions, and most workers' organizations. He also produced an extensive roster of pacifist and anti-Fascist groups, which, he claimed, were well intentioned, but were being manipulated by Moscow. Among these "fellow travelers" were the American and World Youth Congresses and their supporters, the American Farm Bureau Federation, National Council of Jewish Juniors, Girl Scouts of America, the League of Nations Association, National Council of Methodist Youth, American Jewish Congress, and Junior Hadassah, to name but a few of the suspects.[91]

However, his most comprehensive list was one that included virtually every playwright, director, and producer who had even tenuously engaged in or supported workers theatre. Several of those on his list, such as Elmer Rice, Clifford Odets, John Howard Lawson, Mordecai Gorelik, Michael Gold, Herbert Kline, and Paul Robeson, were well known for their support of radical theatre. Others were included because they may have contributed an article to *New Theatre* or worked against censorship. No matter. People like Brooks Atkinson, Lee Strasberg, Walter Pritchard Eaton, Sidney Howard, Robert Sherwood, Dorothy Patton, Claire Stifton, Molly Day Thatcher, and, of course, Hallie Flanagan were all suspect. And their names were duly entered into the record. In the future, any organization or individual who was even remotely connected with progressive theatre, literature, art, music, film or dance would be deemed a subversive.[92]

The Committee began to focus on the FTP specifically on August 19 when Hazel Huffman took the stand. She identified herself as a representative of the Committee of Relief Status Theatrical Employees of the Federal Theatre Project. When Representative Starnes asked the witness the purpose of her testimony, Representative Thomas asked that he might be allowed to answer for her. Dies agreed and Thomas announced: "The purpose of this testimony is to show the communistic activities in the Federal Theatre Project."[93] She then proceeded to regale the Committee with an array of facts, innuendos and suppositions that created the impression that the FTP was a hive of Communist activity. She claimed that the Workers' Alliance dominated the FTP and provided ample "evidence" concerning Flanagan's "active participation and interest in things communistic." She introduced into the record lines from *Can You Hear Their Voices?* that were "communistic," and cited passages from Flanagan's book that praised Soviet theatre. She then pointed out that Flanagan had named Elmer Rice, a known radical playwright to head the New York unit, complained that she persecuted the Veterans' League and insisted that she had approved of the political excesses of the Living Newspaper. While she did not actually accuse Flanagan of being a card-carrying member of the Communist Party, she assured the Committee:

> Mrs. Flanagan was an active participant in Communistic activity, and that her Communistic sympathies, tendencies, and methods of organization are being used in the Federal Theatre Project at the present time, to the detriment of the workers and in violation of the act of Congress.[94]

From that point on, the Committee was off and running and it invited testimony from anyone who had information regarding un-American activities of the FTP. Scores of disgruntled former employees emerged to give incriminating testimony. Francis Verdi explained that he had been hired by Equity and Flanagan to investigate charges that less-qualified members of the Workers' Alliance had kept their jobs during the 1937 summer lay-offs while more experienced actors and stagehands were fired. He told the Committee that he was immediately fired when his report proved the complaint was valid.[95] Charles Walton, a former stage manager, testified that Communist literature was routinely sold and distributed and that he had been passed over for directing jobs because he was not a member of the Workers' Alliance. He also claimed that George Kondolf, director of the New York City project, had confessed that "his hands were tied" by New York unions.[96] Actors testified that FTP employees were paid for marching in a May Day parade, while another former employee claimed that a superior had "urged her to go out with a Negro."[97]

None of the allegations were verified for accuracy and FTP staff members, who had gathered data that refuted these charges, were not called to testify. Still WPA officials did not respond. Finally, Flanagan wrote to Dies asking him to permit her and the six regional directors to cooperate with the Committee by clarifying the inaccurate, biased, and damaging testimony they had heard. Her letter was ignored. She wrote a second time pleading that thousands of jobs were at stake. Still Dies did not reply. Emmet Lavery, director of the National Service Bureau, which approved plays, wrote a passionate letter to Dies telling him that he was a Catholic and had never approved a Communist play for production. This letter, like the others, went unanswered. In the meantime, Representative Thomas told *Herald-Tribune* readers, "practically every play was clear unadulterated propaganda." Lavery invited Thomas to debate the allegation, play by play. That challenge, like all the others, went unanswered.[98]

Finally, in early December the Committee invited Hallie Flanagan and Henry Alsberg, head of the Federal Writers' Project, which was also under attack, to testify. Alsberg told the Committee that there had been trouble with radicals in the past and that he had threatened to shut down the entire project if there were any more sit-down strikes. Apparently, his straightforward responses mollified the Committee and he was excused. Such was not the case with Hallie Flanagan. She brought with her reams of statistics about the composition of audiences, cost of admission, and the number of performances. She attached to that a complete plot synopsis of each play the FTP had performed. She also included a sworn statement that no FTP policy-making administrator was a Communist and that the majority of FTP employees were members of theatre unions that forbade their members from joining the Workers' Alliance.[99] All of her preparation, while it was impressive, was of little interest to the Committee. They were far more interested in Hallie Flanagan – the person – and could barely contain their desire to question her about her exploits. The *Times* reported that she was "heckled" by Committee members, whose "questions tumbled out so fast that sometimes she had to juggle with two or three at a time and was continually cut off from completing her sentences."[100] Had she privileged art over relief? Had she advocated the establishment of a national theatre? Had she used her Guggenheim Fellowship to travel to Russia? Had she written favorably about Russian theatre? Had she visited Russia again? Did she still admire Russian theatre?[101]

The questioning then focused on her book *Shifting Scenes* and "A Theatre Is Born," an article she wrote for *Theatre Arts Monthly* in November 1931, both of which had been extensively quoted by Huffman during her testimony. Starnes led the questioning. Had she not written that workers' theatres had been born in factories and mines and that they were intended to "create a national culture by and for the working class." Flanagan answered that she had, but that she was reporting on the movement for *Theatre Arts Monthly*. She reminded the representative that she was teaching at Vassar College at the time, that she had never established a workers' theatre, and that these groups had nothing to do with the FTP. Starnes would not relent. He was determined to have Flanagan admit that she either participated in or believed in the tenets advanced by radical workers' theatres. He asked whether Flanagan believed that theatre was a "weapon for teaching class consciousness" and that it should "stress strikes and anti-lynching and class consciousness." Once again, she reminded Starnes that she had been quoting the leaders of the workers' theatre movement, not expressing her own beliefs. "The theatre was not born through me," she protested.[102]

Starnes, however, was obsessed with connecting Flanagan to Communism, and once again returned to her *Theatre Arts* article. It was at this point that he received his first theatre history lesson:

MR. STARNES: You are quoting from Marlowe. Is he a Communist?
MRS. FLANAGAN: I am sorry I was quoting from Christopher Marlowe.
MR. STARNES: Tell us who Marlowe is, so we can get the proper reference, because that is all we want to do.
MRS. FLANAGAN: Put in the record, that he was the greatest dramatist in the period of Shakespeare, immediately preceding Shakespeare.
MR. STARNES: Put in the record, because the charge has been made that this article of yours is completely communistic, and we want to help you.
MRS. FLANAGAN: Thank you. That statement will go in the record.

MR. STARNES: Of course, we had what some people call Communists back in the days of the Greek theater.

MRS. FLANAGAN: Quite true.

MR. STARNES: And I believe Mr. Euripides was guilty of teaching class-consciousness also, wasn't he?

MRS. FLANAGAN: I believe that was alleged against all the Greek playwrights.

MR. STARNES: So we cannot say when it began.

MRS. FLANAGAN: Wasn't it alleged also of Gibson and against practically every great dramatist?

MR. STARNES: I think so. All right.[103]

Clearly, the Committee had taken Walter Steele's message during those early hearings quite literally. Anyone, who, at any time, criticized the established power structure, is either a Communist or a fellow traveler. As far as Representative Starnes was concerned, even Euripides was suspect.

Throughout the approximately three hours of testimony, Hallie Flanagan was unflappable. She retained her composure and carefully rebutted even the most artful and incriminating questions. When Dies called for a recess, she replied: "If your Committee isn't convinced that neither I nor the Federal Theatre Project is communistic, I want to come back this afternoon." Representative Thomas laughed, and replied: "We don't want you back. You're a tough witness and we're all worn out." He promised her that her brief, which contained a detailed refutation of all charges, would be published. When the Committee reconvened, Dies did not recall Flanagan, nor did he introduce her brief into the record. WPA officials promised that they would distribute the brief to every senator and representative. No member of Congress ever received a copy of the brief.[104] The Committee filed its report with the House of Representatives on January 3, 1939. Although the Federal Writers' Project was criticized, the Committee's one paragraph indictment of the FTP proved to be far more incriminating:

> We are convinced that a rather large number of the employees on the Federal Theatre Project are either members of the Communist Party or are sympathetic with the Communist Party. It is also clear that certain employees felt under compulsion to join the Workers' Alliance in order to retain their jobs.[105]

The Dies Report wounded the FTP, but did not kill it. That was the job of the House Subcommittee on Appropriations (HSA). By January 1939, Roosevelt and the New Deal were in desperate straits. On January 5, the president requested a supplemental appropriation of $875 million to fund relief programs. Clifton Woodrum (D-Va.) Chairman of the HSA led the fight for the anti-Roosevelt forces. He submitted a committee report that urged Congress to cut the deficit by slashing $150 million from the president's request. The full House agreed with Woodrum. On the following day it passed a Deficit Reduction Bill appropriating only $725 million for relief. The *New York Times* labeled it "open rebellion against the Administration."[106] Woodrum called it "a start on the road to lower appropriations."[107] When an amendment calling for the restoration of $22 million for the Arts Projects was introduced, it was defeated with the "most deafening chorus of 'noes' the House Chamber... had heard in years."[108]

Woodrum continued his assault on the WPA and the FTP throughout the spring of 1939. In hearing after hearing he allowed a parade of witnesses to accuse Flanagan and her colleagues of a litany of malfeasances that he never corroborated. FTP administrators were accused of competing with professional producers, supplementing their salaries by skimming money from ticket sales, using the remainder of the revenue to support Communist causes, and allowing the Workers' Alliance to determine who would and would not be hired by the arts projects.[109]

Although some members of the HSA accused fellow committee members of treating gossip and innuendo as fact, Woodrum's faction won out.[110] On June 12, HSA unveiled its version of the 1940 relief bill, which completely eliminated the federal appropriation for the FTP.[111] On June 16, the full House adopted HSA's recommendations that, in the name of curbing subversives, abolished the FTP.

FTP supporters now turned their attention to the Senate, which could still save the embattled agency. In New York, project employees stationed themselves at street corners and, after explaining that they were acting on their own time, solicited signatures on petitions that pleaded for the continuance of the FTP. Radio commentators denounced the House vote as "fascism at its worst – trial without a jury, trial by prejudice" and pleaded with the Senate to reverse the decision.[112] The Federated Arts Unions representing fourteen AFL (American Federation of Labor) and CIO. organizations pledged its support.[113] Telegrams from Eddie Cantor, Helen Hayes, Lee Shubert, Burgess Meredith, Richard Rodgers, George Abbott, Moss Hart, Clifford Odets, and Harold Clurman urged senators to renew the FTP's appropriation.[114] Stage and screen actress Tallulah Bankhead, whose father was speaker of the House and whose uncle was a senator from Alabama, led a formidable delegation into the Senate Finance Committee hearings. She pleaded: "I ask you from the bottom of my heart not to deprive these people of the chance to hold up their heads with the dignity and self-respect which is the badge of every American."[115]

The Senate Sub-Committee on Appropriations voted to restore some funding to the FTP but did not state an exact amount. The full Senate, after heated debate, passed the measure. The bill then proceeded to a joint House/Senate Appropriations Committee on June 29, 1939, but Congressman Woodrum, who represented the House, maintained that he was going to put the government out of show business. Time was on his side. With the current fiscal year due to end at midnight the following day, Senators were not about to risk the jobs of over 2.5 million WPA employees because of 8,000 FTP workers. They accepted Woodrum's demands and both houses passed the bill. The president faced a lose/lose situation. If he vetoed the measure, the entire WPA would be lost. If he signed the measure, the Federal Theatre Project would cease to exist. He chose the latter course. In a caustic rebuke of the House he said, "[This bill] singles out a special group of professional people for a denial of work in their profession. It is discrimination of the worst type."[116]

The passage of the 1940 Appropriations Bill was a stunning victory for conservative lawmakers. The *Washington Post* called it a "fundamental victory for House conservatives" and a *Newsweek*'s headline read "Rebellious Congress Stymies Pet Plans of the President."[117] The *New York Times* was more subdued in its assessment and devoted two articles to the demise of the Federal Theatre Project. One summarized the short life of the project and described it as having "provided the American public with one lively controversy after another."[118] The second was a poignant description of audience reaction to the final performances of the three FTP shows currently running on Broadway. Even the usually conservative theatre critic of the *Catholic World* mourned its loss, calling it "the finish of one of the most stimulating and educational of social experiments [which contained] . . . the germ of many great ideas for the future."[119]

For her part, Flanagan remained professional to the very last day of her tenure. She contacted regional directors, urged them to remain level-headed, and ordered them to organize all FTP records so that they could be archived in an orderly manner. She did not, however, disappear quietly. Although she refrained from publicly denouncing Congressmen whom she held responsible for the cancellation of the project, she was a frequent contributor to literary magazines and repeatedly made the case that the project had been unjustly condemned. She devoted considerable time to writing *Arena*, her personal history of the Federal Theatre. In it, she reiterated her commitment to the concept of a vigorous, provocative theatre dedicated to social change:

> Thus, Federal Theatre ended as it had begun, with fearless presentation of problems touching American life. If this first government theatre in our country had been less alive, it might have lived longer. But I do not believe anyone who worked on it regrets that it stood from first to last against reaction, against prejudice, against racial, religious, and political intolerance; it fought for a more dramatic statement and a better understanding of the great forces of our life today; it fought for a free theatre as one of the many expressions of a civilized, informed, and vigorous life.[120]

Obviously, Flanagan was an idealist who believed that theatre possessed the power to bring about profound social transformation. She failed to grasp, however, that the majority of any population fears innovation and will defend its laws, traditions, and codes with a ferocity that admits no ethical or moral limits. Flanagan always attested to the capacity of theatre to initiate discussion and inquiry. Yet she seemed to have overlooked its Dionysian power to instigate volatile eruptions within the body politic, an attribute of theatre that her adversaries intuitively comprehended. Although the Federal Theatre Project had not concocted the radical chemistry of the 1930s, its major projects echoed that era's populist idealism. And, like any movement that advocated deviation from the economic, religious, social, political, or sexual status quo, it was targeted for public humiliation and annihilation.

Although the FTP had been eradicated, Congressmen still found reasons to attack theatre. On July 8, 1940, Representative William T. Lambertson, a Kansas Republican, claimed that Communists dominated theatrical unions. As a member of the House Appropriations Committee, he had voted to deny funding to the FTP the previous year, but still felt that New York theatre was a hotbed of subversion. He said: "When the WPA theatre project was killed last year largely because of serious penetration by Communists, Congress assumed that the members of the profession would undertake a house-cleaning. Instead there has been a growing, rather than a diminishing trend of communistic influence in the theatre." He then proceeded to accuse seven members of Equity's governing council – Sam Jaffee, Phillip Loeb, Emily Marsh, Hiram Sherman, Leroy MacLean, Edith Van Cleve, and Alan Hewitt – of belonging to the Communist Party.[121] He also accused George Heller, Executive Secretary of the Radio Actors' Guild, and Hoyt Haddock, Executive Secretary of the American Guild of Variety Artists, of Communist affiliation. The response to his charges was immediate and indignant. Equity maintained that neither the council nor the membership had ever been "dominated or controlled by Communists" and demanded that Lambertson submit the source of his information. After having denied any Communist affiliation, Heller asserted: "It is a scandalous condition that permits any one to issue irresponsible statements that damage the reputation of innocent citizens without at least giving such persons a fair chance to disprove scurrilous allegations."[122] Three days later, Lambertson provided his proof. The individuals he accused had belonged to the American Committee for Democracy, and Intellectual Freedom, the National Emergency Conference for Democratic Rights, the American League for Peace and Democracy, or the Theatre Arts Committee, all of which had been indicted by the Dies Committee as front organizations for the Communist Party.[123] Equity demanded more specific proof. It even requested Dies to conduct hearings on the matter. Of course, neither Dies nor Lambertson replied. In spite of the absence of any concrete evidence, these accusations had a profound effect. After what had happened to the Federal Theatre Project, even groundless charges were enough to strike terror into the souls of those accused of being a Communist. As a result, Equity, as well as other entertainment unions, enlisted in the anti-Communist brigade. For one, Equity proclaimed that Communism was "antagonistic to the purposes of Equity" and would not permit party members to hold elected office.

The frightening forties

The United States' entrance into World War II and its alliance with the Soviet Union considerably reduced the volume of the anti-Communist rhetoric, but did not silence it. Dies kept up a constant drumbeat, and over the course of the next four years he, with the support of fellow conservatives, merged anti-administration rancor with Communist paranoia to the extent that they were virtually indistinguishable from one another. Red baiting intensified during the 1944 presidential campaign during which Republicans equated FDR, labor, and communism. When Roosevelt commuted the jail term of Communist Party Secretary Earl Browder, the rhetoric intensified. GOP presidential nominee Thomas E. Dewey said: "In Russia, a Communist is a man who supports his Government. In America, a Communist supports the fourth term so our form of government may be more easily changed." Clearly, the president's opponents meant to characterize his administration as the antithesis of the "American form of government." After the war, FDR's political and ideological enemies would indict virtually any-one who spoke in favor of change, diversity, or innovation as a subversive.[124]

By the time the shooting stopped in 1945, the United States had emerged as the most powerful nation on earth. Western Europe was a mass of rubble and the Soviet Union was devastated and bankrupt. Inexplicably, however, a collective amnesia gripped the citizenry of the United States. It wiped out all sense of military and economic superiority and in its place a profound paranoia emerged.

The media trumpeted that the United States was encircled by Communists in Europe and Asia and had been betrayed from within. A reactionary Congress responded accordingly. Representative John E. Rankin (D-Miss.), a noted hater of Jews and African Americans, led the charge. On January 3, during a routine reading of a resolution that would reestablish the rules un-der which the House operated, he moved to amend the resolution to include the House Un-American Activities Committee in the list of standing com-mittees. Never before had a representative moved to amend the rules before they were adopted, but Rankin had read the mood of the nation. Commu-nism was the major concern of Americans and the House would not dare to defeat a motion that was aimed at opposing Communism. The measure was overwhelmingly approved, and HUAC became a standing committee of the House of Representatives. Thus, the Dies Committee, which had been arguably the most effective anti-New Deal weapon, was given new life. As *Newsweek* noted, the House was "taking out insurance against the future."[125]

When the Republican Party gained control of the House in the 1946 mid-term elections, the leadership of HUAC passed into the hands of J. Parnell Thomas the New Jersey Republican, who in 1938 claimed that the FTP was awash with Communists. However, Rankin and former chairman Wood remained on the Committee. Democrats J. Hardin Peterson of Florida and Herbert Bonner of North Carolina joined them. The Republican contingent included Karl Mundt of South Dakota, John McDowell of Pennsylvania, John Vail of Illinois, and future president Richard Nixon of California. The Committee quickly became the advance guard of the anti-Communist crusade in the United States.

The Committee might have wreaked less havoc had it not been for President Truman's willing cooperation. Anxious to prove that he, too, wanted to protect the United States from internal subversion, he signed Executive Order 9835 on March 25, 1947, and launched the Federal Em-ployees Loyalty Program. By so doing, he ordered the federal government to dismiss any employee who either belonged to or was "sympathetically associated" with any organization listed by the Attorney General as a subversive organization. With the stroke of a pen he sowed the seeds of the Red Scare of the 1950s. The list, itself a grab bag of left-wing political organizations and peace groups, was quickly adopted by state and local governments, defense contractors, and schools. It became a qualifying test for passports, occupancy of federal housing, and tax exemptions. Within the next few years, it was transmuted into the yardstick by which American loyalty was measured.[126]

Armed with President Truman's formal admission that Communism threatened the security of the United States, HUAC began a series of hearings that was intended to rid the nation of subversives. Long before the war, conservative Congressmen were convinced that Hollywood was awash with Communists, and shortly after peace was established they focused their energies on the film industry. Beginning in September 1947, Chairman Thomas began to investigate Communist influence in Hollywood. One of its first targets was the German composer and former Brecht colleague, Hanns Eisler, whom Robert Stripling, chief investigator for the Committee, accused of being the Karl Marx of music. The Committee questioned him about the political content of the songs he had written during the 1930s, asked if he had been a member of the Communist Party and wanted to know if he had written lyrics for his movie scores. He admitted that his early work had been propagandistic, but explained that it had been composed in a different time and place. He also conceded that he had applied to become a member of the party, but changed his mind. He promised the members that he was no longer a political artist and had not injected any radical ideology into his music. Apparently, Eisler convinced the Congressmen that he was not attempting to topple the American system by injecting films with propagandistic melodies. But the Committee knew that indicting a nervous German composer would hardly prove that Communism had invaded Hollywood. They needed bigger fish to fry if the film industry was to be brought to its knees.[127]

On October 20, 1947, the Committee initiated a series of hearings featuring an array of Hollywood notables that attracted national media attention. As the cameras flashed, the Congressmen quizzed Ronald Reagan, Ayn Rand, Adolphe Menjou, Jack Warner, Walt Disney, Gary Cooper, Robert Montgomery, George Murphy, screenwriter Murray Ryskind, and Mrs. Lila Rogers – Ginger's mother – about Communist infiltration of the film industry. Warner extolled his own patriotism and boasted of firing many employees who advanced un-American ideals. Ryskind told of the Communist influence in the Screen Writers' Guild and Montgomery, Murphy, and Reagan described their activities in the Screen Actors' Guild. The most damaging witnesses were Rand and Menjou who both accused the industry of naively producing films that served to advance the Communist agenda. The Communist message, they asserted, was subtle and often craftily hidden behind an innocent façade and they warned the Committee to be extremely vigilant. The remaining witnesses readily admitted that there were many Communists in Hollywood, but asserted that very few films were propagandistic.[128] Unfortunately, many of these "friendlies," as they came to be known, carelessly tossed off names of individuals whom they believed to be Communists, and it was from this testimony that a list of nineteen "unfriendly" witnesses was assembled. It was the first list that emerged from the hearings, but it would certainly not be the last.

The first of the "unfriendlies" was John Howard Lawson, one of the most radical playwrights of the 1930s and generally regarded as the "Grand Old Man of Hollywood Communism." He took the stand on October 27, 1947, and was indignant and truculent. He insisted upon reading an opening statement, a privilege that was denied to him. He then began to invoke the First rather than the Fifth Amendment. When asked if he had held any office in the Screen Writers' Guild, what films he had written, or whether he had belonged to the Communist Party, he refused to answer, stating that these questions violated freedom of press and communication. He claimed that the Committee, not he, was on trial before the American people. He then accused the Congressmen of attempting to destroy the Bill of Rights. Lawson was ordered to be removed from the witness stand and was later charged with contempt of Congress.[129]

The Committee called ten more witnesses from the "unfriendly" list. They were Albert Maltz, Dalton Trumbo, Ring Lardner, Jr., Edward Dmytryk, Alvah Bessie, Samuel Ornitz, Herbert Biberman, Adrian Scott, Lester Cole, and Bertolt Brecht. When Brecht took the stand on October 30, the Committee seemed more interested in his activities in the 1930s in Germany than in any of his activities in the United States. Brecht assured the Congressmen that his work in Germany was part of a larger anti-Hitler movement and not intended to promote Communism. The Committee seemed convinced by Brecht's version of his life. Chairman Thomas even admitted that he was a much more cooperative witness than any of the other "unfriendlies" who had been subpoenaed.[130] It is also possible that the Committee was much more interested in prominent American screen writers than in a German émigré playwright whose work they did not understand. For whatever reason, the Committee excused Brecht.

Such was not the fate of the nine other "unfriendly" witnesses the Committee called. Like Lawson, they used the hearings to defame the Committee, claiming that the Bill of Rights prohibited the Congressmen from inquiring into their political or religious affiliations. And, like Lawson, each was cited for contempt of Congress. The House upheld the charges 346 to 17 and all were subsequently jailed. For reasons unknown, Thomas suspended the hearings after the "Hollywood Ten" had testified, and the remaining "unfriendlies" were never called. The chairman, however, sounded an ominous note. He warned Hollywood "to clean its own house and not wait for public opinion to force it [Congress] to do so."[131]

The studios took Thomas' warning to heart. The publicity surrounding the "Hollywood Ten" was the type that neither the moguls nor their east coast investors desired. On November 24, fifty members of the Motion Picture Association of America, the Association of Motion Picture Producers, and the Society of Independent Motion Picture Producers met at Manhattan's Waldorf-Astoria and reached a decision that sent shockwaves through the entertainment industry. They voted to discharge the "Hollywood Ten" because "their actions had been a disservice to their employers and have impaired their usefulness to the industry." More importantly, the studios pledged that they would not "knowingly employ a Communist or a member of any party or group which advocates the overthrow of the Government of the United States." After noting that the law of the land did not sanction their decision, the executives urged Congress "to enact legislation to assist American industry to rid itself of subversive, disloyal elements."[132] Although HUAC had called attention to the alleged subversives working in film, it was the studio executives themselves who meted out the punishment. They not only banished Communists from the studios, but also denied work to anyone who spoke in favor of unions, criticized Congress, or advocated disarmament. The studios had repented and had offered up the appropriate sacrifices. The Committee, however, knew that there was more political hay to be made in Hollywood, but they would not resume their harvest until 1951.

Although the patriotism of New York theatre had not been questioned since the demise of the Federal Theatre Project, its morality was still suspect. During the first three years of the decade, Mayor La Guardia and Commissioner Moss closed most of the burlesque theatres in New York and forced the Minsky Brothers into bankruptcy. Actors' Equity, the League of New York Theatres and the Authors' League of America complained that the city had used methods that were "clearly dictatorial and in violation of democratic procedure."[133] La Guardia assured these groups that he had no intention of attacking moral shows, but the mayor's definition of immorality was exceedingly broad. In November 1944, *Trio*, a play written by Dorothy Baker and her husband Howard that was based on her novel by the same name, announced that it would open in New York. It told the story of three people – a middle-aged woman, a young woman, and a young man. Over the course of the play, the young woman attempts to leave the older woman in order to marry the young man. The dialogue hinted at a lesbian relationship, but the authors denied that such a relationship existed. It opened in Philadelphia in October 1944 to mixed reviews, but there was never any talk of suppressing it because of its theme. *Trio*'s producer, Lee Sabinson, planned to move the production into one of the Shubert theatres. However, Lee Shubert was not willing to expose himself to Moss' penalties, and he asked the Commissioner to view the play in Philadelphia to determine if it was indecent. Moss declined, saying that he was not a "censor but a License Commissioner."[134] Without assurances from Moss, Shubert rejected Sabinson's offer. Wittingly or unwittingly, the Broadway theatre moguls, who owned 80 percent of New York theatres, had been co-opted into the censorship apparatus.

Sabinson continued his search for a theatre. He finally rented the Belasco Theatre from Max Jenlin, who had leased it from its owners. *Trio* opened on December 29, 1944, to tepid reviews. When Jenlin came upon hard times, the owners of the Belasco evicted him and applied to have the license transferred back to them, a fairly routine matter. Moss, however, did not immediately act on the application. While he was contemplating his decision, he received a petition signed by sixteen Protestant clergymen and a former Justice of the Domestic Relations Court claiming that the play was injurious to public morals. Two days after he received the petition, Commissioner Moss ruled that he would withhold the Belasco's license unless the owners closed *Trio* within twenty-four hours. He had no idea of the magnitude of the explosion that was to ensue.[135]

The theatre community was up in arms, and another censorship battle had commenced in New York. From the very moment Moss announced his decision, his detractors claimed that he had exceeded his authority. John Chapman accused Moss of being a hopeless dunce. "His mistake," he said, "seems to be in ignoring the fact that there is legal machinery for handling unfit plays – a method designed to make 'the people,' through their prosecutors and courts, decide on what is immoral or dirty."[136] The mayor's office was besieged with complaints. The Equity Council condemned the event as an "arbitrary misuse of licensing power by the License Commissioner acting illegally as a self-appointed censor."[137] On March 1, representatives of most of New York's theatre factions met at the Hotel Astor where they heard the mayor's response. Via a lengthy letter, the mayor informed the assembly that he took full responsibility for the entire affair, but stubbornly maintained that Moss' actions did not constitute censorship:

> No play can be censored in this state except by adjudication of the court in compliance with the laws of the state. No one has been deprived of his rights in court in the case of *Trio*... The Commissioner has the right to deny application for a new license. That is exactly what happened in this instance.[138]

He then went on to blame *Trio*'s producers for not taking the case to court, and maintained that, if they could find another theatre willing to house the production, they were free to move into that space.[139]

The theatre community was far from satisfied with the mayor's response, and insisted on a meeting at City Hall, which was scheduled for March 7. In the meantime, the Executive Director of the American Civil Liberties Union, Roger Baldwin, joined the fray, and Sabinson sued Moss for 1 million dollars. The meeting took place as scheduled and was so raucous that, according to the *Times*, "voices of the participants echoed in the corridors." After the encounter, La Guardia attempted to place a positive spin on the session by saying that it had been "more or less harmonious." While the mayor asserted that he had not changed his mind, he admitted that he had agreed to propose legislation to the State Assembly and City Council that would limit the power of present and future License Commissioners.[140] By the time that these measures were finally introduced to the Council and the Assembly, New York politics had become more tolerant. William O'Dwyer had replaced La Guardia as mayor, and Ben Fielding was the new Commissioner of Licenses. Both openly asserted that they had no intention of subverting the courts in the matter of granting or renewing theatre licenses. Although many theatre critics urged the two bodies to pass the legislation, the various bills that were introduced languished in committee and were never enacted.

While New York, as the center of professional theatre in the United States, may have suffered through the most protracted censorship battles during the 1940s, it was by no means the only city whose reform-minded officials attempted to scour the stage of immorality. Throughout the decade, Boston censors demanded that producers rewrite scenes and lines in *Another*

Love Story (1943), *Early to Bed* (1943), *Peepshow* (1944), and Congreve's *Love for Love* (1947). The Detroit police censor threatened to close O'Neill's *A Moon for the Misbegotten* in 1947 if several lines were not deleted or altered.[141] In Washington, DC a police sergeant ordered an actor in a touring production of *On the Town* to change a line. When the actor refused, he was arrested and fined 25 dollars.[142] The Santa Barbara City Council banned the showing of *Mr. Adam*, a play about the lone male survivor of a nuclear war, because it was "in bad taste."[143] In June 1949, the Chicago producers of *The Respectful Prostitute* were forced to close their production because of continuous court battles and police harassment.[144] The Trenton, New Jersey, Director of Public Safety refused to permit a performance of John Wexley's *They Shall Not Die* in December 1949. The story of the infamous Scottsboro trials of the mid-1930s, the play was to have been used as a benefit to raise funds for the defense of six African American boys accused of murder.[145] The Atlanta Library Board, that city's official censorship body, prohibited Mae West's *Diamond Lil* from opening. It seems that the moral guardians of that city objected to the fact that the play was set in a Bowery saloon and dealt with prostitution.[146] Late in 1952, the Bureau of Licenses in Providence, Rhode Island, refused to issue a permit to *Tobacco Road* because it was "filthy in language, immoral, blasphemous and indecent."[147] When the play's producer, Edward Gould, attempted to open the play, he was arrested for producing an immoral show that "would corrupt the morals of youth."[148]

Although the preservation of traditional moral codes never disappeared from the censorship discourse of the 1940s and 1950s, conservative critics continued to argue that non-conformist theatre threatened the political bulwark of the nation. Communists, they asserted, had been corrupting the United States since the 1930s. They had manipulated our democratic systems and had taken advantage of our *naïveté* to weaken our nation. They were far more wily and crafty than the average citizen and would use our freedoms to destroy us. In order to protect our liberty, these patriots reasoned, our rights would have to be curtailed. Therefore, any demonstration of transgressive behavior, whether it be sexual, religious, or intellectual, was a certain sign that Communists were boring into the political and moral foundations of the nation. As a result, censorship battles were absorbed into a contentious political discourse that pitted anti-Communists against civil libertarians.

The question of freedom versus totalitarianism took an ironic turn when the American Occupation Army in Germany suppressed a production of *Mister Roberts*. Written by Josh Logan and Thomas Heggen, *Mister Roberts* had opened in New York on February 18, 1948, and told the story of sailors on a supply ship serving under a cruel and imperious captain during World War II. Its dialogue was peppered with expletives and several references to the Deity, but, outside of some random objections, it played without interference in the United States and Canada. When a touring production opened in Frankfurt, Germany for American forces in April 1951, the wife and daughter of General Thomas T. Handy, Commanding General of the European armies, left in the middle of the performance. It seems that the candid language had offended the general's family. He immediately suspended performances on the basis that such theatre would corrupt American soldiers. His decision was roundly protested in the United States. After all, the United States Army had been sent to Europe to preserve freedom. Now its own commander was using the tactics of the defeated dictators. The *New York Times* editorialized that soldiers should be able to enjoy the same "simple pleasures" that were available to American civilians. "Surely, if we have to put men into uniform to protect and preserve our freedoms ... we ought to allow them to enjoy some of those freedoms."[149] Logan, who had waived his royalties, was incensed. He noted that he had been in the army for four-and-a-half years and protested that the speech of the characters was mild in comparison to the language of real servicemen.[150] The American Civil Liberties Union interpreted the event as "a serious violation of freedom of speech." In a letter to Handy, Executive Director Patrick Malin reminded the general that the values of democracy were being tested throughout the world and that "no representative group of the United States, least of all the armed forces in the European theatre, should utilize anti-American tactics – censorship and suppression."[151]

Although civil libertarians maintained that military and civilian officials had adopted the same tactics as their Communist adversaries, such logic fell on deaf ears. Communist paranoia dominated American political and social behavior. Freedom of expression or political affiliation was no longer defensible on the basis of the First Amendment. Communism posed an immediate and palpable threat to the American system. It would have to be eradicated even if the most cherished American freedoms had to be sacrificed in the process.

Naming names

The outbreak of hostilities in Korea on June 25, 1950, drastically constricted the government's already limited tolerance of political dissent. In August, Congress passed the Internal Security Act (1950), also known as the

McCarran Act. It banned members of allegedly subversive organizations from government or defense jobs, or from holding passports. It tightened espionage laws; denied entrance to the United States to aliens who had ever belonged to Communist parties; banned picketing of federal buildings; and provided for the detention of suspected spies and saboteurs during a national emergency, the so-called concentration-camp clause. The Immigration and Nationality Act (1952) allowed for denaturalization and deportation of citizens deemed "subversive," as well as for the deportation of resident aliens for political activity.[152]

HUAC, not to be outdone by the actions of their Congressional colleagues, reopened its investigation of the film industry in 1951, but this inquiry was fundamentally different than its 1947 probe. The Hollywood Ten were all members of the Communist Party, and that set of hearings sought to prove that subversives working in the movie industry had imbued American film with propaganda. The later hearings concerned themselves not so much with active members of the party, but with those who had been associated with Communism during the 1930s and early 1940s. Thus, HUAC could give the impression that they were investigating a conspiracy that had been flourishing within the American entertainment industry for over twenty years. However, the Congressmen needed names to support their crusade. They needed names of people who had attended Communist Party gatherings, names of people who made radical speeches at union meetings, and names of people who signed disarmament petitions or marched in peace rallies. Names were literally the fuel that powered the Committee. With names, they could demonstrate that subversives had infiltrated the film, television, radio, and theatre. Without names, their accusations were just idle speculation.

More importantly, by engaging in the ritual of naming names, witnesses, who were themselves suspect, could participate in what Arthur Miller has called a "surreal spiritual transaction." That is, speaking the names of friends and colleagues to the Committee constituted a form of public penance that signified that the speaker had truly regretted his or her past indiscretions and was now a loyal American. It made no difference if the names were already known to the Committee, witnesses had to speak them for the record. Thus, betrayal became a public affirmation of loyalty.[153]

However, the Committee's thirst for names could not have been quenched without the cooperation of the major studios. They welcomed HUAC's obsession with subversive employees and willingly agreed to refuse employment to anyone who did not cooperate with the Committee. In their opinion, it was much easier to fire some malcontents than rewrite scripts and reshoot scenes.

The American Legion significantly fanned the flames of this inquisitorial fire. Joseph Brown Matthews, a key witness and investigator for the original Dies Committee in 1938, had placed himself in the service of the American Legion. His crowning achievement was the publication of *Appendix IX*, a seven-volume work spanning almost 2,000 pages that meticulously described every organization that its author deemed subversive. Most importantly, he provided an index that contained the names of some 22,000 people whom he claimed were either Communists or fellow travelers. Since the studios still employed individuals listed in that index, the American Legion claimed that they were not fully committed to the anti-Communist crusade and threatened nationwide boycotts. Television had already substantially diminished film industry revenue, and an American Legion-led boycott might well result in bankruptcy. Thus, the studios consented to establish internal security divisions that investigated any and all employees to insure that there was no hint of subversive activity in their background. If employees of studios were included for whatever reason on this or any of the other lists that appeared, they were summarily fired. Should the offending party wish to be exonerated, he or she could write a lengthy letter to the American Legion detailing the circumstances surrounding their activities and swearing that they had been the naive victims of a sinister plot. Of course, naming names generally indicated that the offending party was truly contrite.[154]

While the film studios and the American Legion busied themselves with inquiring into the political affiliations of thousands of cameramen, editors, extras, and wardrobe assistants, the Committee had set its sights on bigger game, and the directors, actors, and writers who were involved in the radical theatre of the 1930s proved to be inviting targets. On January 14, 1952, Elia Kazan, renowned theatre and film director, and former member of the Group Theatre, was called to testify. At that time, he admitted that he had been a member of the Communist Party in 1935, but refused to identify others with whom he had associated. Upon learning that Kazan had been an "unfriendly" witness, Spyros Skouras, president of Twentieth Century-Fox, informed him that he if did not cooperate with the Committee, he would never make another film in Hollywood.[155] Kazan contacted the Committee and asked to amend his testimony. His request was granted and on April 10, 1952 he performed his ritual confession by naming the names of other members of the Group Theatre. They included

Phoebe Brand and Morris Carnovsky, her future husband, Paula Miller, later Mrs. Lee Strasberg, Clifford Odets, Lewis Leverett, J. Edward Bromberg, and Tony Kraber.[156] The information that Kazan furnished to the Committee was already a matter of public record. He made no revelations. Still, he performed the ritual penance. He had publicly abased himself by speaking the names of his friends and colleagues and had proven to the Hollywood moguls that he would always be a cooperative employee. Two days later, he purchased advertising space in the theatre section of the *New York Times* that explained his testimony. He claimed that America was faced with "an exceptionally tough problem" and that the nation could only protect itself from "a dangerous and alien conspiracy" if it possessed all of the facts. In his opinion, his disclosure of names simply provided more of these facts. His gesture did not go unrewarded. Skouras made sure that Kazan enjoyed a lucrative and illustrious career.[157]

Perhaps the most unlikely "friendly" was Clifford Odets, the one-time radical playwright and founding member of the Group Theatre. In 1947, when the initial Hollywood hearings took place, Odets bitterly denounced them. By the time he appeared on May 19 and 20, 1952, he had done a complete about-face. He was the model of cooperation. He admitted that he had been a member of the Communist Party for about nine months and identified his recently deceased colleague, Edward Bromberg, as the person who recruited him into the party. He freely named the members of his cell, most of whom were actors and writers and stressed that, as an artist, he had never really embraced Marxism. The once leftist firebrand meekly concluded his testimony by stating that he felt he really had little to say or contribute to the betterment or welfare of the American people.[158]

One day after Odets finished his testimony, Lillian Hellman was sworn in. Prior to her appearance, she sent Chairman Wood a letter outlining the conditions under which she would testify. She maintained that she would waive Fifth Amendment immunity for herself, but she would refuse "to hurt innocent people whom I knew many years ago to save myself." Chairman Wood responded that he could not allow witnesses "to set forth the terms under which they will testify." Moreover, her attorney, Joseph Rauh, warned her that the Fifth Amendment protected witnesses and defendants against self-incrimination not against incriminating others.[159]

True to her word, she refused to respond to inquiries about her associates during her testimony. And, while she answered some questions about her own Communist Party affiliation, she refused to answer others. By so doing, she arguably forfeited any protection that the Fifth Amendment afforded her. Inexplicably, Hellman was dismissed after only sixty-seven minutes of testimony and the Committee issued no contempt citations. The saga, however, had not ended. Hellman was blacklisted in Hollywood for failing to cooperate with the Committee. Moreover, the Internal Revenue Service launched an investigation of her tax history and decreed that she owed tens of thousands of dollars in back taxes. Within a relatively short time she went from earning $140,000 a year to less than $10,000. Although she had not been convicted of any crime, she had been severely punished for her refusal to yield to the Committee.[160]

Throughout the first half of the 1950s, HUAC attempted to establish that Communists were engaged in a long-standing campaign to use the film industry to subvert the government of the United States. It was not until 1955, however, that the Committee attempted to prove a connection between contemporary professional theatre and Communism. Agitated by the fact that actors and writers who had been blacklisted in Hollywood could still find work in New York theatre, HUAC member Francis Walter (D-Penn.) announced that sub-committee hearings would begin at the federal courthouse in Foley Square in New York on August 15. Equity and the American Federation of Television and Radio Artists, fearing that union leadership would be accused of protecting subversives, threatened any member who did not fully cooperate with the Committee with expulsion. Prominent conservatives immediately voiced their support. Alliance, Inc., an ad hoc assemblage of vocal anti-Communists, urged all Americans, "regardless of race, creed, color and political affiliation," to oppose the Communist menace. It praised the Committee for unmasking subversives in the entertainment industry and congratulated it for providing an opportunity for current and former Communists to rehabilitate themselves.[161]

The hearing process, however, never ran smoothly. The *New York Daily Worker* called the investigation a "witch hunt," linked several members of Alliance, Inc. with Senator Joseph McCarthy and organized a demonstration in front of the hotel that housed the Congressmen.[162] The Committee seemed confused and befuddled. Instead of aggressively pursuing prominent directors, actors, producers, or playwrights, it summoned twenty-three journeymen performers who supported themselves by acting in chorus or supporting roles. Upon learning that a less than stellar cast of witnesses had been called, the *Times* sardonically commented: "There may be a few broken hearts and some red faces on Broadway today... After all, if a man or woman has spent a long lifetime climbing slowly toward stage recognition, he or she might well expect to be recognized by Congressional committees as well as by audiences."[163]

As was their strategy, the Congressmen attempted to link witnesses with pre-war Communist causes and then demonstrate that they were still connected to known radicals. They asked witnesses if they had appeared in workers' theatre or were connected with the Federal Theatre Project. The Congressmen also wanted to know if they had signed peace petitions, worked for the Hollywood Ten, or had associated with Communists in Hollywood or New York. Although the Committee was notorious for destroying careers of men and women who refused to cooperate, its reputation seemed to have little impact on the performers who appeared. They invoked the First and Fifth Amendments, and accused the Committee of exceeding its jurisdiction by attempting to establish "control and conformity" in the entertainment field.[164] Actor Elliot Sullivan, when questioned about an anti-FBI skit in which he had acted, responded: "Is it your province to examine the material that goes on the stage anywhere and to comment on it in such a way as to discourage people from expressing their views on what is going on in our country today? It shows that your committee is very clearly encouraging censorship of good American theatre."[165]

From the Committee's perspective, this round of hearings had to be counted an unqualified failure. Of the twenty-three witnesses, only one admitted that he had been a Communist and named others who had associated with the party. The remaining twenty-two either invoked Constitutional protection or simply told the Committee its questions were "improper."[166] Pickets and demonstrators dogged the Congressmen wherever they went. An Alliance, Inc. rally held the night before the hearings began was picketed by over 500 New Yorkers carrying signs that read "Keep Broadway Free," "New York Is a Union Town," "Witch Hunters Go Home," "Bigotry is Un-American," and "Preserve the Bill of Rights! Abolish the Un-American Committee."[167] Demonstrators marched outside the courthouse during the hearings, and at two separate rallies on the night of August 17th thousands of protestors heard speakers accuse the Committee of attempting to intimidate theatrical unions and blacklist actors.[168] HUAC had, for all intents and purposes, been booed off the stage. It had been unable to intimidate actors and did not even attempt to interrogate producers or directors.

Basically, the Committee had failed to comprehend that Broadway in the 1950s was a fairly provincial enterprise. Television networks used shows to sell products, and movie studios depended upon millions of viewers from hundreds of communities to buy tickets. In such cases, boycotts organized by the American Legion or other outraged patriotic groups could very easily cost studios and investors millions of dollars. Broadway, on the other hand, was its own "econosphere." It was financed by an anonymous group of individual investors who depended upon a local rather than national constituency to generate a profit. As such it was considerably more insulated from the economic pressure that dogged its sister industries.

In spite of the embarrassing Foley Square hearings, the Committee was able to rejuvenate itself within a year. In what was perhaps the most transparent act of harassment ever perpetrated by the Congressmen, they called Paul Robeson to testify on June 12, 1956. Robeson, an outspoken critic of racism who lavished praise on the Soviet Union, had been blacklisted in the United States. Moreover, the State Department had revoked his passport, making it virtually impossible for him to earn a living. His every speech and acquaintance had been noted by the FBI and there was very little about Paul Robeson that was a mystery to the Committee. He was nonetheless subpoenaed. A lawyer himself, Robeson proved a formidable witness and effectively neutralized his interrogators. He used his appearance as a forum to attack racism in the United States, and on more than one occasion demanded that the Congressmen protect his people in the South instead of persecuting loyal citizens. He refused to answer any question regarding adulatory statements he had made about Stalin, saying that he would discuss the Soviet leader with Russians not Americans. He praised President Eisenhower for pursuing peace in the world, but blamed the Committee for needlessly inciting anti-Communist paranoia.[169]

The Committee used Robeson as a whipping boy in order to illustrate that the weight of the entire United States government could be brought to bear on unrepentant Communists. But the campaign against Robeson was old news and did not afford the Committee what it desperately needed – proof that Communists still abounded in Hollywood. The Committee's crusades against subversion had effectively purged the entertainment industry of any individual who had maintained even the most anemic association with radical or pacifist causes. Ironically, the Committee desperately needed Communists. Without Communists and the attention they generated, HUAC might unwittingly put itself out of business. Shortly after Robeson appeared, however, the Committee got the witness it needed, playwright Arthur Miller.

By the time he appeared, Miller had already written *All My Sons* (1947), which won the Drama Critics' Award, *Death of a Salesman* (1949), which garnered the Pulitzer Prize, *The Crucible* (1952), and *A View from the Bridge* (1955). Aside from being the most prominent playwright in the United States, he was engaged to marry Marilyn Monroe.[170] Thus, he became the ideal witness. If it could be shown that the Communists had corrupted Miller, an internationally acclaimed artist, the Committee could easily make a case that any thinker who opposed the status quo was suspect. Moreover, Miller's impending marriage to the most glamorous movie star in the United States assured the Committee that all the major media would heap coverage on this hearing.

Miller testified on June 21, 1956, and Staff Director Richard Arens was his most aggressive interrogator. Had Miller urged the State Department to sponsor a production of his play, *All My Sons,* at the World Youth Festival in Prague? Had he labeled the efforts to outlaw the Communist Party of the United States the result of "organized hysteria"? And had he advocated the abolition of the House Un-American Activities Committee? In spite of the prejudicial nature of many of the questions, Miller rarely consulted his counsel, Joseph Rauh, who had also been Lillian Hellman's attorney. Instead, he answered without hesitation and remained composed. Miller admitted that he had made many speeches and signed many petitions on behalf of liberal causes, but adamantly denied that he was "under the discipline or domination of the Party."[171] He argued that artists should not be persecuted for their vision, no matter how controversial. Representative Gordon Scherer (R-Ohio) was incensed. He wanted to know if Miller advocated protecting writers who supported the "violent overthrow of the Government of the United States."[172] Miller responded that he had never met such authors. Scherer continued: "Then you believe that we should allow the Communists in this country to start actual physical violence in the overthrow of the Government before they are prosecuted?" Miller calmly responded: "You fail to draw a line between advocacy and essence. Our law is based upon acts, not thought. How do we know? Anybody in this room might have thoughts of various kinds that could be prosecuted if they were carried into action."[173]

Miller was then asked if he had ever attended Communist meetings. He admitted that he had attended four or five such gatherings for the purpose of understanding in more detail how his plays related to Marxism. When asked to name other writers who were present, he replied, "Mr. Chairman, I understand the philosophy behind this question and I want you to understand mine...I want you to understand that I am not protecting Communists or the Communist Party. I am trying to, and I will, protect my sense of myself. I could not use the name of another person and bring trouble on him." After a few minutes of debate, Congressman Scherer told Miller: "We do not accept the reasons you gave for refusing to answer the question, and it is the opinion of the Committee that, if you do not answer the question, you are placing yourself in contempt."[174] The Committee made good its threat. It filed charges in the full House against Miller and seven others for contempt of Congress. Their colleagues, by a vote of 373 to 9, supported HUAC's claims.

By the end of 1956, however, HUAC's luster had begun to tarnish. Committee Counsel Arens was censured by the California Bar for his "grossly offensive" treatment of lawyers.[175] National opposition to the McCarran–Walter Act had been mounting and the president favored modifying some of its more Draconian provisions. Most importantly, the Supreme Court issued a decision that severely limited the authority that the Committee had appropriated for itself. In April 1954, John T. Watkins, a vice president of the Farm Equipment Workers' Union, refused to name individuals whom he had met when working on projects sponsored by the Communist Party. He was cited for contempt, indicted, found guilty, and given a twelve-month suspended sentence and a fine of $500. The Court of Appeals upheld his conviction, but the Supreme Court reversed this decision in 1957. It maintained that the Committee had a right to question witnesses in order to gain information necessary to draft legislation. It ruled, however, that the names withheld by Watkins were immaterial to any legislative process. By demanding those names the Committee had exceeded its charter and had thus violated the Constitution. The *Washington Post* hailed the Watkins decision as "a landmark in the long struggle to keep Americans free from oppressive and arbitrary government" and *The New Republic* told readers that "civil liberties have come back into fashion."[176] Buoyed by the Watkins verdict, Miller appealed his contempt citation to the United States Court of Appeals and in September 1958 his conviction was overturned.

Toward the end of the 1950s, the nation began to tire of security checks, loyalty oaths, and unending investigations of television and movie stars. Conditions had become somewhat more cordial between the Soviet Union and the United States, and the Communist Party USA virtually disappeared. Moreover, nationalistic uprisings in Eastern Europe and China proved that Communism was not a monolithic juggernaut scourging the earth. Still, anti-Communist crusaders refused to acknowledge that the world was changing. To men such as Arens, J. Edgar Hoover, Chairman Walter, and Congressman Scherer, numbers did not matter. Communism was Communism, and as long as it existed anywhere on earth it posed a mortal threat to the United States.[77]

In May 1960, the Committee scheduled its own death knell. During that month, the Committee planned hearings to investigate Communism in the San Francisco area. It had called an array of witnesses including Communist Party members, teachers, and informers. Student newspapers at the University of California at Berkeley and San Francisco State College had already voiced anti-Committee sentiment. Moreover, thousands of students had mobilized to protest the impending execution of Caryl Chessman, and the anger that they felt at his eventual death hardened into a fierce anti-authoritarian mood. Emotions continued to build as the Committee commenced hearings on May 12. Over a thousand students demonstrated in Union Square, while several hundred marched around City Hall and lined up in front of the doors to the hearing room. The Committee was loath to admit these antagonistic spectators and packed the gallery with its supporters. But refusing admission to the demonstrators only provided the protestors with a powerful cause and a potent rallying cry: "Open the Doors! Open the Doors!" Around 1:15 P.M. police, for no apparent reason, turned high-pressure fire hoses on the crowd. For the next half hour they were washed out of the rotunda and dragged down the steps of City Hall by police who were not shy about using their batons. About sixty demonstrators, two of whom were avowed Communists, were arrested. Congressman Scherer told the press that the riots were "clearly planned at the highest Communist levels." J. Edgar Hoover published a report entitled *Communist Target – Youth; Communist Infiltration and Agitation Tactics.* The Committee even commissioned a movie that was put together from subpoenaed TV newsreel film depicting the events of the riot. A tricky piece of work, it was replete with distortions, irrelevancies, and gossip, not to mention events that were shot out of sequence. Unfortunately, neither Hoover nor the members of the Committee had any idea of what was happening in the country.[178]

By 1960, students were already involved in the civil rights struggle and in a few years they would be staging teach-ins and sit-ins against the Vietnam War. Although the radicals of the 1930s may have resembled those of the 1960s, the two groups were profoundly different. The radicals of the sixties rebelled against an old, fearful generation dominated by unimaginative, unfeeling men. Although many embraced various forms of Marxism, doctrinaire ideologies concerned them far less than spontaneous expressions of freedom. Those who demonstrated against HUAC in San Francisco were merely the vanguard of a generation that would rebel against a deadening hand that reached out from Washington to suffocate heterodoxy and diversity. During this next turbulent decade, theatre, particularly radical theatre produced on college campuses, would be transformed into a crucible in which this generational struggle would ignite.

5

Bye, bye American pie

Civil strife

The "sixties," rather than being a fixed passage of time, were really an altered state of mind brought about by significant changes in the nation's moral, political, and cultural attitudes. If one has to assign a beginning and an end to the period, the Woolworth sit-in in 1960 and the resignation of President Richard Nixon in 1974 seem to be relevant markers. During these years, the rapid evolution of media communication, particularly television, brought gruesome scenes of urban riots, racially motivated beatings, funerals of assassinated leaders, and body-bags from Vietnam into the home of virtually every American. The effect on the population was profound. Conservatives, appalled by dissolute moral behavior, loss of respect for authority figures, and a noticeable decline of patriotism, called for law, order, more discipline, and more police. The "New Left," led by the "baby boomers," challenged the traditional views of their conservative parents. Those that were politically active demonstrated for civil rights and black power, and against the Vietnam War. They marched in Birmingham and Selma. They rallied in Washington, DC, New York, Boston, Chicago, and San Francisco. They seized public buildings and shut down universities. Others embraced pacifism, lived communally, altered their minds with drugs, and dreamed of a benign utopia. On the one hand, the 1960s were beset by violence and demagoguery. On the other, they gave birth to a renewed sense of egalitarianism, pacifism, and hopefulness. Needless to say, it was a complex period.

Once again, theatre was in the eye of the storm. A new generation of visionary directors, producers, and playwrights emerged. Early in the decade, militant black writers virulently attacked the American establishment for its racist policies, and liberal white artists accused the social and political system of hypocrisy and tyranny. By 1968, nudity and sexuality were freely employed by dozens of directors and producers. Many used these new conventions as metaphors to oppose social injustice and war. For some, they functioned as windows through which heretofore unspeakable neuroses could be viewed. Still others used erotic display merely to titillate their audiences. Thus, the radical theatre of the 1960s freely combined the moral license of the 1920s with the political activism of the 1930s to create arguably the most explosive theatre of the century. Although New York complacently tolerated these radical experiments, officials in other cities viewed these productions as attempts by subversives to incite civil and moral chaos. For these officials, the aggressive social and political criticism presented on stage was just another symptom that their culture was under siege and in grave danger of total collapse. These theatre artists could not be allowed to export their anarchistic message to the nation. They had to be stopped.

The sixties, however, were the result of a multitude of domestic and international changes. Internationally, the era began on an anxious note for the United States. In 1959, Nikita Khrushchev told United Nations ambassadors: "Whether you like it or not, history is on our side. We will bury you." During that year, the United States also severed relationships with the new revolutionary government of Cuba, driving the Castro regime into the waiting arms of the Russians. The Soviets, who already dominated 134 million people in Eastern Europe, had now gained a coveted foothold in the Western Hemisphere. Perhaps the most disastrous event came when Francis Gary Powers, who piloted one of the U-2 reconnaissance planes that the United States dispatched from Turkey to photograph missile sites within the Soviet Union, crashed in enemy territory. He confessed that he was a spy. As a result, Khrushchev pilloried the United States for flouting international law. In April 1961, President John Kennedy further compromised the nation by permitting the ill-planned Bay of Pigs invasion, which resulted in the death and capture of hundreds of Cuban ex-patriots. The United States' foreign policy seemed hopelessly incapable of dealing with the rapidly changing international chessboard.

Domestic conditions were equally complex. On February 1, 1960, less than two weeks after John Kennedy assumed the office of president, four African American students from a North Carolina college asked to be served at the all-white Woolworth lunch counter in Greensboro. What started as an unadorned, symbolic demand for equal rights set off a series of events that changed the course of social justice in the United States. Within fourteen days, sit-ins spread throughout the state. After ten weeks, protests involving over 50,000 people were occurring in every southern state. The Civil Rights movement had begun.[1]

Between 1960 and 1963, a growing number of African Americans and whites organized protests in the South. Businesses that refused to hire or serve blacks were picketed and boycotted, and voter registration drives were organized. "Freedom riders," organized by the Committee on Racial Equality (CORE), protested continuing segregation. In Birmingham, Alabama Police Chief Bull Conner had made a secret deal with the Ku Klux Klan that permitted a white mob to attack an interracial group of "freedom riders." The attack was televised nationally and the nation was introduced to the violence that the Civil Rights movement would endure.[2]

President Kennedy initially kept his distance from the Civil Rights movement, but his brother, Attorney General Robert Kennedy, was more aggressive. In September 1962, when Mississippi Governor Ross Barnett personally prevented James Meredith from registering for classes at the all-white University of Mississippi, Robert Kennedy sent 500 federal marshals to Oxford. After an all-white mob, very few of them students, attacked and wounded 160 marshals, the president ordered in 5,000 army troops to stop the violence.[3]

Still, the government's commitment to civil rights was weak, but Dr. Martin Luther King, Jr.'s Birmingham march forced the administration to take action. In full view of the media (and the nation), Chief Conner once again ordered police to attack peaceful protestors, many of whom were children, with clubs and dogs. Civil rights activists in the rest of the nation reacted by staging over 700 more protests in the following months. The president responded by sending Congress a comprehensive civil rights bill in June 1963. In order to demonstrate support for the president's measure, nearly 250,000 Americans rallied on the National Mall in Washington, DC. They heard Dr. King tell the American public that he had a dream.[4]

President Kennedy did not live to see the passage of the Civil Rights Act. He was assassinated in Dallas, Texas on November 22, 1963, the first of many political murders that studded the decade. Although President Johnson, himself a southerner, supported the bill, southern senators filibustered the measure for eighty-one days. When the bill finally passed in 1964, it fundamentally altered American society by prohibiting discrimination based on race or gender, an unexpected victory for American women who, like blacks, had also been treated like second-class citizens. When southern officials assessed poll taxes and applied literacy and constitutional interpretation tests to subvert the aims of the bill, Dr. King organized a march from Selma to Montgomery, the Alabama state capital in March 1965. Once again Alabama state troopers and local policemen attacked the peaceful protesters, while the national media reported violence to a shocked nation. Congress responded in August by passing the 1965 Voting Rights Act that guaranteed all citizens equal access to the voting booth.[5]

For a few months, African American and white activists congratulated themselves on their legislative and political victories, but within the year Stokely Carmichael won control of the Student Nonviolent Coordinating Committee (SNCC). He demanded power and independence for all African Americans. "Black Power," as the movement came to be known, rent the previously unified King-led Civil Rights movement. These young radicals did not desire a Negro–white coalition. They wanted to live in a separate society, one that honored and preserved African American heritage and excluded whites. Their aggressive rhetoric appealed to thousands of young blacks who had no desire to be integrated into white society. As a result, a series of racially motivated riots nearly plunged the nation into a full-scale race war.[6]

The fear and tension that resulted from the racial strife of the period were further exacerbated by the student rights movement, which profoundly changed the face of American higher education. Arguably, the incident that sparked the beginning of this movement occurred in 1964 at the University of California at Berkeley. Mathematics student Jack Weinberg began to collect money to support civil rights efforts in the South. University administrators forbade him to continue his efforts in spite of a long-standing decision by the Supreme Court that included collecting money for political causes among those activities protected by the First Amendment. Weinberg protested the decision, and a major confrontation ensued that pitted administration against students who were supported by 88 percent of the Berkeley faculty. The administration eventually conceded and the Free Speech movement, headed by Mario Savio, had begun and with it a national student rights movement. Early protests were concerned with the civil rights advocacy, and free speech and assembly guarantees. Soon students began to focus on the mission of higher education. They demanded smaller classes and a change in emphasis from a research-centered faculty to a teaching-centered faculty, and pressed for the abolition of the *in loco parentis* administrative control over student lifestyles.[7]

By far the first and most radical of the student organizations was the Students for a Democratic Society (SDS). Founded in 1962 in Port Huron, Michigan, SDS was one of the first groups to articulate the philosophy of the New Left. In its founding manifesto, the Port Huron Statement, drafted by Tom Hayden, SDS stated that the United States had been founded upon the principles of egalitarianism and liberty, but had degenerated into an undemocratic, militaristic bureaucracy.[8] It chastised the right for embracing extremism and criticized the left for accepting the status quo. It furthermore declared that enlightened liberal leadership would emerge not from labor unions, but from college students and a new generation of American youths.[9]

During the first two years of its existence, SDS members identified with President Kennedy's call for self-sacrifice and then with President Johnson's support for civil rights and his war on poverty. By 1964, however, SDS leadership had dramatically altered its stance when Johnson expanded the conflict in Vietnam after winning the 1964 presidential election. It no longer regarded the war as an over-zealous military debacle that was the result of botched foreign policy. Rather, it believed that the war had been initiated and promoted by a small corporate elite who profited from the escalation. By the mid-1960s, SDS leaders had begun to support draft resistance and sponsored rallies that attracted tens of thousands of war protestors to Washington, DC, Chicago, New York, Boston, San Francisco, and Los Angeles.[10] By 1968, student opposition to the war resulted in teach-ins, marches, sit-ins, riots, and building seizures at Harvard, Stanford, Northwestern, San Francisco State University, University of Michigan, University of Wisconsin, and University of California at Berkeley.

Yet these activists were hardly united by a clearly defined agenda. In April 1968, what started as a protest against some innocuous regulations at Columbia University escalated into a full-scale student strike that resulted in the seizure of buildings and the closing of the university. A year later, armed African American students at Cornell demanded that the university institute a Black Studies Program, which meant ridding the current curriculum of everything that, in their opinion, was racist, sexist, or elitist. The faculty, which was held literally at gunpoint, agreed to make the changes. Black faculty and students who refused to support their demands were threatened and the university's president was even assaulted. Perhaps the most tragic event associated with campus demonstrations occurred at Kent State University in Ohio. On May 4, 1970, in response to President Nixon's admission that he had expanded the Vietnam War into Cambodia, students at that campus burned down the ROTC building. The governor deployed the National Guard. When the soldiers hurled tear-gas canisters into a crowd of about 1,000 demonstrators, the crowd panicked. Regrettably, the young guardsmen also panicked and fired at the unarmed students. Four students were killed and nine others wounded.[11]

Student demonstrations were decried as antics staged by privileged, pampered youths who chaffed at the rigors of academia but who did not want to enter the work force. And, when violence erupted, such critics could smugly reply: "They had brought it all on themselves." Yet the volatile chemistry that permeated many campuses was merely a microcosm of the explosive domestic situation brought about by the Vietnam War. The United States had financially supported the French colonial war in that nation during the late 1940s and early 1950s. After the Geneva Accords were signed in 1954, creating North and South Vietnam, the United States supported the South, ruled by Ngo Dinh Diem, against the North, led by Ho Chi Minh, a Communist. In an effort to prop up the unpopular Diem regime, Kennedy sent about 13,000 troops to Vietnam. Johnson gradually added to that number, but on August 4, 1964 the president announced that North Vietnamese patrol boats had attacked the US destroyer *Maddox* in the Gulf of Tonkin. Although the accuracy of the reports was suspect, Congress passed the Gulf of Tonkin Resolution on August 7, giving the president extraordinary powers to expand the conflict.[12]

SDS had already begun to stage protests against the war in 1965 in Washington, DC. Non-student demonstrations commenced in April 1967 when a coalition of anti-war activists organized simultaneous rallies in New York and San Francisco that attracted some 250,000 demonstrators.[13] In October of that year, between 35,000 and 50,000 demonstrators descended on the Pentagon to show their disapproval of the war.[14]

Anti-war protests resulted in a national crisis in 1968. From 1964 to 1968, the number of American forces was increased from 23,000 to 536,000. The majority of Americans, however, still supported the stated aim of the war – to halt the spread of Communism in Asia – but the mood of the nation radically changed. During January and February of 1968, 84,000 North Vietnamese and Vietcong troops launched a massive attack known as the Tet Offensive. They invaded thirty-six of the forty-four provincial capitals in the South as well as hundreds of towns and villages, killing thousands of government officials, teachers, military officers, clergymen, and men of military age. Although these forces were unable to hold the territory they initially captured, the offensive was a devastating blow to the United States' war effort. It demonstrated that South Vietnamese and American forces could not protect the civilian population and that the Communist forces had the capacity to move at will.[15]

According to a Lou Harris poll, support for the war plummeted from 74 percent to 54 percent in a little over two months and 60 percent of the population considered the Tet Offensive a defeat for the United States. Senators Eugene McCarthy (D-Minn.) and Robert Kennedy (D -N.Y.) said they would oppose Johnson in his bid to recapture the Democratic presidential nomination. In the face of rising opposition to his conduct of the war, the president announced that he would not seek reelection on March 31.[16]

In spite of Johnson's decision, the violence continued to escalate. Robert Kennedy and Martin Luther King, Jr. were assassinated. Cities across the nation erupted in flames as a result of racial hatred. Campus demonstrations proliferated and grew more violent; and riots at the 1968 Democratic National Convention in Chicago demonstrated to anyone who owned a television that the nation was on the brink of a meltdown.

Early experiments

Theatre in the beginning of the 1960s was by and large a fairly docile enterprise. Broadway remained thoroughly conventional and commercially motivated. The few regional theatres that existed – the Alley in Houston, Arena Stage in Washington, Mummers Theatre in Oklahoma City, Charles Playhouse in Boston, and Milwaukee Repertory Theatre – produced some new European plays and works which Broadway considered too risky. However, they were located in communities far too conservative for any radical drama to take root. Although some isolated experimental productions appeared Off-Broadway, these theatres were eventually transformed into venues for Broadway tryouts.

However, another tier of producing units, the Off-Off Broadway theatres, quickly became the site of radical experimentation. The direct descendants of "beat" coffee houses, the "Off-Off" theatres retained a penchant for spontaneous, unmediated creations. Although "Off-Off" spawned its own share of commercially successful ventures, it was primarily known as a scene that nurtured playfulness, amateurism, and various forms of deviance all aimed at debunking the establishment. In 1966, *Village Voice* critic Michael Smith rendered this description:

Off-Off Broadway is not a place or an idea or a movement or a method or even a group of people. It has no program, no rules, no image to maintain. It is as varied as its participants and they are constantly changing. At its best it implies a particular point of view: that the procedures of the professional theatre are inadequate; that integrity and the freedom to explore, experiment, and grow count more than respectable or impressive surroundings; that above all it is important to do the work.[17]

Perhaps the first production that fully captured the spirit of "Off-Off" was *The Connection*. Written by a wholly inexperienced playwright, Jack Gelber, it was produced at the Living Theatre by two committed anarchists and pacifists, Judith Malina and Julian Beck, in July 1959.[18] *The Connection* depicted a group of addicts waiting in a squalid apartment for "Cowboy," a black drug dealer – the connection – who is on his way with heroin.[19] For the Becks (Judith Malina was Julian Beck's wife) this piece presented an opportunity for them to theatricalize their political and social beliefs. Malina, who directed the piece, maintained that addicts were "victims of a system that destroys the individual with a pernicious subtlety – that system being Western civilization."[20] Beck asserted, "these dregs of society, as they were regarded, were human, capable of deep and touching feelings and speech worthy of our interest and respect; we had to show that we were all in need of a fix."[21] Both he and his wife believed that the process of theatre could actually undo that tyranny by eliminating the rigid social attitudes that governed behavior.

Gelber had created a text that seemed to him to be more like a piece of jazz music rather than a traditional play.[22] Thus, the piece had very little action in an Aristotelian sense. Most of the evening was taken up with extended monologues supported by an onstage jazz quartet who conversed with the audience during the performance. The actors were visible when the audience entered and, during intermission, they panhandled in the auditorium. By creating the impression of a loosely structured improvisation, Malina completely distorted the ontological distinction that typically existed between actors and audience. While her inventions may seem somewhat simplistic to postmodern audiences, they were extremely controversial for the period.

Critics from the weeklies generally recognized the distinctiveness of *The Connection*. Kenneth Tynan, Harold Clurman, Donald Malcolm, and Robert Brustein lavishly praised Gelber and the Living Theatre for creating a piece of theatre that was "constantly tripping over the boundary between

life and art."[23] However, critics from the New York dailies launched venomous attacks. For the most part they were incredulous at the fact that the
drug environment was too objectively portrayed and that the playwright
refused to censure or make excuses for the addicts' condition. *Times* critic
Louis Calta called it "nothing more than a farrago of dirt, small-time philosophy, empty talk and extended runs of 'cool' music."[24] More importantly,
these critics equated the improvisational informality with an attack on art.
Walter Kerr complained that such productions might signal the end of
traditionally crafted presentations:

> There is a serious and genuine undercurrent running beneath the styles
> and anti-styles of our time, an undercurrent that honestly distrusts art as
> art, a conviction that whatever is organized must therefore be falsified. It
> has led not only in experimental drama but in other media as well − to
> a notion that truth is never to be found in meditation, and certainly not
> in premeditation, but only in what pops out on the spur of the moment,
> only in what is wholly or at least partially improvised.[25]

Within a few years, the Becks would transform the strategy of improvisation into a powerful and problematic performance aesthetic. By obscuring
or completely obviating the convention of characterization, an offensive or
threatening script could no longer be described as a work of fiction performed by actors playing roles. Fiction was totally submerged in reality, as
actor and character seemed to merge.

The Living Theatre and Gelber both won Obies for their efforts and the
former garnered an invitation to perform in the Théâtre des Nations in Paris
in June 1961. The company applied to the State Department for support,
but the government sent the Theatre Guild's *The Skin of Our Teeth* and *The
Miracle Worker* starring Helen Hayes instead to represent the United States.
The Becks were not deterred and raised the $40,000 necessary for the trip
from the New York arts community.[26]

Although the Living Theatre would be the target of police activity during
1968 and 1969, their artistic philosophy began to merge with their anarchistic political views as early as 1963. *The Brig* by Kenneth Brown, which premiered on May 15, 1963, was chosen "to dramatize the excesses of authority
buttressing an unjust system."[27] A profoundly disturbing piece, *The Brig*,
depicts one day in the life of prisoners in a Marine Corps jail or brig. Like
The Connection, *The Brig* was hardly a play in a traditional sense. The "prisoners" were made to execute a series of specific and mindless activities and
failure to do so resulted in brutal punishment. There was no traditional plot

as the production depicted a sadistic system that thoroughly depersonalized those trapped within it.

The production was well received by the critics and won three Obies. Ticket sales were brisk, but the Living Theatre called a press conference for Thursday, October 17, 1963, to announce that they would have to close because they were $45,000 in debt. The largest creditor was, unfortunately, the IRS to whom they owed $28,435.[28] What followed can only be described as the first full-scale, life-sized spectacle staged by the Becks to illustrate their belief that art, life, and politics were all part of a seamless continuum. Within three hours of the announcement, the IRS had dispatched agents to seize the contents of the theatre. The Becks, ever mindful of the theatrical potential of a confrontation with authorities, occupied the building along with many of their friends. The New York City police were called in to quarantine the building. Word began to spread throughout the Village, and the Beck's allies began to picket. They occupied the building all day Friday, but early Saturday morning they discovered that the police had failed to block roof access to the theatre. They decided to challenge the authority of the government by performing *The Brig* one last time. The cast and crew reassembled the set that the IRS agents had dismantled and, by the time the police discovered what had transpired, the audience and press had climbed across the roof and taken their place in the auditorium. Although warrants had been issued for the Becks' arrest, IRS agents correctly reasoned that nothing would be gained if force were used and allowed the performance to take place. With federal agents and city police surrounding the building, this performance of *The Brig* assumed profound symbolic implications.[29]

The Becks acted as their own counsel as the real-life drama shifted to the courtroom. Both were convicted by the twelve-member jury. Julian was sentenced to sixty days in jail, Judith to thirty. At no time, however, did the government prosecutor pursue the original complaint of delinquent taxes. All charges stemmed from "impeding Federal officers in pursuit of their duties," leading to speculation that the Becks had been correct when they claimed they had been harassed because of their anarchist politics and the anti-military content of *The Brig*.[30] Their sentence was postponed to allow them to accompany the Living Theatre to perform in London where they premiered *The Brig* to an enthusiastic English audience. The entire company continued to tour Europe and, in May 1964, Julian and Judith returned to the United States to pay their debt to society for performing "outlaw art." At the end of November, the Living Theatre was lent a farm in Heist-sur-Mer, a bleak village on the Belgian coast. It was here that the Living Theatre began their self-imposed exile. They would not return to the United States until 1968 and, when they did, the fusion of art and political ideology had been completed.

While the case against the Becks may have been an example of veiled censorship, the evolution of radical theatre in New York went virtually unimpeded. Outside of New York, a different history was being written. Plays that contained even the slightest hint of sexual deviation, political revisionism, or religious contempt were met with immediate censure. Groups that wanted to produce controversial plays in public buildings were extremely vulnerable. When Richard Barr, the producer of *The Zoo Story*, attempted to bring that play and *Krapp's Last Tape*, with which it had been paired in New York, to Boston, the only available theatre was owned by the Roman Catholic archdiocese. A spokesman for the Cardinal announced that the productions were too inappropriate to be produced in a church-owned building.[31] In Rockport, Massachusetts, in 1962, the Board of Selectmen voted to deny access to the high-school auditorium to a small New York production company that planned to stage *The Zoo Story* and Michael Shurtleff's *Call Me by My Rightful Name*, a play about an interracial love triangle.[32] In August 1963, Rutherford, New Jersey's Recreation Commission denied a local theatre permission to use the community center to produce *The Immoralist*, a play adapted from the novel by André Gide. A Catholic priest and a Methodist minister opposed the play because it dealt with the impact of homosexuality on a marriage.[33]

College and university theatre programs were also at risk. One of the most publicized cases of the decade occurred in Waco, Texas, at Baylor University, the flagship institution of the Southern Baptist Convention. In December 1962, the Drama Department at Baylor University opened O'Neill's *A Long Day's Journey Into Night*. After consulting with his board of trustees, President Abner McCall forced the department to close the production in mid run. In a letter to Paul Baker, Chairman of the Drama Department, he asserted that plays containing "vulgar, profane or blasphemous language should not be produced by the drama department without deletion of the offensive language." He also stressed that "plays which ridicule the Christian religion were also banned."[34]

McCall's action touched off a storm of controversy within the university. The Student Congress regarded it as a "flagrant violation of academic freedom" and an offense against the Baptist Church, "which is diametrically opposed to the suppression of ideas." On March 7, 1963, Baker and eleven members of his faculty and staff resigned.[35]

The early sixties were, however, generally free of theatrical controversy. With the exception of Shurtleff, Brown, Gelber, and Albee, very few American playwrights authored works that attacked the heterosexual, white, male hegemony in the United States.

Civil rights, black militancy, and guerrilla theatre

By 1964, however, the theatrical landscape had begun to change. Kennedy's assassination in Dallas dashed the hopes of those who believed that an American renaissance was at hand. The center seemed to implode, and new, more radical voices could be heard. Amiri Baraka was arguably the most controversial of these voices. The passage of the 1964 Civil Rights Act marked the zenith of the battle against Jim Crow segregation and institutionalized racism. However, three centuries of oppression could not be eradicated by one piece of legislation, and northern constituencies advocated abandoning integration in favor of Black Nationalism. Malcolm X, originally a follower of Elijah Mohammed and later the leader of his own movement, became the most influential spokesperson of these groups. His message was clear and simple. Whites were devils and were responsible for the humiliation and degradation endured by all blacks. Accordingly, he called for blacks to seize control of their lives by expelling all vestiges of white society and culture from their communities.[36]

Black power denounced all forms of white influence and sought to create an entirely new black culture, based on self-determination, self-definition, and cultural independence. For Amiri Baraka, black power and black culture were inseparable. Thus, the transformation of theatre into a forum that advocated the death of white supremacy seemed a logical step.

Born LeRoi Jones in 1934, Baraka was a struggling writer and poet, and part of the Greenwich Village bohemian scene when the black power movement began to take shape in 1963. He had already written drafts of *The Baptism* and *The Toilet* when he became involved with a playwright's workshop established by Edward Albee and his producers, Richard Barr and Clinton Wilder, at the Cherry Lane Theatre. His success as a playwright was assured after the first performance of *Dutchman*, which he wrote in a single night. It opened in March 1964 at the Cherry Lane and caused an immediate furor.

Dutchman's plot is extremely bare. An alluring white woman, Lulu, meets Clay, a young black student on a New York subway. She immediately sets out to seduce him, telling him that she really knows blacks and accusing him of merely posing as an intellectual. At first, he avoids Lulu's sexual games by hiding behind a façade of middle-class propriety. He finally explodes and unleashes a torrent of rage. Lulu stabs and kills Clay. With the silent complicity of the other passengers, she disposes of the body and readies herself to begin the ritual murder again as the next black man enters the car.

The play disturbed critics, but it won a 1964 Obie Award and Jones' status as a black revolutionary artist grew. He became notorious for his attacks on "whitey," which he conducted in print and in question-and-answer sessions held at various Village clubs. On one occasion, a woman sincerely wanted to know if there was anything whites could do to help. His response typified the anti-white anger that now possessed him. "You can help by dying," he replied. "You are a cancer. You can help the world's people with your death."[37]

The Toilet and *The Slave* opened on December 16, 1964, at St. Marks Theatre. Critcs, liberal and conservative, were appalled. George Dennison of *Commentary* labeled Jones a black racist. "This is what it means to be a demagogue," he claimed. "It is to attempt nothing and resolve nothing, but to amplify the sub-vocal speech of the fanaticist."[38] "Anarchic and prurient in tone, language and style. These two plays present a nightmare of twisted logic," fumed Myrna Bain of the *National Review*.[39] As frightening and/or repellent as these two plays seemed to many observers, they enjoyed a long and prosperous run in New York.

Such was not the case in Los Angeles when *Dutchman* and *The Toilet* opened there in March 1965. During the preceding summer, there had been sixteen urban riots, including those in Harlem and Rochester. However, Los Angeles had escaped this first round of disturbances. The police talked tough and blamed black radicals for the crisis in the nation. They were in no mood to tolerate Jones' provocative dramatizations.[40] The week before the production was to open at the Las Talmas Playhouse, the owner of the theatre canceled his contract because of the language and subject matter of the plays. The producers sued for damages and booked the show into the 335-seat Warner Playhouse. Owner Cy Warner subsequently reported that it had been "suggested" to him that he eject his tenants before his building license was reviewed. Although the plays opened on schedule, the police closed the production after two performances because the producers had allegedly failed to apply for a permit. After several days of intense negotiations, the Police Commission granted the producers a 60-day permit, but warned them that they would be investigated throughout the period to insure that no laws were broken. Cecil Smith, from the *Los Angeles Times*, said the twin bill "exploded like two black furies ... into a searing, devastating, horrifying and incredibly effective evening of theatrical force."[41] Perhaps the program was entirely too powerful. On April 5, the producers reported to the *New York Times* that the *Los Angeles Times* and the *Hollywood Citizens-News* would no longer accept advertisements for the plays. The Authors' League of America protested, as did Howard Taubman, but the production drifted into oblivion.[42] Barely three months later the Watts riots erupted. Eerily, Jones had predicted the future, but very few wanted to listen.

Controversy always seemed to surround Jones' dramas. In May 1968 at the high school in Wellesley, Massachusetts, a prosperous, upper-middle-class suburb of Boston, a ten-minute cutting from Jones' play *The Slave* unleashed a storm of controversy that polarized the community for over five months.[43] The program was developed in response to a state directive that high schools address the implications of civil disorders. The high school's social studies and English departments in conjunction with a community group, the Committee on Racism, arranged a comprehensive program. It featured speeches, panel discussions, a film, several poetry readings, and dramatic presentations intended to give high-school teachers and students better insight into the racial issues. No school funds (i.e., tax dollars) were used for the project. The program was held on Friday, the 31st, barely two months after the King assassination. Within two days, Wellesley was transformed into a crucible of generational and racial conflict.[44]

The obscenities that studded Jones' play, which had not been read by any of the sponsors prior to the performance, stood at the center of the controversy. Adults were outraged that African Americans had dared to speak violent, obscene language at an educational event. That next morning, an irate father filed a complaint that a Massachusetts law prohibiting obscenity had been violated because the performance was "pornographic, lewd and lascivious." About 200 people, half of them students, attended the ensuing School Committee Meeting. A spokesperson for the students read a prepared statement telling the committee that the parents' objections regarding obscenities and violence were "unjustified and invalid":

> We feel that the objections raised, be they concerned with obscenities or violence, are really objections to reality and to a truthful portrayal of life. The play *The Slave* ... was a truly educational experience, something which seems to be (or should be) a concern of the people ... Do they [parents] think that their kids must be sheltered from what is true, from what goes on outside of school, from hate, from issues, from confrontations, from life?[45]

A mother countered that all the four-letter words used during the performance were familiar to teenagers, "but they are not normally used by families at their dinner tables." For this parent at least, decorum and respectful behavior far outweighed the information Jones had to offer about the rage felt by black Americans.

The Board of Selectmen meeting that was held that same evening was attended by invited teachers and parents, but no students. Teachers complained that their rights had been encroached upon because they and the students were "a captive audience, unable to leave." Parents asserted that the program had exposed their children to language and situations that were totally unsuitable. "Where is morality and dignity," lamented one father. "Filth and degradation, sexual matters of intercourse are not part of the educational system...Is there no limitation on how far liberality goes?"[46]

The ordeal had just begun. Nearly 1,200 people attended the next Selectmen meeting on Monday June 10. Several hundred students occupied the front rows to demonstrate support for teachers who were being accused of wrongdoing, but they were outnumbered by nearly a thousand adults.[47] A recent graduate of Wellesley High School, identified as a "model student," quoted a line from the play and calmly explained that he first heard the offensive word contained therein in Wellesley when he was five years old. As he began to explain the etymology of the word, murmurs from the adults grew into a roar. Interspersed among the jeers were shouts of "Kill him!" "Get him out of here!" "Get him!" The student was removed from the auditorium in handcuffs and charged with disorderly conduct.[48] The Wellesley police chief subsequently filed charges against five teachers and community leaders for corrupting the morals of minors.[49]

That next September, the incident was widely discussed. WGBH, the Public Television Station in Boston, produced a 90-minute documentary detailing the events in question. The controversial cutting from *The Slave*, with all of the obscenities excised, was also aired. (Apparently, WGBH did not wish to be charged with obscenity while airing a program on obscenity.) Two discussions formed the major portion of the program. The first featured parents from Wellesley and Roxbury, a predominantly black section of Boston. According to *Boston Globe* critic, Percy Shain, the white parents and educators concerned themselves with the maintenance of an educational system that transmitted traditional knowledge and decorous behavior. The student panels were far more explosive. Language was clearly not a concern, as both groups used a wide array of expletives (also excised) as they discussed state of race relations in America, Boston, and

Wellesley.[50] Earlier that morning, Judge Daniel Rider dismissed charges against the defendants who were accused of corrupting the morals of minors because they could not be linked to the creation or actual production of the play. The judge, however, did announce that the play was definitely obscene.[51]

The issue of racism also provided raw material for the San Francisco Mime Troupe, one of the most controversial companies of the sixties. The group began life as the R. G. Davis Mime Troupe in 1959. Davis had studied in France with Etienne Decroux and worked as an assistant to Herbert Blau and Jules Irving in the early days of the Actors' Workshop. After experimenting with different styles, the company finally decided that it would adopt the techniques of *commedia dell'arte*. What Davis perceived as its working-class origin in the streets and alleys of Renaissance Italy seemed to suit the skills and interests of the company. They improvised on scripts and scenarios from Molière and Goldoni, rewriting scenes and inventing different characters.[52]

The direction that the Mime Troupe took in its first years was not new or original, but in 1964, shortly after the beginning of the Civil Rights movement and the Berkeley Free Speech movement, Davis began his assault on the establishment and the theatre it supported. Although it maintained its connection with *commedia*, the San Francisco Mime Troupe became a "guerrilla theatre," a company of radical performers who struck when least expected, causing chaos and challenging the existing political and cultural bastions. "We try in our own humble way," he said, "to destroy the United States."[53]

For such a theatre to be effective, Davis felt that it had to engage the people in their own environment, not demand that they enter the alien world of the bourgeois auditorium. Consequently, they presented free outdoor park performances in and around San Francisco. The Troupe's first confrontation with police came in August 1965. The San Francisco Parks Commission had agreed to let the company perform in area parks, but withdrew its permission when it was discovered its production, *Candelaio* by Giodano Bruno, a particularly violent play, had been turned into a commentary on American militarism. On August 7 members of the Mime Troupe were arrested and charged with performing without a license. The company thoroughly capitalized on the arrests. They sent out press releases and called press conferences. On November 1, 1965, Davis was found guilty. This conviction cost the Mime Troupe its first grant, $1,000 from the city's Hotel and Motel Tax allocation for the arts. More importantly, the company was forbidden to perform in city parks. In February 1966, the American Civil Liberties Union filed suit against the Parks Commission to show cause why the Mime Troupe should not be granted a permit to perform in city parks. The censure was quickly rescinded.[54]

Like other politically committed artists of the early sixties, Davis wanted to make a statement about civil rights. Unable to decide on a suitable script, he and his company chose to write their own show – *A Minstrel Show*. It would be an American *commedia*, based on decades of minstrel history that resided in the collective unconscious of American theatre. It would have its own repertoire of stereotypical characters, exaggerated gestures, and masks – in this case blackface.[55]

In traditional minstrelsy, an all-white, male cast generally appeared in blackface and generally made African Americans appear to be unsophisticated, untutored, and retarded. *A Minstrel Show* deconstructed this convention to serve the Mime Troupe's political ends. In historical minstrelsy, the "walkabout," the opening number, culminated with the ignorant "darkies" sitting in a semicircle around the "Interlocutor," a pompous white man who was the butt of jokes and insults. The Mime Troupe retained this convention, but blurred the lines between gender and race by having the remainder of the company – Caucasian and African American men and women perform in blackface. As a result, the audience was unable to use race and gender to determine their response to the performers. This assault on traditional markers was followed by "Old Black Joe," a ballad that praised the "good darkie." A "stump speech," given by the Interlocutor attesting to the superiority of whites followed, but, while he spoke, the actor behind him simulated masturbation.

Easily the most controversial piece of *A Minstrel Show* was the "chick/stud" scene. In this piece, an actor in blackface convinced a "white woman" in a bar to return with him to his apartment. However, another male minstrel who wore a white mask over his blackface played the "woman." These various manipulations of sex and race stereotypes collided with one another at every turn, as the cornball racist jokes of minstrelsy became the platforms for radical assaults on white society.[56] In April 1966, the company performed *A Minstrel Show* at St. Martin's College, a Catholic college in Olympia, Washington. As the show progressed, angry students began to boo and leave the auditorium. Finally, the show was halted in mid-performance when technicians turned off the lights. The Mime Troupe also drew the ire of the California State Senate Fact-Finding Subcommittee on Un-American Activities, which accused it of "obscene gestures and

Marxist neighbors."[57] Apparently, Californian politicians had determined that radical theatre artists were a security threat.

Soon the company's transgressions spread eastward. In September 1966, the Troupe performed in several cities en route to an appearance in New York with Dick Gregory. During a performance of *A Minstrel Show* in Denver, the police came backstage at intermission to stop the performance and arrest the company. An actor bolted onto the stage and dared the police to make the arrests in front of the audience. The officers demurred and the show continued. At its conclusion, the performers scurried into the audience. The "guerrilla" tactics of the Troupe so flummoxed the police that they mistakenly arrested black audience members, even though the actors were in blackface, fright wigs, and wearing sky-blue tails.[58] The company was eventually arrested and charged with obscenity and performing "simulated acts of perversion."

The radicals emerge

While the Mime Troupe eventually became a fixture of the Bay Area's counter-cultural ethos, it was New York that continued to push the edges of the theatrical envelope.[59] A little publicized performance art piece at the Bridge Theatre on St. Mark's Place seemed to set the anti-government tone of the next few years. At approximately 1:45 A.M., Jose Rodriguez-Soltero ignited an American flag to protest the nation's involvement in Vietnam as part of his performance, *LBJ: A Live–Multi-Screen-Scrambled-Love–Hate–Paradox USA*. According to the *Village Voice*, the audience, which had never before witnessed such a dramatic anti-American gesture, was "horrified." One onlooker reviled Rodriguez-Soltero as a "pinko . . . fag." Within a few hours, the Department of Licenses issued a "show cause" order demanding that the theatre explain why its license should not be revoked for defacing an American flag. William Kunstler, who represented the Bridge Theatre, claimed that the flag burning was a "symbolic gesture in a theatrical presentation." In the future, defamation and destruction of significant icons, irrespective of their religious or patriotic importance, would become a crucial feature of radical performance.[60]

America Hurrah, performed by Joseph Chaikin's Open Theatre, continued this trend. Although the play was "written" by Jean-Claude van Itallie, he did not function as a traditional playwright. Instead, he attended company classes that explored various social and artistic situations by means of improvisation. As a result, van Itallie crafted a "play" that used the company's ethos as its platform. The final result eliminated the conventions of linear narrative and psychologically consistent characters. Instead, audiences experienced a collage of nightmarish impressions that obliquely commented on the degenerative state of American society.

An Open Theatre acting exercise directly inspired the first piece, *Interview*. It opened with a group of job applicants answering inane interview questions that revealed the abusive absurdity of the situation. The actors, cueing from one another, dissolved the scene into a city street, and then to a party. Traditional attitudes toward character and narrative were completely absent as actors spoke their own thoughts as the scene progressed. *TV*, the second scene, revealed the superficiality of television by juxtaposing the intelligence of actors and producers with the simple-minded reductive messages of the medium. The final piece, *Motel*, was the most daring of the plays. The proprietor of a new motel described her establishment's superior appointments – books in all the rooms and self-flushing toilets – while two guests destroy their room and end up fornicating on what is left of their bed. However, the actors were costumed in oversized bodies, including enormous plaster heads, and the dialogue was taped.

The theatrical and social messages of *America Hurrah* were nightmarishly surreal. Van Itallie and his colleagues in the Open Theatre used improvisation as a means of freeing theatrical energy, of developing meaningful theatrical material, and of fusing the actors into an ensemble. While the company did not invest *America Hurrah* with rigid political ideals, Chaikin described the pieces as "dedicated to the overthrow of public opinion... The group shares a political attitude, unlike Lincoln Center, unlike the commercial theatre. You can't ignore the war like you can... white sugar."[61]

Robert Brustein praised the production for having found "provocative theatrical images of the national malaise we have been suffering in 'Johnsonland' these last three years."[62] *America Hurrah* experienced little or no resistance in New York. The discomfort that it prompted in other parts of the world indicated that American theatre had taken a new and dangerous turn. After a ten-month run in New York, the production opened at the Royal Court Theatre in London in August 1967. It was hailed as a thoroughly new type of American theatre: "Compared to the packaged and neatly labeled America of Hollywood, Bunnies and *Time Magazine* it's like an in-grown toe-nail – non-decorative and nagging."[63]

When producers attempted to move the production from the Royal Court Theatre, which operated as a private club, to the Vaudeville Theatre in the West End, the Lord Chamberlain intervened. His office would prosecute the production unless certain lines referring to President Johnson, his daughter, and the vice president were excised. The producers refused to compromise the integrity of *America Hurrah* and reopened it at the Royal Court where it played for six more weeks.[64]

America Hurrah was not produced extensively in the United States, but, in those locales where it did appear, it encountered rigid opposition. It was literally denied access to Chicago. The owner of a cabaret, the Happy Medium, was told that his liquor license might be in jeopardy if he contracted the show. The producers also contacted St. Alphonsus Catholic Church, which owned the Athenaeum Theatre. The pastor, it was reported, had been advised not to make the theatre available to the production.[65] In Mobile, Alabama city officials closed the University of South Alabama's production. It had played for two nights to packed houses in the city-owned Pixie Theatre. However, Mayor Lambert C. Mims forced university officials to cancel the remaining performances. In his opinion, *America Hurrah* was "filth, pure and simple, and . . . it is a crying shame that Alabama taxpayers' money has been used to produce such degrading trash." Academic freedom and the First Amendment notwithstanding, Mayor Mims was not about to open Mobile to radical social and sexual ideas.[66]

The political commentary of *America Hurrah*, while present, was nonetheless circuitous and indirect. It did not point fingers and name names. Not so with *MacBird!* Based on Shakespeare's *Macbeth*, *MacBird!*, by Barbara Garson, a veteran of the Berkeley Free Speech movement, was a brutal satire that accused Lyndon Johnson of plotting John Kennedy's death. In it, a "good ol' boy" vice president arranges the assassination of a golden boy president only to lose the office to the deceased president's younger brother.[67]

From the very outset, it provoked hostility. Eight days before previews were to begin, Jay Rosenblatt, publisher of *Showcard*, programs for Off-Broadway productions, refused to produce a program for *MacBird!* In his opinion, the show was a crass attempt to profit from a national tragedy.[68] A few days later, Grove Press, which had recently acquired the publishing rights to *MacBird!*, agreed to print the program. WCBS-TV then decided not to air filmed scenes of the play on "Eye on New York," and, only a few days before the opening, fire department officials threatened to revoke the theatre's occupancy permit.[69]

The New York audiences did not seem particularly shocked, but the critics were outraged. The *Village Voice* totally rejected the effort, and called the play "an irresponsible and unedifying relationship to political realities...artistically silly and politically meretricious."[70] Walter Kerr vilified the play. He believed that Americans were too close to the assassination of Kennedy to regard it with anything other than grief. Moreover, he felt that Garson's lack of literary discipline was tantamount to "an anarchy of taste, a sloppiness of mind and hand – a refusal to discriminate."[71]

Peter Brook offered a different viewpoint. He contended that Garson's work should not be regarded as literary theatre, but pop art:

> Through her deliberately simplified language, Barbara Garson is talking about the mechanism of power, about this and nothing else. Her objective is precise, it is the entire Washington establishment, the entire structure of ruling that she wishes to hold up to the light. The fact that the material is flimsy, the idiom pulp, the expectation of literary immortality nil, is a source of strength... Her subversion of traditional dramatic forms was, in fact, a political weapon.[72]

Although Garson never claimed that her burlesque should be regarded as the truth or even a well-grounded accusation, *MacBird!* had touched a nerve. What were the limits of art? Of freedom of expression? Were there certain topics that artists could not visit? Were dramatic texts affidavits attesting to the moral or political beliefs of the playwright? Was theatre bound by some type of moral imperative to "tell the truth"? Or was theatre a fictive domain to be judged by its own discrete rules?

The controversy raged throughout the spring. *The New Yorker* refused to print advertising for *MacBird!* It was the first time in the magazine's forty-two year history that it had rejected an ad for a play. Even J. Edgar Hoover joined the fray:

> lawlessness, unbridled vulgarity, obscenity, blasphemy, perversion and public desecration of every sacred and just symbol [will] destroy the nation...We should be alarmed when widespread recognition and monetary awards go to a person who writes a satirical piece of trash which maliciously defames the President of our country and insinuates he murdered his predecessor...stop deifying offbeat dolts whose ability is measured only by how they can dip their poisonous pens into the pots of blasphemy, filth and falsehood.[73]

The Living Theatre returns

During 1967 urban race riots continued to erupt, but Vietnam was quickly becoming the most pressing national issue. In October, the nation seemed to explode in a frenzy of anti-war protest. In the capitol, a self-proclaimed "irresistible force" of 35,000 gathered at the Lincoln Memorial and descended upon the Pentagon. Ten-thousand citizens marched on the draft induction center in Oakland, California. At the University of Wisconsin in Madison, 2,500 demonstrators clashed with police over the right of Dow Chemical to recruit job applicants. In Boston and New York, demonstrators burned flags and draft cards.[74]

By 1968, the domestic crisis had reached critical mass. In April, Dr. Martin Luther King was assassinated and twenty-one cities burst into flame. Early that summer, Robert Kennedy was murdered. With his death, any hope of a cohesive liberal political presence was permanently fractured. SDS organized a mass protest at the Democratic National Convention in Chicago in August. Ten thousand demonstrators gathered in Lincoln Park to voice their opposition to the war and "the system." Mayor Richard Daley placed his 12,000-man police force on twelve-hour shifts, and called up 5,000 Illinois National Guardsmen and 6,500 federal troops. In addition, a force of 23,000 was on alert. For two days, demonstrators taunted police with shouts of "pig" as well as other more abusive epithets. They mawkishly sang patriotic songs and occasionally hurled bricks and rocks at the troops. Then, on the third day, as a bitterly divided Democratic Party readied itself to nominate Hubert Humphrey for president, the Chicago police mounted an attack on the demonstrators. Flailing batons and hurling tear gas, they charged a small group of protestors who were attempting to make their way to convention headquarters. They even invaded Senator Eugene McCarthy's headquarters and clubbed his volunteers. Three hundred demonstrators and 150 police reported injuries and nearly 600 arrests were made.[75] Hundreds of television and newspaper reporters from Tokyo to Amsterdam described the riot.[76] To the world, Chicago bore a frightening resemblance to Prague, and America appeared to have been transformed into a police state. Conservatives demanded law and order, liberals called for reconciliation, and radicals screamed for revolution. It was amidst this chaos that the most aggressive theatre of the period began to emerge. As it did, the same forces that feared wholesale anarchy rose to suppress it.

The Living Theatre, who returned to the United States less than one month after the violent clashes in Chicago, was by far the most aggressive and provocative political theatre company of the period. The group, still under the direction of Julian Beck and Judith Malina, had lived and worked communally in Europe from November 1964 until September 1968. During this period, the company embraced Artaud's theatrical ideology and attempted to implement his theories by experimenting with a variety of spiritual and metaphysical prescriptions, as well as with mind-expanding drugs that presumably amplified aesthetic consciousness. It also committed itself to pacifism and anarchism, two characteristics that fully permeated their subsequent productions.

Eventually it became impossible to separate the Living Theatre's art from its life. In every sense, the lives of its members were performances and their performances, to which the public was invited, were merely extensions of their political ideologies and personal psychology (or, as some critics contended, personal psychopathology). The Living Theatre, like many radical performance groups, believed that professional theatre was too idealized and unreal. It was too concerned with decoration and ornamentation to address substantive issues. Moreover, the spectator was protected from life and was allowed to return to his home with his prejudices and fears intact, even reinforced.[77] The Becks, however, wanted to transform society. Although their aim was secular, their methodology was based in ancient Jewish beliefs that "the world is in constant process of creation and it is man's sacred duty to assist God in this process." In essence, the Becks held that a radically revisioned theatre was a means of sanctification. Led by committed actor/priests, theatre would transform passive audiences into participants in a world-wide pacifist revolution.[78]

While the Becks' vision of artistic and political revolution catapulted them into an exalted status within the revolutionary ethos of Europe, in the United States their performances came to resemble freak shows. The American tour included a repertory of four productions: (1) *Antigone*, very loosely based on Brecht's adaptation of Sophocles' work, with Malina and Beck in the leading roles; (2) *Mysteries and Smaller Pieces*, composed of communal chanting, a series of *tableaux vivant*, and improvised sound and movement games; (3) *Frankenstein*, whose real attraction was a three-ton, three-tiered scaffold that housed the various scenes; and (4) *Paradise Now*, easily the most controversial of the Living Theatre's American repertory and in the mind of the Becks, the production that most typified the anarchistic, pacifistic ideals of the company.

Paradise Now was developed in 1968 in France for the Avignon Festival. It was intended "to destroy the theatrical form forever" and to illustrate the "mystical and political aspirations of the company."[79] The production consisted of eight sections entitled "rungs." It began with "The Rite of Guerrilla Theatre," in which the actors spoke or screamed five phrases:

"I am not allowed to travel without a passport"; "I don't know how to stop the wars"; "You can't live if you don't have money"; "I'm not allowed to smoke marijuana"; and "I'm not allowed to take my clothes off." This rung was perhaps the most brutal and confrontational, and often demanded that the actors intimidate and/or otherwise insult the audience. It was this section that most offended critics; they claimed that the Living Theatre was little more than an incarnation of the fascist elements they hoped to banish. Rung Four, "The Rite of Universal Intercourse," most agitated censors. The company stripped – bikinis for women and G-strings for men – and proceeded to caress each other and the audience as they formed a mountain of bodies in the middle of the performance space. It was this section that often brought about charges of lewd conduct. Rung Eight, the "Rite of I and Thou," was designed to have the company lead the audience through the doors of the theatre, the metaphorical "Gates of Eden," into the streets of the community, thereby simulating a triumphal return to Paradise. It was a piece of theatre that very few Americans had ever experienced and for many it was extremely disturbing.

The American tour began in New Haven, Connecticut, at Yale University. It was presented in conjunction with the Yale School of Drama whose dean was the eminent critic, Robert Brustein. The company opened with *Mysteries and Smaller Pieces* on September, 16, 1968, and concluded its twelve-day run with three performances of *Paradise Now*. On September 26, Julian, clad only in a G-string, led a company that was similarly attired and an enthusiastic audience into the streets of New Haven to begin the "ritual enactment of revolution."[80] The New Haven police apprehended them within half a block of the theatre. Five members of the company and several audience members were charged with indecent exposure and resisting arrest. At the trial, Julian claimed that his G-string costume and the procession were necessary parts of the production. In his words, they represented "a vertical ascent to greater freedom, greater plenty... We're breaking down the barriers that exist between art and life, barriers that keep most men outside the gates of Paradise." Police Chief James D. Ahern offered a different view. As far as he was concerned: "Art stopped at the door of the theatre, and then we apply community standards." For Chief Ahern, theatre was a fiction designed to take place in a container. Once the confines of the container were violated, it was impossible to determine if the event was a fictional enactment or the beginning of the loudly prophesied revolution. The judge found both Julian and Judith guilty.

Judith was fined $100 for resisting arrest, but all of the other charges were dropped.[81]

The Living Theatre opened in New York at the Brooklyn Academy of Music on October 2 and played there until the 22nd. Even though Richard Schechner stripped to the buff on opening night during "The Rite of Universal Intercourse," the police chose not to act. However, the company concluded the performance in the auditorium rather than marching into the streets.

Establishment critics were violently split in their reaction, and the heated discourse focused primarily on *Paradise Now*. Jack Kroll was exultant. "No one," he claimed, "[who is] concerned with the possibilities of theatre can afford to miss what may now be the most coherent, concentrated and radically effective company in the world ... In one sense they are beyond criticism – exasperating, boring, outrageous and highhanded as they can be, their authenticity of spirit is beyond question as is their desire to settle for nothing but real change in the human beings who are the ultimate substance of both art and life."[82] Edith Oliver was not nearly as enthusiastic. She exclaimed that the company's attempt to involve the audience in the events of *Paradise Now* tended to "numb the mind, making it unfit for any interpretation whatever."[83] Clive Barnes equivocated. He disliked the demagoguery of *Paradise Now*, but gave the company credit for its sincerity.[84] Eric Bentley was outraged over Barnes' reaction and proceeded to attack him personally that next week. In a rambling harangue, he accused his colleague of caring more for his reputation as a critic than for the condition of theatre. He then claimed that the Living Theatre was unethical, and fumed that America might be better off if it were governed by the Nixons and Humphreys rather than the Becks.[85]

Of all the critics, Robert Brustein was the most profoundly disturbed by the Living Theatre. In spite of his support for the company at its New Haven trial, he claimed that the Becks were simply recreating "the youth rallies in Hitler's Nuremberg." In Brustein's imagination, the Living Theatre was both a symptom and a cause of the current political and cultural crisis. Civilization was teetering in the balance, and the Becks, by "radically questioning the prevailing humanism," might only succeed in "pushing everything we value over the precipice."[86] The Living Theatre had not only signified a precipitous, downward spiral for American theatre, it had become synonymous with the cultural and political chaos taking place the world over. If the Becks triumphed, traditional theatre, as well as all of western civilization would be lost. It was a judgment that probably gratified the Living Theatre.

From Brooklyn, the company traveled to Cambridge where it was to perform *Frankenstein* at the Massachusetts Institute of Technology (MIT) on October 31. The entourage was transported in a caravan of buses, cars, and vans and presented a bizarre apparition. The company itself consisted of thirty-four members, nine children and ten or so other "officials" who drove buses, sold poetry books, and baby-sat.[87]

As was often the case, the Living Theatre did not even have to perform in order to generate controversy. In Cambridge, hordes of FBI agents arrived at a performance of *Paradise Now* on November 5 to search for an AWOL soldier. After an initial panic, in which all illegal substances were cleared from dressing rooms, the company performed before an appreciative, loud, activist audience, without incident. They then left for a single performance at Brown University and were expecting to return to Cambridge for two final performances. While in Rhode Island, the company was informed that their MIT engagement would have to be postponed or canceled. The Becks were told that there had been too many people in the audience, the aisles were blocked, and the university's occupancy license would be revoked if such events occurred again. After lengthy meetings with the Director of MIT's Department of Humanities, it was apparent that the programs had been canceled, not postponed, and that this move was taken because irate trustees had complained vociferously to the university administrators. When the Becks attempted to find another Cambridge venue, they discovered that the chief of police would not consent to further performances in the city. The Living Theatre had been banned in Cambridge and the company began its tour on an ignominious note.[88]

In Philadelphia, the Living Theatre once again encountered police opposition. Beck and four members of the company were arrested on charges of indecent exposure. In Madison, Wisconsin, the police refused to issue a permit to perform in Turner Hall. The venue had to be shifted to a Unitarian church, three miles outside of Madison. However, the company, as it was wont, did nothing to endear itself to its hosts. On this occasion, two nude women were persuaded to ascend the pulpit and dive into the waiting arms of the actors.[89]

By the time the company reached California, any semblance of collective political or aesthetic commitment had vanished. Hopeless mismanagement on the part of New York agents had left the members of the company with no money to buy food or pay for accommodation. Moreover, riots and strikes had erupted on several campuses. On February 20, 1969, two days after the Living Theatre arrived at Berkeley, police and striking students and faculty faced each other in Sproul Plaza. The Becks, who had been following the progression of strikes in the newspapers and on television, did not support the students or attempt to use their famed pacifist reputations to restore calm. A bloody melee ensued. That night, when the company performed *Paradise Now* and began to cant its pacifist urgings, the audience, filled with survivors of the riot shouted, "Bull Shit, Bull Shit." When the performance had not progressed beyond the Fifth Rung by 12:30 A.M., building administrators halted the show. By Berkeley standards, the Living Theatre was not at all radical.[90]

When the company moved on to the University of Southern California on February 24 in Los Angeles, it performed under police and fire department surveillance, and a cordon of uniformed policemen stood guard outside Bovard Auditorium. Four days later, the university officials informed the Becks that its final two performances, which were sold out, had been canceled. On March 1, the Living Theatre headed back to New York. Only one more chaotic episode awaited the company, and this one was entirely of its own making. In the minds of some, it proved censorship and abuse were not the exclusive weapons of mayors, police chiefs, and college administrators.[91]

On March 21, 1969, the activities of the Living Theatre were to be discussed by the "Theatre for Ideas," a loosely knit organization that sponsored symposia on cultural and political topics.[92] The discussion was entitled "Theatre or Therapy" and took place in the old Quaker meetinghouse in Gramercy Park. On the program were Robert Brustein and the writer Paul Goodman, speaking in opposition to and support of the Living Theatre, respectively. Brustein spoke first. He maintained that theatre is never therapy and never heals anyone. He then moved on to the Living Theatre, which he claimed had "repudiated everything central to the practice of drama as an art, having renounced structure, ideas, language, and the histrionic imagination in favor of a deadly illiterate amateurism based on acting-out." He described it as "fascist in temperament and methods... anti-intellectual... and a sign of the new anarchy."

Members of the Living Theatre were seated throughout the audience and began to heckle Brustein. When other audience members opposed their interference, they became louder and more belligerent. When Brustein referred at one point to Chekhov, one of the Living Theatre members screamed, "Fuck Chekhov." Goodman, who supported Living Theatre, spoke next. When he maintained that the Living Theatre was not powerful enough to close universities, a member of the company vigorously cursed him. Norman Mailer ascended the podium, took up another microphone, and attempted to bully the audience into submission. He was shouted down, as was Richard Schechner who suggested that everyone meditate for five minutes and "go with it." Pandemonium had taken hold. The "straights," who had paid ten dollars to attend, expressed outrage at the behavior of the company which, in turn, responded with belligerent political and sexual epithets. Judith seized the microphone and praised the spontaneous and genuine beauty of the event in progress. Julian, who assumed a pontifical pose, periodically described the melee as the "coming attraction" and "the shape of meetings to come."

Clearly, the company had no intention of honoring or preserving the conventions of critical discourse. Its goal was to disrupt and destroy. And, judging from descriptions of that evening's events, it was completely satisfied with the conflagration it had ignited. The Living Theatre had created a genuine *agon*, as unwilling, passive spectators were transformed into angry participants. Or, from another point of view, the Living Theatre demonstrated that it was merely an assemblage of foul mouthed hypocrites or, as Brustein claimed, "fascists."

On March 31, the Living Theatre returned to Europe. However, its troubles with the authorities were not done. After splitting into three separate units, Judith and Julian traveled with their portion of the company to Brazil. There they initiated a series of street performances. In mid-August 1971, the *New York Times* reported that they had been arrested for possession of marijuana and were being held for trial. The Becks denied the charges, but had once again taken center stage in an event that spanned continents. The international arts community, including Jean-Paul Sartre, Jean Genet, Jean-Louis Barrault, James Baldwin, Allen Ginsberg, Larry Rivers, Susan Sontag, and Mike Nichols rallied to their support. The Brazilian government claimed that their nation had been slandered and scandalized, and that its security had been compromised. Nonetheless, the international pressure did not abate. The Becks, along with members of the company arrested with them, were expelled from Brazil and they arrived safely in New York in early September 1971.[93]

Pushing the edges of the envelope

The political and military turmoil of the era was further agitated by a sexual revolution. "The pill," first released by G. D. Searle Pharmaceutical

Company in 1960, permanently altered traditional sexual relationships. Un-hampered by the fear of pregnancy, men and women in the sixties inaugu-rated a period of sexual freedom that their parents could barely imagine. Moreover, liberal Supreme Court decisions regarding obscenity created a social and legal climate in which sex was freely explored (and exploited) in film, literature, television, advertising, and theatre. While the baby boomers might have interpreted the marches, demonstrations, love-ins, and race riots as the pangs associated with the birth of a new era, the white middle class saw only the semiotics of anarchy. Convinced that its carefully crafted moral culture was on the verge of collapse, it engaged in a violent struggle to protect its traditions.

The issues of race, Vietnam, and social unrest continued to suffuse the-atre throughout the 1960s. By the end of the decade, however, many radical theatre artists used nudity and sexual displays as metaphors to enhance their anti-establishment positions. These additions presented a host of problems. Many theatre artists used the naked body to signify the fragility and vul-nerability of the human condition. Others used this same type of display to debunk and disrupt Victorian attitudes toward sex. Still others simply wished to titillate audiences by objectifying the female body. Unfortunately, these distinctions never remained discrete as artists, impresarios, judges, prosecutors, and juries rarely agreed on the intent of such displays.

Moreover, nudity and sexuality on the stage further distorted the tradi-tional semiotics of theatre. As in burlesque, the body had become subversive. If the appearance and actions of bodies on stage could not be regulated, the cultural, religious, and economic paradigms that were heavily dependent on conservative interpretations of morality were at great risk. In addition, the manner in which these displays were staged dissolved the distinction between life and theatre, as the differences between actor and spectator were erased. If order in the theatre were not restored, a *regnum diabolus*, dominated by political and sexual excesses, would completely destroy the carefully designed cultural fabric of the nation. Consequently, a bitter strug-gle to suppress these displays took shape.

Although many cultural factors contributed to this controversy, the de-cisions of the Supreme Court regarding obscenity were crucial. As has been noted, obscenity law in the United States was largely based on an English legal decision commonly known as *Regina* v. *Hicklin* (1868). Its most salient feature was a test that stated, that if any part, even a single paragraph, could be adjudged to have a "*tendency*" to "deprave or corrupt" a sensitive or sus-ceptible mind, such as a young child, then the entire work was obscene and could be legally censured (emphasis mine). The beginning of the end of the Hicklin rule came in 1934 when the federal courts were asked to determine if James Joyce's *Ulysses* was obscene after the US Customs Service refused to allow copies of the book to be imported into the United States. US District Court judge John Woolsey of New York ruled that an entire work, not just isolated passages, had to be taken into consideration. Secondly, he ruled that a jury must consider the effect of a work on an average citizen with average sexual instincts, not a child or a person with a susceptible mind.[94]

Because the government did not appeal to the Supreme Court, the case involving *Ulysses* remained an isolated decision. Nonetheless, several judges used the precedent to begin to undo *Hicklin* altogether. In 1957, the Supreme Court entered the fray by agreeing to hear *Roth* v. *United States*. Samuel Roth, a publisher of adult books and magazines, had been convicted under the Comstock Act for sending obscene material through the mail. Ironically, the court upheld his conviction, but in so doing it issued a new test for obscenity. Justice William Brennan wrote the opinion for the six-member majority. He maintained that obscenity was not constitutionally protected, but for materials to be judged obscene they had to be "utterly without redeeming social importance." To make this determination, Brennan developed the following three-pronged test: the "average person . . . applying contemporary community standards" considering the "dominant theme of the material taken as a whole" found that it "appeals to prurient interests."[95]

In the third decision, *Manual Enterprises* v. *Day* (1962), the Post Office Department refused to deliver a homosexual magazine depicting nude males. Justice John Marshall Harlan's opinion for the majority declared that male nudes were no more objectionable that female nudes. However, the most critical aspect of the opinion dealt with the thorny phrase "community standards" that had been introduced in *Roth*. What precisely was the "community"? Harlan responded that he was speaking of a national community. After all, it was a national constitution that he was defining.[96]

Although the Supreme Court's decisions regarding obscenity allowed certain types of erotic materials to enter the marketplace, discussion of sexual matters certainly held no place in the discourse of the moral middle class – not until May 11, 1960, that is. On that date, the Food and Drug Administration approved G. D. Searle Pharmaceutical Company's application to produce the world's first oral contraceptive, thereby permanently liberating the sex act from the responsibility of conception. According to Loren Baritz, this was the first medicine designed for long-term use by people who were not ill. Its hormonal effect fooled the woman's body into "thinking" it was pregnant so it ceased ovulation. For the first time in recorded history, a woman could feel reasonably free from the fear of pregnancy.[97]

From the day the pill was introduced, the Roman Catholic Church was engaged in a furious debate over the morality of it. Did it constitute an artificial means of birth control, or, since its effect was achieved by the introduction of hormones into the woman's body, was it a natural method? Pope Paul VI waited for nearly eight years before issuing his decision that the pill was not to be used by Catholics. By that time, hundreds of thousands of Catholics, Protestants, and non-believers had engaged in a fierce public debate over the purpose of sexual intercourse in and out of marriage. Sex was no longer a sordid topic suitable only for inebriated men in bars, not when it was discussed on the six o'clock news, in the pages of *Newsweek*, *Harper's*, and *Good Housekeeping*, and at the dinner table.

The discussions stemming from sexual emancipation flooded the broad marketplace. *Human Sexual Response* by William H. Masters and Virginia Johnson was published in April 1966 and within one week had become a national bestseller. Although a thoroughly scientific analysis, its dry technical descriptions of every dimension of human sexual arousal and orgasm appealed to millions of Americans. More common, however, were the publications that did not require as much intellectual dedication. Hugh Hefner had published the first issue of *Playboy* in December 1953, and by 1960 subscribers numbered more than a million. By the mid-seventies, there were more than 6 million. However, Hefner marketed more than photographs of nude women. Hefner sold a philosophy of pleasure, a "new hedonism." He urged his readers – almost half of whom were single men – to enjoy what females had to offer without becoming emotionally involved. Marriage, he claimed, was an emotional trap and men should spend their hard-earned money on pleasure, not wives.[98]

Hefner's female counterpart was Helen Gurley Brown who transformed *Cosmopolitan* into a female variant of *Playboy*. Brown seemingly had as little use for marriage as Hefner. Marriage, she wrote, was insurance for a woman's declining years, nothing more. She told her readers that sex was cheaper and more fun "by the dozen," and encouraged them "to play the field."[99]

While erotic magazines certainly aided in transforming the moral consciousness of millions of Americans, a new breed of film directly paved the way for the widespread use of sex and nudity in live theatre. Until 1952, film had been denied protection under the First Amendment because the production, distribution, and showing of motion pictures was a profit-making enterprise and was deemed unworthy of constitutional safeguards. In 1952 in *Burstyn* v. *Wilson*, the Supreme Court reversed this policy. The case involved *The Miracle*, a 1948 Italian film directed by Roberto Rossellini about a woman who imagines that she is giving birth to Jesus. At the urging of Francis Cardinal Spellman, who complained that the film was blasphemous and sacrilegious, the New York State Board of Regents withdrew its license. A unanimous decision of the Supreme Court struck down the Regents' sanction and instituted entirely new standards. It ruled that the rights of free expression could not be denied to film makers simply because they hoped to earn a profit. Essentially, film would now be treated under the rubrics established in *Roth*.[100]

As a result of *Burstyn*, a flood of full-length feature films depicting all manner of erotica appeared in the United States: *Women of the World* (Italy, 1963); *A Stranger Knocks* (Denmark, 1963); *491 Lorna* (Sweden, 1964); *I, a Woman* (Sweden, 1965); *Blow-Up* (United States, 1966); and *Chelsea Girls* (United States, 1966). In 1968, a national battle began over the most sexually transgressive film to be shown in the United States – *I Am Curious – Yellow* (Sweden, 1965). In the film, a young Swedish girl, Lena, intensely concerned about the deteriorating social and political conditions of the world, becomes a peace activist. While her political views were clearly linked to her sexual permissiveness by director Vilgot Sjömannot, it was the latter that overtly disturbed American viewers. She and her boyfriend, a married automobile salesman, fight, play, and make love in a variety of circumstances and locations, many of them very public. Grove Press, the only American publisher under surveillance from the CIA, FBI, and Army, acquired the American distribution rights. The United States Customs Service seized the film, claiming it was obscene. Grove filed suit in federal court and the US Court of Appeals for the Second Circuit held that the film was not obscene. It ruled that, although "sexual conduct is undeniably an important aspect of the picture and may be thought of as constituting one of its principal themes, it cannot be said that the dominant theme of the material taken as a whole appeals to a prurient interest in sex."[101] Given the nature of the decisions that had been recently handed down, the government decided not to appeal to the Supreme Court.

While erotic movies and magazines generated a significant amount of vocal opposition, the advent of nudity and sexuality in live theatre signaled a much more dire set of circumstances. The erotic pleasure provided by a novel or magazine is experienced in private and did not need to be shared to be gratifying. Although graphic sexual exploits depicted in some films may be viewed by a group, they are nonetheless removed in time and space from the audience. Their impact is technologically mediated and is clearly designed to create a fantasy world in which the viewer can only participate imaginatively. Sexuality and nudity in theatre create an entirely different set of conditions. Actors, even when fully clothed, inhabit a precariously ambiguous world. From one point of view, a piece of theatre is merely the "imitation of an action." However, if moralists fully accepted that premise, censorship would rarely if ever occur. Theatre is executed by living, breathing humans who never vanish. As Richard Schechner has stated: "Stage performance is always on the verge of tumbling back into the real world."[102] Stage actors are obviously present and theoretically available. The presence of unclad bodies on stage transforms the conventions of theatre into stark reality. There is no longer any illusion or mystery, only a person whose actual physical being is conspicuously present.

Nudity was tolerated in topless bars and strip joints, but these locales signified the marginal world of drugs and prostitution. They could not be eliminated, but they could be contained. The Off-Off Broadway theatre world of the East Village occupied a similar terrain. These venues may have housed productions that were politically aggressive and morally subversive, but they posed little threat to mainstream behavior. And during the early sixties, while experimentation with nudity and radical politics was confined to smoky clubs and dingy cellars, those who championed traditional social structures were relatively unconcerned. However, once these plays attracted more publicity and wider audiences, their radical stance and the symbols they used to convey their beliefs began to cause concern. Once they moved out of the relatively benign confines of New York and headed for the towns of middle America, blasé disinterest was quickly replaced by vituperative contempt.

On October 24, 1967, Michael McClure's *The Beard* opened at the Evergreen Theatre on E. 11th St. in New York. In the play, two characters, Billy the Kid and Jean Harlow, engage in a fiercely antagonistic Strindbergian sexual battle. There is no action in the Aristotelian sense and the dialogue, which is ritualistically repetitive, is littered with expletives and sexual allusions. Throughout the play, Billy reiterates that both of them are in a state of absolute freedom and attempts to convince Jean to sit on his lap and caress his member. It was the final moment of the play, however, that generated the most furor. With Jean seated in Billy's chair, he gradually manipulates his head between her thighs and begins to simulate oral sex.

New York critics concentrated on the pop-art significance of the characters, but delicately avoided mentioning the obvious sexual display at the end of the play. New Yorkers, at least those who frequented Off-Off Broadway, did not seem disturbed. At least there were no outraged letters to the editor in *The Times* to indicate otherwise.

The Beard met with an entirely different reception when it was performed in California, first at California State College at Fullerton one month after its New York opening and then in Los Angeles in January 1968. The first episode demonstrated how a sexually transgressive representation was linked to subversive politics. Ronald Reagan had been elected governor of California in November 1966 defeating Governor Edmund G. Brown in what was a major step in the formation of the "New Right." Aside from tax cuts, Reagan promised to restore order at California colleges and universities, which had been the sites of frequent student demonstrations. As Reagan appointees to the Board of Regents were establishing control of California's colleges and universities, a theatre student at California State College at Fullerton decided to direct *The Beard*. From the outset, Terry Gorden's choice troubled his teacher, Edwin Duerr. Consequently, the latter surrounded the play with a number of provisos designed to shield students and faculty from any potential fallout that might occur. There were to be no minors in the cast; publicity was limited to notifications displayed on two department bulletin boards; students had to receive written permission to purchase tickets; and no tickets were to be distributed to the press. Duerr attended rehearsals, as did the director's mother. Neither the chair of the department, James D. Young, nor Duerr was enthusiastic about the production, but they allowed it to take place on November 8 and 9, 1967.[103]

In spite of these precautions, a reporter obtained tickets and, on November 15, the *Daily News Tribune* claimed that after sixty minutes of "smutty abuses, the two performers... rang down the final curtain with what viewers call a vile and vulgar act... If the play had been performed any place in the state except on a college campus someone would have been arrested."[104] The issue instantaneously transmuted from an academic and aesthetic concern into a political crusade aimed at justifying tighter state control of higher education. Republican Senator James E. Whetnore and Republican Representative John V. Briggs led the investigation into what the *Los Angeles Times* called the "Vile Play." However, Whetnore and Briggs were less interested in facts than in retribution. Whetnore claimed *The Beard* was worse than an "anti-Vietnam teach-in." Jack Galvin, Briggs' administrative assistant, went even further. He claimed that there was a direct connection between flying the North Vietnamese flag at San Diego State College, anti-Vietnam teach-ins at Berkeley, and *The Beard*.[105]

As the autumn progressed, several bills designed to punish sexually transgressive theatre at state colleges and universities were introduced into the House and Senate. The most notorious of these, Senate Bill 487, would have made it a misdemeanor for directors to teach actors to simulate sexual acts in any play produced by a state college or university. Bill 489 went even further. It prohibited any person speaking to students from advocating or teaching with the intention of indoctrination. A committee report was finally issued on January 25, 1968. It called for the dismissal of Young and Duerr, and criticized the college's president for granting tenure to Duerr and for allowing the *Los Angeles Free Press* to be distributed on campus.[106]

The District Attorney considered pressing charges against the actors for indecency, but a subsequent event involving a production of *The Beard* in Los Angeles captured his attention. On January 23, two days before the legislative report was issued, *The Beard* opened at the Warner Playhouse, the same theatre that housed *Dutchman* and *The Toilet*. In a reprise of their 1965 performance, the Los Angeles Police Department denied the producer a permit because the play contained a simulated sex act, purportedly in violation of a state law prohibiting such behavior on stage. The producer, Robert Barrows, defied the police and opened *The Beard*. On opening night, during a champagne reception, police cited Barrows for operating a theatre without a license and ordered him to appear in court in one week. They warned him that he would be arrested if the play continued, but he ignored the threat. The next night, before curtain, and while reporters and camerapersons waited outside the entrance to the theatre, he and the four other principals in the production were arrested. Barrows, director Robert Gist, and actors Alexandra Hay and Richard Brigh (who had replaced Dennis Hopper) were charged with lewd conduct and using obscene language. Playwright Michael McClure, who yelled obscenities at the reporters, was also charged with disturbing the peace. Ms. Hay was apparently unperturbed. She was pictured in the *Los Angeles Times* waving to reporters, urging them to follow the group to Hollywood police station.[107] The California Supreme Court moved swiftly and stayed the Los Angles Municipal Court from charging the group with obscenity. Such actions when performed within the context of a play, it decided, did not fall within the purview of the state's obscenity statutes.

Hair and *Dionysus* in the heartland

Although *The Beard* controversy lingered in California for several months, the melee caused by *Hair* overshadowed any other debate. Written by Gerome Ragni and James Rado, with music by Galt MacDermot, the team had unsuccessfully attempted to interest producers such as Robert Whitehead, Hal Prince, and David Merrick in the script that centered on vigorous anti-war protest. Finally, Joe Papp, who was vitally interested in the counterculture movement, agreed to produce *Hair*. He hired Gerald Freedman to direct the production that opened on October 29, 1967.[108]

The show was a moderate success, but Papp demonstrated no interest in moving it to Broadway. Enter Michael Butler, the scion of the exceedingly wealthy Chicago-based Butler family, a confidant of John and Robert Kennedy, an advisor to Governor Otto Kerner, and a Liberal Democrat candidate for public office in Illinois. Butler and his partner, Bertrand Castelli, invested $250,000 and moved the show to the Cheetah Discotheque after it closed at the Public. Although the response was less than encouraging, he was convinced that *Hair* had a future. He decided to take the production to Broadway and replaced Freedman with Tom O'Horgan, whom *Cue Magazine* named the "high priest of Off-Off Broadway." O'Horgan, a product of Second City, Chicago's renowned improvisational theatre company, was in tune with Jerzy Grotowski's techniques and had been awarded an Obie in 1967 as best Off-Off Broadway director of the year.[109]

O'Horgan changed *Hair* radically. He and composer MacDermot added thirteen new songs while eliminating three others. With more songs to fill the same two-and-a-half-hour production block, the already thin book was all but eliminated. Plot, character, and theme virtually disappeared. Instead, O'Horgan and MacDermot emphasized picturesque physical activity and bold anti-illusionistic devices that were completely supported by a driving rock score.[110] More importantly, the Broadway *Hair*, although it still voiced opposition to the Vietnam War and racism, took on a new pro-love, pro-sex, and pro-drug stance, as much more emphasis was placed on the "tribal" nature of the hippies.

The New York theatre establishment vehemently opposed *Hair*. Both the Shuberts and the Nederlanders refused to lease a theatre to Castelli and Butler. Finally, Butler's politically influential father convinced David Cogan, owner of the Biltmore Theatre, to make his facility available to *Hair*.[111] Burt Bacharach, Richard Rodgers, and Leonard Bernstein all saw

Hair on opening night, April 29, 1968, and mourned the future of American musical theatre. David Merrick remarked: "I don't know what the hell this is. I don't know why people like it."[112] Several establishment critics voiced similar views. John Chapman of the *Daily News* used the strongest language he could muster to dissuade his readers from visiting the Biltmore. He called it "vulgar, perverted, tasteless, cheap, cynical, offensive and generally lousy, and everybody connected with it should be washed in strong soap and hung up to dry in the sun."[113] Jack O'Brien from the *Daily Column* labeled it "a tangled mad-mod musical whose ultimate obscenities are not shocking though execrably tasteless, whose cast with two exceptions looks permanently bathless, whose points are not irreverent but sacrilegious; its hymns of 'love' are evilly hateful."[114]

Although *Hair* generated a great deal of opposition, it garnered a number of supporters. They applauded its daring score and non-illusionistic staging. Most of all they loved the innocence with which the hippies were portrayed. After admitting to his anxious readership that "yes" the music was loud and "yes" there was nudity, Walter Kerr positively cooed: "The show isn't a hard sell. It isn't even a sell... There is no pressure to buy the bag, no fear in the performers. They aren't wooing you anxiously. Neither are they walloping you desperately. They are simply beside you, like bears coming into your cabin in Yellowstone Park."[115] Richard Watts, Jr. also emerged as a fan. "*Hair* has surprising if perhaps unintentional charm; its high spirits are contagious, and its young zestfulness makes it difficult to resist."[116]

Basically, *Hair* reflected the innocence of the period rather than its angst. As such, it may have been accused of compromising the standards of Broadway but not of corrupting the morals of audiences – at least not in the vast majority of the cities to which it toured. There were, however, exceptions. Demonstrators from the Smite Smut League and the Gay Liberation Front protested the Washington, DC production and an outraged clergyman in St. Paul released twelve mice in the lobby to frighten the audience. These two events, however, were minimal when compared to what happened in Boston and Chattanooga.

By February 20, 1970, when *Hair* was scheduled to open in Boston at the Wilbur Theatre, it had already been successfully produced in fifteen cities world-wide. Bostonians were obviously excited, as advanced sales exceeded $600,000. However, Suffolk County District Attorney Garrett H. Byrne saw a preview performance and asserted that certain scenes in the show violated Massachusetts' obscenity laws. He vowed that he would close the production and prosecute all offending parties. Gerald Berlin, counsel for the producers, requested that the Supreme Judicial Court of Massachusetts grant injunctive relief to the plaintiffs from prosecution by the District Attorney. Each of the judges of the high court of Massachusetts saw a preview performance. They subsequently ruled that *Hair* constituted "in some degree, an obscure form of protest protected under the First Amendment and that viewed apart from the specific incidents mentioned ... it is not lewd and lascivious, whatever other objections there may be to it." However, the justices also announced that they would grant injunctive relief if, and only if, each member of the cast was clothed "to a reasonable extent at all times," and "all simulation of sexual intercourse or deviation" was eliminated.[117] Rather than make the required changes, the producers closed the show on April 10 and appealed to the US District Court to enjoin District Attorney Byrne.

On May 6, 1970, the United States District Court for the District of Massachusetts issued its decision. First, it established that live theatre was entitled to the same First Amendment protection that had been afforded to written material and films. Thus, the judges clearly forbade the state from interfering with live theatre unless they could prove the production to be "constitutionally obscene." Not merely offensive, but "constitutionally obscene."[118]

Second, the judges addressed whether or not the Massachusetts statute punishing lewd and lascivious behavior and the common law prohibiting indecent exposure upon which District Attorney Byrne based his case could be applied to a theatrical performance.[119] The judges reasoned that audiences, unlike unsuspecting bystanders, were willing and forewarned observers. They added, "such other factors as pose, lighting, angle of audience vision, mobility and dramatic context greatly influence what exactly is seen or perceived." Otherwise, "a dim silhouette of a naked form would be as punishable as the most blatant form of eroticism." Similarly, they ruled that the universal application of the "lewd and lascivious behavior" statute to all simulations of sexual deviation might make the portrayal of a deviate in a drama impossible. Finally, they clearly stated an opinion that was utterly crucial to contemporary theatre: "We cannot escape the conclusion that to apply the standards of the street and marketplace to the world behind the footlights would be to sanction a censorship dragnet of unconstitutional proportions ... actors and producers will either avoid Boston altogether or will steer clear of the forbidden zone by excising constitutionally protected material in order to avoid the risk of a three year prison term. Either result is offensive to the First Amendment."[120]

However, the District Attorney was not done. He won a stay to prevent the injunction from taking effect, but, in a 4–4 decision, one vote short of the majority, the Supreme Court voted to rescind the stay. *Hair* reopened in Boston on May 23, 1970. The victory in Boston clearly articulated that theatre, like novels and movies, was a fictional realm to which the rules governing the "street and marketplace" could not be wholly applied. District Attorney Byrne wanted to ban public nudity and eroticism regardless of the context. The Circuit Court, and ultimately the Supreme Court, recognized that there was a fundamental difference between an artistic statement that utilized nudity or sexuality and the world beyond the footlights.

Fourteen months later, *Hair* encountered a different type of opposition. Southwest Productions, Inc., a Little Rock firm, wanted to book the Little Rock Auditorium for a six-night engagement of the musical. The Auditorium Commission refused to grant a contract because it deemed that the musical was obscene. Southwest filed a suit against the Commission in federal District Court claiming that the prohibition constituted illegal prior restraint of First Amendment rights. Federal Judge G. Thomas Eisele concurred and ordered a contract to be issued for the requested dates.[121]

Although the Little Rock case was important, it remained an isolated decision because local authorities did not appeal to the Supreme Court. In October, a similar situation obtained in Chattanooga. Southeast Promotions applied to use the Tivoli Theatre, a privately owned theatre under long-term lease to the city, to present *Hair* for six days beginning November 23, 1971. (By this date *Hair* had been performed in 140 cities in the United and States and had been playing on Broadway for 3 years.) The theatre's governing board rejected the application. The producers petitioned the United States District Court for the Eastern District of Tennessee to issue a temporary restraining order, but the court refused. Some weeks later, the producers petitioned the city to rent the larger Memorial Auditorium for one performance of *Hair*. Once again, their request was rejected, as was their subsequent request for an injunction. On this occasion, the United States District Court, using an advisory jury, ruled that *Hair* was obscene because the group nudity and simulated sex violated city ordinances and state statutes. The US Circuit Court of Appeals affirmed the decision and the case proceeded to the Supreme Court.[122]

Southeast urged the high court to reverse the lower court decisions because (1) the Board's action constituted prior restraint; (2) the courts had applied incorrect standards for the determination of obscenity; and (3) the record did not support the contention that *Hair* was obscene. Luckily, the justices chose to decide the case on the merit of the first contention, and the producers were not called to enter the murky obscenity debate. In a favorable decision, the court ruled that public officials had appropriated the power to deny use of a forum in advance of actual expression. The court, citing numerous precedents, held that the commission had acted illegally when it kept the controversial musical offstage. Rather than allow law-enforcement authorities to prosecute any illegal action that occurred, "they denied the application in anticipation that the production would violate the law."[123]

The court further maintained that the two theatres were public forums designed for and dedicated to expressive activities. Whether the producers might have possibly used another, privately owned facility, did not justify this type of prior restraint of free speech. Citing *Schneider* v. *State*, it stated: "One is not to have the exercise of his liberty of expression in appropriate places abridged on the plea that it may be exercised in some other place ... Only if we were to conclude that live drama is unprotected by the First Amendment – or subject to a totally different standard from that applied to other forms of expression – could we possibly find no prior restraint here."[124]

Thus, by 1975, *Hair* had affirmed (and reaffirmed) several constitutional issues: (1) live stage productions were afforded First Amendment guarantees of free speech; (2) the presence of isolated, objectionable scenes in a stage production did not automatically transform the entire presentation into an obscene presentation; and (3) unpopular or transgressive activities and presentations could not be barred from public facilities without due process. Although it scored some impressive constitutional victories, it must be remembered that *Hair* was a triumphant Broadway production. It had played successfully on three continents and enjoyed the considerable emotional and financial backing of Michael Butler. Moreover, he had engaged a battalion of lawyers to defend its legal rights. *Hair* was, for all intents and purposes, a multinational corporation that enjoyed the protection afforded to such institutions. In the case of other transgressive productions, such conditions rarely if ever obtained.

While *Hair* may have been accused of obscenity, its use of nudity and sexual situations was positively benign when compared to other productions. In June 1968, Richard Schechner and his company, The Performance Group (TPG), opened *Dionysus in 69*, a contemporary reworking of *The Bacchae*. During the course of the production, a chorus of nude and/or partially nude actors staged an orgiastic birth ritual and periodically interacted with the audience. *Futz!*, by Rochelle Owens (directed by O'Horgan), also opened in June. It did not contain nudity but its story about a young man who married a pig nonetheless fueled controversy. In September, the Living Theatre opened *Paradise Now*, which, as previously noted, contained a section entitled "The Rite of Universal Intercourse," performed by the company in G-strings and bikinis. *Sweet Eros* by Terrance McNally in November featured a nude actress who was bound and gagged throughout the entire performance. In December, *The Young Master Dante* explored a sadistic world in which a young man was castrated by a jealous husband. Rochelle Owens' second play, *Beclch*, also appeared in December. It depicted the realistic slaughter of a goat and the strangulation of a naked king. In 1969, the two most controversial plays of the decade opened in New York. *Che!* in March and *Oh! Calcutta!* in June featured complete nudity and, in the case of the former, genital contact and simulated copulation. These and several other sexually transgressive plays encountered little official opposition in New York. Those that ventured out of the city's permissive environs were treated as harbingers of cultural and political anarchy.

Dionysus in 69 opened on June 6, 1968, at the Performance Garage in Soho. As in all of his productions, Schechner wanted to break (or obliterate) theatrical conventions that separated the life of the play from the life of the audience. However, Schechner wanted more than gratuitous participation. He hoped to recreate a communal experience that would bind the audience and actor in an ecstatic moment, which would simultaneously demolish the artificial constraints of western theatre and bourgeois society:

> Underneath whatever repressive machinery civilization constructs to keep itself intact, a counterforce of great unifying, celebratory, sexual, and life-giving power continues to exert its overwhelming and joyful influence. At certain times in everyone's life and during certain periods of each society's history this counterforce is activated ... It seems – when active – to be more authentic than the civilization – the specific social inhibitions – it opposes and frequently obliterates. Dionysus' presence can be beautiful or ugly or both. It seems quite clear that he is present in today's America – showing himself in the hippies, in the "carnival spirit" of black insurrectionists, on campuses ... LSD is contemporary chemistry, but freaking out is ancient. I take this special, ecstatic quality to be essentially theatrical.[125]

For Schechner, nakedness was a crucial feature of this ecstatic state, but he took pains to distinguish between nudity and nakedness. Nakedness was a political and a spiritual statement that revealed the psychic condition, stripped of all protection. Nudity was a creation of the entertainment industry that exploited the erotic potential of the human body for profit.[126]

However, the "nakedness" in *Dionysus in 69* was far more disturbing than the "nudity" in *Hair*. The production opened in June, but the company remained in rehearsal as the show continued to evolve. By December, the actors had decided to appear naked in two scenes – the opening scene depicting the birth ritual of Dionysus and Penthius and again when Agave kills Penthius – in order to heighten the ecstasy of the events. As agents of transformation, the company invited the audience to participate in dances that followed the birth of Dionysus. Audience members who wanted to be transfigured often stripped and participated enthusiastically in the ensuing revels. At this point, theatre and life had not only intersected, but had merged completely, as it became impossible to distinguish between actors and audience.[127]

Once TPG left the protective confines of Soho on a tour of west and Midwest university campuses, the tolerant reception that greeted *Dionysus in 69* evaporated. In Colorado Springs, *Dionysus* was called a "poisonous puss of four-letter words and a senseless display of nudity that seemingly occurred for the sake of nudity alone and for no other reason."[128] When the company arrived at the University of Minnesota in Minneapolis, it was summoned to a meeting with the Student Union Board of Governors (SUBG), consisting of faculty, students, and administrators. The Board maintained that, given the current tensions, onstage nudity would be too provocative. Schechner agreed not to perform in the nude, but the company was outraged over the censorship. As a result, it placed renewed energy into the invitation for the ecstasy dance, and two members of the audience responded by removing their clothing. The SUBG was outraged, accused the company of having planted conspirators, and bought out the contract for the company's final performance. With an open night available to it, the Performance Group performed at Firehouse Theatre, ecstatic scenes intact. In the audience was the mayor of Minneapolis.[129]

By the time TPG arrived at the University of Michigan in Ann Arbor, its exploits had been featured on the front page of the *Michigan Daily* and the town was extremely agitated. On January 26, the day before the company was to perform, President Robert W. Fleming issued a statement asserting that the university was not a "sanctuary" and that the laws of the community were applicable and enforceable on campus. Just hours before the performance, Schechner and another member of the company met with Chief of Police Walter Krasney. They wanted to know if the chief would arrest actors if the birth scene were performed in the nude. The chief refused to commit himself and would say only that he would have to witness the event. TPG's sponsor, the Union Activities Committee would not agree to post bond in the event of arrests. Nonetheless, the company performed the nude scenes. Ten performers were arrested and charged with indecent exposure, a high misdemeanor punishable by a $500 fine and one year in prison. At a post-performance news conference, Schechner, attended by an unidentified male actor clad only in eyeglasses and beads, promised to fight the arrests.[130]

Within forty-eight hours, Michigan lawmakers promised to investigate "subversion" and "corruption" at state colleges and universities. Republican Senator James Fleming, chief sponsor of the resolution, claimed that his constituents were, "sick to death of billy-goated, shaggy-haired idiots with little moral worth" who were interfering with their children's education.[131] Rather than investigating and addressing the issues that generated campus unrest, it was easier to indict outsiders for corrupting the students. As in the "Red Scares" of the previous decades, officials preferred to ignore inherent defects within their various systems in favor of blaming outsiders for the unrest. If only a monolithic, homogeneous community could be maintained, such problems would not occur.

Backlash

Nudity as a theatrical convention reached its apogee – or nadir, depending on one's point of view – in 1969. During that year, two plays, *Che!* and *Oh! Calcutta!*, created a furor inside and outside the theatrical community that has yet to be equaled. The first of these, *Che!*, was the only play to be brought to trial on charges of obscenity during the 1960s in New York. Written by Lennox Raphael, a 29-year-old native Trinidadian, it depicted the last hours of Che Guevara's life as a sexual nightmare. Aside from Che, it featured such characters as the President of the United States, Chilli Billy (Son of King Kong), Mayfang (Intelligence Agent), Sister of Mercy (Viciously Delicious Angelspy), and Breakstone Fearless (Movie Director). The text was meant to reveal that the relationship of a small Latin American nation to the United States was that of a victim and rapist. The 144-page script was an accumulation of stream-of-consciousness one-liners. It described characters who were violent, sexually aggressive, and was littered with obscenities. It was, however, the action that provoked a storm of protest. The actors, nude through most of the performance, presented the unthinkable – simulated sex acts, both homosexual and heterosexual – on stage. While such acts had been described in books and depicted in films, their presentation on stage by live actors transformed avant-garde theatrical practices into a prurient display – or so said *Che!*'s opponents.

Che! previewed on March 12, 1969, and opened on Saturday, March 22 at the Free Store Theatre on Cooper Square. Amos S. Basel, judge for the criminal court, attended a performance the following Monday. He left the theatre, briefly discussed the play with the chief of the New York City Police Department Morals' Squad and signed arrest warrants outside of the theatre. Police immediately entered the theatre and arrested five performers and five members of the production staff.[132] They were arraigned that night on charges of lewdness, consensual sodomy, and obscenity. Defendants and their attorney, Arthur Turco, a member of William Kunstler's defense team, charged that the $500 bail that had been set was excessive. Turco accused Judge Basel of prejudice, claiming, "it was his [Judge Basel's] conscience which was shocked."[133] Two days later, in an effort to have the closing of *Che!* set aside, Kunstler himself argued the case in federal District Court. He asserted that the play dealt with "political realities in sexual terms," and that it did not appeal exclusively to prurient interests. The court disagreed and refused to issue a restraining order.[134] On May 7, a statement of charges was issued. It contained fifty-four counts including consensual sodomy, public lewdness, obscenity, conspiracy to commit the above, and resisting arrest. That night, the company, which had reopened the production, was again arrested.[135]

There had been numerous controversies about nudity in New York theatre, but actors, academics, playwrights, and the media responded as if a bomb had exploded in their midst. An indignant editorial writer for the *New York Post* fumed that *Che!*, as well as other shows of the same ilk, are the "pervading curse of our lives."[136] The *New York Times* editorialized:

> Explicit portrayal on the stage of sexual intercourse is the final step in the erosion of taste and subtlety in the theatre. It reduces actors to mere exhibitionists, turns audiences into voyeurs and debases sexual relationships almost to the level of prostitution. It is difficult to see any great principle of civil liberties involved when persons indulging themselves on-stage in this kind of peep show activity are arrested for "public lewdness and obscenity."[137]

Newsweek called *Che!* "a squalid series of loveless fornications and related sexual gymnastics, performed in the nude and reminiscent of nothing so much as the kind of peep show that used to flourish in Port Said during the reign of the late King Farouk."[138]

For playwrights, the arrests were a divisive event. The joint councils of the Dramatists' Guild and the Authors' League issued a letter to Mayor John Lindsay. In it they maintained that closing the play prior to a judicial decision amounted to censorship by intimidation and seriously endangered the freedom of expression in theatre. They raised a familiar question. Does the law protect mimetic events performed on stage when those same events performed on the street might be a crime? "We believe that it does," they answered. "There is a difference between depicting murder on a stage and committing a murder on the stage. There is a difference between depicting sexual acts on a stage and literally engaging in certain varieties which the law makes criminal."[139]

Che! also raised the question of a hypothetical "outside limit of symbolic communication." For some playwrights, *Che!* had gone beyond that limit, but, for others, the process of establishing any boundary whatsoever would give rise to artists censoring other artists:

> if you start chipping away at the central doctrine, you're really cutting the ground from under your own feet. You'll never know where to stop. It seems to me, no price is too high to pay for a free press, even if the price is allowing something like *Che!* to be exhibited to those people who are willing to go to a box office and pay for it.[140]

Actors were faced with decisions that transcended the issue of censorship. Artistic liberation clashed head on with personal integrity and privacy. As artists, actors were asked to discover and then integrate intimate and some-times painful personal experiences into their characterizations. Now they were being told that nudity was the ultimate form of personal disclosure. Actor Monica Evans, who had turned down roles that demanded nudity, said: "I kept thinking, that wouldn't be me the actress – that would be me . . . Nudity invades the rights of a human being. My body belongs to me – that's my private life, my personal territory." Sally Kirkland who originated the role "The Girl" in *Sweet Eros*, had been an artist's model and a dancer, and her attitude stood in stark opposition to that of Evans. For Kirkland, her body was the artwork, and performing nude seemed entirely natural. "I have no hang-up about nudity," she stated. "I think the human body is beautiful and as long as I feel that what I am doing is artistic, I have no objection to appearing nude."[141]

Meanwhile, Actors' Equity was besieged with complaints from actors who were being asked to disrobe at auditions and for performances. The union responded by issuing a set of guidelines aimed at protecting its members. It stipulated that an actor could be asked to remove his/her clothes only after the singing, dancing, and acting auditions had been completed; that an Equity official had to be present on such occasions, which, in turn, could be attended only by recognized producers, directors, and choreographers; and finally, that any actor had to be informed in writing if the script called for nudity or any simulated sex acts before contracts were signed. Under this policy, a producer had to indemnify a performer in case of arrest, and furnish all fines, bail, and legal fees.[142]

While Equity was hammering out its policy on nudity, *Che!* languished in the courts and finally went to trial in January 1970. Producer David Merrick testified that the performance he saw was "patently offensive," containing all "combinations of physical contact" that he found "prurient, lewd, and vulgar." He said that the playwright, Lennox Raphael, was without any talent whatsoever and should seek vocational guidance. He concluded by claiming that New York theatre was essentially "going to the dogs."[143] Clive Barnes, as well as other expert witnesses, testified that the play was essentially political, and while it was of low quality, it still retained redeeming social value and should not be closed.[144]

On February 25, 1970, in a 2–1 decision, a panel of judges in the Manhattan Criminal Court convicted *Che!* They ruled that the cast, producer, playwright, and set designer were "guilty beyond a reasonable doubt of participating in an obscene performance which predominantly appealed and pandered to prurient interest and went beyond the customary limits of candor in presenting profanity, filth, defecation, masochism, sadism, masturbation, nudity, copulation, sodomy and other deviate sexual intercourse." Judge Arthur H. Goldberg, who wrote the majority opinion, rejected Lennox Raphael's argument that the sexual content of the play was identical to its political message. He stated: "The pretended political content of the play was elusive, both in performance of the play and in its commercial exploitation, and . . . the whole play and performance had no redeeming social value." He also ignored the contention that *Che!* was part of the experimental Off-Off Broadway theatrical movement that dealt openly with sex. He countered: "But it cannot be said that standards of public acceptance and morality so sharply different and shocking can be established by a few commercially inspired producers who try to see how far they can go." He expressed his belief that the legislature's refusal to eliminate New

York's obscenity laws meant that a "line," no matter how blurred, existed between what was permissible and impermissible. And while he admitted that *Che!* had "social value," he did not believe it had "redeeming social value."[145]

The negative response to *Che!* as well as to other sexually transgressive performances received substantial impetus when Richard Nixon was elected president in November 1968. Those who opposed such depictions now had a powerful ally in the White House, and an incipient, but vigorous national opposition emerged. In March 1969, Jim Morrison of "The Doors" was arrested in Miami for exposing himself and using obscene language at a concert attended by thousands of teenagers. In response, a Miami teenager, with support from the Veterans of Foreign Wars (VFW) and local churches, organized a "Rally for Decency" that was attended by over 30,000 people, mostly flag-waving youth. The idea caught on and similar rallies sprang up in Indianapolis, Cincinnati, Minneapolis, Birmingham, and Austin.[146] Self-generated groups calling themselves "Citizens for Decent Literature" sprang up around the nation and promised to appear on the prosecution side in every pornography case that went before the Supreme Court. And by July 1969 over 135 anti-pornography bills were pending before the House Judiciary Committee.[147]

Perhaps the most vivid indication of an organized conservative response to sexually transgressive performances occurred in the fall of 1970. On August 10, a draft of the report of the Presidential Commission on Obscenity and Pornography, which had come into being at the very end of the Johnson administration, was leaked to a House subcommittee. To the representatives' considerable horror, it announced the very opposite of what had been expected. Pornography did not lead to sex crimes and the government should stop policing sexual materials aimed at consenting adults. Nixon called the report morally bankrupt and vowed to continue to appoint justices to the Supreme Court who believed that "American morality is not to be trifled with."[148] However, just as the Commission on Pornography was reaching its much maligned conclusions, and as "Rallies for Decency" were proclaiming the need for moral reclamation, *Oh! Calcutta!*, the first nude musical revue premiered in New York. *Oh! Calcutta!* was the brainchild of English theatre critic Kenneth Tynan. He envisioned it as a revue using "artistic means to achieve erotic stimulation. Nothing that is *merely* funny or *merely* beautiful should be admitted: it must also be sexy... no crap about art or redeeming 'literary merit': this show will be expressly designed to titillate, in the most elegant and outré way."[149]

Tynan originally contacted such luminaries as Peter Brook and Harold Pinter to direct the production, but both demurred. He finally settled on Jacques Levy, who had directed *America Hurrah* for the Open Theatre. He then invited several eminent writers such as John Lennon, Sam Shepard, Samuel Beckett, Leonard Melfi, Jules Feiffer, and David Newman to submit short erotic sketches. (Tynan refused to disclose which writer had written what script, thereby protecting the anonymity of the authors as well as increasing curiosity about the production.)

Unlike other productions of the period that employed nudity, *Oh! Calcutta!* was not a polemic. Sex was never intended as metaphor for international aggression nor was it linked to other controversial issues such as drug use, racism, or student radicalism. *Oh! Calcutta!* was simply a series of sketches, songs, and dances performed wholly or partially nude which reinforced middle-class fantasies about various heterosexual experiences. As such, producer Hillard Elkins was extremely solicitous of New York authorities to insure that the production fell within the limits of the law. "We are not trying to make a revolution," he remarked. "I am simply trying to produce an entertainment in the erotic area in the best possible taste. We do not wish to offend, we want to amuse and we're looking for all the help we can get."[150] As a result, most of the material that the police and District Attorney found unacceptable was deleted from the production. In addition to these officials, Senator Jacob Javits, Rudolf Nureyev, and Jerome Robbins were called in to give their opinions. Consequently, *Oh! Calcutta!* generated a great deal of curiosity, but little passion.[151]

Oh! Calcutta! opened in the old Phoenix Theatre, an off-Broadway house on Second Avenue, provocatively renamed "The Eden," on June 17, 1969. The reviews were, for the most part, unforgiving. Critics, expecting to see "pornography for intellectuals" or "eroticism for sophisticates," were extremely disappointed – and angry. Clive Barnes called the writing "doggedly sophomoric and soporific," and closed by claiming that he would recommend the show only to people who were "extraordinarily underprivileged either sexually, socially or emotionally. Now is your chance to stand up and be counted."[152] Some, like Richard Cooke, seemed genuinely disappointed that Tynan had not delivered on his promise "to make the best of sexual frankness and to present its nuances and its emotional content."[153] Martin Gottfried said that the sketches authored by the literary elite were inferior, and had it not been for the "sexual subject matter and the regular absence of clothes, they would seem still worse ... If you're taking pornography on the simple level of arousal art, stag movies are as good as anything done yet."[154]

Irrespective of the low opinion expressed by New York critics, the show remained opened and played to capacity houses. The police, as expected, did not interfere. Given the nature of the revue, its producers wisely did not attempt to tour for several years. They did, however, license a production for Los Angeles that opened on November 25, 1969. Two municipal judges, vice squad officers, and two city attorneys attended the performance to determine if it violated state obscenity laws. In their opinion it did and they issued warrants for the arrest of the producer, director, and eight members of the cast on December 17. Attorneys for the company told reporters that a constitutional right was at stake and expressed dismay that Los Angeles authorities would prosecute a show that had been seen by over 200,000 people in New York. The December 18 performance had to be cancelled, but a federal District Court issued an injunction against further arrests, thereby allowing the production to reopen until the matter was settled in court.[155]

As the Nixon administration's campaign against indecency gathered strength, *Oh! Calcutta!* came to symbolize all that was immoral in America. No longer was it merely a stage play with nude actors performing in mildly amusing sketches about sex, it was the embodiment of decadence and, within a few months of its opening, the Justice Department and the federal courts would become involved in its suppression. At the center of the turmoil was Charles Keating. A Cincinnati attorney, Keating was a modern-day Anthony Comstock. He headed that city's chapter of Citizens for Decent Literature and was Nixon's only appointee to the notorious Presidential Commission on Obscenity and Pornography. He vigorously opposed the process and findings of the panel, and very nearly succeeded in suppressing the report entirely. After a long struggle, he succeeded in publishing a minority report that voiced the administration's point of view.[156]

In what seemed to be a perverse coincidence, a closed-circuit telecast of *Oh! Calcutta!* was slated to be shown in movie theatres in 200 cities nationwide on September 28, 1970 – the day before Keating's minority report was to be submitted – and Cincinnati, his hometown, was to receive the transmission. Thus, while Keating was alerting the nation to the dangers of pornography, *Oh! Calcutta!* was about to open in his own backyard. He quickly filed suit to block the showing, claiming the production was a public nuisance and appealed only to prurient interests.[157] Thanks also to Keating's efforts, police chiefs and district attorneys across the nation were alerted to *Oh! Calcutta!*'s imminent arrival. Theatres began to renege on their commitments and, at final count, the number of participating sites had dwindled to about seventy-five.[158]

The Orson Welles Cinema in Cambridge, Massachusetts did not cancel its screening. However, nine employees of the theatre were arrested and charged with allowing the premises to be used for showing immoral and obscene entertainment.[159] The Center Theatre in Corpus Christi, Texas also aired the telecast. On May 19, 1971, Attorney General John Mitchell announced that the federal grand jury in that city had issued a single count indictment against Colormedia Corporation. It asserted that the film's producer had used American Telephone and Telegraph's long lines for the interstate transmission of an "obscene, lewd, lascivious and filthy videotape production entitled *Oh! Calcutta!* from New York to Corpus Christi." The federal statute that had presumably been violated was the Comstock Law of 1873.[160] *Oh! Calcutta!* continued to play to sold out houses in New York, but gradually faded from the national consciousness. No local professional theatres dared to produce it, and a tour, at least for the foreseeable future, would be hampered by litigation.

In 1973, the Supreme Court drastically altered the definition of obscenity. During his tenure in office, President Nixon had managed to appoint four new justices to the Supreme Court – Chief Justice Warren Burger, William Rehnquist, Lewis Powell, and Harry Blackmun. These men, along with Byron White, formed the solid conservative majority that, in Burger's words, would reexamine "obscenity doctrine to formulate standards more concrete than those of the past."[161] On June 21, 1973, the court made good on its word and handed down five separate decisions, all of which redefined obscenity – and all decided by 5 to 4 majority.[162] By far the most crucial of these decisions was *Miller* v. *California*. In this case, a California man who mailed unsolicited pictures and drawings was convicted of a misdemeanor. However, the jury had been instructed to apply contemporary community standards of the state rather than national standards when reaching a verdict. The Supreme Court agreed with the California court. The decision, authored by Burger, purged the "national standard of decency," as articulated by Justice Harlan in *Manual Enterprises* v. *Day* in 1962, from the law. In its place stood a new definition of "community," one that permitted each community to create its own definition of obscenity:

Although fundamental First Amendment limitations on the powers of the states as to obscene material do not vary from community to community, nevertheless this does not mean that there are, or should or can be, fixed, uniform national standards of precisely what appeals to the "prurient interest" or is "patently offensive"; *obscenity is to be determined by applying "contemporary community standards," not "national standards."* ... It is neither realistic nor constitutionally sound to read the First Amendment as requiring that people of Maine or Missouri accept public depiction of conduct found tolerable in Las Vegas or New York City. (emphasis mine)[163]

However, the Chief Justice did not stop there. In *Roth* v. *United States*, Justice Brennan had stated that, before a work could be declared obscene, it had to be deemed "utterly worthless." Burger disagreed. He maintained that a work might be judged obscene if it "lacks *serious* literary, artistic, political or scientific value" (emphasis mine). In essence, Burger had completely reversed the burden of proof in obscenity cases. Prior to *Miller*, the prosecution had to prove that a work was "utterly worthless." After June 21, 1973, the defense had to establish that the accused creation had "value." Conspicuously absent from Burger's definition was entertainment value. By omitting this consideration, the Supreme Court specifically stated that a play, book, or movie that was entertaining did not necessarily possess value.[164]

Chief Justice Burger completed his "re-evaluation of obscenity" with *Paris Adult Theatre* v. *Slanton*. The case involved a Georgia Supreme Court's declaration that two films were obscene because they contained simulated sexual conduct. Chief Justice Burger used this opinion to strike down the belief that obscenity laws were unenforceable when consenting adults were involved. He wrote: "We categorically disapprove the theory...that obscene, pornographic films acquire constitutional immunity from state regulation simply because they are exhibited for consenting adults only."[165] While the court declared that an individual had a zone of privacy when at home, it denied that that zone traveled with him/her to a public theatre.[166]

In essence, the Supreme Court returned a prodigious amount of power to communities, which might prosecute whatever displays offended local standards. Moreover, consenting adults could no longer safely choose their own entertainments. Chief Justice Burger clearly affirmed that local governments were fully justified in defining the limits of physical expression. Moreover, he declared that the display of human bodies had a direct impact on the well-being of the state. The response to these rulings was, not surprisingly, divided. Jules Feiffer commented that if Americans looked closely they would see that "the freedom to which we commit ourselves is freedom *from* not freedom *to*. Freedom from those guys, freedom from weird ideas, freedom from bother, freedom from thought, freedom from equality, freedom from art, freedom from sex." Joan Crawford added: "That's it – that's what we'll be missing ultimately – the truth, and without it we will sink back into the unrealities and banalities of the past. To preserve our liberties, we must read and see whatever we please. Boredom will pronounce its own death sentence on repetitive pornography." William F. Buckley commented: "I vigorously applaud the decision of the Supreme Court . . . [It] said nothing more complicated than there is, in fact, a commerce in pornography and obscenity and that it was never a commitment of the First Amendment to protect that commerce against legislation by a self-ruling people."[167] One of the most passionate pleas for censorship came from Diana Ronald, New York Diocesan Chairwoman of Women for Decency, a Roman Catholic organization:

> In this war between good and evil, we must learn to recognize who our enemies are and what weapons they use. Key words and phrases such as "censorship," "freedom of speech," "art," "vigilantes," "puritans," "book burners," and "blue noses," are being used as weapons by those forces which are out to destroy every last vestige of decency and good taste, thus bringing about the moral destruction of our nation.[168]

With these Supreme Court decisions, the radical theatre of the sixties began to wither. It was to be expected. While the Civil Rights Act had addressed some of the more public forms of discrimination, the roots of racial bigotry were still deeply imbedded in the national soil. No amount of student protests had been able to end the Vietnam War, and the National Guard killings at Kent State in 1970 clearly indicated that radical college students would now be treated as enemies of the state. The populace was able to tolerate more sexual freedom, but one was never sure if an enlightened consciousness or Madison Avenue hype was responsible. Yet politics and sex would remain inextricably united as homosexuality and AIDS dominated the cultural landscape of the 1980s and 1990s.

6

The past is prologue

The birth of a movement

"Culture Wars" is the term generally applied to the intense and often violent discourse that erupted during the years between Richard Nixon's reelection in 1972 and the end of the millennium. The period was marked by an unprecedented alliance between conservative political activists who abhorred the growth of the federal government, and fundamentalist Christians who claimed that the liberal political agenda of the previous decade had generated a serious moral decline. Together they formed a coalition that waged a cultural revolution designed to recreate a putative American Golden Age. As political revolutionaries, they preached a doctrine that called for a return to isolationism, larger national defense budgets, smaller human service programs, protection of private property, and support for free enterprise. As cultural revolutionaries, they demanded that American society resurrect the fixed moral code that dominated the ideology of the last quarter of the nineteenth century. Specifically, they demanded a hierarchical arrangement ruled by white heterosexual males and supported by white heterosexual wives all of whom lived within a traditional family structure. It was a paradigm that defined itself by what it rejected, and it indicted homosexuality, promiscuity, divorce, and interracial unions as perversions that had shredded the moral fabric of American society.

This alliance waged several successful high-profile battles including the defeat of the Equal Rights Amendment and the weakening of abortion rights. It opposed television programs that dealt with homosexuality, and organized national boycotts of films that questioned the orthodox Christian interpretations of the Bible. It also targeted visual and performing artists whose creations challenged the authority of the white, heterosexual paradigm that was being urged.

The early salvos of the culture wars were not aimed specifically at theatre. However, the efforts to censure certain theatrical productions that were conducted by local governments in the 1990s were directly inspired by Congress' attempts to eliminate the National Endowment for the Arts. It was these efforts that literally created the terrain upon which subsequent theatrical censorship battles were waged. For this reason it will be helpful to review the evolution of this struggle.

While the most contentious struggles of the conservative revolution were fought from 1989 through 1999, the battle lines began to take shape during the early seventies. During these years, conservative political leaders blamed their opponents for promoting prodigal social legislation that had led to the moral, military, and economic decline of the nation. If the United States was to reclaim its ascendancy, it would have to be led by elected officials who would eliminate costly social service programs, abolish government agencies that interfered with free enterprise, invest heavily in national defense, and support the principles of traditional Christian morality.

This plan first bore fruit during the 1968 presidential campaign that elected Richard Nixon. Although Nixon was never really considered a true conservative and had to beat back a last minute challenge from the supporters of Ronald Regan, he and independent candidate George Wallace polled 57 percent of the popular vote. It was a resounding victory for the conservative movement.[1] During the next four years, strategists developed a plan to build a conservative majority within the Republican Party by stripping Democrats of their traditional constituencies – east-coast Catholics, blue-collar workers, and small farmers. The new Republican gospel preached that drugs, sexual permissiveness, pornography, lack of respect for authority, and the growth of the welfare state were the "consequences of social liberalism" and blamed Democrats for delivering America to the brink of anarchy.[2]

Yet this conservative political gospel could not have taken root if another gospel, the fundamentalist gospel, was not also being preached. The tenets of fundamentalist Christianity were first articulated in 1909 in a series of booklets named *The Fundamentals: A Testimony of Truth* written by a number of ministers and theologians to combat the growing modernization of religion. These essays claimed that traditional Christian beliefs would have to be resuscitated and reclaimed if humankind was to survive. They were primarily concerned with theological purity and preached biblical inerrancy and the divinity of Jesus. Thus, belief in and adherence to ancient Christian beliefs would be able to assure salvation and protect the true believer from the dangers of the outside.[3] For the next sixty years, fundamentalists abjured secular issues and chose to concentrate solely on the challenge of personal salvation. The world, they declared, was beset with sin and strife and should be avoided at all costs. Society would be saved if and only if every individual affirmed the redemptive power of Jesus.

Conservative politicians and Christian fundamentalists agreed in principle on a number of issues, most notably prohibition, opposition to the burgeoning federal bureaucracy, fear of Communism, and the building of a strong national defense. However, they were too suspicious of one another to create a unified and effective political movement. The former feared that "church-going folk" were too naïve to engage in high-level political strategy. The latter believed that politics was corrupt and would only corrupt those who participated in it. On no account could faith in human institutions supplant faith in God.

During the 1960s and early 1970s, however, fundamentalists came to believe that officials running the federal government were determined to obliterate all vestiges of fundamental, Christian religion. Eventually this fear drove these powerful, but politically passive groups into the conservative wing of the Republican Party. This coalition aggressively challenged artists who wished to display or perform any scene that undermined traditional attitudes toward race, gender roles, sexuality, or religion.

Active distrust of the federal government surfaced in 1963 when the Supreme Court proscribed prayers in public schools. Fundamentalists were profoundly shocked. It seemed impossible that in this Christian nation children were not permitted to pray in school. Local control of schools was further eroded when court-ordered busing was established in order to achieve racial balance in public schools. They were again outraged when, in 1971 and 1972, Congress approved the Equal Rights Amendment. Fundamentalists interpreted this amendment, which read, "Equality of rights under the law shall not be denied or abridged by the United States or any state on account of sex," as a blatant threat to Christian families. In their opinion, it would prohibit women from fulfilling their biblical role as submissive wives, serving primarily in the home. Finally in 1973, the Supreme Court in *Roe* v. *Wade* gave women almost complete control of reproduction by legalizing abortion. Tim LaHaye, a leading fundamentalist spokesman, called this aggregate of laws an example of "secular humanism," which he blamed for "today's wave of crime and violence in our streets, promiscuity, divorce, shattered dreams, and broken hearts." He declared it to be the "world's greatest evil" and claimed that its adherents were waging an all-out war on Christianity.[4] If Christians did not take control, the United States, the "city on the hill," would be transformed into a nation of godless heathens. Clearly, secular humanism was considered to be the most pernicious threat Christianity had ever encountered.[5]

Although fundamentalists throughout the nation agreed that "secular humanism" posed a significant danger, Christians in the South embraced this concept with exceptional fervor. At the end of World War II, the South was two-thirds rural, but, by 1960, less than 50 percent of the population lived in the countryside. During that same period, gains in education, a broadening industrial base, air-conditioning, and cheap labor laid the foundation for a massive influx from other parts of the nation. The combination of newcomers, economic prosperity, and urban diversity created a pluralistic environment never before experienced in the South. These changes, combined with the social restructuring brought about by the Civil Rights and Feminist movements, created a culture that native southerners hardly recognized. Beliefs that had sustained their families and their small traditional communities now had to be defended if they were to survive the challenges of the modern world.[6]

In an effort to resist these cultural mutations, fundamentalist Christians undertook a variety of strategies. For decades, fundamentalists had built an infrastructure of revivals, publishing houses, Bible institutes, and radio stations that advanced the causes of doctrinal orthodoxy. Thus it was no surprise when fundamentalists responded to the challenges of secular humanism by creating parallel systems that would protect believers from these pernicious trends. The cornerstone of this development was the "superchurch." The modest, unpretentious meeting hall was replaced by the "superchurch," a facility with thousands of members and multiple buildings that housed choirs, schools, tennis courts, skating rinks, classes, and radio stations.[7]

Equally as important as the superchurches was the emergence of television ministries that began to appear with the advent of cable television. By 1978, television evangelists and religious entrepreneurs such as Jerry Falwell, Pat Robertson, Jim Bakker, Oral Roberts, James Robison, and Rex Humbard had established vast audiences in dozens of cities. They decried threats posed by secular humanism, markedly increased the political content of their programs, encouraged viewers to take individual action, and advanced their own political fortunes. To support their crusades, they built computerized mailing lists and honed sophisticated fund-raising techniques. By January 1980, religious broadcasters claimed audiences in the millions, hundreds of thousands of individual contributors, and bulging treasuries. Although evangelists and reporters often exaggerated the extent of these new religious empires, conservative political strategists quickly recognized that all of the necessary parts of a political machine had already been put into place. As Gary Jarmin, a noted political strategist noted: "The beauty of it is that we don't have to organize these voters. They already have their own television networks, publications, schools, meeting places, and respected leaders who are sympathetic to our goals."[8]

Jarmin, as well as other prominent "New Right" political organizers such as Richard Viguerie, Howard Phillips, Paul Weyrich, and Robert Billings actively targeted this constituency when Jimmy Carter failed to fulfill the dreams of southern evangelicals who had voted in great numbers for him in 1976. By 1978, Jarmin and company transformed these disenchanted voters into what would be known as the "Christian Right," a social movement that mobilized millions of evangelical Protestants and other orthodox Christians on behalf of conservative political apologists. Viguerie, a mass-mailing fund-raising specialist, shared his techniques with evangelical leaders. Jarmin helped to establish Christian Voice, an outgrowth of anti-gay, anti-pornography groups, which was supported nationally on Pat Robertson's "700 Club." Edward McAteer joined forces with James Robison and created Religious Roundtable, especially designed to appeal to fundamentalist ministers who were uneasy with political activism. The best publicized of the Roundtable's "Workshops" was held in August 1980 in Dallas, where these ministers heard speeches from every major New Right figure, many televangelists, southern Baptist president Bailey Smith, and presidential candidate Ronald Reagan, who enthusiastically endorsed the Roundtable's efforts.[9]

It was the Moral Majority, however, that became synonymous with the Christian Right. Originally conceived by Jerry Falwell in July 1979, Robert Billings crafted the organization into a finely tuned political machine that captured the public imagination as well as the attention of the media. More than any other group, it symbolized a revitalized, politically potent fundamentalist movement. With pastors as primary organizers, Moral Majority quickly became a household name in large suburban churches, while television preachers spread its message to their massive audiences. It distributed information through newsletters, seminars, and broadcast ministries, conducted voter registration drives, and lobbied Congress with letters and phone calls. It recruited and trained Christian conservatives to run for local offices, and organized hundreds of independent churches into a comprehensive grass-roots activist network.[10]

Most importantly, the leaders of the Christian Right agreed to define "moral issues" broadly enough to incorporate the New Right's economic and foreign policy stances. By so doing, a host of New Right Congressional heroes were only too happy to make moral regeneration part of a larger conservative platform that included tax cuts, increased defense spending, and curtailment of welfare programs. By far the most important Congressional advocates of the Christian Right was Senator Jesse Helms (R-NC). Helms introduced the Moral Majority's lobbyists to his colleagues, and advised them personally on political strategy. Helms, however, was not the only Congressional advocate of this conservative agenda. He was supported in the Senate by Orrin Hatch (R-Utah), James McClure (R-Ida.), Roger Jepsen (R-Ia.), Gordon Humphrey (R-NH), John Tower (R-Tex.), Alphonse D'Amato (R-N.Y.) and John Danforth (R-Mo.). He was joined by dozens of House members, the most prominent of whom were Larry McDonald (D-Ga.), Daniel Crane (R-Ill.), Robert Dornan (R-Calif.), Dana Rohrabacher (R-Calif.), Richard Armey (R-Tex.), and Newt Gingrich (R-Ga.).

The New Right targets the NEA

The New Right, buttressed by the Christian Right, managed to elect Ronald Regan in 1980 and 1984, and George Bush in 1988, but a floor to ceiling moral revolution failed to materialize. *Roe* v. *Wade*, although somewhat compromised by subsequent Supreme Court decisions, was still the law of the land. Forced prayer was still disallowed in public schools. The Equal Rights Amendment had been defeated, but women and gays continued to acquire more civil rights efforts. In short, the Christian Right, even with the help of their Congressional allies, had not been able to undo the secular humanist agenda that had been put into place during the sixties and seventies. Still, religious and political conservatives searched for a pivotal social issue that could bind these forces in an alliance that could force significant cultural changes. They found their target in 1989. It was the National Endowment for the Arts (NEA), a small government agency that provided financial support to institutions and individual artists. Within months after the original assault launched by Jesse Helms on the floor of the Senate, the NEA became synonymous with every social disease that infected the nation.

The crisis started in an innocuous manner. Andreas Serrano, a black, lapsed Catholic artist living in Brooklyn, had created a series of photographs dealing with bodily fluids – blood, semen, saliva, and urine. "Piss Christ," a 1987 work, depicted a plastic crucifix immersed in a beaker supposedly containing the photographer's urine. His point was twofold: to comment on the cheapening of religion and to examine the transformation and sharing of bodily substances within the Catholic tradition, the most obvious being the transmogrification of bread and water into the body and blood of Jesus. Later that year, he and ten other artists were chosen to receive grants from the Southeastern Center for Contemporary Art (SECCA) in Winston-Salem, North Carolina. Each artist received $15,000, and exhibitions of their works were arranged in three cities – Los Angeles, Pittsburgh, and Richmond. Funding for this SECCA project came from the Rockefeller Foundation, Equitable Life, and the NEA, which, like all government programs, supported the project with taxpayers' dollars.

The tour encountered no opposition until it reached Richmond where an irate viewer interpreted Serrano's work as an attack on Christianity. In a letter to the *Richmond Times-Dispatch* he claimed: "The Virginia Museum should not be in the business of promoting and subsidizing hatred and intolerance. Would they pay the KKK to do a work defaming blacks? Would they display a Jewish symbol under urine? Has Christianity become fair game in our society for any kind of blasphemy and slander?"[11]

Apparently the irate viewer failed to comprehend the basic distinction between Christians, African Americans, and Jews. Christians are a majority in any sense of the word and dominate virtually every governmental, educational, and cultural institution in the United States. And, while Serrano's photograph may not have been flattering, it clearly was not intended as a blanket invitation for non-Christian minorities to deprive Christians of their life, liberty, or property. Nonetheless, the letter was forwarded to The Revd Donald Wildmon, a fundamentalist preacher and president of the American Family Association (AFA) in Tupelo, Mississippi. The AFA, a Christian Right advocacy group organized in the late seventies, targeted media that undermined Christian family values. Its prestige grew immeasurably when Wildmon mobilized some 400,000 members to protest the *Last Temptation of Christ* and convinced Pepsi-Cola to cancel a $5 million advertising contract with Madonna because her music video, *Like a Prayer*, was "blatantly offensive."[12] When Wildmon received this complaint, he sent a letter that reprised the theme of anti-Christian bigotry to every one of his 400,000 supporters. It read in part:

We should have known it would come to this. The bias and bigotry against Christians, which has dominated television and the movies for the past decade or more, has now moved into art museums ... As a young child growing up, I would never, ever have dreamed that I would live to see such demeaning disrespect and desecration of Christ in our country that is present today. Maybe, before the physical persecution of Christians begins, we will gain the courage to stand against such bigotry. I hope so.[13]

In April 1989, Wildmon sent a protest and a reproduction of "Piss Christ" to every member of Congress. Representative Armey spoke about the NEA's support of Serrano in the House and Alfonse D'Amato led the charge in the Senate. On May 18, the latter ripped up a Serrano catalogue, threw it on the floor, and stomped on it. He described how he had received complaints from hundreds of constituents who were outraged at Serrano's photograph and complained bitterly that the NEA had used taxpayers' money to support "trash," "garbage," and "filth."[14] Helms then took the floor. He railed that Serrano's photograph was "blasphemy," seconded D'Amato's accusations, and demanded that the NEA be abolished if it continued to exercise such irresponsible behavior.[15]

Political columnist Patrick Buchanan quickly jumped on the bandwagon and, to a large degree, defined the symbolic parameters of the debate. He claimed that America's art and culture had become openly anti-Christian, anti-American, and nihilistic. Quoting heavily from James Cooper, editor of the *American Arts Quarterly,* he asserted that conservatives had allowed liberals to determine the trajectory of American culture and that they had "meekly embraced without protest a nihilist, existentialist, secular humanist culture ... Those who believe in absolute values such as God and beauty do nothing, and those who believe in existentialist humanism have captured the culture." Thus, while conservative Americans were busy transforming American politics and supporting military adventures in Asia and Central America, liberals had been waging their own war on the "battlefield of the arts within our own borders." And, according to Buchanan and Cooper, they had completely vanquished patriotism and Christian idealism. If America's culture was to be reclaimed for Americans, the decadent artists would have to be silenced. There seemed to be no better method than to attack agencies that supported them financially.[16]

The Congressional attack on decadent and blasphemous art gained momentum in June of that year when the Corcoran Gallery in Washington stunned the art world. It cancelled "The Perfect Moment," a 150-piece exhibition of photographs by Robert Mapplethorpe. The University of Pennsylvania's Institute of Contemporary Art (ICA), assisted by a $30,000 grant from the NEA, assembled the show. The exhibition contained a wide range of Mapplethorpe's work. It was not, however, the photographs of flowers and character studies that disturbed the Corcoran's leadership. A number of the photographs portrayed children with exposed genitalia and homoerotic images that included erect penises of African Americans, as well as various sadomasochistic poses.[7] The controversy was further heightened by Mapplethorpe's recent death. The artist, an openly proclaimed homosexual, had died of AIDS in March 1989.

Various Corcoran officials justified their actions by contending that the exhibition would have embroiled the gallery in the volatile cultural debate that had erupted in Congress and might have further damaged the NEA. Moreover, it might also have jeopardized the Corcoran's funding from the NEA, as well as the National Capital Arts and Cultural Activities Program, another federal program that provided grants to Washington institutions. The president and chair of the Corcoran's Board of Trustees said: "It is indeed our function to ensure that the Corcoran does not damage itself or the NEA and the greater arts community. Weighing these considerations, and being fully aware of the public controversy ... the director and the board of trustees on June 26 reaffirmed the Corcoran's withdrawal from the tour of the Mapplethorpe exhibition as the prudent and wise course of action at this time."[18]

Artists and arts advocates pilloried the Corcoran for its decision. Board members resigned, donors canceled their pledges and changed their wills, and artists withdrew their works from upcoming shows. The National Committee Against Censorship in the Arts circulated petitions against the Corcoran at other galleries; and the National Association of Artists' Organizations bitterly complained: "It [the Corcoran] has betrayed all who believe in democracy and the right to freedom of expression. It has weakened all of our efforts to withstand the bullying cry of a vocal few."[19] The question of artistic freedom was debated at great length and with great ferocity. Samuel Lipman railed that artists had no right to expect that so-called works of art could only be judged by aesthetic criteria. The artist was also responsible for the content of the work. More importantly, audiences who failed to assess the impact of this content ignored responsibility for the "dreadful changes made in our lives, and the lives of our children, [caused] by the availability of this decadence everywhere, from high art to popular culture."[20] Robert Brustein, while he did not necessarily affirm the aesthetic merit of any artist who liked "to flout prevailing codes," nonetheless opposed "punitive moral constraints on independent aesthetic activity." "Once we allow law-makers to become art critics," he maintained, "we take the first step into the world of the Ayatollah Khomeini, whose murderous review of *The Satanic Verses* still chills the heart of everyone committed to free expression."[21] The abstract issue of artistic freedom, as discussed by many who debated the Corcoran decision, quickly became subsumed in the homosexual question – arguably the most contentious cultural discourse of the 1990s. Writing in the *Washington Post*, art historian Joshua Smith concisely summarized the salient issues. Contemporary viewers, because they are familiar with family albums, newspapers, and the evening news, assume that photographs capture an action that, whether candid or staged, actually transpired. Thus, the actual target of political and religious interest groups was not the work of art but the lifestyles portrayed.[22] Mapplethorpe's artistic preeminence coupled with the tragic circumstances of his death only added to the furor of the debate. He had proudly displayed his homoerotic fantasies and encounters, and used his genius to transform raw brutality into art; and the NEA, which had given money to the ICA to organize the exhibition, was indicted as the advance guard of a liberal juggernaut that intended to corrupt the morals of the nation by elevating pornography into art. Not since the 1980 presidential election had political and religious conserva-tives found such a unifying issue. Together they unleashed a withering attack.

The 1989 appropriations process for fiscal year 1990 had just gotten un-derway when the Serrano/Mapplethorpe controversy exploded. On July 12, Representative Rohrabacher introduced a proposal to eliminate the NEA entirely.[23] When the Senate began debating the budget, Wildmon once again entered the fray. On July 25, the AFA blanketed Congress and the media with a press release attacking the NEA for establishing an elite group of pornographic artists subsidized by taxpayers. Wildmon urged the Senate "to stop all funding to the National Endowment for the Arts... The First Amendment guarantees freedom of speech, not funding of speech. The American taxpayer should no longer be forced to support artists such as Mapplethorpe and Serrano."[24] On July 26, one day after Wildmon sent his press release, Helms introduced an amendment to the Senate appropria-tions bill. Officially titled Amendment 420, it was more commonly known as the "Helms Amendment." It read:

None of the funds authorized to be appropriated pursuant to this Act may be used to promote, disseminate, or produce – (1) obscene or indecent materials, including but not limited to depiction of sadomasochism, homo-eroticism, the exploitation of children, or individuals engaged in sex acts; or (2) material which denigrates the objects or beliefs of the adherents of a particular religion or non-religion; or (3) material which denigrates, debases, or reviles a person, group or class of citizens on the basis of race, creed, sex, handicap, age or national origin.[25]

He emphasized that he was not advocating censorship. He explained: "A difference exists between an artist's right to free expression, and his right to have the Government, that is to say the taxpayers, pay him for his work... I reiterate that there is a fundamental difference between government censorship, the preemption of publication or production, and government's refusal to pay for such publication and production."[26] Since Helms was clever enough to introduce his amendment late at night before a nearly empty Senate chamber, it easily passed.

The battle over the Helms Amendment raged throughout the summer and fall of 1989. Buchanan urged the country to "defund the poisoners of culture, the polluters of art; we can sweep up the debris that passes for modern art outside so many public buildings; we can discredit self-anointed critics who have forfeited our trust... tell Jesse to hold the fort; help is on the way."[27] Other commentators claimed that contemporary art thrived on a "belief system of deliberate contempt for the public... The flaw is not with a public that refuses to nourish the arts. Rather it is with a practice of art that refuses to nourish the public."[28]

Opponents of the amendment feared that the measure would emasculate artists who produced harsh and offensive social critiques by denying them government funding. Robert Hughes, *Time*'s art critic, wrote that the Helms Amendment, "would make the NEA hostage to every crank, ideologue and God botherer in America... In short, what the amendment proposes is a loony parody of cultural democracy in which everyone becomes his or her own Cato, the Censor."[29] Anthropologist Carole Vance feared that Congress was attempting to create the fiction of a singular "public" with a universally shared "taste" that would replace diverse constituencies with multiple ideas. According to Dr. Vance, the fundamentalist attack on the NEA was not a silly outburst of "Yahoo-ism." Rather it was a plan carefully constructed by the right wing to restore "traditional social arrangements and reduce heterogeneity by manipulating what symbols might be seen by the public."[30]

Thus, the struggle over the NEA symbolized a much larger argument than whether or not the government would support transgressive artists. The NEA, and by extension the federal government, had instigated an extremely threatening discourse, one that sanctioned homoeroticism and challenged traditional religion. To combat this situation, conservative lawmakers designed what Michel Foucault called "rules of exclusion." Such systems police the boundaries of discourse and, by extension, power relations within a society by establishing a web of regulations that severely limit the range of that discourse. For these lawmakers, art was not meant to challenge traditional notions of sexuality or religion. It was meant to buttress the existing cultural paradigm by creating images that affirmed the balance, beauty, and righteousness of the dominant ideology. And the NEA, because it financially supported some programs that promoted such cultural revisions, became the target of Congressional conservatives for the next eight years.

Heartache in the heartland

The culture wars were not, however, confined to Washington, and regional skirmishes erupted throughout the nation. In spring 1989, the Theatre Department of Southwest Missouri State University (SMSU) in Springfield decided that it would open its fall season with a production of Larry Kramer's compelling AIDS drama, *The Normal Heart*. Department head Robert Bradley commented that he and his colleagues had chosen the play because it addressed the AIDS "cover-up" that had kept the public ignorant and to honor two recent graduates who had just died of the disease.[31] The department also spearheaded an AIDS awareness week on campus that involved guest speakers, the campus health service, and the Ozarks AIDS Council. By so doing, theatre faculty and students hoped to create an environment of awareness and compassion. They did not, however, anticipate that their actions would generate heated opposition from those who considered homosexuality a sin and viewed AIDS as a just punishment.

Although Springfield was, in most respects, a sleepy town nestled in the Ozarks, it was nonetheless the national headquarters of the Assembly of God and home to three Bible colleges. The current anti-gay, anti-NEA rhetoric resonated loudly in this Bible-belt town. In mid-September 1989, State Representative Jean Dixon (R-Springfield) sounded the alarm. Using Helms' strategy, she complained that SMSU was using taxpayers' money to promote the homosexual agenda and, in a three-and-a-half-hour meeting with university president Dr. Marshall Goodman, she insisted that the play was pornographic and obscene, and could not be presented. The president refused to yield to Dixon's demands, but sent a copy of the script to the university attorney for a legal opinion.[32]

In the meantime, Springfield's fundamentalist churches enlisted in the battle. Copies of certain offensive passages and stage directions were sent to various pastors. On Sunday October 17, 1989, the debate became public when ministers denounced the upcoming production from their pulpits and exhorted their congregations to make their opinions known. The protest was designed to coincide with a meeting of the Board of Regents that was scheduled for the following week. Dixon, two other state representatives, and scores of her Bible-bearing supporters were on hand to press their case. The board set aside its rules and allowed Dixon to speak, whereupon she delivered a harangue that equated homosexuality with pornography, sex offenses, child molestation, and rock music, and accused *The Normal Heart* of contributing to the moral decline in America. After a brief recess, the board refused to act on Dixon's demands and moved on to the next agenda item. The production would go forward.

Ten days later, the committee supporting Dixon, Citizens Demanding Standards (CDS), took out a full-page advertisement in the *Springfield News-Leader*. It claimed that various university and state officials were "using your tax money to promote a homosexual political agenda in our university" and asked readers if they wanted their "tax dollars to promote homosexual, anti-family life style[s]." It then turned its attention to the play itself. It labeled *The Normal Heart* a "homosexual play" and asserted that it was written by a "militant homosexual political activist" and used excessive profanity.[33]

Local television stations saw the advertisement and demanded interviews and access to rehearsals. Kathleen Turner, Tess Harper, and John Goodman, all SMSU alumni, made public statements on behalf of the production. Lanford Wilson, who was born in the Ozarks and whose mother still lived about twenty miles from Springfield, wrote a guest editorial for the *News-Leader*. In it, he argued that theatre was supposed to upset prevailing notions of propriety and morality:

> It is for those people who are willing to be challenged, who expect to be challenged. You have an obligation to protest if you are not challenged there... Come to the theatre to be assaulted. Don't even think about protesting the theatre for carrying out its job. Don't come to the theatre expecting us to conform to the community standards of morality. That's not our job. We would rather die first. If you can't stand up under the mandate of art, turn on the television set. Go to a movie. Stay home.[34]

Regional and national media picked up the story and consistently compared Dixon's crusade to Helms' attack on the NEA. CNN contacted Bradley, and articles appeared in the *Los Angeles Times, St. Louis Post Dispatch, Arizona Republic*, and *Kansas City Times*. Suddenly the stakes became higher as Springfield was catapulted into the national spotlight. Tess Harper flew from Dallas to appear at a campus rally and Kathleen Turner spoke on behalf of Citizens for the American Way. Dr. Mervyn F. Silverman, president of the American Foundation for AIDS Research, commented: "Just when the Berlin Wall is coming down, just when people have been fighting for the chance to hear everything they might want to hear and make their own decisions, we see almost an attempt to put a Berlin Wall around this theatre on this campus."[35]

Dixon and her supporters also understood the importance of this conflict. The governor and the legislature received hundreds of telegrams and calls opposing the production. A rally attended by some 1,200 people heard Gene Antonio, author of *The AIDS Cover-Up*, declare that homosexuals were threatening "warfare." And Dixon personally presented President Marshall Gordon with a petition signed by nearly 5,000 people who protested that taxpayers' money had been used to promote a "homosexual political agenda."[36]

On campus, People Acting with Compassion and Tolerance (PACT), a student organization, sponsored frequent rallies that called for understanding and tolerance. Bradley and various administrators met daily to plan for the safety of the cast, crew, and audience. And audience there would be. The complete run of eight performances was sold out in a matter of hours. Opening night arrived, and a security force accompanied by bomb-sniffing dogs inspected the building from lobby to loading dock. Cast and crew were issued identity badges and only ticket holders were permitted to enter the building. Undercover detectives posed as audience members and police patrolled the theatre twenty-four hours a day during the run of the show.[37] The only violent incident occurred off campus. The student leader of PACT, Brad Evans, was the target of arson. While he was leading a candlelight service, his small rent house was burned to the ground.[38] In response to the attack on Evans, university officials decided to house the cast in motels and local police were dispatched to their residences.

The SMSU production of *The Normal Heart* significantly raised AIDS awareness in Springfield. The university health clinic distributed more information in four weeks than they had during the previous year, and the county health agency exhausted its supply of AIDS literature. In addition, the production also generated a gay rights backlash that was responsible for defeating Dixon in the Republican primary the following August.[39]

The NEA, Congress, and the courts

While the controversy over *The Normal Heart* was raging in Missouri, New Right Congressmen were still attempting to gut the NEA. In July, 1989, President Bush appointed John Frohnmayer, a Portland, Oregon attorney, to succeed Frank Hodsoll as chair of the Endowment. Although Frohnmayer had served as chair of the Oregon Arts Commission and had been a member of the NEA Opera/Musical Theatre panel, he was totally unfamiliar with the arcane rituals of Washington politics. He also lacked any connection to or understanding of the east-coast arts oligarchy that included some of the nation's most powerful institutions – the National Gallery, the Metropolitan Opera, the Boston Symphony, the Lincoln Center for the Performing Arts, etc. It was this inexperience, claims Joseph Zeigler, that precipitated the chaos which reigned during the next few years. Doubtlessly Frohnmayer's *naïveté* contributed to the ensuing debacle.[40] In his defense, however, from the day of his appointment he encountered scores of hostile lawmakers who were supported by an extensive network of fundamentalist activists who were set to launch a cultural revolution. Frohnmayer had absolutely no opportunity to construct a map that might have allowed him to negotiate these dangerous shoals.

Less than a month after Frohnmayer took office, Congress passed Public Law 101–121. The law specifically punished SECCA and ICA for their role in the Serrano and Mapplethorpe controversies. More importantly, Congress defined the type of art that the NEA could not fund by including a version of the Helms Amendment in the legislation. It stated:

> None of the funds authorized to be appropriated for the National Endowment for the Arts . . . may be used to promote, disseminate, or produce materials which in the judgment of the National Endowment for the Arts . . . may be considered obscene, including but not limited to, depictions of sadomasochism, homoeroticism, the sexual exploitation of children, or individuals engaged in sex acts and which, when taken as a whole, do not have serious literary, artistic, political, or scientific value.[41]

By including this clause, Congress obligated the NEA to censor artists and shifted the determination of obscenity from the judicial branch – the courts – to the executive branch – a federal agency. Although Jesse Helms failed to get his amendment included as part of the NEA's 1990 appropriation, he had nonetheless triumphed. He had convinced Congress that the NEA, rather than encourage and support the arts, should act as a censor.[42]

The Bush–Quayle emphasis on family values only made the NEA more vulnerable to attack. New Right Congressmen pointed with self-satisfied glee whenever they found (or thought they had found) that the NEA had funded projects that might outrage conservative sensibilities. In February 1990, Congressman Rohrabacher claimed that part of a $500,000 grant that the NEA had awarded to the New York State Council for the Arts had, in turn, been awarded to the Kitchen Theatre in New York. The theatre, according to Rohrabacher, had used a portion of its grant to present *Annie Sprinkle: Post-Porn Modernist*. A former star of porn films turned performance artist, Sprinkle had devised for herself a one-woman show that consisted of simulated masturbation, oral tricks with rubber toys, and various forms of audience participation. In a "Dear Colleague" letter, Rohrabacher described Sprinkle's act in explicit detail, attacked Frohnmayer for allowing taxpayer's money to be used to finance such a vile exhibition, and closed on a threatening note. "If the NEA can't hold itself responsible to the U.S. taxpayer," he said, "it's our job to make them responsible."[43]

A week after Rohrabacher's letter landed on the desks of his fellow representatives, Pat Williams (D-Mont.), an NEA supporter, released his own "Dear Colleague" letter. In it he pointed out several glaring inaccuracies in his colleague's epistle. Neither Kitchen Theatre nor Sprinkle received "one penny of funding" from the NEA or the New York Council for the Arts. The state agency had specifically excluded any funding for the X-rated performer. He went on to assert that such "Dear Colleague" letters were part of an organized attack on the NEA and on the Congressmen who supported it. He claimed the anti-NEA forces wanted to make "the American public believe that the Endowment has deliberately set out to fund works that are offensive to the average American, and that a vote by members of Congress to support funding for the Endowment is a vote to support obscenity and pornography."[44]

Wildmon, like Rohrabacher, did not place a premium on accuracy. In a fundraising advertisement he purchased in the *Washington Times* on February 13, he accused the Endowment of directly supporting Serrano, Mapplethorpe, Sprinkle, and wide range of galleries and performances that presented descriptions and depictions of lesbians and gay lifestyles and attacks on traditional religion. He ended his appeal for funding by listing the names of 262 Congressmen who had voted against the original Helms

Amendment and urged readers to oppose the "abuse and misuse of your tax dollars."[45] The NEA issued its own fact sheet that rebutted Wildmon charge by charge and called attention to AFA's deliberate distortion of the facts.[46] Wildmon did not bother to respond.

The limits of speech continued to be hotly debated throughout the year. In April, the Cincinnati police arrested Dennis Barrie, Director of the Contemporary Arts Center (CAC), when it opened Robert Mapplethorpe's exhibition of photographs "The Perfect Moment." Barrie and the CAC were both indicted on charges of pandering obscenity and child pornography. If convicted, Barrie would face $2,000 in fines and up to a year in jail and the CAC could have been fined up to $10,000. Opponents of Mapplethorpe clearly recognized that they stood a good chance of obtaining an obscenity conviction in Cincinnati, long known for its opposition to transgressive art. It was, after all, the home of Charles Keating, who led the battle to have the closed circuit telecast of *Oh! Calcutta!* banned in nearly 125 cities in 1970. More recently, its "Citizens for Community Values" had engineered the proscription of *Last Tango in Paris, The Last Temptation of Christ*, and *Equus.* The case went to trial on September 24 before a jury of four men and four women, some of whom had never been in a museum. Defense lawyers based their defense on the opinion of a number of art critics who testified that the seven contested photographs had serious artistic merit. In his summation, the defense attorney admitted that Mapplethorpe's images were "rough" and "undoubtedly controversial," but, he reminded the jury, "Person upon person, from the East Coast to the West Coast to the middle of this country, people with credentials, people who are knowledgeable have said that those photographs have serious artistic value." The prosecutor attempted to pit the jury against the art world by depicting the CAC and its artists as an effete cadre who believed they were immune from the judgments of ordinary individuals. On October 5, the jury returned a verdict of not guilty. Using the three-prong *Miller* test, they agreed that the photographs appealed to prurient interests and were patently offensive, but that they possessed serious artistic merit and therefore were not obscene. Barrie's attorneys called the whole affair a "sad battle" but hailed the verdict as a victory for the First Amendment.[47]

Meanwhile, Frohnmayer took drastic steps that he hoped would insulate the NEA from further Congressional attacks. In November 1989, he inserted the text of Public Law 101–121 into the "General Information and Guidance for Grant Recipients." During that same month, he also revoked a $10,000 grant to Art Space, an alternative gallery in the TriBeCa neighborhood of Manhattan. The exhibition in question dealt with AIDS and depicted homosexual unions. Helms applauded the decision of the new chair, but the art community reviled him.[48] Frohnmayer further alienated the arts community by inserting the infamous anti-obscenity clause into the "General Terms and Conditions for Grant Recipients," a form that each award recipient had to sign and return to the Endowment. Within weeks, the arts community began to attack the Endowment for surrendering to Congressional pressure. On April 27, Joseph Papp, Artistic Director of the New York Shakespeare Festival, refused to accept a $50,000 grant from the NEA. He stated: "I cannot in all good conscience accept any money from the NEA as long as the Helms-inspired amendment on obscenity is part of our agreement."[49] Papp's refusal to sign what came to be known as the "loyalty oath" prompted fourteen other organizations to return their awards, and the art world began to view the NEA as an enemy instead of an ally.[50]

The attack on theatre gathered momentum in June when Frohnmayer threw more fuel onto the censorship fire. In the spring of 1990, the NEA's Solo Performance Theatre Peer-Review Panel approved grants ranging from $5,000 to $8,000 for four artists, Karen Finley, Holly Hughes, John Fleck, and Tim Miller. Frohnmayer disagreed with the panel's recommendation and rescinded the awards. The "NEA 4," as these artists came to be known, shot back. Holly Hughes claimed that Frohnmayer had overturned the panel recommendation because her work was "chock-full of good old feminist satire and...I am openly lesbian."[51] Tim Miller asserted that he had the right to "create art about my identity as a gay person, art that confronts my society, art that criticizes our government and elected officials, and maybe even some art that deserves a few tax dollars from the 20 million lesbians and gay men who pay the IRS." John Fleck asked: "How can we as citizens in a land of multicultural diversity, allow our government to suppress certain points of view? To only validate images of a select few is to limit the freedom of expression and the choices available to the American public." It was Karen Finley, however, who emerged as the primary spokesperson for her colleagues as well as for many artists who produced transgressive work. "As an American artist," she said, "I have made a commitment in creating work that deals with victims in our society, and I use the language of how our society treats these victims: women, people living with AIDS, minorities, homosexuals and lesbians, the homeless, the victims of child abuse, incest and violent sexual crimes."[52]

Frohnmayer vehemently denied that "anti-lesbian/gay discrimination exists at the National Endowment for the Arts." He insisted, "The basis for giving grants...is now and has always been artistic excellence and artistic merit," but thousands of artists nationwide doubted his sincerity.[53] Joseph Papp railed: "Senator Jesse Helms...is now joined by apprentice, John E. Frohnmayer, the endowment's chairman...Here's to the National Endowment for the Arts, the new cultural Federal Bureau of Investigation."[54]

In September 1990, the American Civil Liberties Union in cooperation with the National Campaign for Freedom of Expression and the Center for Constitutional Rights filed a lawsuit on behalf of the NEA 4. The suit stated that Frohnmayer, by imposing content restrictions, had violated both the NEA's governing laws and the First Amendment.[55] The suit would remain in the federal courts for the next eight years until the Supreme Court finally rendered its verdict in 1998.

The 1990 appropriations process for fiscal year 1991 was a melee even by Congressional standards. The original administration bill called for a five-year reauthorization without content restrictions, but representatives and senators sought to weaken the agency by attaching amendments intended to hobble the endowment and intimidate applicants. One suggested that organizations found guilty in a court of law of producing obscene material with federal funds be barred from receiving NEA grants for a year. Another would have channeled 60 percent of NEA funds to state arts agencies thereby paralyzing the agency's grant making capacity. Congressman Rohrabacher, ever the NEA foe, demanded content restrictions. Finally Daniel Crane (R-Ill.) introduced a proposal to abolish the NEA entirely.[56]

Given the general state of confusion and animosity, it is fortunate that the NEA survived at all, but its mandate and guidelines were altered significantly. The appropriations bill that was passed in October reauthorized the NEA for three, not five years. Funds allocated to state arts agencies increased from 20 to 35 percent over the next three years. More funds were earmarked for rural and inner-city projects, which, it was argued, shifted the emphasis more toward social service and away from artistic excellence. The bill did not contain specific anti-obscenity restrictions and did not require grant recipients to sign a loyalty oath. Instead it inserted an amendment known as section 954(d)(1) that charged the chairperson to take into consideration "general standards of decency and respect for the diverse beliefs and values of the American public" during the grant-making process.[57] While the anti-obscenity oath had been deleted from the appropriation bill, Congress had clearly intended for the NEA to establish boundaries for artistic expression beyond which grant recipients could not travel.

David Chambers, chairman of the NEA Theatre Program, predicted that the attack on the arts was "simply the first skirmish in a larger battle-ground. We were an easy target. A precedent has now been established in the national debate about issues of decency and expression, and language has now been created that will soon migrate into education, health, science and all other areas where the federal pot and free expression intersect." Jesse Helms seemed to validate Chambers' fears when he declared: "I say to all the arts community and homosexuals who may be upset... What is past is prologue. You ain't seen nothing yet."[58]

Freedom of expression, particularly performative expression, was dealt another severe blow in June 1991. On the 21st of that month, the Supreme Court upheld a section of Indiana's public indecency law that made it a misdemeanor to appear in a public place "in a state of nudity." At issue was the attempt of two clubs to present totally nude dancing as entertainment. An Indiana statute required the dancers wear at least "pasties" and a "G-string," and the United States District Court for the Northern District of Indiana concurred, stating that "nude dancing was not protected expressive activity." The United States Court of Appeals for the Seventh Circuit overturned the lower court's decision, but the Supreme Court upheld the Indiana statute.[59] Chief Justice Rehnquist reminded the litigants that the court was not obligated to protect all forms of expression. He also asserted: "The requirements that the dancers don pasties and G-strings does not deprive the dance of whatever erotic message it conveys; it simply makes the message slightly less graphic."[60] Justice Scalia argued that laws "regulating conduct and not specifically directed at expression" are not subject to First Amendment scrutiny. He went on to assert that the state possessed the inherent right to control the presentation of the body:

> Perhaps the dissenters believe that "offense to others" *ought* to be the only reason for restricting nudity in public places generally, but there is no basis for thinking that our society has ever shared that Thoreauvian "you-may-do-what-you-like-so-long-as-it-does-not-injure-someone-else" beau ideal – much less for thinking that it was written into the Constitution. The purpose of Indiana's nudity law would be violated, I think, if 60,000 fully consenting adults crowded into the Hoosier Dome to display their genitals to one another, even if there were not an offended innocent in the crowd. Our society prohibits, and all human societies have prohibited, certain activities not because they harm others but because they are considered, in the traditional phrase, "*contra bonos mores*," i.e., immoral.[61]

Thus, the Supreme Court had affirmed that certain actions, even when performed within the limited confines of an entertainment environment for adults who wished to avail themselves of that communication, were, by definition, a threat to the state. It was a chilling decision.

The *Barnes* v. *Glenn Theatre* decision, combined with the recent attack on transgressive performers that was unfolding at the NEA, set the stage for an all-out assault on any production that challenged the moral status quo. Buoyed by a groundswell of conservative support, many local authorities began to police their own backyards. The first major local crusade was launched in Chattanooga, Tennessee, and the target was that warhorse from the 1970s, *Oh! Calcutta!* The review had been touring nationally since 1988. It had managed to avoid openly hostile communities and had played successfully in Atlanta, Knoxville, Nashville, and Memphis. When, however, the tour's producer attempted to rent the city owned auditorium for a January 1991 run, Chattanooga's city attorney filed suit to have the production banned. After all, Chattanooga had lost a Supreme Court battle over *Hair* in the early seventies and, as Marjorie Heins, Executive Director of the American Civil Liberties Union, has argued, city officials probably wanted to test the limits of *Barnes* to avenge that defeat.[62]

Since the city attorney sought a court order rather than damages, Judge Vann Owens could have rendered a verdict on his own. He chose instead to empanel an "advisory jury" in order to obtain a verdict from the community. On November 15, after deliberating more than three hours, the jury reached its decision. Relying more on *Miller* than on *Barnes*, the panel ruled that, while the play was sexually offensive, it nonetheless contained artistic, literary, and political value and was "not obscene under today's community standards." Judge Owens reluctantly agreed with the jury and admitted that the First Amendment was intended to protect "unpopular and seemingly unworthy messages." He claimed, however, that times had changed. Plays that advocated "free sex" might have been appropriate in the sixties, but were ill-advised in the nineties. He warned, "The horror of the AIDS epidemic which has resulted from casual sex makes any such advocacy especially untimely today."[63]

Congressional copycats

By 1993, however, local officials seemed less concerned about nudity in a heterosexual play than the sympathetic discussion of homosexuality and AIDS. Since 1989, when New Right politicians had fired their first salvo at pornographic art, homosexual themes and the AIDS discourse were featured in lavish Broadway productions and were increasingly embraced by mainstream audiences. The most successful musical of 1993, *Kiss of the Spider Woman*, merged a homoerotic love story with campy homage to bygone movies told from a gay perspective. *Angels in America* was the first gay-centered play to win the Pulitzer Prize. The runner-up, *The Destiny of Me* by AIDS activist Larry Kramer, was selected the best show of the Off-Broadway season. Lynn Redgrave's *Shakespeare for My Father* alluded to the bisexuality of Sir Michael Redgrave, while the rock opera *Tommy* contained numerous references to homosexuality and pedophilia. William Finn and James Lapine's *Falsettos*, a mordantly witty musical about facing death in the age of AIDS, began a successful national tour by emphasizing that it was a celebration of families of all types. *Angels'* author Tony Kushner claimed that homosexuals had gained "legitimacy" and that their rights were "taken seriously." "We're winning," he proclaimed, "and that gives things a certain electricity."[64]

The spark of which Kushner spoke also provided a galvanizing stimulus for those who wished to censure theatrical presentations that challenged the status quo. Political conservatives who believed the arts, regardless of content, should pay for themselves, found enthusiastic allies among groups that opposed plays that treated homosexuality with candor and compassion. It was an alliance that experienced a significant amount of success. Its primary targets were small local theatres and, like their Washington colleagues, they insisted that the Constitution did not obligate taxpayers to support presentations that offended the sensibilities of the majority.

Using this strategy, city and county governments that were dominated by conservative forces sought to cripple producing organizations that dealt with homosexual themes. The first of these episodes involved a small professional theatre in Marietta, Georgia, the county seat of Cobb County. Located about eighteen miles north of Atlanta, this upper-middle-class community, the home of some of the nation's largest defense contractors and the nerve center of Newt Gingrich's North Georgia Congressional district, was notorious for its iconoclastic politics. In the summer of 1993, however, it gained a nationwide reputation for its blatant attack on homosexuals.

The Marietta furor over homosexuality had been brewing for some time. The Atlanta City Council had recently passed a measure that granted domestic partners health benefits and was attempting to bring the 1998 Gay Games to that city. In Marietta, a contentious debate over sex education in elementary schools had erupted. In November 1992, a committee of educators, health professionals, and teachers recommended teaching fourth graders about AIDS. Public hearings were held and opponents attended in record numbers. Initially, they insisted that nine year olds were too young to learn about sexually transmitted diseases. Later debates revealed that many parents wanted to transform the AIDS debate from a public health discourse into an ersatz sermon depicting AIDS as a form of divine punishment.

During the summer of 1993, the AIDS discussion spilled over from the hearing room into the theatre. Unlike New York, Marietta, Georgia was not eager to embrace sympathetic depictions of gays, but the play that censors challenged was a highly unlikely target. *Lips Together, Teeth Apart*, by Terrance McNally opened in May 1993 at Theatre in the Square, a small but very successful professional theatre. It concerns two "post-yuppie" couples exploring marriage and mortality in a beach house that one of the women had inherited from a friend who had died of AIDS. Dan Hulbert, theatre critic for the *Atlanta Constitution*, called *Lips* "an insightful, dramatically nuanced production."[65] *Lips Together, Teeth Apart* had been running for two months before the storm struck. Apparently, two citizens complained to Gordon Wysong, a first-term member of the Cobb County Commission, that taxpayers' money had been used to support a production that favored homosexuality. Without ever having seen the production or read the play, Wysong introduced an ordinance on July 21 that would prohibit the county from funding any arts groups that supported the "gay lifestyle." Wysong steadfastly denied that he was practicing censorship. "We're not trying to censor people," he maintained, "but we're not going to use taxpayer money to show support for a lifestyle that's contrary to the community standards."[66] Apparently the commissioner believed that tax dollars were not to be used to promote a discourse that challenged the dominant ideology. In his opinion, government was obligated to use its economic power to suppress rather than promote the discussion of divergent opinions.

The issue immediately polarized Cobb County residents as opponents of the measure accused Cobb officials of "gay bashing":

> The only threats to Cobb County are intolerance, homophobia, bigotry and an unhealthy aversion to diversity. As for the "family values" ploy – it is more than slightly egotistical for those who would support this hateful resolution to assume that they corner the market on families and family values. Are condemnation and alienation the "family values" that are to be taught in Cobb County?[67]

The Artistic Director of Theatre in the Square, Michael Horne, was incredulous. He argued that his ten-year-old operation was the only professional theatre outside of Atlanta proper, that his budget exceeded $800,000, and that his season subscription renewal rate was an astonishing 94 percent. "We're in touch with the community. You don't have [our success] ... by being out of touch with the community."[68]

About three weeks later, the battle over the depiction of homosexuality on stage assumed much larger proportions. The Cobb County commissioners adopted a resolution, also introduced by Wysong, which stated that the "gay lifestyle" was "incompatible with the standards to which this community subscribes."[69] Although the resolution was not legally binding, opponents and supporters reacted strongly. Commission Chairman Bill Byrne said the resolution was not intended to be a "lambasting of gays" and complained that Cobb County was now characterized as the home of "racists, bigots, mongers and rednecks because we're singling out one group of people."[70] Gays and lesbians were irate and staged several rallies protesting the resolution. On Sunday August 22, they held a "Queer Family Picnic" in Glover Park to protest the commissioners' action. Several churches responded with a "prayer and praise rally." Virtually every peace officer in Cobb County had been called in to maintain order.[71]

The furor, however, had not ended. On Tuesday, August 24, the commissioners stunned most of Cobb County and a substantial portion of the nation. Rather than attempt to determine which groups supported family values and which did not, they simply eliminated all funding for the arts. The Associated Press, National Public Radio, and a number of newspapers across the nation reported the story. Arts organizations as well as gay rights groups responded with cries of censorship. Arts supporters complained that the commissioners' vote reinforced the "image of Cobb and the South as a bunch of hicks and rednecks." The Georgia ACLU announced that it would probably file suit. Several gay organizations launched a national campaign that urged businesses to boycott Cobb County. Commissioner Byrne sidestepped the issue by asserting that the vote would reduce government spending and insure that tax dollars would be used "to serve every member of the community." In essence, the Cobb County Commission had achieved what Rohrabacher, Helms, and their conservative colleagues had only hoped to do; it had officially declared that the arts did not benefit the public and had completely dismantled the apparatus that linked the government to the arts. By so doing, it assured its constituencies that their political system had severed any and all relationship with individuals who might advocate diverse social and sexual arrangements.[72]

It is unlikely that either of these measures would have passed without the support of the city's most powerful ministers who applauded the Commission's effort to link the political administration of Cobb County to orthodox Christianity. "Homosexuality is incompatible with the teachings of Jesus Christ," preached Revd Randell R. Mickler from the pulpit of the Mount Bethel United Methodist Church. "I deeply resent one dollar of my taxes going to support a lifestyle my faith considers an abomination."[73] Nelson Price, pastor of the largest Southern Baptist congregation in the area, the 9,500-member Roswell Street Baptist Church, was particularly supportive. A long-time friend of Wysong, he privately helped the commissioner draft the resolutions and sent letters to other ministers soliciting support. Price justified his action by claiming that indicting the gay lifestyle would serve the community well. He stated: "Communities all over the nation have had to act remedially, and it was thought to be to our advantage to act preventatively."[74] For Price, any objective or compassionate discussion of the gay issues constituted an attack on the family and he was completely unable to regard homosexuality as anything other than sinfully corrupt. When asked how he felt about ending funding for the arts in Cobb County, he replied: "Theatre should feed the aesthetic taste and inspire and uplift rather than glamorize sexual distortion."[75] And, while he personally wanted to assist groups who worked within the parameters of Christian morality, he asserted: "There is a radical element within the arts community that is not going to stand for any kind of parameters."[76] Other ministers attacked the media for characterizing them as bigots. They insisted that as Christian ministers they were not condemning individual homosexuals, but were attacking a "sinful activity." Still others congratulated the Commission for drawing "a line in the sand" and saying "we are not going to accommodate the forward progress of the homosexual agenda."[77]

The total amount lost to Cobb County Arts groups was $110,000. The largest amount, $40,950, would have gone to Theatre in the Square. At first, the commissioners' actions only boosted Theatre in the Square's reputation and swelled its coffers. In April 1994, Managing Director Palmer Wells announced that local businesses and art patrons had contributed a whopping $115,000 to the theatre. Paul Newman and Joanne Woodward, a native of Cobb County, led the field with a $20,000 gift.[78] By 1996, however, the theatre had fallen on hard times. Many private donors assumed the crisis had passed and ceased contributing. In addition, the controversy had cost the theatre one third of its season subscribers. Theatre in the Square failed to meet its payroll, and Horne and Wells were forced to lay off employees, cut advertising budgets, take out loans, and spend their own savings to keep the theatre afloat. Eventually, the theatre's fortunes rebounded, but at a cost. In order to win back subscribers, Horne and Wells introduced programming aimed at "family-oriented theatergoers." "We did what we had to do to survive," Horne said. The story does not have an altogether happy ending. Michael Horne died in 1996 of cardiopulmonary arrest, and county funding for the arts was never restored. However, Theatre in the Square survived and is prospering under the direction of Palmer Wells, Horne's long-time partner and colleague.[79]

Meanwhile, Congress continued to attack the NEA. It decreased its appropriation from $167.4 million in fiscal year 1995 to $99.5 million in fiscal year 1996, a reduction of 40 percent. It continued to insist upon content restrictions and, with the exception of those who applied to the literature program, it eliminated all grants to individuals. By so doing, it made sure that performance artists such as Annie Sprinkle and the NEA 4 would never receive a dime of taxpayers' money.

Other governmental entities enthusiastically followed Congress' lead. In 1996, lawmakers in Charlotte, North Carolina attempted to suppress *Angels in America*, Tony Kushner's Pulitzer Prize-winning play, because of its candid treatment of gay life and AIDS. The struggle in Charlotte resembled the battle in Marietta in several salient respects, but Marietta was generally regarded as a suburb of Atlanta whose cultural identity was bound up in traditional southern conservatism. Charlotte, however, was one of the brightest jewels in the crown of the New South. In 1998, BF Goodrich, America's largest manufacturer of tires, decided to move its corporate headquarters to Charlotte. When San Francisco's BankAmerica merged with NationsBank, Charlotte became the second largest banking center in the nation. And Charlotte had recently acquired a National Football League expansion franchise. This new prosperity was clearly visible in downtown Charlotte, which had been transformed into a glittering arena full of shining glass and steel corporate towers. The tenants of these new buildings, like the seventeenth-century merchant princes of Venice, commissioned giant sculptures and paintings to advertise their wealth and power. The $55 million Blumenthal Performing Arts Center was built with the blessing (and the donations) of these corporate patrons, and the powerful Charlotte Arts and Science Council dispensed $8 million per year to various cultural agencies.[80]

In the spring of 1996, Charlotte was convinced that it would soon overtake Atlanta as the cultural and economic leader of the New South. However, these new cultural barons completely underestimated the power of the New Right. Christian conservatives had gained significant power in the state's burgeoning Republican Party and they were ready to flex their muscles, even if it meant challenging the powerful downtown business community.[81]

The precipitating incident occurred in the spring of 1996 when the Charlotte Repertory Theatre (the Rep) announced that it would produce both parts of Tony Kushner's Pulitzer Prize drama, *Angels in America / A Gay Fantasia on National Themes* – Part One, *Millennium Approaches* and Part Two, *Perestroika*. Two members of its Board of Directors resigned in protest, and Keith Martin, the company's producer and managing director, failed to convince corporate sponsors to underwrite the production. Although the two plays had been presented at the University of North Carolina at Greensboro and at Duke University by touring companies, the Rep's production was more problematic. One of Charlotte's most elite organizations would mount these plays and present them in a building constructed and supported by taxpayers' dollars. For conservative politicians and fundamentalist Christians, such an example of cultural liberalism was intolerable.

When rehearsals started, the controversy became public. The Revd Joseph R. Chambers, pastor of a non-denominational, fundamentalist congregation appeared on the theatre's doorsteps and demanded that it cancel the production. Chambers, who had campaigned against the children's television show "Barney and Friends" because it was "clearly occultic" and the movie *The Lion King* because it depicted "voodooism," was upset about the play's brief nude scene and its homosexual themes. He insisted: "This is a play filled with vulgarity, filled with explicit scenes, filled with unsafe sex... There is something in this drama to offend everyone but those who accept the worst pornography."[82] He appealed to other fundamentalist ministers who, in turn, exhorted their congregations to express their opinions on radio talk shows and in letters to the editor.

Chambers was not content to mobilize the court of public opinion. He also enlisted the aid of several conservative politicians. Together they attempted to have the play suppressed by invoking the state's obscenity law. When they encountered Supreme Court decisions that protected works of "intrinsic artistic or literary merit" from the purview of such laws, they changed tactics. Because *Angels in America* contained an eight-second scene in which a male performer appeared nude, he convinced local officials that the play violated the state's indecent exposure law. Although the misdemeanor statute was intended to combat nude dancing, the police and District Attorney warned the Rep that anyone who exposed their genitals to a member of the opposite sex was violating the law. Thus, if actor Alan Poindexter stood naked on stage while he was posing as an AIDS patient undergoing a physical examination, he and the other members of the cast would be arrested. Kushner was outraged. He wrote: "I strongly object to the characterization of the protest against *Angels in America* as a holy war. There is nothing holy about the protest or the protestors. The protestors' objection to a nude scene is just thinly veiled homophobia; nothing more."[83]

When the directors of the Blumenthal Center learned of possible police interference, they issued a cease-and-desist order to the Rep in order to prevent the opening. Attorneys for the theatre sought protection from the courts and, three hours before curtain, Superior Court Judge Marvin Gray ruled that the nudity in the play "appears to constitute artistic expression" and enjoined the police, District Attorney, or any representative of the Blumenthal Center from impeding the opening.[84] The scene outside the Blumenthal Center was pandemonium. There were bells, whistles, protesters, police, television cameras, and a drag queen. Backstage, the actors were tense and exhausted from weeks of controversy. Kushner buoyed their spirits with a good-luck fax. He wrote: "Be splendid tonight, be focused, have fun, make theatre: That's our way of repudiating the bullies, the killjoys, the busybodies and the blowhards."[85]

The opening performance was unimpeded and the run attracted record audiences. However, the battle of Charlotte was not over. About one year later, the Rep announced that it would present *Six Degrees of Separation* by John Guare, another play that featured nudity and homosexual subject matter. Conservatives were frothing and set out to punish not just the Rep, but all arts organizations.

Ironically, the most aggressive spokesman for this group was Hoyle Martin, a retired African American college instructor and Democratic County Commissioner. On most social issues he was considered a liberal, but he found the homosexual discourse intolerable. He issued a spate of scurrilous statements that seriously marred Charlotte's carefully crafted progressive image. On one occasion he stated: "If I had my way, we'd shove these people [homosexuals] off the face of the earth."[86] In response to Ellen DeGeneres' appearance on the cover of *Time Magazine*, he demanded: "Why can't homosexuals keep their private lives private?"[87] On another occasion he indicted gays because "they are so aggressive":

Since they can't reproduce themselves with the kind of sex they have, the only way they can survive is to recruit or seduce other people and children into their lifestyle ... Homosexuality is immoral. It's unnatural. It's unhealthy. And therefore it causes AIDS.[88]

An array of local leaders joined forces to oppose Martin and his backers. Dozens of clergy, academicians, CEOs, the president of the Chamber of Commerce, and former North Carolina governor Jim Martin spoke on behalf of tolerance, diversity, and preserving Charlotte's image.

The debate reached a climax on the night of April 1 when over 700 people jammed themselves into commission chambers to watch Charlotte air its dirty laundry. At issue was a measure that, if passed, would abolish the county's $2.5 million subsidy to the Arts and Science Council. The first draft of the resolution, crafted by Martin, justified this action because "the aggressive homosexual agenda seeks to undermine the values of the traditional American family." When county attorneys informed him that the resolution was unconstitutional because it singled out one group for punishment, he hastily reworded the measure to read: "Any activities by private agencies that seek to undermine and deviate from the value and society role of the traditional American family are not compatible with our community's moral beliefs."[89]

Bible-carrying supporters filled the hall with cheers when the wording was approved, but opponents were equally as vocal. Joe Martin, a NationsBank executive and an elder in the Presbyterian Church, delivered a stinging six-minute lecture that accused Charlotte city councilmen of being the modern day Puritans and Inquisitors who were quite willing to abuse power in the name of religion.[90] Although Joe Martin was greeted with a standing ovation, the four Republican commissioners teamed with Hoyle Martin to pass one of the most infamous anti-art bills of the decade.

This story, however, has a relatively happy ending, for the arts groups at least. The action of the "gang of five," as they came to be known, was covered by every major newspaper from New York to Los Angeles. For the business community, the entire affair turned out to be a public-relations nightmare. Within seven days of the vote, a committee of corporate leaders, arts patrons, and gay activists joined forces to unseat Martin and his four Republican colleagues. The strategy worked. In the 1998 elections, three of the four commissioners lost at the polls and a fourth did not run. Within months, the new commission passed a measure to restore the $2.5 million cuts.[91]

By 1997, conservative politicians and religious leaders had made it abundantly clear that a state of war existed between them and any group or individual that sought to discuss AIDS, homosexuality, incest, or religious hypocrisy. Any discourse that admitted compassion and/or objectivity was, by definition, an attack on the family, the community, and the nation. They asserted that the white, male, heterosexual Christian hegemony was a divine invention and not, as their critics suggested, a social construct. In their opinion, society had been built upon moral imperatives that were fixed and immutable. They were unwilling to conceive of a world in which disease and love, decay and beauty, and corruption and salvation were all components in a constantly evolving chemistry. Those who dared to make such an assertion frequently incurred the wrath of public officials across the nation who attempted to silence such transgressors by depriving them of public financial support. And, while the attacks on transgressive artists were not linked by conscious design, they all followed the model established by Donald Wildmon, Jesse Helms, and Dana Rohrabacher – artists who question the authority of traditional morality should not be supported with tax dollars.

A few months after the Mecklenburg County Commission defunded the Arts and Science Commission, the San Antonio, Texas City Council voted to decrease city funding for the arts, but completely eliminated its support of the Esperanza Peace & Justice Center. A small, controversial agency that produced programs addressing issues of importance to women, people of color, gays, lesbians, and other marginal groups, Esperanza was planning to produce the San Antonio Lesbian and Gay Media Project.[92] Mayor Howard Peak steadfastly maintained that neither he nor the council had been motivated by any anti-art or anti-gay prejudice. He argued that the across-the-board reduction was necessary because basic city services such as streets and drainage should take priority over the arts. Councilman Robert Marbut, who led the fight for reduction, added: "City government is no longer a trough where arts groups can line up for handouts."[93] Peak admitted, however, that the decision to withdraw funding from Esperanza was motivated by punitive rather than financial concerns. Esperanza, he claimed, used the arts to advance a liberal political agenda. He maintained: "They [Esperanza] are not an arts agency, or not just an arts agency. They get involved in other kinds of activities and what we were funding through our arts programs were arts agencies and not other kinds of activities."[94] Another Esperanza opponent maintained: "Esperanza used the arts as a tool to achieve their goals of a better society not to better the arts... Arts funding should go to organizations which use teaching, exhibitions, performances,

etc. to further understanding of and excellence in the arts."[95] Esperanza supporters claimed, however, that it was an arts organization that emphasized
social issues and insisted that the council had surrendered to religious groups
who opposed its gay and lesbian programming. Although groups such as the
Christian Pro-Life Foundation and the Bexar County Christian Coalition
organized letter-writing campaigns and flooded San Antonio's talk-radio
shows with calls that denounced the organization, it was fairly obvious that
the councilmen did not have to be heavily lobbied.[96] An unidentified councilman called some of its programs "borderline pornography." Peak labeled it
an "in your face" group that was "rubbing people's noses" in its philosophy.[97]
Marbut repeated the same mantra that had been voiced by Jesse Helms eight
years earlier. When asked about Esperanza's gay and lesbian activities, he
responded: "I don't have a problem if they promote that, but that doesn't
mean that taxpayers have to pay for it."[98]

San Antonio officials had zealously applied the strategy of conservative
opponents of the NEA, but this event clearly exposed another dimension
of this battle. Up until the decision to cut Esperanza's funding, groups
that addressed homosexual issues were derided as a threat to the traditional
American family. However, this case had clearly demonstrated that gays
and lesbians were regarded as a potent political force that might undo the
traditional power structure that governed San Antonio.

The efforts to silence arts organizations that dealt openly with homosexuality were not confined to the South. Out North Theatre in Anchorage,
Alaska, was also denied funding because its directors, who were openly
homosexual, used their institution to give gays and other disenfranchised
groups a cultural voice. Like the episode in Marietta, theatre censorship
in Anchorage was closely linked to a contentious debate that began in
1996 regarding how (or if) human sexuality, particularly homosexuality and
AIDS, was to be taught in public schools. Prior to that year, the approach was
relatively liberal. Homosexuality was discussed in a non-judgmental manner
and AIDS was treated as a virus. Opponents of this approach vehemently
opposed this strategy. "Homosexuality is destructive," claimed one parent,
"and it kills people." In the end, the Anchorage School Board agreed with
the outraged parent and greatly limited the type of information that could
be distributed about AIDS and homosexuality.[99]

In November 1997, while the debate over sex education in public schools
still raged on, the Anchorage Assembly, that city's governing legislative
body, voted to eliminate funding for the Out North Theatre. As the city's
most cutting-edge theatre, it was known for its plays that supported racial

and sexual diversity. The British drag group, Bloolips, performed there in 1995. In 1996, it sponsored Silamiut, a three-person theatre/dance troupe from Greenland that integrated native myths, dances, masks, drumming, and singing into captivating performance. That same year it also presented *Mommy Dance*, a one-woman performance piece based on the harrowing experiences of a new mother. One its most acclaimed productions, Susan Miller's *My Left Breast*, which premiered in 1997, told the story of a 36-year-old lesbian mother who discovers she has breast cancer. Later in 1997, Donny Lee's *Superbeast*, an original one-man show, dealt with racism aimed at Alaska's indigenous peoples. As a result of Out North's committed and daring programming, it was voted the most outstanding theatre in Anchorage for two years running and had received state as well as NEA funding. However, the co-artistic directors of Out North, Jay Brause and Gene Dugan, were eighteen-year life partners. One week before the Assembly's action, the two men appeared in State Superior Court to challenge an Alaska law that refused to grant legal status to same-sex unions. They claimed that they and other gay couples had been denied health insurance and other benefits that had been granted to married and unmarried heterosexual couples.[100]

Brause and Dugan's bold assertion of gay rights, coupled with the widespread distribution of an Out North advertisement that featured partial female nudity, profoundly agitated several assemblymen. On November 18, 1997, by a 6 to 5 vote, the Assembly refused to renew a grant of $22,000 to the Out North Theatre. The sum represented 10 percent of its annual budget. Ted Carlson, the leader of the opposition, claimed that Out North was too degenerate to merit support: "We don't want to use tax money to pay for something that the whole family can't go to."[101] Brause and Dugan claimed that they were being punished because they were gay. Their supporters claimed that the Assembly was afraid of controversy and did not want to encounter unfamiliar or uncomfortable ideas.

In the meantime, Brause and Dugan's suit demanding that Alaska recognize same-sex unions was proceeding. Judge Peter Michalski had contended that the state had to prove a compelling interest in regulating the gender of life partners if this law was to remain on the books. The legislature interpreted the suit as an attempt to legalize homosexual marriage and passed an amendment to the state constitution that limited marriage to one man and one woman. The measure was placed on the 1998 general election ballot and passed by a margin of 2 to 1. Within a year, Judge Michalski dismissed the

Brause and Dugan's suit. Both the city of Anchorage and the state of Alaska had demonstrated that homosexual unions and homosexual discourse would not be condoned in the foreseeable future.[102]

While Brause and Dugan were battling Alaska's legislature, the United States Supreme Court reentered the censorship debate. After eight years, the suit filed by the NEA 4 against the National Endowment for the Arts was heard by the high court. The four performance artists claimed that their First Amendment freedoms had been violated and later amended their petition to include a challenge to section 954(d)(1) of the 1990 NEA reauthorization, which they claimed was unconstitutionally vague. A federal District Court and Circuit Court of Appeals sided with the artists, but not the Supreme Court. In an 8 to 1 decision, the court agreed with the NEA. The justices maintained that section 954(d)(1) was "hortatory . . . and stops well short of an absolute restriction." The opinion, written by Justice Sandra Day O'Connor, asserted that the "decency and respect" criteria placed no condition on grants nor did they "disallow any particular viewpoints." They were instead among the many inherently subjective factors to be considered in the NEA's "assessment of artistic merit."[103] By so doing, Justice O'Connor effected a compromise of sorts. She permitted Congress to have some say in what its constituencies would pay for, but allowed the NEA to interpret the "decency and respect" directive subjectively.

Both sides considered the decision a victory. Newt Gingrich applauded the court for vindicating "the right of the American people to not pay for art that offends their sensibilities." The American Civil Liberties Union expressed relief that the court had rendered the law meaningless.[104]

Terrance McNally's gay Jesus

While the Supreme Court was deliberating the legality of section 954(d)(1), another censorship battle erupted, this time in New York. On May 1, 1998 the *New York Post* reported that the Manhattan Theatre Club would produce a play by Terrance McNally that featured a "Christ-like character who has sex with his apostles." Although the script was not available (it had not been completed when the story broke), the Roman Catholic Archdiocese of New York went on record as opposing the production. "That would be horrifying," a spokesman for John Cardinal O'Connor uttered. William Donahue, president of the Catholic League for Religious and Civil Rights (CLRCR), a quasi-official arm of the archdiocese dedicated to defending the Catholic Church against criticism, called it "sick beyond words." More importantly, he interpreted the play, *Corpus Christi*, as proof that the gay and artistic community was engaged in all-out "Catholic bashing":

> There's obviously a very deep problem in the artistic community. The animus against Roman Catholicism is so pervasive that it warrants immediate attention. The reticence on the part of the gay and artistic community over blasphemy targeted at Catholics is astounding. The fact that McNally is an established artist makes it all the more disturbing.[105]

CLRCR immediately launched an all-out campaign to generate support for its position. It sent news releases to newspapers across the country and scheduled radio and televisions interviews. Donahue wrote McNally asking him to alter his script:

> In your upcoming play, *Corpus Christi*, the script calls for an offstage comment by the apostles regarding their having sex with Jesus. As you know, this part of your work is deeply offensive to Christians. That is why I am asking you to delete any such reference from the script.[106]

When McNally did not respond, CLRCR focused its attack on the Manhattan Theatre Club. Although Donahue still did not have access to a script, he urged CLRCR members to write public officials at every level to urge them to withdraw support for the Manhattan Theatre Club. He also asked his constituents to contact their Congressmen and senators to demand that they cease funding the NEA.[107] The League was no stranger to this type of major league arm-twisting. In 1997, it mounted a fierce campaign against "Nothing Sacred," a seriocomic television series featuring a young priest beset with moral and libidinous temptations. It took out a $13,000 advertisement in *Advertising Age* urging advertisers to move their money and advertisements to another show. It also threatened sponsors with a massive Catholic consumer boycott. Within a few weeks, ABC cancelled the series.[108] Although the League had learned how to intimidate commercial sponsors and networks, its conflict with the Manhattan Theatre Club (MTC) was its first encounter with a major New York theatre. Needless to say, the altercation would be a fierce one.

Initially, it seemed that CLRCR had scored a first-round knockout. On May 22, MTC Artistic Director Lynne Meadow and Executive Producer Barry Grove announced: "Because of security problems that have arisen around the production of this play, Manhattan Theatre Club is unable to mount this production responsibly."[109] Although they would not elaborate, Broadway insiders reported that an avalanche of phone calls and letters had deluged the theatre. Meadow and Grove later told the *Times* that the theatre had received anonymous threats to "burn down the theatre, kill the staff and 'exterminate' Mr. McNally." Donahue, while he steadfastly denied any connection to the threats and maintained he was not an advocate of censorship, was elated. "We are delighted," he said, "that the Manhattan Theatre Club pulled the plug from this despicable play. While McNally has every legal right to insult Christians, he has no moral right to do so." He also cautioned other production companies from sponsoring *Corpus Christi*. He warned, "They had better not be thin-skinned: we'll wage a war that no one will forget."[110]

McNally was unusually taciturn. He simply said he regretted that the Manhattan Theatre Club had decided not to go forward with plans to produce *Corpus Christi* and expressed hope that "audiences would have the opportunity to see the play in another venue."[111] The remainder of the professional theatre community, however, was exceedingly vocal. Several groups, including the Williamstown Theatre Festival in western Massachusetts, one of the nation's leading summer theatres, offered to produce *Corpus Christi*. Athol Fugard withdrew permission for the MTC to stage his latest play, *The Captain's Tiger*. He confessed that he was "shocked and disturbed" at the theatre's decision. He continued: "In yielding to the blackmail and threats of the Catholic League the theatre management has compromised one of the basic freedoms of democracy – the Freedom of Speech – and they have done it by censoring themselves and collaborating in an attempt to silence McNally."[112] Tony Kushner called MTC's decision "appalling." He said: "It's shocking that in New York City a major theatre succumbs to pressure like this. This is a medieval notion that the arts in the U.S. need to follow the Roman Catholic theological line." He asserted that it was not the specifics of the play that mattered, but the principle of artistic freedom, and called on the mayor to take a stand against the threats.[113] Craig Lucas lamented that it was a "very, very bad piece of news that in New York City an artist could be silenced with bomb threats and threats on his life . . . No one has a monopoly on views of Jesus."[114]

Perhaps the most eloquent defense of *Corpus Christi* appeared in a *New York Times* editorial. The writer maintained that the "practitioners and beneficiaries of religious freedom" were attacking freedom of speech without realizing that the two liberties could not be defended separately:

There is no essential difference between suppressing the production of a controversial play and suppressing a form of worship. No one would ever have been forced to see *Corpus Christi* had it been produced, but now everyone is forced not to see it...That there is a native strain of bigotry, violence and contempt for artistic expression in this country is not news. But it is news whenever someone as well regarded as the head of the Manhattan Theatre Club capitulates to it instead of standing firm and relying on the police for protection. This is not only a land of freedom; it is a land where freedom is always contested. When courage for that contest is lacking, freedom itself – religious or artistic – is terribly diminished.[115]

Then on May 29, MTC reversed itself. Saying that she was "outraged" by the accusations of censorship hurled at the Manhattan Theatre Club, Meadow announced that her theatre would produce *Corpus Christi* after all. The decision drew enthusiastic response from artists and civil libertarians. Fugard said he would be happy to bring his play back. In a show of support, thirty of the nation's leading playwrights, including Kushner, Lucas, Arthur Miller, Christopher Durang, A. R. Gurney, Stephen Sondheim, and Wendy Wasserstein signed a statement congratulating MTC for making a "brave and honorable decision."[116]

As might be expected, Meadow's announcement drew stinging criticism from CLRCR. League spokesman Rick Henshaw called the on-again, off-again status of the production a "publicity stunt."[117] He also labeled the play "a form of bigotry that would not be countenanced if it were directed at blacks, Jews or other minorities."[118] At no time did the leadership of CLRCR ever regard *Corpus Christi* as worthy of serious dramatic investigation. The very idea that a traditionally celibate Jesus could be reconfigured as a human being with homosexual desires was beyond the pale. To permit such a challenge to go unchecked would simply serve to advance a blasphemous, homosexual agenda. On no account would they be permitted to deconstruct the most sacred of all myths. Religious conservatives continued to attack the play throughout the summer. The *Post* lent its pages to several guest columnists who characterized *Corpus Christi* as a bigoted and intolerant attack on the Catholic Church. One columnist remarked: "In this day and age, who can openly insult a religious group and be not only tolerated but hailed? Oops, that's right, Catholic-bashers can."[119] Another described the League as "an organization that defends Jesus." "If there was ever a time for Christians to draw a line in the sand," the writer continued, "this is it."[120] Toward the end of the summer, Patrick Buchanan railed: "McNally's purpose is to insult, offend, wound and outrage Catholics and all Christians by blaspheming their savior and mocking their moral code." He called the play "a hate crime of modernity directed against Christians, the moral equivalent of Nazis marching in Skokie" and castigated the "New York cultural elite" for defending the anti-Christian bigotry by claiming that it was art:

> While that elite would never be so gauche as to say, "Good for Terry for giving those (expletive) Christian homophobes what they deserve," it defends his bigotry on First Amendment grounds. But behind the customary claptrap about no censorship, our elite shares McNally's hatred of Christianity, especially its teaching on sexual morality. Thus, it will reflexively rise to the defense of any Catholic-basher or Christian-baiter who cloaks his hatred in art.[121]

The activity outside of the auditorium of City Center on W. 55th Street on the night of September 23, the first preview of *Corpus Christi*, provided just as much, if not more, excitement than the production. The police installed metal detectors and dispatched a brigade of bomb-sniffing dogs to make sure that no explosives or weapons were smuggled into the house. Outside, dozens of police were on hand to make sure that protestors did not get too close to the theatre. The security was so tight that the dutiful officers even handcuffed and arrested a seventy-year-old woman for disorderly conduct. Several Franciscan friars held a prayer vigil, and about 100 other people, some of them carrying placards reading, "You call this art?" and "Don't mock God," marched and sang hymns.[122]

When *Corpus Christi* officially opened on October 12, supporters and opponents of the play took full advantage of their First Amendment freedoms. Donahue had convinced over 2,000 people representing 50 religious and civic organizations from 7 states to march outside the theatre. In a rousing speech, he characterized McNally's drama as "gay hate speech" and claimed: "These people want to spit on us." He promised: "We are not going to be nice little altar boys and girls anymore." The People for the American Way, founded by television producer Norman Lear, staged a counter-demonstration described as a "quiet walk for the First Amendment." Among the counter-protestors were Tony Kushner and Wallace Shawn.[123]

A tragic coincidence gave *Corpus Christi* compelling immediacy. A few days before McNally's play opened, Matthew Shepard, a young gay man, was kidnapped, robbed, and beaten to death in Wyoming. Virtually every critic mentioned this event as an example of the bigotry that McNally was seeking to combat. Shepard's death served as a brutal reminder that young men like

McNally's innocent hero, Joshua, were actually being murdered because of their lifestyle. Unfortunately, McNally was unable to find a dramatic metaphor that would transform Jesus' death in Palestine 2,000 years ago into a modern tragedy. His effort began promisingly. He set the beginning of the play in Corpus Christi, Texas, his own hometown. Joshua is born in a shabby motel room and "comes to manhood as a gay geek in a high school full of jocks and bimbos."[124] Then, for some inexplicable reason, he transports his characters and his audience into the biblical world complete with centurions, street vendors, and crucifixions. From that point on, the plot simply retells the events of the New Testament from a gay perspective. Joshua baptizes his disciples and tells each of them: "I bless you and I baptize you and I recognize your divinity as a human being." Mary Magdalene is a male prostitute and Judas is depicted as Joshua's lover. McNally's hero presides over a gay marriage, greets a man infected with AIDS with a hug and a kiss, and is crucified because he is the "king of the queers." The central message, that no one should be persecuted for being different, was a worthy one, but one that did not generate enough dramatic energy to sustain a two-hour play.

Most critics were aware that the tempest that preceded *Corpus Christi* had raised their expectations to an unrealistic height, but the threats, demonstrations, and metal detectors were generally credited with providing more drama than the production. Moreover, McNally's play was unable to provide a compelling dramatic lens through which to review the ancient Christian mythology. "The excitement stops right after the metal detectors," quipped Ben Brantley. "As a piece of writing *Corpus Christi* feels lazy. It rides piggyback on the mighty resonances guaranteed by the story that inspired it, and rarely reaches beyond the easy novelty of making its central character gay."[125] Clive Barnes was similarly intrigued by the metal detectors and spent the first two paragraphs of his review describing the surrender of his key chain to which was attached his Swiss Army penknife to authorities. He was far less intrigued by the show. "Blasphemy," he said, "is one thing. Boredom is entirely another. I can't judge the blasphemy content, but as for boredom, *Corpus Christi* exemplifies it."[126] Martin Gottfried agreed that McNally had preached a noteworthy sermon but asserted that "the validity of a point, however, does not mean it is well made and certainly does not guarantee dramatic effectiveness."[127] Michael Feingold echoed Gottfried's sentiments. He congratulated McNally for his courage, but characterized him as a "middle-class entertainer" who had said nothing that had not been expressed by countless artists who preceded him. He asserted: "The religion that has survived Renan, Genet, Kazantzakis, Fellini, Arrabal, Dali, Max Ernst, and Oskar Panizza has no need to panic over *Corpus Christi*.[128]

The Catholic League for Religious and Civil Rights only had to contend with *Corpus Christi* for a few weeks, but it had failed in its mission. Since these religious conservatives did not have the support of political allies, it was impossible for them to silence the Manhattan Theatre Club by threatening to withdraw public funding. And, by generating an avalanche of publicity for the production and MTC, they gave new meaning to the old adage that sometimes your enemies can do more for you than your friends.

Angels in east Texas

By the end of the century, the alliance of political and religious conservatives had lost much of its clout. The National Endowment for the Arts had survived a decade of attacks; 60 percent of the American people still approved of President Clinton in spite of his sexual indiscretions; and Newt Gingrich resigned as Speaker of the House of Representatives as a result of the embarrassment he suffered during the impeachment debacle. Nonetheless, many communities still feared that homosexuals were using the arts to advance a monstrous conspiracy. Nowhere was this fact more evident than in Kilgore, Texas, a sleepy, conservative east-Texas town of 14,000 that is the home of Kilgore College, a publicly funded, two-year educational institution. During the summer of 1999, Raymond Caldwell, chairman of the Drama Department and artistic director of the Texas Shakespeare Festival, which calls Kilgore College home, was troubled that the plays presented by his program were so dated:

> At Kilgore, we have done *The Crucible*, *The Glass Menagerie*, and *Our Town*, which are great plays...But they're done to death. This summer, it began to get on my conscience. We hadn't produced a play that was written since 1980...We had not done anything since these kids were born. I knew we should do something that spoke to them and came from their generation.[129]

He decided to remedy this situation by choosing to direct Kushner's *Angels in America / A Gay Fantasia on National Themes / Part One: Millennium Approaches*. Caldwell knew that his decision would generate controversy and made several alterations to the script. He deleted the scene where an AIDS patient removes his clothes for a medical examination, cut several expletives, and carefully masked a gay-sex scene so that the action was heard but not seen. He also demonstrated a great deal of sensitivity toward his students. He waived the rule that required all majors to audition for departmental productions, thereby giving them the option of not participating in the project. He printed extensive disclaimers on audition posters and encouraged students to consult with their parents before auditioning. He also sent copies of the play to college administrators. Unfortunately, most of them, including President William Holda, did not read the script until the storm struck.[130]

The melee began on September 24 when a writer for the *Flare*, the Kilgore College newspaper, ran a front-page article surveying the play's gay theme and the cast's reaction. It also ran a feature headline in bold letters that announced the play's subtitle – *A Gay Fantasia*. When Caldwell saw the headline, he knew there would be far more trouble than he originally anticipated. Six days later, Donald Bebee, pastor of Grace Baptist Church, phoned Caldwell and demanded a copy of the script. After reading the play, he wrote a letter to the *Kilgore News Herald*. In it he chastised Caldwell for choosing a play that contained "four-letter words" and "vulgar and explicit scenes including two men embracing and kissing." He accused Caldwell of identifying with the Roy Cohn character and attacked students associated with the production for blatantly disregarding community sensibilities. He then echoed the sentiments of Jesse Helms and Dana Rohrabacher when he stated: "If our tax dollars are so carelessly being used without consideration to the affect [*sic*] and offense toward people in the community, perhaps it is time to consider withdrawing support for additional activities such as the Shakespeare Festival in which the drama department at Kilgore College engages." Other prominent citizens followed Bebee's lead, including Dave Kucifer, the publisher of the *News Herald*. Although he had not read the script, he editorialized that the school's drama department should not produce *Angels in America* because it dealt with an "alternate lifestyle foreign to Kilgore and the East Texas area."[131]

MTV, *USA Today*, and the Associated Press, as well as newspapers and television stations across the state, publicized the struggle, and local ministers seized upon the homosexual themes of the play as topics for their Sunday sermons. Within a matter of hours, the phones in Caldwell and Holda's offices started ringing. On October 4, 5, and 6, the college received approximately 100 phone calls per day, forcing the president to install separate phone lines and e-mail addresses. People who had never read the play accused Caldwell of perpetrating evil on innocent youth and destroying their morals. One caller wished him a painful death from AIDS, and an anonymous letter writer said: "Fuck you, you arrogant asshole. I hope you die of AIDS, too."[132]

Letters poured into the Gregg County Commission demanding that the commissioners revoke the $50,000 emergency grant it had just given to the Texas Shakespeare Festival. Several of the commissioners agreed. "We're a Bible Belt, conservative, religious area," stated Commissioner Mickey Smith "and I'd like to keep it that way." Hundreds of phone calls, letters, and e-mails urged the college's board of trustees to cancel the production. An unidentified citizen even purchased 150 of the Van Cliburn Theatre's 264 tickets hoping to diminish the number of people who could see the show.[133]

However, the conservative activists who opposed *Angels in America* chose college president William Holda as their primary target. Holda, by all accounts, was a pillar of the church community. He was an ordained Roman Catholic deacon and long-time minister of music at the First Presbyterian Church. Irrespective of his church affiliations, he was publicly vilified. On the Sunday before opening night, a group of protesters parked their pink van across the street from the Presbyterian Church. On its roof was a large bill board that read "DR. HOLDA: THE CONSTITUTION LIKE GRACE IS NOT A LICENSE TO DO EVIL." The group heckled members of the congregation and screamed Holda was headed for hell. After services they handed out flyers that attacked the president at local stores. On the Sunday after the play closed, Holda and his friends were greeted with a sign that read "GOV. BUSH, CALL THE POLICE!! DR. HOLDA & HIS SEWER-SUCKING SODOMITES AT K.C. HAVE RAPED AND SODOMIZED THE VIRGIN VILLAGE OF KILGORE, TX." That week he answered dozens of complaints and met with his trustees to make sure that they supported his decision to allow the play to be produced. Throughout the entire ordeal, he steadfastly defended Calder's First Amendment rights and the academic freedoms set forth in the college's mission statements.[134]

On opening night, the religious fringe descended upon the Kilgore campus like a swarm of locusts. Particularly aggressive demonstrators from Baptist churches in Lindale and Mount Enterprise, both neighboring communities, carried placards with sayings that were more graphic than any lines written by Kushner. One sign depicted stick figures engaged in anal intercourse. Another read "God Hates Fags." A protestor handed out press releases titled "God hates the workers of iniquity." It went on to say that "God has prepared a place for the cursed 'angels'... a place of everlasting torment called hell!"[135] When the pastor in charge of the demonstrators encountered a placard claiming, "God Doesn't Hate," he responded, "God does hate. God wouldn't create hell if He didn't hate."[136]

The protestors disappeared shortly after opening night and the remaining performances of Kilgore College's production of *Angels* played to packed houses. However, other aspects of this ongoing drama had not yet unfolded. The Texas Shakespeare Festival had been produced by Kilgore College Drama Department since 1985, and the college had provided it with substantial support. In the late 1990s, the college was forced to reduce its contribution. Because the Festival attracted a significant number of tourists to the region, Holda asked the Gregg County Commission to contribute $50,000 to the Festival's operating budget. The commissioners were not enthusiastic about the proposal, but approved the request by a narrow 3 to 2 vote. When Holda and Caldwell refused to cancel *Angels*, they rescinded the county's support. However, Caldwell was indefatigable. He sent a chain letter to every one of his colleagues and it soon worked its way into the media. The commissioners' decision was publicized and criticized in *The Nation*, *Back Stage*, and *The Chronicle of Higher Education*. *Texas Monthly* awarded the Gregg County Commission one of its infamous "Bum Steer Awards." Such accolades are handed out to only the most obstreperous, corrupt, and/or invidious individuals and organizations in the state. As a result of the widespread attention, the Texas Shakespeare Festival received over $35,000 in contributions from associations, individuals, and foundations from across the nation. To date, the Texas Shakespeare Foundation is a viable producing organization.[137] It is, however, unclear whether or not the Festival can count on this outpouring of sympathy. Ultimately, local production organizations must depend on local patrons, and it is unclear whether or not such support will reappear.

While the majority of censorship incidents that occurred in theatre during the period under consideration transpired in the 1990s, the climate that provoked them had been germinating since the early 1970s. Riots, assassinations, Vietnam, and Watergate had driven Americans, particularly conservative Americans, to the brink of despair. They found themselves in a country beset by a sprawling government and dominated by a generation that had lost respect for traditional forms of authority. More devastating, however, was the effacement of moral boundaries that had separated the corrupt from the virtuous. *Roe* v. *Wade* had given women exclusive rights over their reproductive systems. The Equal Rights Amendment threatened to destroy the age-old hierarchical arrangement that kept women subordinate to men. The Gay Rights movement challenged the hetero-sexual dominance of American society as it affirmed the legitimacy and morality of same-sex relationships.

This cultural despair ultimately led conservatives of all stripes to band together to arrest what they considered to be a precipitous political and moral decline. By the late 1980s, fundamentalist Christians and conservative Republicans had forged a powerful coalition that commenced an all-out assault on the National Endowment for the Arts as well as on several theatres that demonstrated any tendency to question traditional religious dogma or discuss transgressive sexuality.

Yet none of these cultural critics claimed that they were anti-art or anti-theatre. They argued convincingly that they were not censoring artists that opposed the status quo. They simply claimed that taxpayers' money should be used to support institutions that advanced the ideals of the majority of the taxpayers. It was a seductive argument, one that appealed to a culture whose buttresses seemed to be collapsing. They wanted artists who would support established systems, systems that honored tradition not evolution.

Yet many contemporary artists, playwrights, and directors were funda-mentally opposed to such restrictions. They reasoned that prevailing social, sexual, and religious attitudes were supported by governments, corporations, advertisers, and the media. These assertive artists hoped to illustrate that the rules and boundaries that define society are merely constructs, erected and sustained by those who benefit from the arrangements they support.

There is a momentary lull in the battle between these two forces. It will, however, erupt again because much contemporary theatre does not seek to preserve what playwright Stephen Dietz called "nostalgia." It does not want to create ideological museums meant to enshrine the behavior of the past. It wants to expose audiences to ideas, images, and language that question and often defy traditional beliefs and behaviors. Defenders of the moral and cultural status quo will oppose what these playwrights, performers, and producers do and speak. They will attempt to maintain (or restore) the boundaries that preserve economic systems, prescribe sexual behavior, and separate the genders. These censors will arrest actors, enact legislation, boycott sponsors, or initiate any other action that will silence the voices of transgressive artists. Battles between the agents of change and the defenders of tradition are ancient, and there is little reason to believe that such encounters will ever abate.

Notes

Introduction

1 Karen Armstrong, *The Battle for God* (New York: Ballentine Books, 2001), 34–35.
2 Quoted in Richard Wattenberg, "Finding the Heat of Current Theatre," *The Sunday Oregonian*, October 28, 2001, F, 6.

1 Overture: theatrical censorship from the Puritans to Anthony Comstock

1 Winton Solberg, *Redeem the Time: The Puritan Sabbath in Early America* (Cambridge, MA: Harvard University Press, 1977), 127.
2 James Ford, "Social Life (1630–1689)," in *Commonwealth History of Massachusetts*, edited by Albert Bushnell Hart, 5 vols. (New York: States History, 1927), I, 272.
3 Increase Mather, *A Testimony Against Several Prophane and Superstitious Customs Now Practised by some in New England* (London, 1687).
4 Increase Mather, *An Arrow against Profane and Promiscuous Dancing Drawn out of the Quiver of the Scriptures* (Boston, 1684), 14.
5 Bruce C. Daniels, *Puritans at Play: Leisure and Recreation in Colonial New England* (New York: St. Martins Press, 1995), 61 and 112.
6 Ibid., 54 and 59.
7 "Letter Book of Samuel Sewall," *Collections of the Massachusetts Historical Society*, 6th series (1888), II, 29–30.
8 George B. Bryan, *American Theatrical Regulation: 1607 to 1900* (Metuchen, NJ: The Scarecrow Press, 1993), 13–16.
9 Carl and Jessica Bridenbaugh, *Rebels and Gentlemen: Philadelphia in the Age of Franklin* (New York: Reynal & Hitchcock, 1942), 2.
10 Quoted in Bryan, *American Theatrical Regulation*, 7.
11 Quoted in ibid., 7.
12 Paul Judson Little, "Reactions to the Theatre: Virginia, Massachusetts, and Pennsylvania, 1665–1793," Ph.D. dissertation, Syracuse University, 1969, 140–148.
13 Henry Steele Commager, *The Empire of Reason* (New York: Anchor Press, 1977), 16.
14 Bridenbaugh and Bridenbaugh, *Rebels and Gentlemen*, 76.
15 Ibid., 146–178.

16 Thomas Clark Pollack, *The Philadelphia Theatre in the Eighteenth Century* (New York: Greenwood Press, 1968), 4–7.
17 Quoted in William Clapp, *A Record of the Boston Stage* (New York: Benjamin Bloom, Inc., 1968), 2–3.
18 Ibid., 2.
19 Little, "Reactions to the Theatre," 50–55.
20 Hugh F. Rankin, *The Theatre in Colonial America* (Chapel Hill: University of North Carolina Press, 1965), 62.
21 William Dunlap, *A History of the American Theatre* (New York: J. & J. Harper, 1832), 47.
22 *Pennsylvania Gazette,* March 19, 1754.
23 *Pennsylvania Gazette,* March 26, 1754.
24 *Pennsylvania Gazette,* April 25, 1754.
25 Little, "Reactions to the Theatre," 155–156.
26 *New York Mercury,* November 6 and December 11, 1758.
27 *Pennsylvania Gazette,* July 5, 1759.
28 Little, "Reactions to the Theatre," 157–158.
29 Pollack, *Philadelphia Theatre,* 11.
30 B. W. Brown, "The Colonial Theatre in New England," *Special Bulletin of the Newport Historical Society,* 76 (July 1930), 7.
31 Rankin, *Theatre in Colonial America,* 93–94.
32 Brown, "Colonial Theatre," 9–11.
33 *Weyman's Gazette,* December 21, 1761.
34 *New York Mercury,* December 28, 1761.
35 Quoted in Brown, "Colonial Theatre," 20.
36 Ibid., 21–22; Rankin, *Theatre in Colonial America,* 100.
37 George C. D. Odell, *Annals of the New York Stage,* 15 vols. (New York: Columbia University Press, 1927), 1, 95.
38 Douglas McDermott, "Structure and Management in the American Theatre," in *The Cambridge History of American Theatre,* edited by Don B. Wilmeth and Christopher Bigsby, 3 vols. (Cambridge University Press, 1998), 1, 188–189.
39 *The Pennsylvania Chronicle and Universal Advertiser,* February 2–9, 1767.
40 *The Pennsylvania Chronicle and Universal Advertiser,* March 2–9, 1767.
41 *The Pennsylvania Chronicle and Universal Advertiser,* March 23–30, 1767.
42 Gordon Wood, ed., *The Rising Glory of America: 1760–1820* (Boston: Northeastern University Press, 1990), 5.
43 Quoted in ibid., 5–6.
44 Ibid., 20.
45 *The Pennsylvania Chronicle and Universal Advertiser,* February 9–16, 1767.
46 *The Pennsylvania Gazette,* July 31, 1766.
47 *The Pennsylvania Chronicle and Universal Advertiser,* January 26 – Febuary 2, 1767.
48 *The Pennsylvania Gazette,* April 30, 1767.
49 Pollock, *Philadelphia Theatre,* 100–101.
50 In the South, a second company, the Virginia Company, headed by William Verling began producing plays in Norfolk, Virginia, in January 1768. Rankin, *Theatre in Colonial America,* 140.

51 Quoted in ibid., 187.

52 Jared Brown, *The Theatre in America during the Revolution* (Cambridge, UK and New York: Cambridge University Press, 1995), 58.

53 Odell, *Annals of the New York Stage*, I, 148.

54 Quoted in Paul Leicester Ford, *Washington and the Theatre* (New York: Burt Franklin, 1899; repr. 1970), 26–27.

55 Quoted in Brown, *Theatre in America*, 63.

56 Pollack, *Philadelphia Theatre*, 41–43.

57 Ibid., 44.

58 Carl Van Kussrow, "On with the Show," Ph.D. dissertation, University of Indiana, 1959, 211.

59 Ibid., 211.

60 *The Independent Gazetteer or the Chronicle of Freedom*, November 11, 1788.

61 *Federal Gazette*, February 17, 1789.

62 *The Independent Gazetteer, or the Chronicle of Freedom*, March 6, 1789.

63 *Statutes at Large*, vol. XVIII. 184; *Federal Gazette*, February 28, 1789.

64 "The Speech of Joseph T-sd-le, Esq; in the House of Representatives," June 1767.

65 *Columbian Centinel*, October 26, 1791.

66 *Columbian Centinel*, November 9, 1791.

67 *Columbian Centinel*, November 26, 1791.

68 *Columbian Centinel*, December 3, 1791.

69 *Columbian Centinel*, January 7, 1792.

70 John Gardiner, *A Speech Delivered to the Massachusetts House of Representatives, Jan. 26, 1792, On the Subject of the Report of the Committee Appointed to Consider the Expediency of Repealing the Law Against Theatrical Exhibitions within this Commonwealth*. Boston, 1792, vii–ix.

71 Clapp, *Record of the Boston Stage*, 6.

72 Ibid., 7.

73 *Columbian Centinel*, September 8, 1792.

74 Loren K. Ruff, "Joseph Harper and Boston's Board Alley Theatre, 1792–1793," *Educational Theatre Journal*, 26 (March 1974), 48.

75 Clapp, *Record of the Boston Stage*, 12.

76 Ruff, "Joseph Harper," 50.

77 Marilyn Wood Hill, *Their Sisters' Keepers: Prostitution in New York City, 1830–1870* (Berkeley: University of California Press, 1993), 199.

78 Sean Wilentz, *Chants Democratic: New York City and the Rise of the American Working Class* (New York: Oxford University Press, 1984), 4; Richard Butsch, *The Making of American Audiences: From Stage to Television, 1750–1990* (Cambridge University Press, 2000), 5.

79 *New York Evening Post*, June 17, 1826 quoted in Peter George Buckley, "To the Opera House," unpublished Ph.D. dissertation, State University of New York at Stony Brook, 1984, 151.

80 Luke Sante, *Low Life* (New York: Farrar, Straus & Giroux, 1991), 74.

81 Butsch, *Making of American Audiences*, 47–49.

82 Buckley, "To the Opera House," 83.

83 Between 1825 and 1850, New York grew threefold from 156,000 to 515,000. Moreover, its character changed, from a major seaport whose citizens were native-born, to a city where more than half the population had been born abroad. The Irish, however, were the most numerous immigrant nationality. From 1838 to 1844, 200,000 Irish sailed to the United States. During the famine years of 1845–55, 1.5 million arrived in America. Most lacked marketable skills, and were destitute and Roman Catholic. Kerby A. Miller, *Emigrants and Exiles: Ireland and the Irish Exodus to North America* (New York: Oxford University Press, 1985), 199 and 291; Edward K. Spann, *The New Metropolis: New York City, 1840–1857* (New York: Columbia University Press, 1981), 148.

84 Bryan, *American Theatrical Regulation*, 101

85 Ibid., 60–63.

86 Robert C. Allen, *Horrible Prettiness* (Chapel Hill: University of North Carolina Press, 1991), 73.

87 Bruce McConachie, "American Theatre in Context," in *The Cambridge History of American Theatre*, 1, 161–162.

88 Quoted in Bluford Adams, *E Pluribus Barnum: The Great Showman and the Making of U.S. Popular Culture* (Minneapolis: University of Minnesota Press, 1997), 99.

89 Quoted in ibid., 118.

90 Neil Harris, *Humbug: The Art of P. T. Barnum* (University of Chicago Press, 1973), 105–106; T. Allston Brown, *A History of the New York Stage* (New York: Benjamin Bloom, repr. 1964), 71–73.

91 Allen, *Horrible Prettiness*, 61.

92 Quoted in Brooks McNamara, " 'A Congress of Wonders': The Rise and Fall of the Dime Museum," *Emerson Society Quarterly*, 20 (1974), 220.

93 Claudia Johnson, "That Guilty Third Tier: Prostitution in Nineteenth Century American Theatres," *American Quarterly*, 27 (1975), 578–579. For an interesting and provocative study of this subject as well as other aspects of audience composition and dynamics see Rosemarie K. Bank, *Theatre Culture in America, 1825–1860* (Cambridge University Press, 1997).

94 Brown, *History of the New York Stage*, 125.

95 *The Liberator*, September 9, 1853.

96 *The New York Atlas*, October 16, 1863.

97 Allen, *Horrible Prettiness*, 73.

98 Ibid., 7.

99 Ibid., 13.

100 *New York Times*, September 29, 1868, 4.

101 *New York Times*, October 1, 1868, 6.

102 Allen, *Horrible Prettiness*, 15.

103 *New York Times*, November 8, 1868, 4.

104 Allen, *Horrible Prettiness*, 17.

105 Richard Grant White, "The Age of Burlesque," *Galaxy*, August 1869, 256.

106 *New York Times*, May 15, 1869, 5.

107 Olive Logan, *Apropos of Women and Theatres* (New York: Carleton, 1869), 128 and 136.

108 Allen, *Horrible Prettiness*, 145.

109 Logan, *Apropos*, 135.
110 Allen, *Horrible Prettiness*, 126–127.
111 Charles Gallaudet Trumbell, *Anthony Comstock, Fighter* (New York: Fleming H. Revell Company, 1913), 52.
112 Walter Kendrick, *The Secret Museum: Pornography in Modern Culture* (New York: Viking Press, 1987), 132–133.
113 Anthony Comstock, *Traps for the Young* (New York: Funk and Wagnalls, 1883), xi.
114 Sanger returned to the United States in mid October of that year. Charges against her were dismissed on February 18, 1916. By that time Comstock had died and escaped humiliation. Kendrick, *Secret Museum*, 150–155.
115 Ibid., 144–145.

2 Bad girls, tough guys, and the changing of the guard

1 In his recent dissertation, Randy Kalpelke presents a thorough investigation of the press attacks on Olga Nethersole and *Sapho* and links them to a desire on the part of "yellow" newspapers to increase circulation. Randy Kalpelke, "Artistic Victories: How the Legitimate Theatre Overcame New York City's Efforts to Impose Censorship on *Sapho* in 1900, *Mrs Warren's Profession* in 1905 and Other Productions to 1927," unpublished Ph.D. dissertation, Tufts University, 1998.
2 "Woman to Woman," *New York World*, February 23, 1900.
3 "Nethersole Is Indicted," *New York Sun*, March 23, 1900.
4 John D'Emilio and Estelle B. Freedman, *Intimate Matters: A History of Sexuality in America* (New York: Harper and Row, 1988), 141.
5 David J. Pivar, *Purity Crusade: Sexual Morality and Social Control, 1868–1900* (Westport, CT: Greenwood Press, 1973), 158.
6 D'Emilio and Freedman, *Intimate Matters*, 143.
7 Barbara Meil Hobson, *Uneasy Virtue: The Politics of Prostitution and the American Reform Movement* (New York: Basic Books, 1987), 64–65.
8 Ibid., 49.
9 The penalties for men involved with prostitution in New York clearly supported this double standard. As late as the 1920s, men who engaged prostitutes were not charged with a crime. Pimps and procurers were routinely given lighter fines and jail sentences than their female partners. Willoughby Cyrus Waterman, *Prostitution and Its Repression in New York City, 1900–1931* (New York: AMS Press, repr., 1968), 71–77.
10 In actuality, unmarried, pregnant women faced insurmountable biases. Domestic servants as well as factory workers were summarily dismissed because their condition cast doubt on the moral rectitude of the workplace. Charitable organizations denied support; and, in an era when most women gave birth at home, the only institutions willing to assist with childbirth were alms-houses or public lying-in hospitals, both of which were depressing last resorts for the most destitute women. Hobson, *Uneasy Virtue*, 72.
11 David Grimstead, *Melodrama Unveiled* (Berkeley: University of California Press, 1987), 172.

12　Quoted in Arthur Hobson Quinn, *A History of the American Drama from the Civil War to the Present Day* (New York: Appleton-Century-Crofts, 1936), 44–45.

13　Quoted in "Sapho Convicted in Critics' Court," *New York World*, February 7, 1900.

14　"City Superintendent Maxwell Warns Parents and Teachers," *New York World*, February 19, 1900.

15　"Sapho-Crazed Women Throng to See Nethersole Play," *New York World*, February 18, 1900.

16　"Rev. Dr. Newell Hillis Scores the Sapho Plague," *New York World*, February 19, 1900.

17　D'Emilio and Freedman, *Intimate Matters*, 176–177.

18　Ibid., 130–133 and 167.

19　"Sapho Arouses Sense of Disgusted Pity," *New York World*, February 14, 1900.

20　"Sapho at Wallack's," *New York Times*, February 6, 1900.

21　"The Police Stop Sapho," *New York Sun*, March 6, 1900.

22　"Sapho Plague to Spread Far," *New York World*, February 18, 1900.

23　"Another Sapho Worse Than the First," *New York World*, February 21, 1900.

24　"This Sapho Was Mild," *New York World*, February 24, 1900.

25　"A Burlesque of Sapho," *New York Tribune*, March 9, 1900; "Columbia Students Air Satire of Sapho," *New York World*, February 23, 1900.

26　Adele Heller and Lois Rudnick, eds., *1915: The Cultural Moment* (New Brunswick, NJ: Rutgers University Press, 1991), 70–71.

27　"Are Cardinal Gibbons Startling Charges True?," *New York World*, February 11, 1900.

28　"At the Play and with the Players," *New York Times*, February 25, 1900.

29　"Zaza, Sapho and Co.–Unlimited," *New York Tribune*, November 11, 1900.

30　"Will Corrupt Young, Miss Hart Declares," *New York World*, February 6, 1900.

31　"I Thank the Women; Men Will Follow," *New York World*, February 18, 1900. Within days, however, the *World* published a petition signed by scores of female teachers urging that the "Sapho plague" be suppressed.

32　"Arrest of Nethersole," *New York Sun*, February 22, 1900.

33　"Rev. Dr. Easton's Statements," *New York Times*, May 7, 1900.

34　"Nethersole in Sapho," *New York Sun*, April 8, 1900.

35　Program for *Sapho*, The Columbia Theatre, Brooklyn, New York, January 1901. Clipping file, Billy Rose Theatre Collection.

36　Olga Nethersole eventually became an outspoken advocate for children's health issues and an ardent feminist, appearing on several occasions with the noted British suffragist Christabel Pankhurst. At the outbreak of World War I, she retired permanently from the stage to become a nurse. She died in England in 1951, still unmarried. "Olga Nethersole Dies at Age of 80," *New York Times*, January 9, 1951.

37　"Bernard Shaw Resents Action of Librarian," *New York Times*, September 26, 1905, 1.

38　"Comstock Responds to Shaw," *New York Times*, September 28, 1905, 9.

39　"The Shackles on Dramatic Inspiration," *New York Times*, October 1, 1905, III, 9.

40　Quoted in "Is Bernard Shaw a Menace to Morals?," *Current Literature*, 39 (October 1905), 551–552.

41　"Chicago Comstockery," *New York Times*, October 6, 1905.

42　Shaw never uses words such as sex, brothel, or prostitution in his play. To do so would have invited certain censure.

43 "Comstock at It Again," *New York Times*, October 25, 1905, 1.

44 "Comstock Won't See Bernard Shaw's Play," *New York Times*, October 26, 1905, 9. Obscenity law in the United States was largely based on an English legal decision commonly known as *Regina* v. *Hicklin* (1868). Its most salient feature was a test which stated that if *any* part, even a single paragraph, could be adjudged to have a *tendency* to "deprave or corrupt" a sensitive or susceptible mind, such as a young child, then the entire work was obscene and could be legally censured.

45 "Daly's New Shaw Play Barred in New Haven," *New York Times*, October 29, 1905, 1

46 "M'Adoo Will See Shaw Play Here," *New York Herald*, October 29, 1905, 8.

47 Mary Shaw, "My 'Immoral' Play: The Story of the First American Production of *Mrs Warren's Profession*," *McClure Magazine*, April 1912, 688.

48 "Shaw's Play Unfit; the Critics Unanimous," *New York Times*, October 31, 1905, 9.

49 "Shaw's Play unfit . . . ," *New York Times*, October 31, 1905.

50 "Shaw Play The Limit of Stage Indecency," *New York Herald*, October 31, 1905, 3.

51 "Shaw's Play Stopped; The Manager Arrested," *New York Times*, November 1, 1905, 1.

52 Ibid.

53 *New York Sun*, November 1, 1905. Quoted in the preface to *Mrs Warren's Profession*.

54 "Shaw's Play Not a Public Nuisance," *New York Herald*, July 7, 1906, 8.

55 Mary Shaw blamed the entire episode on New York politics. William Randolph Hearst was trying to unseat Tammany-backed Mayor George B. McClellan. The Hearst papers attacked *Mrs Warren's Profession* in a futile attempt to show that Tammany Hall had even corrupted New York's theatres. Shaw, "My Immoral Play," 689 and 692.

56 "Representative Boston Men Criticize Play: *Playboy of the Western World*" *Boston Globe*, Morning Edition, October 17, 1911, 9.

57 "Double Bill at the Plymouth," *Boston Herald*, Morning Edition, October 17, 1911, 12.

58 "The Embattled *Playboy*," *Boston Evening Transcript*, October 17, 1911, 13.

59 "Doesn't Need Expurgation," *Boston Globe*, Evening Edition, October 17, 1911, 6.

60 "Object to Irish Play," *New York Times*, October 9, 1911, 2; "Irish Players Fear No Riot," *New York Times*, November 26, 1911, 15.

61 "Riot in Theatre Over Irish Play," *New York Times*, November 28, 1911, 1.

62 "Groans and Hisses for Irish Players," *New York Times*, November 29, 1911, 2.

63 "Approves the *Playboy*," *New York Times*, November 30, 1911, 13.

64 "The *Playboy* Row," *New York Times*, November 29, 1911, 10.

65 "Irish Play Row in Philadelphia," *New York Times*, January 16, 1912, 8; "More Theatre Riots Greet *The Playboy*," *New York Times*, January 17, 1912, 2; "Irish Players Arrested," *New York Times*, January 18, 1912, 13; "At Least Better than Riot," *New York Times*, January 19, 1912, 4; "Shaw Scores Philadelphia," *New York Times*, January 20, 1912, 3.

66 "Peaceful at the Playboy," *New York Times*, February 13, 1913, 13.

67 Quoted in Eliza O'Brien Lummis, *Daughters of the Faith: Serious Thoughts for Catholic Women* (New York: The Knickerbocker Press, 1905), xx.

68 "The Drama League of America," *The Drama*, 1 (February 1911), 119.

69 Susan Duffy and Bernard K. Duffy, "Watchdogs of the American Theatre 1910–1940," *Journal of American Culture*, 6 (Spring 1983), 53.

70 "The Stage," *America*, 5 (September 2, 1911), 488.

71 Ibid.

72 "Reforming the Stage," *America*, 8 (December 28, 1912), 278. The Roman Catholic Church was not the only denomination to exhibit concern that contemporary theatre threatened the morals of Christians. Both the Methodists and Congregationalists initiated programs to protect the faithful from contamination. "Lifting the Ban on the Theatre," *The Literary Digest*, 46 (April 26, 1913), 952.

73 Frances Panchock, "The Catholic Church and the Theatre in New York, 1890–1920," unpublished Ph.D. dissertation, The Catholic University of America, 1976, 149–151. Amazingly, Lummis did not consider this strategy censorship. If a majority of citizens desired protection from vulgar, sensual, and materialistic productions, the state would have no other option than to establish formal means to shield them from such displays. Lummis felt completely secure in this demand because state film censorship boards had been established in Pennsylvania, Ohio, Maryland, and Kansas, and dozens of other states were considering them.

74 Ibsen's *Ghosts* premiered in New York exactly one year before *Damaged Goods*. However, it ran for a mere four performances.

75 "That Moral Play," *New York Times*, March 2, 1913, III, 6. Brieux was keenly aware of the rigorous taboo which existed around the discussion sexual topics, and judiciously omitted the words "prostitute," "syphilis," and "sex." In a short speech written to be delivered before the start of each performance, he assured his audiences that they would not be embarrassed: "It [*Damaged Goods*] contains no scene to provoke scandal or arouse disgust, nor is there in it any obscene word: and it may be witnessed by everyone, unless we must believe that folly and ignorance are necessary conditions of female virtue." Eugene Brieux, *Damaged Goods*, translated by John Pollock in *Three Plays by Brieux* (New York: Brentano's Books, 1913), 186.

76 "Brieux Play on March 9," *New York Times*, February 8, 1913, 13.

77 As Barbara Meil Hobson points out, the term "white slavery" was grossly misleading. There was also a significant amount of trade in Asian and African women in the United States and Europe. Hobson, *Uneasy Virtue*, 142.

78 Mary de Young, "Help, I'm Being Held Captive! The White Slave Fairy Tale of the Progressive Era," *Journal of American Culture*, 6 (Spring 1983), 97; D'Emilio and Freedman, *Intimate Matters*, 209.

79 Ibid., 208. The first documented case of white slavery occurred in Michigan in 1887 and involved a compound for prostitutes that serviced lumberjacks, Pivar, *Purity Crusade*, 135–136.

80 As Kathy Peiss points out, single working-class women – foreign-born and daughters of immigrants – dominated the female labor force. By 1900, 80 percent of the 343,000 wage-earning women in New York were single. Almost one-third were between the ages of sixteen and twenty and nearly 60 percent of all women in New York in this age group worked in the early 1900s. Equally as important, the context in which these women labored differed dramatically from their Victorian forebears. New jobs in department stores, large factories, and offices provided alternatives to domestic service, household production and sweat work in small shops. These employment opportunities coupled with declining hours of labor altered the relationship between work and leisure. Leisure came to be viewed and experienced as a realm distinct

from that of the workplace. It connoted independence, pleasure, and heterosexual adventures. Kathy Peiss, *Working Women and Leisure: Working Women and Leisure in Turn-of-the-Century New York* (Philadelphia: Temple University Press, 1986), 34–35.

81 The use of "white slave" plays to control the sexuality of young, independent women has been addressed by M. Joan McDermott and Sarah J. Blackstone in "White Slavery Plays of the 1910s: Fear of Victimization and the Social Control of Sexuality," *Theatre History Studies*, 16 (June 1996), 141–156.

82 "Drama: Filth on Stage," *The Nation*, 97 (September 11, 1913), 246.

83 *America*, IX (August 30, 1913), 494; *America*, X (October 11, 1913), 20; *America*, X (December 20, 1913), 261. *America*, one of the Catholic Church's most powerful organs, instituted "The Drama" a weekly column devoted exclusively to the censure of what were held to be impure or profane plays. The column continued for a year.

84 In his autobiography, Veiller admits that he and his producer added the notorious bordello scene to increase attendance. Bayard Veiller, *The Fun I've Had* (New York: Reynal & Hitchcock, 1941), 213–216.

85 "Pornography for Hire," *The Nation*, 97 (December 18, 1913), 585.

86 "Police May Close *Fight* and *Lure*," *New York Times*, September 7, 1913, 11, 3.

87 "Suffragists Approve *Lure*," *New York Times*, September 7, 1913, 1.

88 "To Issue Warrants for Play Managers," *New York Times*, September 9, 1913,1.

89 "Women and Stage Indecency," *New York Times*, September 12, 1913, 10.

90 "Women Approve *Fight*," *New York Times*, October 15, 1913, 11.

91 "Defend Social Evil Play," *New York Times*, October 13, 1913, 9.

92 "Mrs. Pankhurst's Most Quiet Day," *New York Times*, October 23, 1913, 7.

93 "Arrest of Actress Stops Vice Play," *New York Times*, December 10, 1913, 1.

94 Alan Dale, *"House of Bondage,"* Billy Rose Theatre Collection.

95 "The Traffic," *Chicago Inter Ocean*, November 24, 1913, 9.

96 "Bad Plays," *New York Times*, December 12, 1913, 12.

97 Burns Mantle and Garrison P. Sherwood, eds., *The Best Plays of 1909–1919* (New York: Dodd, Mead and Company, 1933), 539.

98 Brooks McNamara, *The Shuberts of Broadway* (New York: Oxford University Press, 1990), 65.

99 See note 82.

100 "Brieux Play...," *New York Times*, February 8, 1915.

3 Flappers and fanatics

1 George E. Mowry, ed., *The Twenties: Fords, Flappers and Fanatics* (Englewood Cliffs, NJ: Prentice Hall, 1965), 3.

2 Geoffrey Perrett, *America in the Twenties: A History* (New York: Touchstone Books, 1983), 251.

3 Ibid., 224.

4 Robert L. Duffus, "The Age of Play," *The Independent*, December 20, 1924, 539.

5 Quoted in Loren Baritz, ed., *The Culture of the Twenties* (New York: Bobbs-Merrill, 1970), viii.

6 George Santayana, *Character and Opinion in the United States* (Garden City, NY: Doubleday Anchor, 1956), 89.

7 F. Scott Fitzgerald, *This Side of Paradise* (New York: C. Scribner Sons, 1920), 282.

8 Quoted in Loren Baritz, ed., *The Good Life: The Meaning of Success for the American Middle Class* (New York: Harper and Row, 1982), 59.

9 Ibid., 67.

10 Baritz, *The Culture of the Twenties*, 75 and 85.

11 Harley Erdman, "Jewish Anxiety in 'Days of Judgment.' Community Conflict, Anti-Semitism, and the *God of Vengeance* Obscenity Case." *Theatre Survey*, 40 (May 1999), 64.

12 Baritz, *The Good Life*, 68.

13 "Our Lawless Age," *The Literary Digest*, October 8, 1921, 30.

14 D'Emilio and Freedman, *Intimate Matters*, 240.

15 McNamara, *The Shuberts of Broadway*, 96; Abe Laufe, *The Wicked Stage* (New York: Frederick Ungar, 1978), 50.

16 Ronald Wainscott, "Attracting Censorship to the Popular Theatre: Al Woods Produces Avery Hopwood's *The Demi-Virgin*," *Theatre History Studies*, 10 (1990), 128.

17 Perrett, *America in the Twenties*, 225–226.

18 Wainscott, "Attracting Censorship," 131.

19 Alexander Woollcott, "The Play," *New York Times*, October 19, 1921, 22.

20 "*The Demi-Virgin*," *Variety*, October 21, 1921, 16.

21 H. Z. Torres, "*The Demi-Virgin* Needs the Censor," *New York Commercial*, October 19, 1921, 2.

22 "Complain of *Demi-Virgin*," *New York Times*, November 3, 1921, 22.

23 Quoted in Wainscott, "Attracting Censorship," 134.

24 "Play Censor Soon, Vice Crusader's Theatre as Court Scores *Demi-Virgin*," *Variety*, November 11, 1921, 28.

25 Wainscott, "Attracting Censorship," 135.

26 Edward de Grazia and Roger K. Newman, *Banned Films: Movies, Censors and the First Amendment* (New York: R. R. Bowker, 1982), 15.

27 "*Demi-Virgin* Gets Reprieve," *New York Times*, November 26, 1921, 18.

28 Wainscott, "Attracting Censorship," 136.

29 "*The Demi-Virgin* Ban is Upheld By Court," *New York Times*, January 4, 1922, 8.

30 "Woods Wins Suit Over *Demi-Virgin*," *New York Times*, February 21, 1922, 18. The Justices also noted that decisions regarding content of films were the responsibility of a board appointed by the governor and approved by the Senate, and could not be exercised by one official.

31 Wainscott, "Attracting Censorship," 136.

32 "Against Stage Censorship," *New York Times*, February 4, 1922, 14. An important precedent already existed in New York. In 1921 the Assembly established a film censorship board to rule on the content of movies.

33 "Pussyfoot in the Theatre," *The New Republic*, 29 (December 7, 1921), 33.

34 Alexander Woollcott, "Second Thoughts on First Nights," *New York Times*, January 1, 1922, VI, 1.

35 "The Stage and the Censor," *The Nation*, January 18, 1922, 60.

36 "Straton and Brady Clash in Church Over Stage Morals," *New York Times*, February 13, 1922, 1.
37 William McAdoo, "The Theatre and the Law," *The Saturday Evening Post*, January 28, 1922, 47.
38 David K. Rod, "Trial by Jury: An Alternative Form of Theatrical Censorship in New York, 1921–1925," *Theatre Survey*, 26 (May 1985), 51.
39 Kaier Curtin, *We Can Always Call Them Bulgarians* (Boston: Alyson Publications, 1987), 26.
40 Erdman, "Jewish Anxiety," 55.
41 Heywood Broun, "The New Play," *New York World*, December 21, 1922, 13.
42 "Rudolf Schildkraut Stars in *The God of Vengeance*," *New York Sun*, December 20, 1922, 18.
43 "The Play," *New York Evening Post*, December 20, 1922.
44 Arthur Hornblow, "Mr. Hornblow Goes To The Play," *Theatre Magazine*, April 1923, 68.
45 Erdman, "Jewish Anxiety," 64.
46 Quoted in Baritz, *The Culture of the Twenties*, 78.
47 "*God of Vengeance* Immoral; 11 Actors in Play Convicted," *New York World*, May 24, 1923, 1.
48 "Better Than Censorship," *New York Times*, May 25, 1923, 5.
49 Erdman, "Jewish Anxiety," 62.
50 "A Naked Challenge," *The Nation*, September 5, 1923, 229.
51 Quoted in Curtin, *Call Them Bulgarians*, 38.
52 Arthur Hornblow, "Olla Podrida," *Theatre Magazine*, June 1923, 7.
53 James S. Metcalfe, "Is a Theatre Censorship Inevitable?" *Theatre Magazine*, 28 (November 1923), 9.
54 John Sumner, "The Sewer on the Stage," *Theatre Magazine*, 38 (December 1923), 9.
55 Ibid., 10.
56 Quoted in Arthur Gelb and Barbara Gelb, *O'Neill* (New York: Harper and Rowe, 1973), 547–548.
57 Ibid., 551–552.
58 "O'Neill Defends His Play of Negro," *New York Times*, May 11, 1924, IX, 11.
59 Gelb and Gelb, *O'Neill*, 553.
60 "Prologue of *All God's Chillun* Is Read, as Child Actors Are Barred," *New York World*, May 16, 1924; Gelb and Gelb, *O'Neill*, 553–555.
61 Ibid., 555.
62 Originally, the title of the play did not contain a question mark.
63 Quoted in Barnard Hewitt, *Theatre U.S.A.* (New York: McGraw-Hill, 1959), 358.
64 Stark Young, "The Play," *New York Times*, September 6, 1924, 14.
65 "Hylan Acts Against New Broadway Play," *New York Times*, September 24, 1924, 1. "Police Put Censors On Broadway Plays," *New York Times*, September 25, 1924, 22; "Broadway Shows Chastened Before Police Interfere," *New York Times*, September 25, 1924, 1. Aside from *What Price Glory*, police squads threatened Earl Carroll with arrest if he did not provide more clothes for his *Vanities'* chorus girls. Carroll flatly refused to make any alterations to the costumes. He declared that the number in question – nearly naked women swinging on a pendulum – was neither immoral nor

indecent. It was "merely a display of beautiful figures." "Broadway Shows...," *New York Times*, September 25, 1924, 1.

66 "Police Put Censors...," *New York Times*, September 25, 1924.

67 "Arms and the Baby," *The New Republic*, October 15, 1924, 160.

68 Burns Mantle, *The Best Plays of the 1924–1925 Season* (Boston: Small, Maynard & Company, 1925), 608.

69 "Clergy at Theatre Criticize the Stage," *New York Times*, December 5, 1924, 29.

70 Fred Niblo, "O'Neill New Play Sinks to Depths," *New York Morning Telegraph*, November 12, 1924.

71 Stark Young, "Eugene O'Neill's Latest Play," *New York Times*, November 12, 1924, 20.

72 Joseph Wood Krutch, "The God of the Stumps," *Nation*, November 26, 1924, 578.

73 "Pastors Denounce Stage Immorality," *New York Times*, February 23, 1925, 5. New York's theatre problems may have been the most widely publicized, but it seemed that the censorship hysteria had swept across the nation. Between the 7th and the 17th of that month, Cincinnati appointed a nine-member board to judge plays. It immediately elected to remove hundreds of posters advertising the Shubert revue *The Passing Show* upon a complaint from the Federation of Churches. The Philadelphia Board of Censors voted to close Earl Carroll's *Vanities*. Even Congress joined the crusade as Representative Dallinger of Massachusetts introduced a resolution in the House to inquire about establishing a censor for the District of Columbia. In April, ministers from New Bedford, Massachusetts, protested against the reading of *Desire Under the Elms*, and in October the Mayor of Boston refused to allow it to open in that city. "Cincinnati to Have Nine Play Censors," *New York Times*, February 13, 1925, 19; "Ban *Passing Show* Posters," *New York Times*, February 17, 1925, 13; "Carroll Defies Censors," *New York Times*, February 17, 1925, 13; "Asks Stage Censor for Washington," *New York Times*, February 17, 1925, 13; "New Bedford Ministers Protest," *New York Times*, April 23, 1925, 23; "*Desire Under the Elms* Will Not Be Seen in Boston," *New York Times*, November 14, 1925, 16.

74 "Belasco to Rewrite 2 Plays by Tuesday," *New York Times*, February 21, 1925, 1.

75 "Play Juries Acquit 2 Shows as Clean," *New York Times*, March 14, 1925, 15.

76 "Cardinal Condemns Indecency on Stage," *New York Times*, March 16, 1925, 21.

77 "To Boycott Profane Plays," *New York Times*, March 16, 1925, 21.

78 "Preachers Attack Play Jury System," *New York Times*, March 31, 1925, 23.

79 "The Editor's Uneasy Chair," *Theatre Magazine*, 42 (July 1925), 7.

80 J. Brooks Atkinson, "The Play," *New York Times*, February 10, 1926, 20.

81 Ibid.

82 "The New Yorker," *The Bookman*, 63 (April 1926), 216.

83 Arthur Hornblow, "Mr. Hornblow Goes to the Play," *Theatre Magazine*, 43 (April 1926), 15.

84 Burns Mantle, *Best Plays of 1926–1927* (New York: Dodd, Mead and Company, 1927), 536.

85 Marybeth Hamilton, *The Queen of Camp: Mae West, Sex and Popular Culture* (London: HarperCollins Publishers, 1995), 64.

86 George Eells and Stanley Musgrove, *Mae West* (London: Robson, 1984), 87.

87 Ibid., 61.

88 Hamilton, *Queen of Camp*, 45.

89 Quoted in Lillian Schlissel, ed., *Three Plays by Mae West* (London: Nick Hern Books, 1997), 10.

90 Ibid., 10.

91 "The Theatre," *The New Yorker*, May 8, 1926, 26.

92 "Sex," *Variety*, April 28, 1926, 79.

93 Edouard Bourdet, *The Captive*, Arthur Hornblow, Jr., trans. (New York: Brentano's Books, 1926), 145.

94 "*The Captive* from Paris," *New York Sun*, September 30, 1926, 38.

95 Arthur Hornblow, "Mr. Hornblow Goes to the Play," *Theatre Magazine* (December 1926), 16.

96 George Jean Nathan, "The Theatre," *The American Mercury*, March 1927, 373–374.

97 "Newer Hit Shows on B'way Hurting Older Attractions," *Variety*, October 6, 1926, 75.

98 "Don't Relax Mayor! Wipe Out Those Evil Plays Now Menacing the Future of the Theatre," *New York American*, January 26, 1927, Editorial Section, 1.

99 Matthew and Hannah Josephson, *Al Smith: Hero of the Cities* (Boston: Houghton Mifflin, 1969), 266–269.

100 "Drama Censor Bill Drafted," *New York Sun*, January 27, 1927.

101 *Variety*, January 12, 1927, 37; Hamilton, *Queen of Camp*, 53.

102 Schlissel, *Three Plays*, 120.

103 Hamilton, *Queen of Camp*, 54.

104 *Rain* was adapted by John Colton and Clemence Randolf from a short story by Somerset Maugham. It opened on November 7, 1922, and was considered a fine example of modern realism. It is set on a South Sea island and tells of a loose woman's encounter with a missionary. Burns Mantle chose it as one of the ten best plays of the season. It was revived in September 1924. Mantle, *The Best Plays of 1922–1923*, 29–74 and *The Best Plays of 1924–25*, 443.

105 "Plays Out of Town," *Variety*, February 2, 1927.

106 "Police Ready to Raid Theatre with Dirt Plays," *Variety*, February 9, 1927, 34.

107 "Police Raid Three Shows, *Sex, Captive* and *Virgin Man*; Hold Actors and Managers, *New York Times*, February 10, 1927, 1.

108 "Raided Shows Play to Crowded Houses," *New York Times*, February 13, 1927, 1.

109 "Cast of *Virgin Man* is Held for Trial: Two Plays up Today," *New York Times*, February 15, 1927, 1.

110 "*Virgin Man* Author Is Arrested Again Trying to Stop It," *New York Times*, February 22, 1927, 1.

111 "Three Sent to Jail in *Virgin Man* Case," *New York Times*, March 29, 1927, 1.

112 "*The Captive* Quits, But New Producer Will Defy Police," *New York Times*, February 17, 1927, 1.

113 "Press Old Charge Against Liveright," *New York Times*, February 18, 1927, 1.

114 "Fight to Save *Captive* Like 'Scopes Case,'" *New York Herald Tribune*, February 19, 1927, 6.

115 "*Captive* Immoral, Mahoney Decides," *New York Times*, March 9, 1927, 1.

116 "Play *Sex* Closes: Move Voluntary," *New York Times*, March 21, 1927, 21.

117 "Stage Censor Defeat Seen After Hearing," *New York Tribune*, March 9, 1927.

118 "Plan To Put Power To Close Theatres Into City's Hands," *New York Times*, March 18, 1927, 1.

119 "Senate Approves Stage Padlocking," *New York Sun*, March 23, 1927, 1.

120 "Theatre Padlock Law Held to Fill a Long-Felt Want," *New York Times*, April 17, 1927, 24.

121 "Ready to Enforce New Padlock Law," *New York Times*, April 9, 1927, 1.

122 "Padlocks for Plays," *The Nation*, 124 (April 6, 1927), 360.

123 "*Sex* Cast Is Guilty with Two Backers; 22 Face Jail Terms," *New York Times*, April 6, 1927, 1.

124 "Mae West Jailed with 2 Producers," *New York Times*, April 20, 1927, 1.

125 "Ready To Enforce New Padlock Law," *New York Times*, April 19, 1927, 1.

126 "Mae West Wears Workhouse Garb," *New York Times*, April 21, 1927, 29.

127 "Mae West Departs From Workhouse," *New York Times*, April 28, 1927, 28.

128 Alexander Woollcott, "The Stage," *New York World*, February 22, 1928. Clipping file, Billy Rose Theatre Collection. No page number.

129 J. Brooks Atkinson, "The Play," *New York Times*, February 22, 1928. Clipping file, Billy Rose Theatre Collection. No page number.

130 Gilbert Gabriel, "*Maya*, the Play That Launched a Thousand Frowns, Slides Slowly Into Town," *New York Sun*, February 22, 1928. Clipping file, Billy Rose Theatre Collection. No page number.

131 John Anderson, "*Maya* at the Comedy," *New York Journal*, February 22, 1928. Clipping file, Billy Rose Theatre Collection. No page number.

132 "Censor Reports Findings to Police For Further Action," *New York Morning Telegraph*, February 24, 1928. Clipping file, Billy Rose Theatre Collection. No page number.

133 "Shuberts Move to Bar *Maya* From Theatre," *New York Herald Tribune*, February 26, 1928. Clipping file, Billy Rose Theatre Collection. No page number.

134 "The Threat to Padlock a Theatre," *New York World*, March 2, 1928. Clipping file, Billy Rose Theatre Collection. No page number.

135 Heywood Broun, "It Seems to Me," *Cleveland News*, March 8, 1928. Clipping file, Billy Rose Theatre Collection. No page number.

136 Barrett H. Clark, "The Padlock Law in New York," *Drama* 18 (April 1928), 200.

137 "Shubert Aid Asks Padlock on Guild," *New York World*, April 25, 1928. Clipping file, Billy Rose Theatre Collection. No page number.

138 "*Interlude, Volpone* Called Raw," *New York Telegraph*, April 25, 1928. Clipping file, Billy Rose Theatre Collection. No page number. As it so happened, *Volpone* was appearing at the Guild Theatre. If a conviction had been obtained against the Jonson play, the Theatre Guild might have gone bankrupt.

139 "Banton O.K.'s *Interlude*; Guild to Renovate Play," *New York Evening Post*, May 1, 1928. Clipping file, Billy Rose Theatre Collection. No page number.

140 "Oh, My Dear, Here's Mae West's New Show – Get a Load of It and Weep," *Variety*, September 19, 1928, 46.

141 Quoted in Curtin, *Call Them Bulgarians*, 133–134.

142 "West Play a Hodge Podge," *New York Times*, October 2, 1928, 34.

143 "Court Stays Police on Mae West Play," *New York Times*, October 3, 1928, 33.

144 "Mayor Takes a Hand, Show Again Raided," *New York Times*, October 4, 1928, 1.

145 "Mayor Takes a Hand..." *New York Times*, October 4, 1928.

146 Quoted in Curtin, *Call Them Bulgarians*, 136.

147 Quoted in ibid., 133.

148 "New Play Weapon in Mae West Ruling," *New York Times*, March 29, 1930; Acrobats Perform for Mae West Jury," *New York Times*, April 1, 1930, 12.

149 "Jury Fails to Agree at Mae West Trial," *New York Times*, April 4, 1930, 1.

150 "Censorship Urged by Mae West Jury," *New York Times*, April 6, 1930, 13.

151 "O'Neill's *Interlude* Banned by Mayor, *Boston Daily Globe*, September 17, 1929, 1. "Mayor Rejects Plea to Remove Play Ban; Guild Continues to Fight," *Boston Herald*, September 19, 1929, 1.

152 "How Little Rollo Came to Rule The Mind of Boston," *Boston Evening Transcript*, September 21, 1929, Magazine Section, 1.

153 "Theatre Guild Ready to Fight Ban on O'Neill," *Boston Evening Transcript*, September 17, 1929, 1.

154 "*Strange Interlude*," *Boston Herald*, September 18, 1929, 18. On the day the mayor announced his ban, the tenth edition of George White's *Scandals*, noted for their scantily clad female choruses, opened in Boston. Two burlesques entitled *Ginger Girls* and *Oriental Girls* were also running. Announcements and reviews appearing in the *Boston Globe*, September 17, 1929.

155 "Forever and Forever," *Boston Globe*, September 18, 1929, 18.

156 Quoted in "*Strange Interlude*," *Boston Herald*, September 18, 1929, 18.

157 "Battle Over Play Is Heard On Radio," *Boston Globe*, September 20, 1929, 1; "Mayor Rejects Plea...," *Boston Herald*, September 19, 1929.

158 "Churches Support Nichols Ban," *Boston Herald*, September 23, 1929, 1

159 "Rev. L. J. Radcliff Hits New Morality," *Boston Herald*, September 23, 1929, 4.

160 "Pastor Scores Boston Censors," *Boston Herald*, September 23, 1929, 4.

161 "Hits Complex Toward Drama," *Boston Herald*, September 23, 1929, 4.

162 "Quincy will See *Strange Interlude*," *Boston Globe*, September 25, 1929, 1; "Play Jury Will Pass on O'Neill Drama in Quincy," *Boston Herald*, September 26, 1929, 1. From the moment that Mayor Nichols announced his ban of *Strange Interlude*, theatre owners from surrounding communities, including Lynn, Salem, Concord, Revere, Malden, Chelsea, and Quincy, offered to house the production. Although Cambridge was the Guild's first choice, Mayor Quinn expressed some doubt about the production.

163 "Play Jury..." *Boston Herald*, September 26, 1929.

164 "McGrath To Judge *Interlude* Staged," *Boston Globe*, September 26, 1929, 6.

165 "Quincy Clears Deck for Banned Play," *Boston Globe*, September 27, 1929, 8.

166 "Guild Rushes Its Plans for the Quincy Opening," *Boston Evening Transcript*, September 25, 1929, 1.

167 "Quincy Clergy Will Withhold Judgment," *Boston Evening Transcript*, September 26, 1929, 1.

168 "Strange Merits of *Strange Interlude*," *Boston Globe*, October 1, 1929.

169 "Innes Indorses It – Several Lines Cut," *Boston Globe*, October 1, 1929, 1.

170 "Clean Bill Certain For O'Neill Drama; Notables Applaud," *Boston Herald*, October 1, 1929, 1.
171 "Departure, Retrospect and Residue," *Boston Evening Herald*, October 25, 1929, 8.

4 Have you now or have you ever . . .

1 Joshua Freeman, Nelson Lichtenstein, and Stephen Brier et al., *Who Built America: Working People and the Nation's Economy, Politics, Culture, and Society*, 2 vols. (New York: Pantheon Books, 1992), II, 318–319.
2 Ibid., 319.
3 Russell Lynes, *The Lively Audience: A Social History of the Visual and the Performing Arts in America 1890–1950* (New York: Harper & Rowe, 1985), 42.
4 Hewitt, *Theatre U.S.A*, 383.
5 Howard Taubman, *The Making of the American Theatre* (New York: Coward McCann, 1965), 210.
6 "*Lysistrata* Here With Broad Humor," *New York Times*, June 6, 1930, 20; "Aristophanes Meets With Police Approval," *New York Times*, June 7, 1930, 10.
7 "Carroll's *Vanities* Raided As Indecent," *New York Times*, July 10, 1930, 1.
8 "Catholics Crusade For Stage Clean-Up; Attack Two Plays," *New York Times*, August 11, 1930, 1.
9 "Denies Catholics Seek Play Censor," *New York Times*, August 16, 1930, 6.
10 "Producers Decry Cardinal's Views," *New York Times*, October 4, 1930, 6.
11 "Play *Frankie and Johnnie* Raided by Police As Indecent; Fifteen Arrests Are Made," *New York Times*, September 11, 1930, 1.
12 "*Bad Girl*, Cast Summoned," *New York Times*, September 20, 1930, 15.
13 "Mastick Halts Bill To Aid Stage Move," *New York Times*, March 8, 1931, 17.
14 "Carroll Show Raided as Obscene in Chicago; Police Arrest 29 in Cast of *Sketch Book*," *New York Times*, February 14, 1931, 1.
15 "Cermak To Ban Plays On Chicago Gang Life," *New York Times*, April 29, 1931, 27.
16 "*Lysistrata* Subdued For Pittsburgh Stage," *New York Times*, March 20, 1931, 29.
17 "Raids Close *Lysistrata*," *New York Times*, January 20, 1932, 17.
18 Gene Fowler, *Beau James* (New York: Viking Press, 1949), 314, 325.
19 "Censorship Conference," *New York Times*, January 5, 1935, 23.
20 "Burlesque Show Raided," *New York Times*, April 6, 1935, 11.
21 "Girls in Show Freed At Hearing," *New York Times*, November 15, 1935, 21; "Burlesque Wins License Appeal," *New York Times*, December 28, 1935, 17.
22 "Two Thumbs Down on *Within the Gates*," *Boston Transcript*, January 15, 1936, 1.
23 "Catholic View of *Within the Gates*," *Boston Transcript*, February 2, 1935. *Within the Gates* clipping file, Harvard Theatre Collection. No page number.
24 "O'Casey's Play 'Not Bad Enough to Be Banned,'" *Boston Transcript*, January 16, 1935. The *New York Herald Tribune* noted that *Within the Gates*, had it been allowed to open, would have run simultaneously with *The First Legion*, a play about Jesuits that affirms miracles and the power of religion. "Boston Mayor Bars O'Casey's *Within Gates*," *New York Herald Tribune*, January 16, 1935. *Within the Gates* clipping file, Harvard Theatre Collection. No page number.

25 Burns Mantle, *The Best Plays of 1934–1935* (New York: Dodd, Mead and Company, 1935), 33.

26 "The Theatre," *Time*, December 3, 1934, 24.

27 Young, "Two New Plays," *The New Republic*, December 19, 1934, 169.

28 Brooks Atkinson, "The Play," *New York Times*, November 21, 1934, 23.

29 "*Children's Hour*, Banned by Mayor, May Be Produced in Nearby City," *Boston Herald*, December 15, 1935, 1.

30 "It Should Not Be Banned," *Boston Post*, December 22, 1935. *The Children's Hour* clipping file, Harvard Theatre Collection. No page number.

31 "Mayor Is Sued for $250,000," *Boston Globe*, December 26, 1935, 1.

32 Daniel M. Doherty, "Censorship of Theatre in Boston," Unpublished Masters thesis, Boston University, 1950, 41–42.

33 Ibid., 50.

34 "Court Refuses to Halt Ban on *Children's Hour*," *New York Herald Tribune*, February 25, 1936.

35 *Tobacco Road*, Jack Kirkland and Erskine Caldwell (New York: The Macmillan Company, 1934), 15.

36 "All Shows Now Face Censor," *Chicago American*, October 22, 1935, 1. *Tobacco Road* opened in Boston at the Plymouth Theatre on April 13, 1936.

37 "Judge Will Read *Tobacco Road*," *Chicago American*, October 23, 1935.

38 "*Tobacco Road* Ban Kept," *New York Times*, November 22, 1935, 18.

39 Freeman, et al., *Who Built America*, II, 339–341.

40 Arthur M. Schlesinger, Jr., *The Coming of the New Deal* (Boston: Houghton Mifflin, 1959), 387–394.

41 Sam Smiley, *The Drama of Attack* (Columbia: University of Missouri Press, 1972), 28.

42 Burns Mantle, ed., *The Best Plays of 1933–1934* (New York: Dodd, Mead and Company, 1935), 9.

43 Smiley, *Drama of Attack*, 30.

44 Quoted in Herbert Kline, ed., *New Theatre and Film 1934 to 1937: An Anthology* (New York: Harcourt Brace Jovanovich, 1985), 31. *New Theatre* was by far the most influential of all leftist cultural periodicals. It began as a mimeographed magazine in the early thirties, but was redesigned and printed for the first time in January 1934. It contained criticism and reviews of theatre, film, and dance and dozens of the United States most prominent leftist artists and critics contributed to it. Some of the most recognizable were, Mordecai Gorelik, Ben Blake, Herbert Kline, King Vidor, Alfred Saxe, Lee Strasberg, Ben Shawn, John Gassner, Michael Chekhov, Paul Robeson, Lincoln Kirstein, and Harold Clurman.

45 The following summary was compiled from Richard Pack, *Censored: A Record of Present Terror and Censorship in the American Theatre* (New York: National Committee Against Censorship of the Theatre Arts, 1935), 15–24 and Ben Blake, *The Awakening of the American Theatre* (New York: Tomorrow Publishers, 1935) 52–57.

46 Harry L. Hopkins, *Spending to Save* (New York: W. W. Norton & Company, 1936), 174–178; Jane De Hart Matthews, "Arts and the People: The New Deal Quest for a Cultural Democracy," *The Journal of American History* 62 (September 1975), 316–320.

47 Hallie Flanagan, *Arena: The History of the Federal Theatre* (New York: Arno Press, 1980), 20.
48 Rena Fraden, *Blueprints for a Black Federal Theatre, 1935–1939* (New York: Cambridge University Press, 1994), 34–35.
49 Jane De Hart Matthews, *The Federal Theatre, 1935–1939* (Princeton University Press, 1967), 51.
50 William F. McDonald, *Federal Relief Administration and the Arts* (Columbus: University of Ohio Press), 529.
51 Matthews, *Federal Theatre*, 52–53.
52 Freeman, et al., *Who Built America*, 381.
53 Flanagan, *Arena*, 35.
54 McDonald, *Federal Relief*, 105; Matthews, *Federal Theatre*, 50.
55 Wilson Whitman, *Bread and Circuses* (New York: Oxford University Press, 1937), 175–191.
56 Carol Anne Highsaw, "A Theatre of Action: The Living Newspapers of the Federal Theatre Project," Unpublished Ph.D. dissertation, Princeton University, 1988, 11.
57 Quoted in Kline, *New Theatre and Film*, 102.
58 Pierre De Rohan, ed., *Federal Theatre Plays: Triple-A, Power, Spirochete* (New York: Da Capo Press, 1973), x.
59 Quoted in Matthews, *Federal Theatre*, 72.
60 John Mason Brown, "'The Living Newspaper' Acted at the Biltmore," *New York Post*, March 16, 1936, 8.
61 "The Raw Deal Presents," *New York Evening Journal*, March 16, 1936, 28.
62 Richard Lockridge, "The Stage in Review: Terrors of Impartiality," *New York Sun*, March 21, 1936, 9.
63 Flanagan, *Arena*, 72–73.
64 W.B., "WPA Play Picture of Labor Fight," *New York World-Telegram*, July 25, 1936, 15.
65 Quoted in Highsaw, "Theatre of Action," 17.
66 Quoted in ibid., 218.
67 Matthews, *Federal Theatre*, 78–79.
68 Lewis had sold the movie rights to MGM but a film was never made, presumably because the story was too controversial.
69 Flanagan, *Arena*, 117.
70 Ibid., 127 and 129.
71 Ibid., 129.
72 Ibid., 184.
73 Ibid., 185.
74 Quoted in Highsaw, "Theatre of Action," 282–283.
75 Flanagan, *Arena*, 201.
76 Quoted in John Houseman, *Unfinished Business: Memoirs 1902–1988* (New York: Applause Books, 1989), 130.
77 Ibid., 131.
78 Ibid., 131–136.
79 Ibid., 138–139.
80 Ibid., 139.

81 Richard Lockridge, "The New Play," *New York Sun*, December 6, 1937, 26.

82 Brooks Atkinson, "The Play," *New York Times*, December 6, 1937.

83 Stark Young, "The Mercury and London," *The New Republic*, 93 (January 19, 1938), 310–311.

84 After protracted discussions with the senator, Flanagan finally directed the Living Newspaper to insert a line into the script after his speech: "LOUDSPEAKER: Despite his position during the debate, Senator Andrews voted for and supported the bill in its final form." Highsaw, "Theatre of Action," 347–350.

85 Walter Goodman, *The Committee: The Extraordinary Career of the House Committee on Un-American Activities* (New York: Farrar, Straus and Giroux, 1968), 14. The official name of the Committee as adopted by Congress was House Committee on Un-American Activities. However, the acronym HUAC, which reverses the order of the words, quickly came to be used by the press and became the moniker by which the Committee was known. Thus, I have chosen to use that order of words and that acronym when referring to this investigative body.

86 Goodman, *The Committee*, 15 and 19.

87 Ibid., 21–23.

88 Ibid., 24.

89 "Washington Notes," *The New Republic*, August 31, 1938, 102.

90 "Dies Inquiry Gets Income Tax Books," *New York Times*, August 10, 1938, 6. Thomas was subsequently tried and convicted for defrauding the United States government.

91 *Hearings Before a Special Committee on Un-American Activities*, 13 vols. (Washington, DC: Government Printing Office, 1938), I, 616. Hereafter, all citations from this source will be referred to as *Hearings*.

92 *Hearings*, I, 538–554.

93 According to Paul Edwards, administrator of Project One in New York, Huffman had never been employed by the FTP.

94 *Hearings*, I, 780.

95 Ibid., I, 833–839.

96 Ibid., I, 843.

97 Ibid., I, 847 and 859.

98 Flanagan, *Arena*, 336–337.

99 Ibid., 338–339.

100 "WPA Writers' Head Hits Communists," *New York Times*, December 7, 1938, 2.

101 *Hearings*, IV, 2838–2885.

102 Ibid., 2849.

103 Ibid., 2857–2858.

104 Flanagan, *Arena*, 345–346.

105 Quoted in ibid., 347.

106 "House Rebellion Passes Relief Bill at $725,000,000, Restricts Use of Funds," *New York Times*, January 14, 1939, 1.

107 Ibid.

108 Ibid.

109 "WPA Witness Says Soviet Trained Him In Street Fighting," *New York Times*, June 7, 1939, 1; "House Group Told of Red Domination Over WPA Writers," *New York Times*, May 2, 1939, 1.

110 Flanagan, *Arena*, 350.
111 "Relief Bill Aimed At WPA Radicals Ready for House," *New York Times*, June 13, 1939, 1.
112 "Federal Theatre Ban Is Attacked On Radio," *New York Times*, June 21, 1939, 3.
113 "Stage, Music Favor WPA Arts Projects," *New York Times*, June 20, 1939, 24.
114 Matthews, *Federal Theatre*, 282–283.
115 "Miss Bankhead Asks Aid For Stage," *New York Times*, June 21, 1939, 1.
116 "Roosevelt Signs Relief Bill, But Condemns It as Hardship," *New York Times*, July 1, 1939, 2.
117 "Relief Bill Passed; Bans WPA Theatre," *Washington Post*, July 1, 1939, 1; *Newsweek*, July 10, 1939, 11. This same article also pointed out that this Congress, which anointed itself the "Economy Congress," had approved much higher appropriations than Roosevelt had requested to run the government. The only program that was reduced was the relief budget.
118 "Uncle Sam in the Show Business Had Hits, Flops and Always Rows," *New York Times*, July 1, 1939, 2; "Three WPA Shows Close Amid Hot Protests," *New York Times*, July 1, 1939, 2.
119 Euphemia Van Rensselaer Wyatt, "The Drama," *Catholic World*, 149 (August 1939), 598.
120 Flanagan, *Arena*, 367.
121 "Refusal to Revive WPA Theatre Laid to Red Rule of Actor Unions," *New York Times*, July 9, 1940, 23.
122 "Equity Denies Reds Sit on Ruling Board," *New York Times*, July 10, 1940, 15.
123 "Lambertson Returns to Attack Equity," *New York Times*, July 13, 1940, 16.
124 Quoted in Richard M. Fried, *Nightmare in Red: The McCarthy Era in Perspective* (New York: Oxford University Press, 1990), 57.
125 "Rebirth of a Committee," *Newsweek*, January 15, 1945, 34.
126 From 1947 to 1953, loyalty boards investigated 26,236 persons. More than 13,000 interrogatories and letters of charges were issued and more than 4,000 hearings were held. Griffin Fariello, *Red Scare* (New York: W. W. Norton & Company, 1995), 17.
127 Eric Bentley, ed., *Thirty Years of Treason* (New York: Viking, 1971), 86.
128 "Menjou Testifies Communists Taint the Film Industry," *New York Times*, October 22, 1947, 1.
129 Bentley, *Thirty Years of Treason*, 153–165.
130 Ibid., 220.
131 John Cogley, *Report on Blacklisting*, 2 vols. (New York: Arno Press and *The New York Times*, 1972), 1, 21 and 74.
132 Quoted in ibid., 22.
133 "Mayor Is Criticized For Burlesque Ban," *New York Times*, March 4, 1942, 4.
134 "The Case Of Trio," *New York Times*, November 19, 1944, 11, 1.
135 "A United Theatre Defeats Official Censorship," *Equity*, 30 (March 1945), 5.
136 "Moss Keeps Things Humming in Theatre By Making Mistakes," *New York Daily News*, February 27, 1945. *Trio* clipping file, Billy Rose Theatre Collection. No page number.
137 "A United Theatre...," *Equity*, 6.

138 "A United Theatre . . . ," *Equity*, 6–7.

139 "A United Theatre . . . ," *Equity*, 7.

140 "Mayor Approves Plan To Curb Moss," *New York Times*, March 8, 1945, 1.

141 "O'Neill Play Cleaned Up," *Detroit News*, March 12, 1947, 1.

142 "Play Censored in Capitol," *New York Times*, August 12, 1949, 12.

143 "Santa Barbara Bans Kirkland's *Mr. Adam*," *New York Times*, February 28, 1949, 18.

144 "Chicago Officials Blamed," *New York Times*, June 7, 1949, 27.

145 "Ban on Play Assailed," *New York Times*, December 27, 1949, 25.

146 Paul Jones, "Mae West's Play Is Banned Here," *Atlanta Constitution*, January 31, 1951, 2.

147 "*Tobacco Road* Banned Here; 'Filthy, Immoral, Indecent,'" *Providence Journal*, December 31, 1952, 8.

148 "Producer Arrested Over *Tobacco Road*," *New York Times*, January 10, 1953, 19.

149 "Soldiers Are People Too, *New York Times*, April 14, 1951, 14.

150 "U.S. Occupation Army in Germany Closes Its *Mister Roberts* for 'Strong' Language," *New York Times*, April 11, 1951, 35.

151 "Mister Roberts Ban Criticized," *New York Times*, August 6, 1951, 17.

152 Fried, *Nightmare in Red*, 113–114.

153 Arthur Miller, *Timebends* (New York: Grove Press, 1987), 331.

154 Cogley, *Report on Blacklisting* I, 121. The practice of blacklisting had rapidly spread to the radio and television industries. *Counterattack, the Newsletter of Facts on Communism* and *Red Channels, The Report of Communist Influence in Radio and Television* were the most influential and effective "blacklists." In addition to publishing alarming news about the spread of Communism in the United States they provided their readers with a series of "special reports," listed scores of "Communist front" organizations, and revealed the names of thousands of individuals supposedly connected to them. These lists, as well as the copy-cat lists they spawned, were responsible for hundreds if not thousands of lost careers. For a full account of the pernicious effects of blacklisting in the movie, television, and radio industries see Cogley, *Report on Blacklisting*, I and II.

155 Lillian Hellman, *Scoundrel Time* (Boston: Little, Brown and Company, 1976), 69. More than likely, Kazan knew that director Edward Dmytryk, one of the Hollywood Ten, appeared again before the Committee in 1951 and listed the names of persons he had known to be Communists. Although these individuals were already known to the Committee, he was allowed to resume his career after he had undertaken the ritual betrayal. Goodman, *The Committee*, 302–303.

156 *Hearings Before the Committee on Un-American Activities, House of Representatives, Eighty Second Congress, Second Session*, "Communist Infiltration of the Hollywood Motion-Picture Industry – Part 7," 2409–2410.

157 Elia Kazan, "A Statement," *New York Times*, April 12, 1952, 7. Eric Bentley notes that Tony Kraber informed the Committee that Skouras rewarded Kazan with a new $500,000 contract the day after he concluded his testimony. Bentley, *Thirty Years of Treason*, 486.

158 Ibid., 531. The reasons for Odets' sudden docility have never been adequately explained. Many critics assumed that he, like Kazan, feared that he would never again

work in Hollywood if he did not cooperate with the Committee. Odets, however, claimed that he never should have been grouped with other friendly witnesses and that his testimony was unfairly presented in the press. Gabriel Miller insists that Odets was profoundly injured by the abuse heaped on him by his colleagues and that the experience ruined him as a writer. Gabriel Miller, *Clifford Odets* (New York: Continuum, 1989), 203–204.

159 Hellman, *Scoundrel Time*, 97–98. William Wright, *Lillian Hellman: The Image, The Woman* (New York: Simon and Schuster, 1986), 248.

160 Ibid., 248–260.

161 "70 Back Inquiry Into Stage Reds," *New York Times*, August 13, 1955, 6.

162 David Platt, "Theatre Witchhunt Opening Here Today," *Daily Worker*, August 15, 1955, 1.

163 "All-Star Cast," *New York Times*, August 12, 1955, 18.

164 David Platt, "Actors Defy Walter in Stormy Hearing," *Daily Worker*, August 17, 1955, 1.

165 "Actor Rips Walter Probe . . . ," *Daily Worker*, August 17, 1955, 1.

166 Milton Bracker, "Six Witnesses Balk As Inquiry Ends," *New York Times*, August 19, 1955, 1.

167 "500 Picket, Chant 'Go Home, Walter'!" *Daily Worker*, August 17, 1955, 2.

168 "Hearings Attacked At Two Rallies," *New York Times*, August 18, 1955, 14.

169 Bentley, *Thirty Years of Treason*, 787.

170 Miller also knew how to use the public-relations potential of the hearings. He announced during a recess that he would marry Ms. Monroe before July 13, the date that she was slated to begin a film project in London. Robert E. Thompson, "Playwright Will Marry Marilyn," *The Washington Post and Times Herald*, June 22, 1956, 2. It was rumored that Committee Chairman Francis Walter offered to call off the hearing if Miller consented to have a photograph taken with the Congressman and Ms. Monroe.

171 Bentley, *Thirty Years of Treason*, 798–801.

172 Ibid., 807.

173 Ibid., 808.

174 Ibid., 820–822.

175 Goodman, *The Committee*, 396.

176 Quoted in ibid., 360.

177 Ibid., 397–400.

178 Ibid., 431.

5 Bye, bye American pie

1 David Farber and Beth Bailey, eds., *The Columbia Guide to America in the 1960s* (New York: Columbia University Press, 2001), 16.

2 Ibid., 16–17.

3 Ibid., 17.

4 Carl Singleton, ed., *The Sixties in America*, 3 vols. (Pasadena, CA: Salem Press, Inc., 1999), I, 83–85; II, 416.

5 Farber and Bailey, *Columbia Guide*, 20–21.

6 "Civil Rights: Black Power," *Newsweek*, June 27, 1966, 36; In 1967 alone, the President's Commission on Civil Disorders reported that there were 164 racially motivated disturbances in 122 cities. "As Another Riot Season Nears," *US News and World Report*, March 11, 1968, 33.

7 Singleton, *The Sixties*, III, 688.

8 Alexander Bloom and Wini Breines, eds., *Takin' It to the Streets* (New York: Oxford University Press, 1995), 61–74.

9 Farber and Bailey, *Columbia Guide*, 248–249.

10 Singleton, *The Sixties*, III, 691–692.

11 Blake Bailey, *The 60's* (New York: Mallard Press, 1992), 62–65.

12 Singleton, *The Sixties*, III, 753–755.

13 Farber and Bailey, *Columbia Guide*, 41.

14 "The Nation: Protest," *Time Magazine*, October 27, 1967, 23.

15 Singleton, *The Sixties*, III, 714 and 755.

16 Ibid., 716.

17 Michael Smith, "The Good Scene Off Off-Broadway," *TDR*, 10 (1966), 159.

18 Although the Living Theatre was one of the original members of the League of Off-Broadway Theatres, the improvisatory style and self-consciously theatrical attitude of this production, combined with Beck's unyielding political commitment, clearly link this production with the ethos of Off-Off.

19 The topic of narcotics was a daring theatrical choice. In 1959 addicts were believed to be moral degenerates who lived in decaying urban slums. This belief about addicts persisted in spite of the fact that 1.2 million pounds of the tranquilizer Milltown had been prescribed to middle-class suburbanites by the end of the 1950s. Baritz, *The Good Life*, 200.

20 Pierre Biner, *The Living Theatre* (New York: Horizon, 1972), 51.

21 Quoted in John Tytell, *The Living Theatre: Art, Exile and Outrage* (New York: Grove, 1995), 155.

22 "Young Playwright," *The New Yorker*, July 9, 1960, 24–25.

23 Robert Brustein, "Junkies and Jazz," *The New Republic*, September 28, 1959, 39.

24 Louis Calta, "Theatre: World of Narcotics Addicts," *New York Times*, July 16, 1959, 30.

25 Quoted in Stuart W. Little, *Off-Broadway: The Prophetic Theatre* (New York: Coward, McCann & Geoghegan, Inc., 1972), 206–207.

26 Ibid., 208.

27 Tytell, *Living Theatre*, 183.

28 Ibid., 186.

29 "The Living Theatre goes Broke; Becks Brigged by Feds," *The Village Voice*, October 24, 1963, 1.

30 Renfreu Neff, *The Living Theatre: USA* (New York: The Bobbs-Merrill Company, 1970), 9–11.

31 "Church-Owned Theatre in Boston Rejects Plays," *New York Times*, February 15, 1960, 23.

32 "Rockport, Mass. Bans Two Plays," *New York Times*, July 14, 1960, 11.

33 "Rutherford Board Bans Play by Gide," *New York Times*, August 18, 1963, 52.

34 "Paul Baker Quits Baylor for Trinity; 11 Drama Dept. Aides Also Resign," *Waco Times-Herald*, March 8, 1963, 1.

35 As it turned out, Baker was not injured by his willingness to challenge such a formidable foe. He was named artistic director of the Dallas Theatre Center and Chair of Trinity University's Speech and Drama Department. However, as the 1960s progressed, very few college directors would be able to emerge from such encounters with their reputations intact and futures secure.

36 Bloom and Breines, *Takin' It to the Streets*, 141.

37 Amiri Baraka, *The Autobiography of LeRoi Jones* (New York: Fruendlich Books, 1984), 93.

38 George Dennison, "The Demagogy of LeRoi Jones," *Commentary*, February 1965, 68–69.

39 Myrna Bain, "Everybody's Protest Play," *The National Review*, March 23, 1965, 249.

40 "A Police Chief Talks of 'Police Brutality,'" *US News and World Report*, August 10, 1964, 33.

41 Cecil Smith, "Jones Hits With Nightmares," *Los Angeles Times*, March 26, 1965, v, 11.

42 "Harassment Hurts Le Roi Jones Plays," *New York Times*, April 6, 1965, 31; "Advertising Ban Is Protested," *New York Times*, April 9, 19; "The Right To Have His Say," *New York Times*, April 25, 1965, 11, 1.

43 Population data for 1968 are unavailable. However, the 1963 data indicates that, of the 26,071 residents of Wellesley, thirty-seven were black (0.14%). In 1973 the total population was 28,051 and the number of black residents had risen to 201 (0.7%). Source: Wellesley Local Growth Committee, Comparative Statistics.

44 "Obscenity Fight Splits City of Wellesley After LeRoi Jones Play is Given at High School," *New York Times*, September 10, 1968, 25.

45 "Controversial Program At High School Last Friday Raises Storm Of Protest At Meetings of Town Boards," *Wellesley Townsman*, June 6, 1968, 1.

46 Ibid.

47 "Obscenity Fight . . . ," *New York Times*, September 10, 1968.

48 Ibid. This incident was omitted from coverage by the *Wellesley Townsman*.

49 "Hundreds Hear Vehement Arguments On *The Slave*, Moderates Urge Town to 'Cool It'; Court Action Deferred," *Wellesley Townsman*, June 13, 1968, 1.

50 "'Wellesley Incident' Explosive," *Boston Globe*, September 10, 1968, 39. There are no extant prints of this particular documentary.

51 "*The Slave* Ruled Obscene," *Wellesley Townsman*, September 12, 1968, 7.

52 R. G. Davis, *The San Francisco Mime: The First Ten Years* (Palo Alto, CA: Ramparts Press, 1975), 32.

53 "The Theatre," *Time*, October 18, 1968, 72.

54 Davis, *San Francisco Mime*, 69, 202–203.

55 Ibid., 51–52.

56 Ibid., 56–57.

57 Ibid., 20.

58 Ibid., 72.

59 In 1968, the Troupe won an Obie Award for "uniting theatre and revolution and grooving in the park." Davis, *San Francisco Mime*, 211. Later in 1968, the Troupe hosted the Radical Theatre Festival at San Francisco State College. Included were the Mime Troupe, Bread and Puppet Theatre, El Teatro Campesino, Gut Theatre, and Berkeley Agit Prop. *Time*, October 18, 1968, 72.

60 "American Flag Burned In Theatre Spectacle," *Village Voice*, April 14, 1966, 7.

61 "The Man-Not-in-the-Street On Stage Off-Broadway," *Village Voice*, November 8, 1966, 24.

62 Robert Brustein, "Three Views of America," *The New Republic*, December 3, 1966, 31.

63 "America Undone," *London Observer*, August 6, 1967. *America Hurrah* clipping file, Billy Rose Theatre Collection. No page number.

64 "*America Hurrah* Returns To Private London Theatre," *New York Times*, September 4, 1967, 25.

65 "Chicago Is Closed To *America Hurrah*," *New York Times*, November 8, 1967, 56.

66 "*America Hurrah* Closed In Alabama as a Disgrace," *New York Times*, August 1, 1968, 24.

67 As a piece of political satire, it could not have been more perfectly timed. The production opened on February 22, 1967. In March, results of the most recent Gallup Poll revealed that the president's approval rating had plummeted. Only 45% of Americans approved of Johnson as president, and only 37% agreed with his handling of the Vietnam War, down from 56% and 50%, respectively, the preceding year. "LBJ and the War," *US News and World Report*, March 20, 1967, 8.

68 "Program Printer Rejects *M'Bird*," *New York Times*, January, 11, 1967, 53.

69 "Ready *M'Bird*," *New York Times*, February 19, 1967, 11, 1.

70 "Theatre Journal," *Village Voice*, March 2, 1967, 24.

71 "Truth, Taste and *M'Bird*," *New York Times*, March 12, 1967, 11, 1.

72 "Is *M'Bird*, Pro-American," *New York Times*, March 19, 1967, 11, 1.

73 "Hoover Assails *M'Bird* Author," *New York Times*, April 1, 1967, 29. Hoover's comments originally appeared in the FBI monthly, *Law Enforcement Bulletin*, which was distributed to approximately 57,000 policemen. *Macbird!*'s notoriety nonetheless made for packed houses; it returned its $30,000 investment to 50 backers by May 5, and ran for over 300 performances. "*M'Bird*, in the Black," *New York Times*, May 5, 1967, 34.

74 "The Nation," *Time Magazine*, October 27, 1967, 23–25.

75 " 'Police State' Or Model City? Chicago In Perspective," *US News and World Report*, September 16, 1968, 65.

76 The organizers of the Chicago demonstration were very clear about the value of television as a means of disseminating the message of revolution. The *US News and World Report* description referred to above makes frequent reference to the fact that organizers of the protest wanted the police to attack. They knew full well that the ensuing battle would be broadcast around the world. In a very real way, television transformed the "revolution" into a "media event." Moreover, the leaders of the radical movement, recognizing the desire of the media for celebrities, crafted revolutionary personas for themselves which were assured copious media coverage.

For a provocative analysis of this strategy, see Robert Brustein's "Revolution As Theatre," in *Revolution As Theatre* (New York: Liveright, 1971), 15–28.

77 Biner, *Living Theatre*, 97.

78 Ibid., 98.

79 Neff, *Living Theatre*, 204.

80 Tytell, *Living Theatre*, 244.

81 "Indecent Exposure Charged to Becks," *New York Times*, September 28, 1968, 27; Neff, *Living Theatre*, 35–36.

82 Jack Kroll, "The Monster," *Newsweek*, October 14, 1968, 117; Jack Kroll, "The 'Living,'" *Newsweek*, October 28, 1968, 134.

83 Edith Oliver, "Off Broadway," *The New Yorker*, October 12, 1968, 106.

84 Clive Barnes, "Stage: Living Theatre's *Paradise Now* a Collective Creation," *New York Times*, October 15, 1968, 39.

85 Eric Bentley, "I Reject the Living Theatre," *New York Times*, October 20, 1968, II, 1.

86 Robert Brustein, "The Third Theatre Revisited," *NY Review of Books*, 12 (February 13, 1969), 26.

87 By the time the tour ended, the total of "officials" and joiners was more than sixty. This figure does not include a constantly shifting number of hangers on and groupies. Neff, *Living Theatre*, 92–94.

88 Ibid., 100–105.

89 Ibid., 117.

90 Ibid., 161–167.

91 Ibid., 179 183.

92 The following description was compiled from Richard Gilman, "The Theatre Of Ignorance," *The Atlantic*, July 1969, 40–42 and Brustein, *Revolution As Theatre*, 31–48.

93 "Living Theatre Jailed in Brazil," *New York Times*, August 15, 1971, 11, 1; "Becks, In Brazil, Work Despite Trial," *New York Times*, August 24, 1971, 30; "Brazil to Expel Living Theatre Troupe," *New York Times*, August 26, 1971, 15; and "The Becks Return After 65 Days In Brazil Jail," *New York Times*, September 5, 1971, 28.

94 Robert J. Wagman, *The First Amendment Book* (New York: Pharos Books, 1991), 202–203.

95 For his first fifteen years, Brennan was the court's strongest anti-obscenity voice. In the 1970s, admitting the futility of attempting to define and control obscenity, he became an advocate of the broadest possible definition of freedom of expression.

96 Quoted in Wagman, *First Amendement*, 207.

97 Baritz, *The Good Life*, 229–230.

98 D'Emilio and Freedman, *Intimate Matters*, 302–303.

99 Ibid., 303–305.

100 DeGrazia and Newman, *Banned Films*, 80–83.

101 Ibid., 121–125, 299–301.

102 Richard Schechner, *Public Domain* (New York: Bobbs-Merrill, 1969), 141.

103 William I. Oliver, "The Censor in the Ivy," *TDR*, 15 (Fall 1970), 32–33.

104 *Fullerton Daily News Tribune*, November 15, 1967, quoted in Oliver, "The Censor in the Ivy," 33.

105 *Fullerton Daily News Tribune*, November 15, 1967, quoted in Oliver, "The Censor in the Ivy," 35.

106 Ibid., 37–38.

107 "Producer Presents *Beard* in Spite of Court Order," *Los Angeles Times*, January 25, 1968, 1, 3; "5 Principals in *The Beard* Arrested by Vice Officers," *Los Angeles Times*, January 26, 1968, 1, 3.

108 Barbara Lee Horn, *The Age of Hair* (Westport, CT: Greenwood Press, 1991), 25–31.

109 Ibid., 40.

110 Ibid., 45–46.

111 Ibid., 42.

112 Ibid., 86.

113 Quoted in William Goldman, *The Season* (New York: Harcourt, Brace and World), 386.

114 Quoted in ibid., 386.

115 Walter Kerr, "*Hair*: Not in Fear, But in Delight," *New York Times*, May 19, 1968, II, 3.

116 Quoted in Horn, *Age of Hair*, 87.

117 Supreme Judicial Court of Massachusetts, *P.B.I.C. Inc. et al.* v. *District Attorney of Suffolk County*, April 9, 1970.

118 United States District Court for the District of Massachusetts, *P.B.I.C., Inc., Natoma Productions, Inc.*, v. *Garrett H. Byrne*, May 6, 1970. While this part of the decision may not seem remarkable today, no Supreme Court decisions had yet been issued on the First Amendment privileges of live theatre if it employed nudity or sexual situations.

119 Lewd and lascivious behavior is generally regarded as self-explanatory and typically consists of public and intentional exposure of private or intimate body parts in such a way as to connote or denote sexual activity. Indecent exposure is defined as "offensively exposing [oneself] without necessity or reasonable excuse, and in such a way as to produce alarm."

120 United States District Court for the District of Massachusetts, *P.B.I.C., Inc., Natoma Productions, Inc.*, v. *Garrett H. Byrne*, May 6, 1970.

121 Mike Trimble, "Allow *Hair* at LR For Six-day Run, Judge Eisele Orders," *Arkansas Gazette*, August 12, 1971, 1.

122 United States Supreme Court, *Southeastern Promotions, Ltd.* v. *Conrad et al.*, March 18, 1975. Neither the District Court judges nor the Appeals Court judges had seen a production of *Hair*.

123 United States Supreme Court, *Southeastern Promotions* v. *Conrad*.

124 Ibid.

125 Schechner, *Public Domain*, 217.

126 Richard Schechner, *Environmental Theatre* (New York: Applause Books, 1994), 61.

127 Actors quickly began to feel sexually violated and it was clear that many audience members had no notion of what was expected of them. This confusion and antipathy proved to be generally destructive to the ethos which Schechner had hoped to create, and such scenes eventually had to be rigorously controlled. Schechner, *Environmental Theatre*, 117.

128 Quoted in Richard Schechner, "Speculations on Radicalism, Sexuality, & Performance," *TDR*, 13 (Summer, 1969), 93.

129 Schechner, "Speculations . . . ," 94.
130 "10 Nude Actors Feel Cold Arm of the Law at U. of M.," *Detroit News*, January 27, 1969, 1.
131 "Nudity Spurs Campus Probe," *Detroit News*, January 28, 1969, 13.
132 John Mullane, "*Che!* Cast Vows to Carry On and Take It Off," *New York Post*, March 25, 1969, 24.
133 "Sex in Film and Play Put to the Courts," *New York Times*, March 26, 1969, 37.
134 "Bid to Reopen *Che!* Fails in U.S. Court," *New York Times*, March 28, 1969, 38.
135 "Actors and Author of *Che!* Arrested After Performance," *New York Times*, May 8, 1969, 33.
136 Murray Kempton, "Looking at Obscenity," *New York Post*, March 26, 1969. *Che!* Clipping file Billy Rose Theatre Collection. No page number.
137 "Beyond the (Garbage) Pale," *New York Times*, April 1, 1969, 46.
138 "Morals: Backlash," *Newsweek*, April 7, 1969, 31.
139 "Letter to John V. Lindsay and District Attorney Frank S. Hogan," *Dramatists Guild Quarterly*, Spring 1969, 8.
140 "A Discussion of Censorship and the *Che!* Case," *Dramatists Guild Quarterly*, Spring 1969, 7–8.
141 "Actresses Talk About Onstage Nudity," *New York Times*, February 17, 1969, 28.
142 "Actors Equity [*sic*] Sets Rules For Nudity in the Theatre," *New York Times*, May 20, 1969, 41.
143 Morris Kaplin, "David Merrick, at Cast's Trial, Assails *Che!* as Without Value," *New York Times*, January 20, 1970, 46.
144 "Barnes Testifies on *Che!" New York Times*, Jan 31, 1970, 36.
145 Criminal Court of the City of New York, New York County, *People* v. *Larry Bercowicz, et al.*, February 25, 1970.
146 "Morals: Backlash," *Newsweek*, April 7, 1969, 31. Nixon responded by sending a personal letter of congratulations to Mike Levesque, the organizer of the rally.
147 "Modern Living," *Time*, July 11, 1969, 61.
148 Wagman, *First Amendment*, 209–210.
149 Kathleen Tynan, *The Life of Kenneth Tynan* (London: Methuen, 1988), 277. According to Tynan's wife, Kathleen, the title *Oh! Calcutta!* was inspired by a Clovis Trouille painting featuring the backside of a Turkish concubine. One of a series that was greatly admired by Tynan, it was entitled, *Oh! Calcutta!*. Later she discovered that it was also a French pun, *O quel cul t'as*.
150 Lewis Funke, "City Officials Consulting with *Oh! Calcutta!* Staff," *New York Times*, May 24, 1969, 27.
151 Tynan felt as though the final result was a tawdry burlesque and wanted his name removed from the credits three days before the production opened. Tynan, *Life of Kenneth Tynan*, 283.
152 Clive Barnes, "Theatre: *Oh! Calcutta!* A Most Innocent Dirty Play," *New York Times*, June 18, 1969, 33.
153 Richard F. Cooke, "The Theatre: For Buffs Only," *The Wall Street Journal*, June 19, 1969.
154 Martin Gottfried, "Theatre," *Women's Wear Daily*, June 18, 1969.

155 John Kendall, "Show Cancelled After Arrest of *Oh! Calcutta!* Performers," *Los Angeles Times*, December 18, 1969, II, 1.

156 "Porno Report Cleared for Publication," *Publishers Weekly*, September 28, 1970, 59.

157 "Nixon Obscenity-Unit Man Sues to Block *Calcutta*," *New York Times*, September 23, 1970, 39.

158 "*Oh! Calcutta!* in 60 Cities," *New York Times*, September 29, 1970, 37.

159 "*Oh! Calcutta!* Tape Seized, 9 Arrested," *Boston Globe*, September 29, 1970, 39.

160 "*Oh! Calcutta!* Showing Here Results in Federal Indictment," *Corpus Christi Caller*, May 20, 1971, 1; "TV *Oh! Calcutta!* Leads To Charges," *New York Times*, May 20, 1971, 83.

161 Wagman, *First Amendment*, 211.

162 Each of the five obscenity decisions announced on June 21 were 5–4 decisions. In each case, the five justices for and the four against were exactly the same. Wagman, *First Amendment*, 213.

163 Quoted in ibid., 213.

164 Ibid., 212.

165 Quoted in ibid., 213.

166 Ibid., 213.

167 "Has the Supreme Court Saved Us From Obscenity," *New York Times*, August 5, 1973, II, 1.

168 "'Decent Americans Hail Supreme Court Rulings,'" *New York Times*, September 9, 1973, II, 16.

6 The past is prologue

 1 Jerome L. Himmelstein, *To the Right: The Transformation of American Conservatism* (Berkeley: University of California Press, 1990), 71.

 2 William Rusher, *The Rise of the Right* (New York: Morrow, 1984), 154–155.

 3 Ed Dobson and Cal Thomas, *Blinded by the Might: Can the Religious Right Save America?* (Grand Rapids, MI: Zondervan, 1999), 31–32.

 4 Tim LaHaye, *The Battle for the Mind* (Old Tappan, NJ: Fleming H. Revell, 1980), 26 and 57.

 5 Nancy T. Ammerman, "North American Protestant Fundamentalism," in *Media, Culture and the Religious Right*, edited by Linda Kintz and Julia Lesage (Minneapolis: University of Minnesota Press, 1998), 92–93.

 6 Ibid., 92.

 7 Himmelstein, *To the Right*, 115–116.

 8 Quoted in James L. Guth, "The Politics of the Christian Right," in *Religion and the Culture Wars*, edited by John C. Green, James L. Guth, Corwin E. Smidt and Lyman A. Kellstedt (Lanham, MD: Rowman & Littlefield Publishers, Inc., 1996), 15.

 9 Ibid., 17.

10 Ammerman, "Protestant Fundamentalism," 97

11 Quoted by Peter J. Boyer, "Mean for Jesus," *Vanity Fair*, September 1990, 225.

12 Wildmon founded the AFA, originally incorporated as the Federation for Decency, in 1977. The AFA is a tax-exempt, not-for-profit corporation that seeks to promote family values by stripping television and other media of images and situations that it considers detrimental to Christian families. AFA links the increase in teenage pregnancies, sexually transmitted diseases such as AIDS, and abortion to the entertainment industry. www.afa.net/General_Info/general_info.html, June 21, 2000, and Joseph Wesley Zeigler, *The Arts in Crisis* (New York: A. Cappella Books, 1994), 70.

13 Quoted in Zeigler, ibid., 72–73.

14 Quoted in *Culture Wars*, edited by Richard Bolton (New York: New Press, 1992), 28–30.

15 Ibid., 30–31.

16 Ibid., 32. Patrick Buchanan, "Losing the War for America's Culture?" *Washington Times*, May 22, 1989.

17 Zeigler, *Arts in Crisis*, 73.

18 Freeborn G. Jewett and David Lloyd Kreeger, "The Corcoran: We Did the Right Thing," *Washington Post*, June 29, 1989, A, 24.

19 Charlotte R. Murphy, "At the Corcoran, a Chilling Case of Censorship," *Washington Post*, June 18, 1989, C, 8.

20 Samuel Lipman, "Just Say No to Trash," *New York Times*, June 23, 1989, A, 29.

21 Robert Brustein, "Don't Punish the Arts," *New York Times*, June 23, 1989, A, 29.

22 Joshua P. Smith, "Why the Corcoran Made a Big Mistake," *Washington Post*, June 18, 1989, G, 1.

23 Although Rohrabacher's measure was defeated, the House voted to cut the NEA's budget by $45,000, the total amount that was spent on the Serrano and Mapplethorpe exhibitions. It also voted to transfer $400,000 from the agency's Visual Arts Program, which had supported the controversial exhibitions, to the Folk Arts Program, and to impose a five-year ban on grants to SECCA and ICA, sponsors of Serrano and Mapplethorpe, respectively. Zeigler, *Arts in Crisis*, 79.

24 American Family Association Press Release on the NEA, July 25, 1989, quoted in Bolton, *Culture Wars*, 72.

25 Debate in Senate over Amendment 420, quoted in Bolton, *Culture Wars*, 73.

26 Ibid., 78.

27 Patrick Buchanan, "Pursued by Baying Yahoos," *Washington Times*, August 2, 1989; Bolton, *Culture Wars*, 86.

28 Frederick Hart, "Contemporary Art Is Perverted Art," *Washington Post*, August 22, 1989, A, 19.

29 Robert Hughes, "A Loony Parody of Cultural Democracy," *Time*, August 14, 1989, 82.

30 Carole S. Vance, "The War on Culture," *Art in America*, September 1989, 39.

31 Robert Bradley, "The Abnormal Affair of *The Normal Heart*," unpublished paper presented at the Speech Communication Association, November 2, 1990.

32 Ibid.

33 CDS advertisement, *Springfield News-Leader*, October 29, 1989.

34 Lanford Wilson, "If You Can't Stand Honest Theatre, Stay Home," *Springfield News-Leader*, November 12, 1989.

35 Robert Koehler, "*Normal Heart* Stirs Up the Heartland," *Los Angeles Times*, December 3, 1989, 41.

36 Bradley, "The Abnormal Affair."

37 Ibid.

38 All of Evans' possessions were destroyed and his two cats were killed. When told of the fire, Dixon said it was "terrible" but claimed that Evans was a "Satan worshiper" and suggested that he set the fire himself. She later recanted her statement about Satanism, stating that she did not know she was being interviewed. Bradley, "The Abnormal Affair"; Rick Harding, "Springfield's Shame," *The Advocate*, December 19, 1989, 9.

39 Bradley, "The Abnormal Affair"; Harding, "Springfield's Shame," *The Advocate*, December 19, 1989, 9.

40 Zeigler, *Arts in Crisis*, 67–68.

41 Quoted in Bolton, *Culture Wars*, 121.

42 Zeigler, *Arts in Crisis*, 81.

43 Quoted in Bolton, *Culture Wars*, 147.

44 Quoted in ibid., 150–151.

45 "Is This How You Want Your Tax Dollars Spent?" *Washington Times*, February 13, 1990, quoted in Bolton, *Culture Wars*, 150–151.

46 Ibid., 152.

47 Isabel Wilkerson, "Cincinnati Jury Acquits Museum In Mapplethorpe Obscenity Case," *New York Times*, October 6, 1990, 1; Andy Grundberg, "The Cincinnati Obscenity Trial and What Makes Photos Art," *New York Times*, October 18, 1990, B, 1.

48 A few days after his initial decision, he allowed Art Space to keep the money as long as they did not use federal funds to produce the catalogue for the exhibition. The catalogue in question contained an essay by artist David Wojnarowicz, who was dying of AIDS. In his essay he called Cardinal O'Connor a "fat cannibal" and told of fantasizing about dousing Jesse Helms with gasoline and "setting his putrid ass on fire." Ziegler, *Arts in Crisis*, 109.

49 Quoted in Bolton, *Culture Wars*, 353–354.

50 See Zeigler, 115–116 for a list of these organizations.

51 Barbara Gamarekian, "Arts Agency Denies Four Grants Suggested by Advisory Panel," *New York Times*, June 30, 1990, 1.

52 Quotations by Miller, Fleck, and Hughes were taken from Gamarekian, "Arts Agency," *New York Times*, June 30, 1990. Karen Finley's response appeared in "The NEA 4," *National Association of Artists' Newsletter*, July 1990, 1.

53 Response of John E. Frohnmayer to a letter from the National Gay and Lesbian Task Force, November 23, 1990, quoted in the *National Association of Artists' Organizations Newsletter*, December 1990, n.p.

54 Quoted in Zeigler, *Arts in Crisis*, 114.

55 "Status Reports," *The American Civil Liberties Union Arts Censorship Project Newsletter*, 1:1 (Fall 1991), 1.

56 Barbara Janowitz, "Will the NEA Weather the Continuing Storm?" *American Theatre* (September 1990), 41.

57 Barbara Janowitz, "A Last-Minute Save?" *American Theatre* (December 1990), 36.

58 "First Takes," *American Theatre* (December 1990), 37.

59 Supreme Court of the United States, *Barnes* v. *Glenn Theatre, Inc., et al.*, June 21, 1991.

60 Ibid.

61 Ibid.

62 Marjorie Heins, *Sex, Sin and Blasphemy: A Guide to America's Censorship Wars* (New York: New Press, 1993), 99.

63 Quoted in ibid., 102.

64 William T. Henry III, "The Gay White Way," *Time*, May 17, 1993, 62.

65 Dan Hulbert, "Critics' Choices Theatre," *Atlanta Constitution*, June 4, 1993, F, 2.

66 Kathy Alexander, "Plan Would Cut Groups Supporting Gay Lifestyle," *Atlanta Constitution*, July 22, 1993, D, 3.

67 "From Our Readers," *Atlanta Constitution*, July 31, A, 17.

68 Howard Pousner, "Furor Takes Marietta Theatre by Surprise," *Atlanta Constitution*, August 20, 1993, C, 1.

69 Kathy Alexander, "Anti-Homosexual Resolution," *Atlanta Constitution*, August 11, 1993, A, 1.

70 Bill Vejnoska, "Cobb's Stand," *The Atlanta Constitution*, August 15, 1993, A, 1.

71 Kathey Alexander and Holly Morris, "Cobb Prays and Picnic Over Rights of Gays," *Atlanta Constitution*, August 23, 1993, B, 1.

72 Kristine Anderson, "Georgia County Sparks Furor," *The Christian Science Monitor*, September 8, 1993, 8.

73 Alexander, "Anti-Homosexual..." *Atlanta Constitution*, August 11, 1993.

74 James Dotson, "Resolution Against Homosexuality Puts Spotlight on Cobb County," *The Christian Index*, September 2, 1993, n.p.

75 Anderson, "Georgia County...," *The Christian Science Monitor*, September 8, 1993.

76 Dotson, "Resolution...," *The Christian Index*, September 2, 1993.

77 Ibid., It is, however, unfair to assume that the majority of churches in Cobb County supported these measures. Price mailed a letter to 280 priests, rabbis, and ministers asking for their support, and was "tremendously amazed at the lack of response of ministers."

78 Cathy Clelan, "Woodward, Newman Give $20,000 to Help Cobb Theatre Stay on Stage," *Atlanta Constitution*, September 23, 1993, G, 3.

79 Dan Hulbert, "Obituaries: An Appreciation," *Atlanta Constitution*, B, 6; interview with Palmer Wells conducted by author, August 23, 2000.

80 Stephen Nunns, "Is Charlotte Burning?" *American Theatre*, February 1999, 23.

81 Ibid.

82 Kevin Sack, "Play Displays a Growing City's Cultural Tensions," *New York Times*, March 22, 1996, 12; "Hot Plays Boil in Carolina Cauldron," *Variety*, April 1–7, 1996, 59.

83 Tony Kushner, "Editorial," *The News and Observer* (Raleigh, NC), March 26, 1996, 8.

84 "Around the South," *Atlanta Constitution*, March 22, 1996, C, 1.

85 Ibid.

86 Quoted in Nunns, "Is Charlotte...," *American Theatre*, February, 1999.

87 Quoted in Eric Harrison, "Showcase City of the South Rebels at Anti-Gay Vote," *Los Angeles Times*, A, 1.

88 Quoted in Nunns, "Is Charlotte...," *American Theatre*, February, 1999.

89 Scott Huler, "Bid to Restrict Arts Funding Splits Charlotte," *The News and Observer* (Raleigh, NC), March 30, 1997, B, 1.

90 Byron Woods, "N.C. County Ends Arts Funding Due to Plays," *Back Stage*, April 11, 1997, 3.

91 Paul Nowell, "Board Poised to Restore Arts Funding Cuts in *Angels in America* Flap," *The Associated Press State and Local Wire*, February 16, 1999.

92 Elda Silva, "Esperanza's Agenda Seen As Root of Its Defunding," *San Antonio Express News*, November 16, 1997, H, 8.

93 Thaddeus Herrick, "Debate Over Budget Cuts in Arts; San Antonio accused of 'Economic Censorship,'" *Houston Chronicle*, October 5, 1997, State Section, 1.

94 Silva, "Esperanza Agenda . . . ," *San Antonio Express News*, November 16, 1997.

95 Ibid.

96 Panel discussion at 1998 conference of the Association for Theatre in Higher Education held in San Antonio.

97 Herrick, "Debate Over Budget Cuts . . . ," *Houston Chronicle*, October 5, 1997.

98 Judith H. Dobrzynski, "In Texas, a Showdown on Money for the Arts," *New York Times*, September 11, 1997, C, 13.

99 Rosemary Shinohara, "Board OK's New Sex Ed Guidelines," *Anchorage Daily News*, November 27, 1996, B, 12.

100 Peter Shaughnessy, "Alaskan Theatre Loses Funding; Claims Bias," *Back Stage*, December 5, 1997, 1.

101 Tom Bell, "Assembly Nixes Funds for Theatre," *Anchorage Daily News*, November 19, 1997, B, 1.

102 Jim Clarke, "Same Sex Marriage Ban Heads to Voters," *Associated Press State and Local Wire*, November 4, 1998; "Lawyer Files Motion to Dismiss Same-Sex Marriage Lawsuit," *Associated Press State and Local Wire*, November 9, 1998; "Judge Dismisses Same-Sex Marriage Lawsuit," *Associated Press State and Local Wire*, September 23, 1999.

103 United States Supreme Court, *National Endowment for the Arts, et al.* v. *Karen Finley, et al.*, June 25, 1998.

104 Stuart Taylor, "More of O'Connor's Muddled Moderation," *American Lawyer Media, L.P., Fulton County Daily Report*, July 8, 1998, n.p.

105 Ward Morehouse III and Tracy Connor, "Gay Jesus May Star on B'Way," *New York Post*, May 1, 1998, 5.

106 "'Gay Jesus' Coming to Broadway," *Catalyst*, June 1998, 3.

107 "*Corpus Christi* to Run in Fall; Protest Mounts," *Catalyst*, July/August 1998, 2; Roger Armbrust, "Catholic League Scourges McNally Play," *Backstage*, May 15–21, 1998, 1.

108 Ibid.

109 Ralph Blumenthal, "New McNally Play Canceled After Protests and Threats," *New York Times*, May 23, 1998, B, 9.

110 Ralph Blumenthal, "Discord Mounts after Play is Cancelled," *New York Times*, May 27, 1998, E, 1.

111 Ibid.

112 Ibid.

113 Ibid.

114 Ibid.

115 "Censoring Terrance McNally," *New York Times*, May 28, 1998, A, 28.

116 Peter Applebome, "In Rehearsal, Theatre Vows to Stage Play That Drew Threats," *New York Times*, May 29, 1998, A, 1.

117 Ward Morehouse III and Andy Geller, "McNally's 'Gay Jesus' Is Resurrected," *New York Post*, May 29, 1998, 14.

118 Applebome, "In Rehearsal . . . ," *New York Times*, May 29, 1998.

119 Susan Brady Konig. "Theatre Club of the Absurd," *New York Post*, June 2, 1998, 29.

120 Brent Bozell, "*Corpus Christi*: The Mother of Sick Plays," *New York Post*, June 26, 1998, 33.

121 Patrick Buchanan, "The Art of Good Hate Crimes," *New York Post*, August 8, 1998, 19.

122 Michael Riedel, Virginia Breen, and Leo Standora, "Anger at Play on Gay 'Christ,' " *New York Daily News*, September 23, 1998, 22.

123 Katherine Roth, "Competing Protests on Tap for Opening of Controversial Play," *Associated Press State and Local Wire*, October 13, 1998.

124 Fintan O'Toole, "Protests at Play Opening a Texas Chainsaw Massacre of Bible," *New York Daily News*, October 14, 1998, 19.

125 Ben Brantley, "Nice Young Man and Disciples Appeal for Tolerance," *New York Times*, October 14, 1998, E, 1.

126 Clive Barnes, "Just How Boring is the 'Gay Jesus' Play?; Alas *Corpus Christi* Is Boring, Says our Clive Barnes," *New York Post*, October 14, 1998, 41.

127 Martin Gottfried, "The Body of *Corpus* Needs More Soul," *New York Law Journal*, October 16, 1998, 6.

128 Michael Feingold, "Texas Nativity," *Village Voice*, October 20, 1998, 175.

129 Murdoch McBride, "Community Ends Funding For TX Shakespeare Fest After *Angels* Is Blasted From Local College," *Playbill On-Line*, November 10, 1999, 1.

130 Cynthia Greenwood, "Where *Angels* Fear to Tread," *Houston Press*, January 20, 2000, Features Section, n.p.

131 Quoted in ibid.

132 Ibid.

133 "Gay-Themed Play Sparks Outrage in East Texas,"*Associated Press State and Local Wire*," October 14, 1999.

134 Brad Rollins, "For Holda, 'It's Been Very Tough,' " *Kilgore College Flare*, October 15, 1999; Greenwood, "Where *Angels* . . . ," *Houston Press*, January 20, 2000.

135 Brad Rollins, "Play Opens Under Protests," *Kilgore College Flare*, October 15, 1999.

136 Ibid.; Greenwood, "Where *Angels* . . . ," *Houston Press*, January 20, 2000.

137 Richard Stewart, "Gay Drama Furor Puts Cash in Festival's Coffers," *Houston Chronicle*, February 6, 2000, State, 1; interview with Raymond Caldwell, December 4, 2002.

Bibliography

Adams, Bluford. *E Pluribus Barnum: The Greatest Showman and the Making of U.S. Popular Culture*. Minneapolis: University of Minnesota Press, 1997.

Allen, Robert C. *Horrible Prettiness*. Chapel Hill: University of North Carolina Press, 1991.

America, IX (Aug. 30, 1913), 194; X (Oct. 11, 1913), 20; X (Dec. 20, 1913), 261.

The American Family Association Online. June 21, 2000, www.afa.net/General_Info/general_info.html.

Ammerman, Nancy T. "North American Protestant Fundamentalism." In *Media Culture and the Religious Right*. Eds. Linda Kintz and Julia Lesage. Minneapolis: University of Minnesota Press, 1998.

Armbrust, Roger. "Catholic League Scourges McNally Play." *Backstage* 15 May 1998: 1.

"Arms and the Baby." *The New Republic* Oct. 15, 1924: 160.

"As Another Riot Season Nears." *US News and World Report* Mar. 11, 1968: 33.

Bailey, Blake. *The 60's*. New York: Mallard, 1992.

Bain, Myrna. "Everybody's Protest Play." *The National Review* Mar. 23, 1965, 249–250.

Bank, Rosemarie K. *Theatre Culture in America, 1825–1860*. Cambridge University Press, 1997.

Baraka, Amiri. *The Autobiography of LeRoi Jones*. New York: Fruendlich Books, 1984.

Barish, Jonas. *The Anti-Theatrical Prejudice*. Berkeley: University of California Press, 1981.

Baritz, Loren, ed. *The Culture of the Twenties*. New York: Bobbs-Merrill, 1970.
   The Good Life: The Meaning of Success for the American Middle Class. New York: Harper and Row, 1982.

Bentley, Eric, ed. *Thirty Years of Treason*. New York: Viking, 1971.

Biner, Pierre. *The Living Theatre*. New York: Horizon, 1972.

Blake, Ben. *The Awakening of the American Theatre*. New York: Tomorrow Publishers, 1935.

Bloom, Alexander and Wini Breines. *Takin' It to the Streets*. New York: Oxford University Press, 1995.

Bolton, Richard, ed. *Culture Wars*. New York: New Press, 1992.

Bourdet, Edouard. *The Captive*. Trans. Arthur Hornblow, Jr. New York: Brentano's Books, 1926.

Boyd, Ernest. "Readers and Writers." *The Independent* 114 (1925): 272.

Boyer, Peter J. "Mean for Jesus." *Vanity Fair* Sept. 1990: 225.

Bradley, Robert. "The Abnormal Affair of the *The Normal Heart*." Unpublished paper presented at the Speech Communication Association, November 2, 1990.

Bridenbaugh, Carl and Jessica Bridenbaugh. *Rebels and Gentlemen: Philadelphia in the Age of Franklin*. New York: Reynal & Hitchcock, 1942.

Brieux, Eugene. *Damaged Goods*. In *Three Plays by Brieux*. Trans. John Pollock. New York: Brentano's Books, 1913.

Brockett, Oscar G. *History of the Theatre*. 7th edn. Boston: Allyn and Bacon, 1995.

Brown, B. W. "The Colonial Theatre in New England." *Special Bulletin of the Newport Historical Society* 77 (July 1930): 7, 9–11, 20–22.

Brown, Jared. *The Theatre in America during the Revolution*. Cambridge, UK and New York: Cambridge University Press, 1995.

Brown, T. Allston. *A History of the New York Stage*. 1903. New York: Benjamin Bloom, 1964.

Brustein, Robert. *Revolution As Theatre*. New York: Liveright, 1971.

"The Third Theatre Revisited." *New York Review of Books* Feb. 13, 1969: 26.

"Three Views of America," *The New Republic*. Dec. 3, 1966, 31–33.

"Junkies and Jazz." *The New Republic*. Sept. 28, 1959: 39–40.

Bryan, George B. *American Theatrical Regulation: 1607 to 1900*. Metuchen, NJ: Scarecrow, 1993.

Buckley, Peter George. "To the Opera House." Ph.D. dissertation. State University of New York at Stoney Brook, 1984.

Butsch, Richard. *The Making of American Audiences: From Stage to Television, 1750–1990*. Cambridge University Press, 2000.

Caldwell, Erskine. *Tobacco Road*. Adapted for the stage by Jack Kirkland. New York: The Macmillan Company, 1934.

Citizens Demanding Standards. Advertisement. *Springfield News-Leader* Oct. 29, 1989: n.p.

"Civil Rights: Black Power." *Newsweek* June 27, 1966: 36.

Clapp, William. *A Record of the Boston Stage*. 1853. New York: Benjamin Bloom, 1968.

Clark, Barrett H. "The Padlock Law in New York." *Drama* Apr. 1928: 200.

Cogley, John. *Report on Blacklisting*. 2 vols. New York: Arno Press and *The New York Times*, 1972.

Commager, Henry Steele. *The Empire of Reason*. New York: Anchor, 1977.

Committee on Un-American Activities, House of Representatives. Communist Infiltration of the Hollywood Motion-Picture Industry – Part 7. 82nd Congress, 2nd session.

Comstock, Anthony. *Traps for the Young*. New York: Funk and Wagnalls, 1883.

"*Corpus Christi* to Run in Fall; Protest Mounts." *Catalyst* July/Aug. 1998: 2.

Criminal Court of the City of New York. *People* v. *Larry Bercowicz, et. al*. New York County, Feb. 25, 1970.

Cross, Gary. *A Social History of Leisure since 1600*. Ventura: State College, 1990.

Curtin, Kaier. *We Can Always Call Them Bulgarians*. Boston: Alyson, 1987.

Daniels, Bruce C. *Puritans at Play: Leisure and Recreation in Colonial New England*. New York: St. Martins, 1995.

Davis, R. G. *The San Francisco Mime: The First Ten Years*. Palo Alto, CA: Ramparts, 1975.

De Grazia, Edward and Roger K. Newman. *Banned Films: Movies, Censors and the First Amendment*. New York: R. R. Bowker, 1982.

D'Emilio, John and Estelle B. Freedman. *Intimate Matters: A History of Sexuality in America*. New York: Harper and Row, 1988.

Dennison, George. "The Demagogy of LeRoi Jones." *Commentary* Feb. 1965: 68–69.

De Rohan, Pierre, ed. *Federal Theatre Plays: Triple-A, Power, Spirochete*. New York: Da Capo, 1973.

De Young, Mary. "Help, I'm Being Held Captive! The White Slave Fairy Tale of the Progressive Era." *Journal of American Culture* 6 (Spring 1983): 96–99.

Dietz, Steven. "An Audience Manifesto." *American Theatre* Jan. 1993: 9.

"A Discussion of Censorship and the 'Che!' Case." *Dramatists Guild Quarterly* (Spring 1969): 7–8.

Dobson, Ed and Cal Thomas. *Blinded by the Might: Can the Religious Right Save America?* Grand Rapids, MI: Zondervan, 1999.

Doherty, Daniel M. "Censorship of Theatre in Boston." Unpublished Masters Thesis. Boston University, 1950.

"The Drama League of America." *Drama* 1 (1911): 117.

"Dramatizing Vice." *Literary Digest* 47 (1913): 577.

Duffus, Robert L. "The Age of Play." *The Independent* Dec. 20, 1924: 539.

Duffy, Susan and Bernard K. Duffy. "Watchdogs of the American Theatre 1910–1940." *Journal of American Culture* 6 (Spring 1983): 52–59.

Dunlap, William. *A History of the American Theatre*. New York: J. & J. Harper, 1832.

Eaton, Walter Pritchard. "The Theatre." *The American Magazine* Feb. 1914: 105.

"The Editor's Uneasy Chair." *Theatre Magazine* 42 (1925): 7.

Eells, George and Stanley Musgrove. *Mae West*. London: Robson, 1984.

Erdman, Harley. "Jewish Anxiety in 'Days of Judgment.' Community Conflict, Anti-Semitism, and the 'God of Vengeance' Obscenity Case." *Theatre Survey* 40 (1999): 51–74.

Evans, Hiram Wesley. "The Klan's Fight for Americanism." *The North American Review* Mar. 1926: 33.

Farber, David and Beth Bailey, eds. *The Columbia Guide to America in the 1960s*. New York: Columbia University Press, 2001.

Fariello, Griffin. *Red Scare*. New York: W. W. Norton & Company, 1995.

"First Takes." *American Theatre* Dec. 1990: 37.

Fitzgerald, F. Scott. *This Side of Paradise*. New York: C. Scribner Sons, 1920.

Flanagan, Hallie. *Arena: The History of the Federal Theatre*. New York: Arno, 1980.
"Somebody Must Be Wrong." *Survey Graphic* Dec. 1939: 774–81.

Ford, Paul Leicester. *Washington and the Theatre*. 1899. New York: Burt Franklin, 1970.

Fowler, Gene. *Beau James*. New York: Viking, 1949.

Fraden, Rena. *Blueprints for a Black Federal Theatre, 1935–1939*. New York: Cambridge University Press, 1994.

Freeman, Joshua, Nelson Lichtenstein, and Stephen Brier et al., *Who Built America: Working People and the Nation's Economy, Politics, Culture, and Society*. 2 vols. New York: Pantheon Books, 1992. Vol. 2.

Fried, Richard M. *Nightmare in Red: The McCarthy Era in Perspective*. New York: Oxford University Press, 1990.

Frohnmayer, John E. "Letter to the National Gay and Lesbian Task Force." Nov. 23, 1990. *National Association of Artists' Organizations Newsletter*. Dec. 1990.

Garber, Marjorie. *Vested Interests: Cross Dressing and Cultural Anxiety*. New York: Routledge, 1992.

Gardiner, John. *A Speech Delivered to the Massachusetts House of Representatives. Boston, Jan. 26, 1792, On the Report of the Committee Appointed to Consider the Expediency of Repealing the Law Against Theatrical Exhibitions within this Commonwealth*. Boston, 1792.

" 'Gay Jesus' Coming to Broadway." *Catalyst* June 1998: 3.

Gelb, Arthur and Barbara Gelb. *O'Neill*. New York: Harper and Row, 1973.

Gilman, Richard. "The Theatre of Ignorance." *Atlantic* July 1969: 40–42.

"The God of Vengeance." *Outlook* June 6, 1923: 117–118.

Goldman, William. *The Season: A Candid Look at Broadway*. New York: Harcourt, Brace and World, 1969.

Goodman, Walter. *The Committee: The Extraordinary Career of the House Committee on Un-American Activities*. New York: Farrar, Straus and Giroux, 1968.

Gottfried, Martin. "The Body of 'Corpus' Needs More Soul." *New York Law Journal* Oct. 16, 1998: 6.

Grimsted, David. *Melodrama Unveiled*. Berkeley: University of California Press, 1987.

Guth, James L. "The Politics of the Christian Right." In *Religion and the Culture Wars*. Eds. John C. Green, James L. Guth, Corwin E. Smidt, and Lyman A. Kellstedt. New York: Rowman & Littlefield, 1996.

Hamilton, Marybeth. *The Queen of Camp: Mae West, Sex and Popular Culture*. London: HarperCollins Publishers, 1995.

"Mae West Live: *Sex, The Drag*, and 1920's Broadway." *Drama Review* 36 (1992): 82–100.

Harding, Rick. "Springfield's Shame." *The Advocate* Dec. 19, 1989: 8–9.

Harris, Neil. *Humbug: The Art of P. T. Barnum*. University of Chicago Press, 1973.

Hart, Albert Bushnell, ed. *Commonwealth History of Massachusetts*. 5 vols. New York: States History, 1927.

Havelock, Eric. *Preface to Plato*. Cambridge, MA: Harvard University Press, 1963.

Hearings Before a Special Committee on Un-American Activities. 13 vols. Washington: United States Government Printing Office, 1938.

Heins, Marjorie. *Sex, Sin and Blasphemy: A Guide to America's Censorship Wars*. New York: New Press, 1993.

Heller, Adele and Lois Rudnick, eds. *1915: The Cultural Moment*. New Brunswick, NJ: Rutgers University Press, 1991.

Hellman, Lillian. *Scoundrel Time*. Boston: Little, Brown and Company, 1976.

Henry, William T. III. "The Gay White Way." *Time* May 17, 1993: 62.

Hewitt, Bernard. *Theatre U.S.A: 1665 to 1957*. New York: McGraw-Hill, 1959.

Highsaw, Carol Anne. "A Theatre of Action: The Living Newspapers of the Federal Theatre Project." Ph.D. dissertation, Princeton University, 1988.

Hill, Marilyn Wood. *Their Sisters' Keepers: Prostitution in New York City, 1830–1870*. Berkeley: University of California Press, 1993.

Himmelstein, Jerome L. *To the Right: The Transformation of American Conservatism*. Berkeley: University of California Press, 1990.

Hobson, Barbara Meil. *Uneasy Virtue: The Politics of Prostitution and the American Reform Movement*. New York: Basic Books, 1987.

Hopkins, Harry L. *Spending to Save*. New York: W. W. Norton & Company, 1936.

Horn, Barbara Lee. *The Age of Hair*. Westport, CT: Greenwood, 1991.

Hornblow, Arthur. "Mr. Hornblow Goes to the Play." *Theatre Magazine* Apr. 1923: 20, 68.

"Olla Podrida." *Theatre Magazine* June 1923: 7.

"Mr. Hornblow Goes to the Play." *Theatre Magazine* Apr. 1926: 15–19, 64, 66, 72.

"Mr. Hornblow Goes to the Play." *Theatre Magazine* Dec. 1926: 15–18, 68, 72, 74.

Houseman, John. *Unfinished Business: Memoirs 1902–1988*. New York: Applause Books, 1989.

Hughes, Robert. "A Loony Parody of Cultural Democracy." *Time* Aug. 14, 1989: 82.

"Is Bernard Shaw a Menace to Morals?" *Current Literature* 39 (1905): 551–552.

Janowitz, Barbara. "NEA Chronicle: 30 Days That Shook the Arts." *American Theatre* Sept. 1990: 41–48.

"A Last-Minute Save?" *American Theatre* Dec. 1990: 36–39.

Johnson, Claudia. "That Guilty Third Tier: Prostitution in Nineteenth Century American Theatres." *American Quarterly* 27 (1975): 575–584.

Josephson, Matthew and Hannah Josephson. *Al Smith: Hero of the Cities*. Boston: Houghton Mifflin, 1969.

"Judge Will Read *Tobacco Road*," *Chicago American*, Oct. 23, 1935.

Kalpelke, Randy. "Artistic Victories: How the Legitimate Theatre Overcame New York City's Efforts to Impose Censorship on *Sapho* in 1900, *Mrs. Warren's Profession* in 1905 and Other Productions to 1927." Ph.D. dissertation. Tufts University, 1998.

Kendrick, Walter. *The Secret Museum: Pornography in Modern Culture*. New York: Viking, 1987.

Kline, Herbert, ed. *New Theatre and Film 1934 to 1937: An Anthology*. New York: Harcourt Brace Jovanovich, 1985.

Kroll, Jack. "The Creature." *Newsweek* Oct. 14, 1968: 117–118.

"The 'Living'." *Newsweek* Oct. 28, 1968: 134–135.

Krutch, Joseph Wood. "The God of the Stumps." *Nation* Nov. 26, 1924: 578.

Kussrow, Van Carl, Jr. "On with the Show." Ph.D. dissertation, University of Indiana, 1959.

LaHaye, Tim. *The Battle for the Mind*. Old Tappan, NJ: Fleming H. Revell, 1980.

Laufe, Abe. *The Wicked Stage*. New York: Frederick Ungar, 1978.

"Letter to John V. Lindsay and District Attorney Frank S. Hogan." *Dramatists' Guild Quarterly* Spring 1969: 8.

"Lifting the Ban on the Theatre." *Literary Digest* 46 (1913): 952.

Little, Paul Judson. "Reactions to the Theatre: Virginia, Massachusetts, and Pennsylvania, 1665–1793." Ph.D. dissertation Syracuse University, 1969.

Little, Stuart W. *Off-Broadway: The Prophetic Theatre*. New York: Coward, McCann & Geoghegan, 1972.

Logan, Olive. *Apropos of Women and Theatres*. New York: Carleton, 1869.

Lynes, Russell. *The Lively Audience: A Social History of the Visual and the Performing Arts in America 1890–1950*. New York: Harper and Row, 1985.

Mantle, Burns, ed. *The Best Plays of 1922–1923*. New York: Dodd, Mead and Company, 1934.

The Best Plays of the 1924–1925 Season. 1935. Boston: Small, Maynard & Company, 1925.

The Best Plays of 1926–1927. 1936. New York: Dodd, Mead and Company, 1927.

The Best Plays of 1933–1934. 1937. New York: Dodd, Mead and Company, 1935.

The Best Plays of 1934–1935. 1938. New York: Dodd, Mead and Company, 1935.

Mantle, Burns and Garrison P. Sherwood, eds. *The Best Plays of 1909–1919*. New York: Dodd, Mead and Company, 1933.

Mather, Increase. *An Arrow against Profane and Promiscuous Dancing Drawn out of the Quiver of the Scriptures*. Boston, 1684.

A Testimony Against Several Prophane and Superstitious Customs Now Practised by Some in New England. London, 1687.

Matthews, Jane De Hart. *The Federal Theatre, 1935–1939*. Princeton University Press, 1967.

"Arts and the People: The New Deal Quest for a Cultural Democracy." *The Journal of American History* 62 (Sept. 1975): 316–320.

Maya Program. Billy Rose Theatre Collection.

McAdoo, William. "The Theatre and the Law." *The Saturday Evening Post*, Jan. 28, 1922: 6–7, 44, 47, 49, 51.

McBride, Murdoch. "Community Ends Funding for TX Shakespeare Fest After *Angels* Is Blasted From Local College." *Playbill On-Line* Nov. 10, 1999: 1.

McConachie, Bruce. "American Theatre in Context." In *The Cambridge History of American Theatre*. Eds. Don B. Wilmeth and Christopher Bigsby. 3 vols. Cambridge University Press, 1998. Vol. 1.

McDermott, Douglas. "Structure and Management in the American Theatre." In *The Cambridge History of American Theatre*. Eds. Don B. Wilmeth and Christopher Bigsby. 3 vols. Cambridge University Press, 1998. Vol. 1.

McDermott, M. Joan and Sarah J. B. Blackstone. "'White Slavery Plays of the 1910s' Fear of Victimization and the Social Control of Sexuality." *Theatre History Studies* 16 (1996): 141–156.

McDonald, William F. *Federal Relief Administration and the Arts*. Columbus: University of Ohio Press, 1969.

McNamara, Brooks. *The Shuberts of Broadway*. New York: Oxford University Press, 1990.

"'A Congress of Wonders': Rise and Fall of the Dime Museum." *Emerson Society Quarterly* 20 (1974): 216–232.

Metcalfe, James S. "Is a Theatre Censorship Inevitable?" *Theatre Magazine* 28 (Nov. 1923): 8.

Miller, Arthur. *Timebends*. New York: Grove, 1987.

Miller, Gabriel. *Clifford Odets*. New York: Continuum, 1989.

Miller, Kerby A. *Emigrants and Exiles: Ireland and the Irish Exodus to North America*. New York: Oxford University Press, 1985.

"Modern Living." *Time* July 11, 1969: 61.

" Morals Backlash." *Newsweek* Apr. 7, 1969: 31.

Morgan, Edmund S. "Puritan Hostility to the Theatre." *Proceedings of the American Philosophical Society* 110 (1966): 340–347.

Mowry, George E., ed. *The Twenties: Fords, Flappers and Fanatics*. Englewood Cliffs: Prentice Hall, 1965.

"A Naked Challenge." *Nation* Sept. 5, 1923: 229.

"The Nation." *Time* Oct. 27, 1967: 23–25.

Nathan, George Jean. "The Theatre." *American Mercury* Mar. 1927: 373–374.

"The NEA 4." *National Association of Artists' Newsletter* July 1990: 1.

Neff, Renfreu. *The Living Theatre: USA*. New York: Bobbs-Merrill, 1970.

"New Play in Manhattan: 'Power.'" *Time* Mar. 8, 1937: 37.

"Newspaper into Theatre." *Nation* Mar. 12, 1937: 256.

Nunns, Stephen. "Is Charlotte Burning?" *American Theatre* Feb. 1999: 31.

Odell, George C. D. *Annals of the New York Stage*, 15 vols. New York: Columbia University Press, 1927. Vol. 1.

Oliver, Edith. "Off Broadway." *New Yorker* Oct. 12, 1968: 106–108.

Oliver, William I. "The Censor in the Ivy." *TDR* 15 (Fall 1970): 31–55.

"Our Lawless Age." *Literary Digest* 71 (1921): 30.

Pack, Richard. *Censored: A Record of Present Terror and Censorship in the American Theatre*. New York: National Committee Against Censorship of the Theatre Arts, 1935.

"Padlocks for Plays." *Nation* (April 6, 1927): 360.

Palmer, A. Mitchell. "The Case Against Reds." *Forum* (Feb. 1920): 78, 173–176, 179–185.

Peiss, Kathy. *Cheap Amusements: Working Women and Leisure in Turn-of-the-Century New York*. Philadelphia: Temple University Press, 1986.

Perrett, Geoffrey. *America in the Twenties: A History*. New York: Touchstone Books, 1983.

Pivar, David J. *Purity Crusade: Sexual Morality and Social Control, 1868–1900*. Westport, CT: Greenwood Press, 1973.

Plato. *The Republic*. Trans. Francis M. Cornford. New York: Oxford University Press, 1945.

"A Police Chief Talks of 'Police Brutality.'" *US News and World Report*. Aug. 10, 1964: 33–35.

Pollack, Thomas Clark. *The Philadelphia Theatre in the Eighteenth Century*. New York: Greenwood Press, 1968.

Pope Pius X. "Letter to Eliza O'Brien Lummis." Eliza O'Brien Lummis. *Daughters of the Faith Serious Thoughts for Catholic Women*. New York: Knickerbocker, 1905.

"Pornography and Politics." *Newsweek* Aug. 17, 1970: 81.

"Pornography for Hire." *Nation* Dec. 18, 1913: 585.

"Porno Report Cleared for Publication." *Publishers Weekly*. Sept. 28, 1970: 59.

"Pussyfoot in the Theatre." *The New Republic*, Dec. 7, 1921: 33.

Quinn, Arthur Hobson. *A History of the American Drama from the Civil War to the Present Day*. New York: Appleton-Century-Crofts, 1936.

Rankin, Hugh F. *The Theatre in Colonial America*. Chapel Hill: University of North Carolina Press, 1965.

"Rebirth of a Committee." *Newsweek* Jan. 15, 1945: 32–34.

"Reforming the Stage." *America* Dec. 28, 1912: 278.

Rod, David K. "Trial by Jury: An Alternative Form of Theatrical Censorship in New York, 1921–1925." *Theatre Survey* 26 (1985): 47–61.

Ruff, Loren K. "Joseph Harper and Boston's Board Alley Theatre, 1792–1793." *Educational Theatre Journal* 26 (March 1974): 45–48.

Rusher, William. *The Rise of the Right*. New York: Morrow, 1984.

"Samuel Sewall to Isaac Addington" in "Letter Book of Samuel Sewall." *Collections of the Massachusetts Historical Society*. Series 6. Vol. 2 (1888): 29–30.

Santayana, George. *Character and Opinion in the United States*. Garden City: Doubleday Anchor, 1956.

Sante, Luc. *Low Life: Lures and Snares of Old New York*. New York: Farrar, Straus and Girou, 1991.

Sapho Program. Columbia Theatre, New York. Jan. 1901.

Schechner, Richard. *Public Domain*. New York: Bobbs-Merrill, 1969.

"Speculations on Radicalism, Sexuality and Performance." *TDR* 13 (Summer 1969): 89–109.

Environmental Theatre. New York: Applause Books, 1994.

Schlesinger, Arthur M., Jr. *The Coming of the New Deal*. Boston: Houghton Mifflin, 1959.

Schlissel, Lillian, ed. *Three Plays by Mae West*. London: Nick Hern Books, 1997.

Shaw, Mary. "My 'Immoral' Play: The Story of the First American Production of 'Mrs. Warren's Profession.'" *McClure Magazine* Apr. 1912: 688–692.

Singleton, Carl, ed. *The Sixties in America*. 3 vols. Pasadena, CA: Salem Press, Inc. 1999.

Smiley, Sam. *The Drama of Attack*. Columbia: University of Missouri Press, 1972.

Smith, Michael. "The Good Scene: Off Off-Broadway." *Tulane Drama Review* 10 (Summer 1966): 159–175.

Snowman, Daniel and Malcom Bradbury. "The Sixties and Seventies." In *Introduction to American Studies*. Eds. Malcolm Bradbury and Howard Temperley. New York: Longman, 1989.

Solberg, Winton. *Redeem the Time: The Puritan Sabbath in Early America*. Cambridge, MA: Harvard University Press, 1977.

Spann, Edward K. *The New Metropolis: New York City, 1840–1857*. New York: Columbia University Press, 1981.

"A Sponge for the Stage." *Literary Digest* Dec. 23, 1923: 29.

"The Stage." *America* Sept. 2, 1911: 488–489.

"The Stage and the Censor." *Nation* Jan. 18, 1922: 59–60.

"Stage: Federal Theatre Strikes at Utilities' Evils with 'Power.'" *Newsweek* Mar. 6, 1937: 30.

"Status Reports." *American Civil Liberties Union Arts Censorship Project Newsletter* Fall 1991: 1.

"Students: The Free Sex Movement." *Time* Mar. 11, 1966: 66.

Sumner, John. "The Sewer on the Stage." *Theatre Magazine* 38 (1923): 9–10.

Supreme Court of the United States. *Paris Adult Theater* v. *Slanton*. June 21, 1973.

Miller v. *California*. June 21, 1973.

Southeastern Promotions, Ltd. v. *Conrad et al.* Mar. 18, 1975.

Barnes v. *Glen Theatre, Inc., et al.* June 21, 1991.

National Endowment for the Arts, et al. v. Karen Finley, et al. June 25, 1998.

Supreme Judicial Court of Massachusetts. *P. B.I.C., Inc. et al. v. District Attorney of Suffolk County*. Apr. 9, 1970.

Taubman, Howard. *The Making of the American Theatre*. New York: Coward McCann, 1965.

Taylor, Stuart. "More of O'Connor's Muddled Moderation." *American Lawyer Media, L.P., Fulton County Daily Report. Academic Universe*, July 8, 1998.

"The Theatre." *Time* Oct. 18, 72–73.

"The Theatre." *New Yorker* May 8, 1926: 26.

"The Theatre." *Time* Dec. 3, 1934: 24.

"'The Traffic.'" *Chicago Inter Ocean* Nov. 24, 1913: 9.

Trumbell, Charles Gallaudet. *Anthony Comstock, Fighter*. New York: Fleming H. Revell, 1913.

T-sd-le, Joseph, Esq. Speech delivered to the Massachusetts House of Representatives June 1767.

Tynan, Kathleen. *The Life of Kenneth Tynan*. London: Methuen, 1988.

Tytell, John. *The Living Theatre: Art, Exile and Outrage*. New York: Grove Press, 1995.

"A United Theatre Defeats Official Censorship." *Equity* Mar. 1945: 5–7, 10.

Vance, Carole S. "The War on Culture." *Art in America* (Sept. 1989): 39–45.

Veiller, Bayard. *The Fun I've Had*. New York: Reynal & Hitchcock, 1941.

Vernon, Grenville. "Injunction Granted" *Commonweal* Aug. 21, 1936: 407.

"Power" *Commonweal* Mar. 12, 1937: 556.

Wagman, Robert J. *The First Amendment Book*. New York: Pharos Books, 1991.

Wainscott, Ronald. "Attracting Censorship to the Popular Theatre: Al Woods Produces Avery Hopwood's *The Demi-Virgin*." *Theatre History Studies* 10 (1990): 127–140.

Waterman, Willoughby Cyrus. *Prostitution and Its Repression in New York City, 1900–1931*. 1932. New York: AMS, 1968.

Wellesley Local Growth Committee, *Comparative Population Statistics*, 1968.

West, Mae. *The Drag*. In *The Plays of Mae West*. Ed. Lillian Schlissel. London: Nick Hern Books, 1997.

White, Richard Grant. "The Age of Burlesque." *Galaxy* Aug. 1869: 256.

Whitman, Wilson. *Bread and Circuses*. New York: Oxford University Press, 1937.

Wilentz, Sean. *Chants Democratic: New York City and the Rise of the American Working Class*. New York: Oxford University Press, 1984.

Wilmeth, Don B. and Christopher Bigsby, eds. *The Cambridge History of American Theatre*. 3 vols. Cambridge University Press, 1998.

Wood, Gordon, ed. *The Rising Glory of America: 1760–1820*. Boston: Northeastern University Press, 1990.

Wright, William. *Lillian Hellman: The Image, the Woman*. New York: Simon & Schuster, 1986.

Wyatt, Euphemia Van Rensselaer. "The Drama." *Catholic World* Aug. 1939: 598–602.

"Young Playwright." *New Yorker* July 9, 1960: 24–25.

Young, Stark. "Two New Plays." *The New Republic* Dec. 19, 1934: 169.

"The Mercury and London," *The New Republic*, Jan. 19, 1938: 310–311.

Zeigler, Joseph Wesley. *The Arts in Crisis*. New York: A. Cappella, 1994.

Newspapers

Anchorage Daily News, yrs: 1996–97.

Associated Press State and Local Wire, yrs: 1998–99.

Atlanta Constitution, yrs: 1951, 1993, 1996.

Backstage, yrs: 1997–98.

Boston Evening Herald, yr: 1929.

Boston Evening Transcript, yrs: 1911, 1923, 1929.

Boston Globe, yrs: 1911, 1929, 1935, 1968, 1970.

Boston Herald, yrs: 1911, 1929, 1935.

Boston Post, yr: 1935.

Boston Transcript, yrs: 1935–36.

Christian Index, yr: 1993.

Christian Science Monitor, yr: 1993.

Cincinnati Examiner, yr: (undated).

Cleveland News, yr: 1928.

Colorado Springs Gazette-Telegraph, yr: 1969.

Columbian Centinel, yrs: 1791–92.

Corpus Christi Caller, yr: 1971.

Daily Worker, yr: 1955.

Detroit News, yrs: 1947, 1969.

Federal Gazette, yr: 1789.

Fullerton Daily New Tribune, yr: 1967.

Houston Chronicle, yr: 2000.

Houston Press, yr: 2000.

Independent Gazetteer or the Chronicle of Freedom, yrs: 1788–89.

Liberator, yr: 1853.

Little Rock Gazette, yr: 1971.

London Observer, yr: 1967.

Los Angeles Times, yrs: 1965, 1967–69 1989, 1996.

News and Observer (Raleigh, NC), yrs: 1996–97.

New York American, yr: 1923.

New York Atlas, yr: 1863.

New York Daily News, yrs: 1945, 1998.

New York Evening Journal, yr: 1936.

New York Evening Post, yrs: 1926, 1928, 1968–69.

New York Herald, yrs: 1901, 1905, 1922–23.

New York Herald Tribune, yrs: 1925, 1927, 1928, 1935–37.

New York Journal, yr: 1928.

New York Journal or General Advertiser, yrs: 1767–68.

New York Mercury, yrs: 1758, 1761.

New York Morning Telegraph, yrs: 1924, 1928.

New York Post, yrs: 1936, 1998.

New York Sun, yrs: 1900, 1926–28, 1936–37.
New York Telegraph, yr: 1928.
New York Times, yrs: 1868–69, 1900, 1905, 1911–13, 1921–32, 1934–40, 1942, 1944–45, 1947, 1949, 1951–53, 1955, 1959–60, 1963, 1965–71, 1973, 1989–90, 1996–98.
New York Tribune, yr: 1900.
New York World, yrs: 1900, 1905, 1923–24, 1928.
New York World-Telegram, yr: 1936.
Pennsylvania Chronicle and Universal Advertiser, yr: 1767.
Pennsylvania Gazette, yrs: 1754, 1759, 1766–67.
Providence Journal (Rhode Island), yr: 1952.
San Antonio Express News, yr: 1997.
Springfield News-Leader (Missouri), yr: 1989.
US News and World Report, yrs: 1964, 1968.
Variety, yrs: 1921, 1926–28, 1996.
Village Voice, yrs: 1963, 1966–67, 1998.
Waco Times-Herald, yr: 1963.
The Wall Street Journal, yr: 1969.
Washington Post, yrs: 1939, 1989.
Washington Post and Times Herald, yr: 1956.
Washington Times, yrs: 1989–90.
Wellesley Townsman, yr: 1968.
Weyman's Gazette, yr: 1761.
Women's Wear Daily, yr: 1969.

Archives

Billy Rose Theatre Collection, New York Public Library for the Performing and Visual Arts at Lincoln Center.
Harvard Theatre Collection, Pussey Library, Harvard University.

Index

Munro, A. G., 124, 125
Murder in the Cathedral, 136
Murphy, George, 156
Murray, Walter, 10, 11, 13
Mussolini, Benito, 135
My Left Breast, 256
Mysteries and Smaller Pieces, 195, 196

Nashville, Tennessee, 245
Nathan, George Jean, 86, 89, 97
Nation, The, 65, 80, 85, 141, 266
National Association of Artists'
    Organizations, 233
National Campaign for Freedom of
    Expression, 243
National Capital Arts and Cultural
    Activities Program, 233
National Committee Against Censorship
    in the Arts, 233
National Council of Jewish Juniors, 146
National Council of Methodist Youth,
    146
National Emergency Conference for
    Democratic Rights, 154
National Football League, 250
National Gallery, 239
National Guard, 129, 178, 224
National Public Radio, 248
National Recovery Act, 134
National Review, 185
National Service Bureau, 148
NationsBank, 250, 253
naturalism, 41, 60, 70, 82, 88
NEA (National Endowment for the
    Arts), 226, 230, 231, 232, 233, 234, 235,
    236, 238, 239, 240, 241, 242, 243, 244,
    245, 250, 255, 256, 257, 258, 263, 267
Negro People's Theatre, 130
Neighborhood Playhouse, 105
Nethersole, Olga, 41, 42, 46, 48, 49, 50, 51,
    52, 57, 68
New Deal, 137, 138, 139, 140, 141, 145, 150,
    155
New England, 6, 14, 15, 16, 115, 123
New Exhibition Room, 25

New Hampshire, 24, 230
New Haven Register, 54
New Haven, Connecticut, 54, 58, 131, 196,
    197
New Jersey, 49, 129, 145, 155
New Left, 173, 177
New Mexico, 145
New Orleans, Louisiana, 32, 144
New Republic, 170
New Right, 206, 229, 230, 239, 240, 245,
    251
New South, 250, 251
New Theatre, 130, 147
New Theatre Group, 131
New Theatre League, 130, 131
New Waverly Theatre, 34
New Woman, 40, 49
New York American, 87
New York City, 10, 11, 13, 14, 15, 16, 19, 20,
    26, 27, 28, 31, 32, 33, 34, 37, 38, 41, 44,
    48, 49, 52, 54, 55, 57, 58, 59, 60, 61, 62,
    65, 66, 67, 68, 70, 72, 73, 76, 78, 79,
    82, 83, 85, 86, 89, 90, 91, 92, 93, 94,
    95, 98, 99, 100, 101, 102, 103, 104, 105,
    109, 110, 111, 117, 118, 119, 120, 121, 122,
    123, 124, 125, 126, 127, 128, 129, 130,
    132, 133, 134, 135, 137, 140, 142, 144,
    148, 151, 153, 158, 159, 160, 166, 167,
    173, 174, 177, 178, 181, 182, 183, 184, 185,
    190, 191, 192, 194, 197, 198, 199, 200,
    202, 205, 206, 208, 213, 215, 216, 218,
    219, 220, 221, 222, 223, 224, 240, 247,
    253, 257, 258, 259, 261, 262
New York City Police Department, 216
New York Daily Column, 209
New York Daily News, 206, 209
New York Daily Worker, 166
New York Evening Journal, 137
New York Evening Post, 109
New York Globe, 89
New York Herald, 55
New York Herald-Tribune, 141, 148
New York Morning Telegraph, 91
New York Post, 216, 257
New York Public Library, 52